P9-DHI-892

THE RIGHT APPROACH

Anitra Frazier understands that each cat is unique, and she believes that respecting a cat is just as important as loving and caring for him or her. This fully updated and expanded edition of her groundbreaking cat care manual not only offers invaluable information on cat nutrition, grooming, and safety but also answers many of the most common questions cat owners ask. Frazier provides specific advice on acceptable commercial foods . . . a Super-Finicky Cat Owner's I'll-Do-Anything-for-My-Cat Diet . . . communication techniques and solutions to "impossible"problems . . . plus eye-opening information about immunization and medications. Written in a warm, personal, and reassuring style, this extraordinary guide also provides a unique perspective on holistic health care for your pet, including complete information on herbal remedies, homeopathy, and other alternative therapies. It is indispensable for anyone who loves and cares for a cat.

ANITRA FRAZIER is a nationally known feline nutritionist, groomer, and behaviorist. She lives with and cares for eleven (sometimes more) cats. Her human clients have included many celebrities from the worlds of entertainment and fashion. She is the author of *The Natural Cat*, *It's a Cat's Life*, and the annual *Natural Cat Calendar*. She lives in New York City.

NORMA ECKROATE is a writer. She also has extensive experience in theater management and producing on Broadway and across the country. She lives in Virginia Beach, Virginia.

THE
NEW
NATURAL
CAT

A COMPLETE GUIDE FOR
FINICKY OWNERS

by

Anitra Frazier

with

Norma Eckroate

Foreword by Richard H. Pitcairn, D.V.M., Ph.D.
Illustrated by Glenna Hartwell

A PLUME BOOK

This book is not a veterinary reference book. The advice it contains is general, not specific, and neither the authors nor the publishers can be held responsible for any adverse reactions to the recipes, formulas, recommendations or instructions contained herein. Do not try to diagnose or treat a feline health problem without consulting a qualified veterinarian, preferably one with a holistic practice. The recommendations in this book should not be instituted without seeking professional advice for your cat's specific needs.

PLUME
Published by the Penguin Group
Penguin Books USA Inc., 375 Hudson Street, New York, New York 10014, U.S.A.
Penguin Books Ltd, 27 Wrights Lane, London W8 5TZ, England
Penguin Books Australia Ltd, Ringwood, Victoria, Australia
Penguin Books Canada Ltd, 10 Alcorn Ave, Toronto, Ontario, Canada M4V 3B2
Penguin Books (N.Z.) Ltd, 182-190 Wairau Road, Auckland 10, New Zealand

Penguin Books Ltd, Registered Offices: Harmondsworth, Middlesex, England

Published by Plume, an imprint of New American Library,
a division of Penguin Books USA Inc. Simultaneously printed in a Dutton hardcover edition.

First Printing, November, 1990
10 9 8 7 6 5

Copyright © Anitra Frazier and Norma Eckroate, 1981, 1983, 1990
All rights reserved. For information address

Ⓟ REGISTERED TRADEMARK—MARCA REGISTRADA

Library of Congress Cataloging-in-Publication Data

Frazier, Anitra, 1936–
    The new Natural cat : a complete guide for finicky owners / Anitra
Frazier with Norma Eckroate ; Foreword by Richard H. Pitcairn;
illustrated by Glenna Hartwell.—Newly rev. and expanded.
        p. cm.
    Includes bibliographical references and index.
    ISBN 0-452-26517-7
    1. Cats. 2. Cats—Health.   I. Eckroate, Norma, 1951–
II. Frazier, Anitra, 1936– Natural cat. III. Title.
SF447.F7 1990b
636.8—dc20   90-41223
                                                            CIP
Printed in the United States of America
Set in Palatino
Designed by Soloway · Mitchell Design Associates

Without limiting the rights under copyright reserved above, no part of this publication may be reproduced, stored in or introduced into a retrieval system, or transmitted, in any form, or by any means (electronic, mechanical, photocopying, recording, or otherwise), without the prior written permission of both the copyright owner and the above publisher of this book.

BOOKS ARE AVAILABLE AT QUANTITY DISCOUNTS WHEN USED TO PROMOTE PRODUCTS OR SERVICES. FOR INFORMATION PLEASE WRITE TO PREMIUM MARKETING DIVISION, PENGUIN BOOKS USA INC., 375 HUDSON STREET, NEW YORK, NEW YORK 10014

Dedicated to
the owners who asked
and the cats who taught

Acknowledgments

Special thanks go to Dr. Richard H. Pitcairn for his encouragement and guidance through the years, his generous contribution of recipes and information, and his astute editing of the veterinary medical material in Chapters 9 and 10.

Our heartfelt thanks for their contributions to this book also go to:

Phyllis Levy, our guiding light

Doctors, healers, and teachers: Dr. Paul Rowan, Dr. Gerald Johnson, Dr. Edwina Ho, and Dr. Amrita McLanahan

Sources of information and inspiration: Integral Yoga Institute and Association for Research and Enlightenment

And the many supporters who cheered us on, especially: Alicia Perez, Matt Sartwell, Sandra Martin, Margaret Blackstone, Andrew Lewis, Sharon and Steve Sherman, Lucy and Dan Kaplan, Olga Aparicio, Lynne and Gus Gustavson, Ursula Jahoda, Swami Gurucharanananda, Phyllis Embleton, Mark MacCauley, and J. David Stites.

Contents

Contents

Contents

Chapter
10
273   A Guide to
       Common Feline Health Problems

Contents

Foreword

This is a very special book. It is written by a woman who was willing to put aside a mass of opinion and ignorance and find out for herself the truth about cats.

What strikes me as her greatest contribution (besides a wealth of practical and useful information) is her approach toward understanding. Rather than letting herself be captivated by ideas and images passed on by many sources, she determined to find out firsthand how to care for cats—by asking the animals themselves.

I am reminded of a conversation that took place some years ago between the author J. Allen Boone and Mojave Dan, a desert hermit who had close communion with animals. As he wrote in his fascinating book *Kinship with All Life*, Boone had been struggling to find out the real truth about the nature of a remarkable dog who was his companion. So he put the issue to his friend Dan. After a long silence, Dan's cogent reply was "There's facts about dogs, and there's opinions about them. The dogs have the facts, and the humans have the opinions. . . . If you want facts about a dog, always get them straight from the dog. If you want opinions, get them from the human."

Much of what Anita Frazier has learned about cats has come in just such a way, and she has reaped a wealth of information about them. Her book invites you to travel the same road. As you read it, you can see how she evolved the process of watching cats without a screen of preconceptions. This kind of learning does not end.

There is another hidden value in all of this. Many people have learned through relating to animals what it is to care for and accept responsibility for another being. All the basic elements of relationship are there—the same elements found in relationship with a friend, husband or wife, child, or even a plant. If one can discover how to relate fully to an animal, without exploitation, with real care and concern for its welfare and continued physical and psychological well-being, then one can relate to anyone. The skills involved are universal.

Many people have found in themselves a compassion they did not know existed, by relating to an animal in their life. This potential is meant to be extended to all relationships. Some, however, focus their affections on only one or two animals, and in so doing become withdrawn into themselves. Later, when the animal dies, as it inevitably will, such people may suffer terrible anguish. I bring this up here because I see it so often. Reading Anitra's book reminded me again of the potential that can be realized through relationship with a cat or any animal. Not stopping at this point—extending that potential to ever wider circles of both people and animals—can allow for a continuous learning that is immensely rewarding.

The Natural Cat is also extremely practical and covers common and mundane problems in a unique way—holistically. That is, the author considers all aspects of the animal's life and environment, both psychological and physical.

I want to emphasize Anitra's sections on declawing and over-population. As a veterinarian, I have seen firsthand the incredible suffering of cats who have an amputation of what is to them their fingers. And my work in an SPCA clinic (Society for the Prevention of Cruelty to Animals) brings me face-to-face daily with the suffering and neglect of unwanted animals. It is a blight on our society that such conditions should exist.

I heartily recommend this book to you. Use it as a learning tool and as a source of practical information. May both you and your animal friends profit!

Richard H. Pitcairn, D.V.M., Ph.D.

Introduction

"Cats?"

"Yes. Holistic health care—for cats."

People find it hard to believe that such a career exists. "However did you get started doing *that*!?" they usually ask.

When I was little I had two alternative goals of what I wanted to do when I grew up. One was to work somehow with animals; the other was to perform on the stage.

I attended Lebanon Valley College, a Pennsylvania Dutch institution, which had a top-notch conservatory of music, and I lucked out with a great voice teacher. Thanks to them I ended up in show business. I landed my first job with a professional summer stock theater three days after graduation and my first career was launched. I was never famous, but then I didn't want to be. "Stars don't get to work as often," actress Barbara Barrie pointed out to me.

I enjoyed my career to the hilt, from the exciting Broadway openings to the television commercials and the national tours. It was during this period that two new elements entered my life that were to have profound effects in the not-too-distant future: I became a student at Integral Yoga Institute, and somebody gave me a cat. She was my first, a huge female Siamese named Eurydice. It was she who began my cat education.

I'd probably still be cavorting around on Broadway if I hadn't taken a working vacation with Club Med. I went to teach yoga in Yugoslavia, and there I picked up hepatitis. I nearly died. When I got back enough strength to work again, I still looked too awful to think of appearing on stage or before a camera. So I started looking for something else.

The job that came my way was working for Dr. Paul Rowan, who was a cat specialist in Greenwich Village at that time. I learned a lot about cats working with Dr. Rowan and his staff, but I learned a lot more about what people don't know about cats. Dr. Rowan had specialized in cats because cats were "treated like second-class citizens or 'difficult' dogs." Paul Rowan found better ways of doing a lot of things where cats were concerned, and he and his staff were constantly revising and improving their standard operating procedures.

The day they decided to send me out to groom cats in their own homes, my life was to change completely. A white hatbox marked "grooming kit" was shoved into my hands along with a ragged piece of tablet paper listing the names and addresses of five cats that needed grooming. I knew next to nothing about grooming cats in their own home, or anywhere else for that matter, and there was nowhere I could go to learn. "Nobody's ever done it before," they said. "Why don't you just give it a try."

That little suggestion turned out to be a pattern that was to be repeated over and over during the next sixteen years. Although I didn't know it at the time, when I accepted that white hatbox one door clicked shut behind me and another opened and I stepped through. The actress who put on costumes and makeup and sang and danced onstage seemed like an acquaintance I had once known, but didn't anymore. It was as if I were reincarnated into a new life without dying in between.

When I was "thrown to the cats," so to speak, the cats caught me. They taught me everything I needed to know from there on in. I *had* to learn from the cats—there was no one else to teach me. I was the slowest student in all Creation at first while I was learning anatomy, skin tensions, fur texture, and scissor angles. The pussycats persevered with me, and I also learned patience and concentration. I watched the cats, I felt the cats, I listened to the cats, and I loved the cats. The love between us opened the doors of communication, and the cats gave me lessons in all the things a cat thinks are most important. Cat lessons are there for everybody, you only have to love and ask—not what you want to know but what it is that they would like you to know. My first cat lessons were on how to groom them and how to keep every part of their external bodies just the way they most like them to be.

Because I visited them in their home environment, I was soon made aware of problems and unanswered questions that owners all over New York City had in common—about random wetting, how to train to the scratching post, persistent health problems, and special home-nursing care—things that were outside the realm of grooming.

Of course, my first move was to refer all problems to the veterinarians, assuming that they would have the answers. In this I found I was mistaken. Many of these problems were not in their field. In fact, before long I had a whole collection of problems that did not seem to be in anybody's field. So I looked for the answers. I asked. I read. But in the end it was the cats themselves that came through for me once again. "Stick as close as you can to nature," Dr. Rowan used to say, "and you'll never go very far wrong." So I researched how cats handle some of these problems in the wild. What is the purpose of their behavior? As possible answers began to emerge they all seemed to fall under that old heading, "Nobody's ever done it that way before; why don't you just try it?"

Many answers came from the sick cats and the castoffs—cats so old or sick, so smelly or ugly, that no one wanted them. When I invited them to spend whatever time they had left with me, I never dreamed that they would pay for their keep in the solid gold coin of knowledge gained. You don't learn much from a cat that is young and strong, healthy and well adjusted. These castoff cats taught me with their bodies, their patience, and their love. Home care of the sick cat I learned from sick cats. My recommendations concerning proper diet and feeding habits are largely a distillation of what is found in nature. I didn't create any of this information. I only asked the questions, and, by the grace of the cat goddess, the answers came.

By the time I met Norma Eckroate and her big red Maine coon cat, Clarence, I had seven years of experience behind me. I could handle just about any cat, keep him calm, and convince him to let me do whatever was needed.

Norma, like so many owners, had been doing everything she was told to do for the cat she loved, but still his health was sliding downhill and she was in fear of losing him. "One more attack of feline urologic syndrome," the veterinarian had said, "and we'll have to do a urethrostomy or put him to sleep." Norma and Clarence were at their wits' end.

I took one look at greasy, sick, matted, flea-ridden Clarence and I totally flipped out. I became so upset that I lost what little tact I had ever possessed. I cut the commercial flea collar off his neck and flung it into the wastebasket. All through the grooming and bath I lectured poor Norma on the horrors and futility of most commercial flea products. Then I went on and on about the food she was feeding Clarence and how it could contribute to his disease. Clarence's brush was *wrong*; his diet was *wrong*; the litter box was *wrong*—I didn't have one good word to say to that poor, distraught, concerned owner.

Norma did not become discouraged; she did not become angry—far from it, she seemed immensely relieved and buoyed by the new information, which she believed would turn the tide in Clarence's favor. "Everything you're saying makes perfect sense," she exclaimed. "You really must write it all down in a book!"

By that time Clarence was looking and feeling much more comfortable and I was calmer. So I just laughed. "I can't type," I replied, "and I can't spell, and I'm not organized."

"Oh, I can do all that," she said, smiling. "I'll help you." And so she did.

While we were writing the book we were warned by level-headed friends that such a work would probably never be published. We would be sued, they said, for suggesting that grocery-store cat foods were far from perfect. As for encouraging owners to start telling their veterinarians how to reduce stress while their cats were hospitalized, well, it just wasn't done! Sympathetic friends described the book as being "too far in the vanguard and ahead of its time." Others, less sympathetic, declared us to be out on the lunatic fringe.

Nevertheless, I did have a lot of new information and I did feel responsible for its perpetuation. All those new facts and techniques could not be left in one person's head. After all, what if something were to happen to me? Bop! Information disappears!

Introduction

There turned out to be an awful lot of finicky owners out there whose main concern was "What is the best for my cat?" Our little *Natural Cat* didn't land us in jail after all; it survived two publishers going bankrupt and still managed to sell 115,000 copies.

Ten years after it was first published, *The Natural Cat* is no longer "far in the vanguard" or "out on the lunatic fringe." Instead, we find ourselves smack-dab in the middle of the establishment and that won't do at all. An updated and vastly expanded edition was clearly called for. After all, much progress had been made in the world of natural and holistic health care. Owners have become increasingly aware of the new applications and of research into traditional fields such as homeopathy, acupuncture, and herbs.

Owners haven't stopped asking questions. Far from it: *The Natural Cat* opened their minds to new possibilities and seemed to generate as many questions as it gave answers. Now owners want to know about visualization, Bach flower remedies, interspecies communication, and all manner of new and expanded home-nursing techniques that can be applied to those wonderful cats who cherish them.

The book you have in your hands right now contains all the old information that is still applicable plus all of the new information, techniques, and discoveries that have accumulated in my head over the past ten years. The cats have continued to teach me. They have entrusted me with their bodies and honored me by opening their minds, and they have made of themselves a bridge to link me with other humans who have shared with me their knowledge and their own wonderful questions.

So, you see, this book isn't really by me. The information is coming through me but not from me. Knowledge is like the air; it's there for you to use and pass along but not to possess.

New knowledge seems to evolve out of the old. It is my hope that the knowledge contained in this book will generate further new knowledge in the mind of each reader. After all, each cat is unique, just as each one of us is unique. I know that with this in mind you will not make the mistake of thinking of anything in this book as "the last word." There is always the possibility of finding an even better way. Perhaps it will be your cat, giving cat lessons to you, who will reveal this even better way. All you have to do is keep your mind open, and love, and ask.

1
Desirable Behavior
in Cats and Owners

Communication and understanding are the two most important links between cats and their owners. It is obvious to sensitive and caring owners that their cats are aware when the owners are unhappy or in ill health. Likewise, the cats respond with joyful play when the owner's mood is jolly.

By understanding the cat's psyche, you are better able to open the pathways to a rewarding and fulfilling relationship—for you and for your feline friend. All you have to do is look at any situation from your cat's point of view.

Communicating with Your Cat

The golden rule for the finicky cat owner is "Don't limit yourself." In your relationship with a pussycat, you will discover new dimensions of sensitivity. When new owners discover petting, they first learn the pleasures of medium and firm stroking. However, there is another dimension of stroking in which you deliberately hold yourself back.

Because cats are much more sensitive than we are, both physically and emotionally, they are fascinated by the very light touch. Actually, if you want to experiment, you can try what I call the "feather" touch, and the "almost" touch. For the "feather" touch, your hand touches only the very tips of the hair throughout the entire stroking motion. Your cat will probably respond by arching his back up against your hand and purring encouragement for you to proceed on to a medium and then firm stroke.

To describe the "almost" touch, which is the most tantalizing of all, I'll share with you a charming scene I witnessed during a retreat at the Integral Yoga Ashram in Virginia. One afternoon, while walking down a woodland path, I came upon one of the swamis surrounded by a little group of kindergarten children. She had apparently been conducting a nature walk when I happened upon them. One little fellow was crouched down on all fours in the middle of the path nose-to-nose with a big Monarch butterfly. Of course, the child reached out to touch the beautiful creature, and, as he did, the swami said softly, "Just pet his aura, Michael, that's the way to pet a butterfly."

"Just pet the aura" is a good description of the "almost" touch. Just pet the aura and you may be very surprised at the response.

Both of these techniques are especially good for cats who are old, ill, or arthritic. They also work magic on frightened cats who have been abused in the past.

The very best lesson in the soft approach can be learned from your cat. First, put your hands behind your back and, bending over, reach out to your cat with just your nose. Then stop about six inches away, be still, and wait—and your cat will demonstrate to you how very softly it is possible to touch somebody. This approach to a cat—this overture with the nose—demonstrates great trust and friendliness, because you are exposing your eyes and face without having any defense in reserve. It conveys the message "I love you and trust you" very nicely. I use it often when greeting a cat client with whom I am already acquainted. However, I never use this approach on a strange cat until I have first ascertained that he or she is fairly calm—although this action does serve to calm a nervous cat.

Another dimension in interacting with your cat is throwing a "cat kiss" from across the room. A cat kiss is a long, slow blink with your gaze and attention fixed on the cat's eyes before, during, and after the blink. When throwing a cat kiss, I always think the phrase "I love you" ("I" before, "love" during, and "you" after the blink).

Cats don't communicate with sound only—in fact, they seldom

communicate that way. I notice that cats use the slow eye blink communication when they are feeling relaxed, contented, and secure. I started practicing every time I could get a cat's eye attention and found that I received a return blink from the cat by the third try. Delighted with my break in the language barrier, I began throwing these cat kisses to any and all cats with whom I came in eye contact.

If you'd like to perfect the technique, you need to be aware that you are really doing two things at the same time: the physical focus and blink plus the mental message "I love you." Practice them separately; then put them together. Think the "I love you" with emotional warmth but do not get so enthusiastic you screw up your face or squeeze your eyes shut. That only clouds the issue. The blink is slow and gentle; the mental message is warm and strong.

The supreme test came for me when I began throwing cat kisses to strange felines on the other side of closed windows as I walked down the street. After my technique was perfected, I was thrilled to discover that these strangers would automatically throw back a leisurely reply. They seemed to take it in stride that a human walking by would casually throw them a kiss. Only twice have I had the experience of a cat doing a sort of double-take afterward. Looking rather surprised, they seemed to be thinking, "Hey, she speaks Cat!"

Keep in mind that, because cats are so much more sensitive than we are, they will always enjoy the kiss or loving word thrown from afar. Also remember that cats, being so small, feel very much at our mercy. Often a cat's hiss is a defensive act to try to make the large and threatening human back off just enough so the cat can slip away unharmed. A hissing cat is a frightened cat. Whenever you deal with a cat who is nervous, frightened, or just standoffish, you must become totally permissive. If the cat doesn't want to be touched, don't touch; if he wants to leave, let him go. You must take great pains to be polite—polite in the cat sense. In this way, you will leave the door open for your relationship to progress at a later date.

A really top-notch finicky owner will always be polite with any cat, as a matter of course. Never walk up to cats and scoop them up without first announcing your presence and your intent and asking permission. If you have more than one cat, you can see a demonstration of this sort of politeness by watching a performance of the cats' "I want to sit next to you" ritual. The ritual usually goes like this: Marbles is sleeping on a chair, and Roger jumps up next to her. Roger begins licking the sleeping Marbles, thereby announcing his presence and begging leave to stay. Marbles (1) returns the grooming with a casual lick or two, indicating acceptance; (2) ignores Roger, indicating basic neutrality with "You better not disturb me" undertones; or (3) she can lift her head and growl a rejection, indicating that Roger had better jump down. A cat never just plops down next to another cat. Those tentative licks are our equivalent for saying, "May I?" Impolite cats are simply not acceptable to other cats. Cats are willing to make all sorts of allowances for the humans they love, but isn't it much nicer to slip gracefully into their society by being polite on their terms?

Because cats seldom express themselves with sound (except for the Siamese), people sometimes think that they are uncommunicative. In reality, cats have a vast and rich vocabulary of body postures, poses, mental pictures, emotions, and actions with which they communicate among themselves—or with anyone else who knows the language.

The carriage of the tail is often a clue to how your cat is feeling. A tail held high is jaunty, enthusiastic, or playful. A tail between the legs or wrapped very tightly around the ankles indicates fear. A tail carried in a low graceful arc is casual as is a tail loosely wrapped around a reclining cat. A cat uses his tail for balance when he leaps. He can also use it to control nervousness and excitement by swinging or lashing the tail as an outlet for tension or to drain off excess energy.

The human mind is better equipped than the cat's for learning other languages. Therefore, it makes more sense for us to make the effort to learn and practice cat communication and etiquette than to expect a cat to act like a person.

However, when a close and loving relationship exists between a cat and a human, do not be surprised if, under certain circumstances, the cat begins to express himself in a very human way. Meowing or calling to get your attention is probably the most common example. Cats seldom communicate vocally with each other except when mating, fighting, or rounding up the kittens.

Modern science is now verifying the mental communication between cats. But your cat may have noticed that we humans gain each other's attention by making noise (how crude!) and so he decides to give it a try. Lo and behold, it works—so your cat has learned to call you.

The cat performs many of our hand skills, such as picking up, carrying, and petting, with his mouth. Instead of petting, licking and grooming are used as signs of affection. However, many years ago when I used to hold my first cat, Eurydice, in my arms, she would reach up and tap my cheek or chin several times with her paw. I cannot think of any other explanation except that, out of her deep love for me, she was trying to express affection in a way that I would understand. She was copying my way of showing love. Eurydice was my first cat and, at that time, I assumed that her behavior was altogether unique. She was my darling and I was quite convinced that I was living with the most intelligent, the most loving, the most wonderful cat in the world. Be that as it may, I have, over the years, seen this same loving communication displayed between many cats and their owners. I'm sure anyone who has enjoyed close relationships with cats could say the same. Mind you, I'm not saying that my Eurydice was not the most wonderful cat in the world; but I am admitting that in this one thing she was not unique.

Years later, Priscilla, my tiny blue point Siamese, would express affection to those with whom she was intimate by giving "hugs" with her teeth. I would always pick Priscilla up in my arms and hug her to me as soon as I arrived home. Priscilla knew that what humans do with the hands, cats do with the mouth, so she would reach up and take my chin between her teeth and "hug" it. I have since met several affectionate felines who express their love in this way, "hugging" the owner's arm or hand or ear. The cat's teeth close firmly but gently, denting but never breaking the skin. It is really an enormous compliment to the owner and shows a great depth of understanding between cat and human for, without that deep and loving rapport, a human might react with surprise, and if he should pull away quickly, he could scratch himself on the cat's eye teeth. Sometimes, when I stayed out too long, Priscilla would be so overcome with happiness and relief that I was safely back that she would "hug" a bit too hard. I never told her for fear

11

she might misconstrue and stop altogether, thinking that all "hugging with mouth" was unpleasant to me.

Emotions and Well-Being

It's often said that dogs resemble their owners in one way or another. I've observed that cats too can resemble their owners in temperament and emotional tendencies.

Recent studies have shown that cats "pick up" their owner's thoughts just as they have always picked up the thoughts of their cat friends. You may walk into the kitchen twenty times a day, but the cat seems to know when it's his meal you're about to prepare, and then he comes running, even if you don't stick to a regular time schedule every day. It's also possible that they pick up mental images. For example, your thought of feeding Muffy is tied to an image in your own mind of your getting a can of food out of the cupboard, opening it, etc., and your cat "sees" that image.

In the same way, cats react to their owner's attitudes, emotions, and physical condition. Deborah, a client of mine who had an invalid mother in another state, noticed that time after time she would return from a family visit when her mother had a turn for the worse to find her cat, Dizzy, in the beginning stages of feline urologic syndrome (FUS), a stress-triggered disease. Knowing that FUS can be fatal if not caught in the very early stages, she was extremely upset. After this occurred several times, she also noticed that the cat was always healthy when she returned from routine business trips. Dizzy was used to being left alone since Deborah frequently made business trips, and in every case, the same kindly neighbor was coming in to feed Dizzy the same high quality food with the same special vitamins and supplements for an FUS prone cat.

I suspected that Dizzy was picking up Deborah's own emotional upset at her mother's condition and that this created a chemical imbalance within the cat's body, making him more susceptible to the disease. FUS is usually triggered by negative emotions.

So we tried a little experiment. First, whenever she went away anywhere, she would leave a cardboard carton on the floor for Dizzy to lounge and play in. She lined the bottom with a blouse or pajama she had worn so that Dizzy would have the comfort of her scent while she was gone, thus providing both a new distraction and more security. Since Dizzy seemed to be picking up Deborah's thoughts and emotions anyway, I asked her to try consciously sending him some thoughts—the kind of thoughts that would make him feel the way she wanted him to feel: calm and happy.

It has been scientifically proven that thoughts can be transferred in picture form. "Sending love" is wonderful but only part of the picture. So two or three times a day Deborah would sit quietly and picture Dizzy lounging happily in the box just the way she hoped he would. Cats have very acute senses so she would also remind herself (and Dizzy) how pleasant and clean a cardboard box can smell, how quiet the world is when sounds are muffled by the walls of the box, and how soft and comforting the pajamas in the bottom were. She pictured herself sitting close by the box and feeling happy as she looked at Dizzy and loved him.

It worked. The FUS attacks stopped, and Dizzy greeted her with the same joyous excitement no matter where she was returning from. And there was an extra bonus as well. Those three-minute mental visits with Dizzy seemed to calm Deborah's mind as well. They were like little mini-vacations in the midst of a difficult situation. She found she could handle the problems better and return home less fatigued than she used to.

Controlling Your Cat's Behavior Patterns

One of the cat's greatest fears is fear of the unknown. Conversely, familiarity breeds contentment. Cats love familiar things, patterns, places, and sounds. The very fact that a thing is well known and familiar makes it dear to the cat. We can use this love of sameness as a tool to direct the cat's behavior patterns. If we make certain ground familiar, that is the path the cat will want to take. And to engineer a situation so that the cat wants to do what we want him to do is really the only way to control a cat's behavior patterns.

You can't train a cat the way you would train a dog or a child. A dog positively enjoys learning to do anything that will please you. And if you're training children you can explain reasons and advantages for behavior patterns you wish them to adopt.

There is, however, one golden rule in all three cases. In training a cat, a dog, or a young child, it is most important that you be consistent. If there is something that you don't want the cat to do, such as jumping on a table when there is food on it, then don't *ever* invite the cat up onto the table. *Never*. Not for any reason. If you see the cat on the table, shove him or her unceremoniously onto the floor with a word of disapproval. You must keep it simple—not confusing.

It is difficult to train a cat not to jump up onto the table and/ or rifle the wastepaper basket, because they are negative lessons. It is much easier to train the cat *to* do something. For example, if you want a cat *not* to scratch the couch and *to* scratch the scratching post, just forget about the couch, which is the "no-no," and concentrate on building fascinating rituals around the scratching post, which is the "yes-yes." (See the section in Chapter 4, "Encouraging Use of the Scratching Post.")

Velvet Paws for Human Flesh; Claws for Toys and Scratching Post

The same principle applies when you're teaching a cat not to use teeth or claws on human flesh or clothing. Don't let anyone play with the cat using their hands or flesh or any part of their own bodies. The cat cannot make the distinction between being allowed to roughhouse with the man of the house and not being allowed to play rough with Great Aunt Ethel when she extends a delicately veined hand to stroke an ear. And heaven forbid you should have young children come to visit who want to hug and kiss a pussycat who has been taught that the use of teeth and claws on human flesh is okay.

My Big Purr was almost a year old when he was left at my door. He had evidently been encouraged to play roughly by someone in his past. About a week after he arrived, we were lying on the floor together and I was stroking him. He was all purrs and stretches. His purrs got louder and louder. Then suddenly, without warning, his body contracted, he trapped my arm in his front claws, pulled my hand into his teeth, and pressed his hind claws into the soft flesh of my inner arm, preparing to rake the claws down my skin. I froze, afraid to move.

I didn't know what to do. Purr was not angry with me; he

was just so overcome by happiness and love that his emotions overflowed and expressed themselves in this very wild and primitive way. Many cats bite softly to express affection. But Purr's former owner must have made the mistake of playing roughly with him, using his hands instead of a toy. This naturally taught Purr that using claws on skin was okay. When a cat like that grows up, continuing the pattern, what was amusing in a kitten becomes downright dangerous in a large animal. And Purr at one year old was definitely not small.

Few people know how to break this pattern once they have inadvertently established it. Some begin by hitting the cat, which only reinforces the feeling of roughness and brutality. Some even go so far as to mutilate their pet with a declawing operation. In this case, the cat automatically becomes a biter. In both cases, the situation becomes progressively worse instead of better. The cat adores the owner and reaches out for physical closeness and play in the very way the owner has taught him as a kitten. The cat and the owner both end up sad and lonely. They miss the closeness and fun but don't know how to get it back without the owner getting scratched and the cat getting yelled at.

Of course, the easiest way out is never to start the pattern in the first place. *Never* play with a cat or kitten with your bare hands. Use a toy, a sash, or ball—never your hand (and, incidentally, never use a grooming tool as a toy). In short, if you don't want the cat to scratch something, don't even begin to suggest it. Never let the cat start in the first place.

Use your hands for stroking, petting, grooming, transporting, sometimes medicating, but never for play. To cats, play means teeth and claws—catch and kill. If they are not scratching, pouncing, and biting, it's not play, not really; it's love and cuddle. Show them from the start that hands and skin are for love and cuddle; toys are for play.

If you are dealing with a kitten who gets carried away and carelessly uses claws on the skin, just stop dead and relax *toward* him and disengage the claws, unhooking them by pushing the feet *forward*, never pull away. Then immediately put the offending kitten gently but firmly away from you with words of deep disappointment. Do not become excited in any way or raise your voice; you want to put a big damper on all exuberance or emotion. Then ignore the kitten for at least three minutes—don't even allow eye contact. Thus you are demonstrating that claws on skin are socially unacceptable—and cats are very social animals. Do the same thing in exactly the same way every time the kitten uses claws on skin. A kitten learns faster if your reaction does not vary. After five or six calm repetitions of you being disappointed and him being ostracized, the kitten will become very careful not to initiate the undesirable chain of events by being too rough or careless in the first place.

At the same time that you are repatterning your pet's behavior, be sure to offer plenty of fascinating alternatives to help drain off the negative emotions. Play catch and kill games two or three times a day using a ball, a toy mouse, or a sash. Get creative, use your imagination to devise ways to refocus his energy.

Years ago, when this situation arose with Purr, I was at a loss and completely at his mercy. Purr was no longer a kitten one could calmly unhook and place on the floor. Also, the problem was very strongly established. Obviously it was one more reason why he was put on my doorstep in the first place (besides his spraying problem, because he was unneutered when he arrived). A big strong cat with weapons like that could easily put a large dog to flight. An inexperienced owner might well be frightened.

It was fortunate that I had enough knowledge to stop Purr's action. By relaxing toward him, I confused him. Prey always pulls away and so, unfortunately, do most people. Press *toward* a cat's teeth and claws, and the cat will stop, totally confused, for a second or two. In those two seconds, then, I had to somehow distract him before he resumed the action. My arm was still encircled in a ring of front claws, my hand clamped to his teeth, the teeth ready to chomp. Those miniature scimitars in the back were denting my soft underarm and preparing to rake down.

I didn't know what to do. I had a heartbeat to decide, and I had no answer. No past experience to help me, no bit of forgotten lore bubbling to the surface of consciousness out of all the book learning stored in the depths of my memory. Nothing. My beautiful Purr, my soft and loving friend, was about to injure me and I was helpless. I loved him, and he was hurting me, and my heart was broken. I started to cry.

Purr pulled away! From the look on his face, I knew I had

stumbled on an answer. He was so startled he unhooked his claws. So I whimpered and mewed, translating emotion into sound, trying very hard to sound like an injured kitten. Purr looked as if he were dying of embarrassment. Evidently no one had ever gotten through to him before that claws hurt skin. Purr was so upset he didn't know what to do—he couldn't stand to see me cry. Carefully he rolled onto his feet. His ears were sort of sticking out at right angles; his muzzle was all stiff and wrinkling as if he was smelling something that hurt his nose. He moved off, looking so confused and sheepish that I felt almost as bad as when he had me "captured."

I didn't want to change him. But how could I live with this breathtaking animal if he periodically displayed the manners of a cougar? I loved his wildness. But I needed him to learn when to be wild and when to be a velvet-pawed pussycat.

To change an undesirable behavior pattern you have to (1) stop the bad action, (2) distract the cat's attention away from it, and (3) focus attention on a new and desirable action.

After only four or five repetitions of the "crying because of claws" pattern, Purr never again unsheathed a claw to me. However, I do not consider my actions in this case a success. Evidently the old owner had played roughly with Purr while lying on the floor next to him. Lying together on the floor must have triggered the old teeth and claws impulse, and this frightened him for my safety. The last thing he wanted was to see me cry again. So now he always moves away if I try to lie down next to him to pet him. Instead I must be standing or sitting, and he must be perched above or below me—the same level won't do.

I did not successfully fulfill step 3—focusing his attention on a new and desirable activity. In the tension of that situation, I didn't retain his attention long enough to do it. I shocked and embarrassed him, and now he won't lie next to me on the floor.

Dealing with Abused or Neglected Animals

Just as you would feed a starving animal frequent small meals but never a large meal, give the emotionally deprived cat frequent light contact for very short periods. In some cases it may be necessary to pull yourself back all the way to just eye and voice contact. When you add petting, move slowly, use the light touch, and *keep it short*. Always stop soon enough to leave him wanting more. The object is to repeat the desirable pattern: love and petting make love and purring, over and over again. Never ever allow your actions to go on so long that you trigger the undesirable response of biting, scratching, or hiding in fear.

Patience is all important; it's better to go too slow than too fast. When I start repatterning a cat who has been abused or locked in a cage for a long time, I know before I start that I can expect to work with the patient for several weeks before he begins to relax and enjoy a normal relationship.

From time to time I come upon an owner who is unwittingly initiating the scratch and bite response by overstimulating a hypersensitive cat. When some cats are petted they will first react with a typical purring, stretching, and kneading response. However, if the petting becomes too vigorous or is simply carried on too long, the cat's emotions are stimulated beyond the point where the cat can either understand or control himself. The emotions engulf the cat, his own emotions frightening him, and he lashes out at the cause of this emotional tidal wave: you. I see this reaction most often in cats who have come out of a situation where there was very little demonstration of love. They are taken into a new home starving for affection and physical closeness, and when they get it they experience a kind of emotional indigestion. When this happens, keep calm. The cat will be as frightened of his sudden and unexpected reaction as you are. Gently withdraw and try to remember how long you were petting your friend before this reaction occurred. Next time, you must stop earlier. Remember, until he settles down, *always leave him wanting more*.

The Proper Way to Pick Up a Cat

When I go into someone's home to groom, I always ask the owner to pick up the cat and place him or her on the grooming area. This is because I want to demonstrate to the cat that the beloved, trusted owner approves of the proceedings. I was amazed to see how many owners did not know how to pick up a cat comfortably. I saw cats dangling by their midriffs, gasping for breath over the owner's arm, and, even more frequently, cats clasped under the armpits with their heavy hindquarters swinging in the air, and their shoulders hunched up to their cheeks with a look of long-suffering patience on their little faces. In such cases, I would always delay the grooming session a moment to give a few pointers on how to pick up the cat comfortably.

Here are a few rules to remember before you begin:

1. Before you pick up the cat, announce your intentions of doing so.
2. Before you pick up the cat, *face the cat away from you.*
3. Hindquarters must be supported comfortably. They are the heaviest part of the cat's body.
4. Leave the legs as free as possible to give the cat a feeling of freedom and safety. Cats hate to have their forelegs or paws held.
5. Don't squeeze or grasp too hard.
6. Never breathe into the cat's ears, eyes, or nose—it tickles.

Once the cat is facing away from you, all you have to do is slip one hand under the cat's chest and the other hand under a thigh from behind. In both picking up and putting down, move the head slightly ahead of the hindlegs. When picking him up, this tilts the cat's weight back onto the hand that supports the rear. When putting the cat down, it allows the cat to see where he is going. Because the legs are always left free and pointing toward the floor, the cat feels very safe and secure.

My Big Purr wanted no part of being picked up when I first got him. I had no wish to impose my will on an affectionate and exciting pet but, for the sake of practicality, I knew that I had to be able to pick Purr up to place him in the carry case for the annual trip to the veterinarian, and there were bound to be other times when I would need to pick him up. So, using cats' love of ritual, I invented a wonderful new game that we called "Pick up/Put down."

Ritual, to *be* ritual, must be repeated frequently. So, for a few weeks, we played Pick up/Put down two or three times a day. I would come up behind Purr, announce my intention by rubbing my thumb against my other fingers, which made a "shushing" sound near his ear, and repeat the ritual phrase "Do you want to come?" His natural reaction was usually to jump up with glee and face me, with an expectant look on his face. I would then turn him around to face away from me, stroke my hands around and underneath his chest and hindquarters, and lift him up a bit, just barely disengaging his feet from the ground. During this action, I always repeated the second ritual phrase, "There's my good boy." The trick is, while cats are learning, you must put their feet back down again *before* they begin to get nervous or upset. Design calmness into the pattern, and *leave them wanting more*. Always follow this ritual with stroking and lavish praise and approval.

For the first few days, the whole procedure took less than ten seconds. By the third day, I was lifting him up about three feet, always keeping my face close to the back of his neck to help him feel secure. Because I was bent over, I was able to nuzzle my nose and my mouth against his ruff and murmur loving words. The ritual still lasted less than ten seconds. In two weeks, I could lift him up, straighten up myself, and tuck his hindquarters between my arm and body at the side of my waist. His front feet were still left dangling floorward, while my right hand supported his chest— so he still had a feeling of security. I learned from Purr that a cat doesn't wiggle as much if you move about while you're carrying him. So it's easier if you have a definite place to go or a reason for picking him up. If you stand still, keep yourself in control by putting the cat down before he starts wiggling to jump down.

The Carry Case

When you choose the carry case, remember above all that you and your feline companion are going to depend upon that case for the next twenty years or more. You'll be using it for the yearly trip to the veterinarian and for any other trips such as moving or vacations. But, even more important, the proper case is like an insurance policy. Come fire or flood, come sickness or accident, come hell or high water, you and your beloved cat can pick up and *go* in security and comfort.

Keeping in mind the number of years you're going to be using the case, you will not choose a case because it is on sale or because it matches your luggage; you will choose a case because:

1. *It fits your cat.* The case should be large enough for the occupant to be able to stand up, turn around, and sit down. It should not be so large that the passenger will slide around. That would be frightening. Cats like to be able to brace themselves against the sides. It gives a cat a feeling of still having some sort of control over what's happening to his body. Size small is fine for a kitten, but your cat will soon outgrow it. My solution is to get a size medium and put a smaller cardboard box inside, nicely braced with newspapers or towels, until the kitten grows into the medium size case. I have met a few very large males, like Clarence, my Maine coon friend, who do require a size large case.

2. *It feels safe and comfortable to your cat.* Choose a hard-sided case. Those soft collapsible cases are very frightening. Every time you put the thing down the sides and top start collapsing inward and sag down on top of the poor little pussycat trapped inside. Avoid the soft-sided collapsible cases.

3. *It's simple and easy to put your cat in and take her out.* Choose a case that hinges open from the top and allows you to lower your cat in from above, not the kind where you're expected to push and cram the cat in through a little door in the end.

4. *It is designed with your cat's comfort and pleasure in mind.* The case must have several large ventilation holes in *both* ends. To avoid motion sickness, choose a case with a transparent lid so your passenger can see out and enjoy his trip, and potential admirers can see in. If you ever choose to do so, you can always make such a case opaque by simply draping a scarf across the top.

5. *It is well built and safe.* Examine all hinges, clasps, and handles to be sure all are secure and strong enough to support easily at least twice your cat's actual weight. Open it and close it and swing it around with some books in it before you buy it.

6. *It feels good to your hand and is comfortable to carry.* This is just as important as all of the above. After all, you, the owner, are an equal partner in using the case.

Warning: *Do not get a case large enough for two cats!* You'll hate it for the next twenty years and so will your cats. A two-cat case, even if there's only one cat inside, is heavy, awkward, and unmanageable. As for the two cats inside, how would you like it if you were traveling in very cramped quarters and your companion "had a little accident" all over the floor?

If you need a case to tide you over until you find the right one, I suggest the disposable cardboard type. They have no see-through top, but otherwise they work well as a temporary case. They're light, comfortable for cat and owner, and quite strong as long as you put them together exactly as directed.

Once in a great while I have found myself in some dire situation where I must transport a cat and the only case available is obviously on its last legs. To insure that the thing won't fall open after we're out on the street, I loop a belt or a couple of those stretchy luggage hooks around the case.

Once you acquire the carry case you feel good about, the next step is to introduce your fuzzy friend to all the positive aspects of his "private module." Leave it out and open one or two days a week for him to play or nap in. Most cases are a bit top-heavy so be sure it's braced securely so it doesn't tip over and make a bad impression. Serve a treat or some catnip in the case every week or so to build positive associations. If your cat is the timid type, once a week put him in the case and take him for a little jaunt around the living room, followed by a play session and a treat.

There is yet another nice advantage to owning the ideal carry case: you can make it cool in the summer and turn it into a snug little heated compartment in winter. You should be able to weatherproof your cat's carry case easily. This is difficult if you have the type with a lot of screen or grill-work suitable only for warm climates.

Let's assume for the sake of illustration, that (heaven forbid) your cat is taken ill in the middle of a snowstorm. Prepare the carry case in the following way. First, fold two kitchen towels (or paper towels) to fit over the air holes in both ends of the case and tape the towel in place with masking tape. Also tape closed any additional holes in the case with masking tape. That way, air can filter in through the towel but the case will be breezeproof.

Now you need a plastic bottle. Empty your shampoo into a mixing bowl and fill your shampoo bottle with water as hot as you can handle. The hotter, the better. Screw on the lid and drop the bottle into a thick woolen sock, preferably one that you've recently worn. Thus you are providing both heat and the comfortable, familiar scent of your beloved foot. Fold a towel into the bottom of the case—preferably a towel of a becoming color so it will subliminally affect the mind of the veterinarian or whomever you are going to see. Drop the sock-covered bottle into the case.

Grab a large brown paper bag and container of your cat's high-quality food in case the cat must stay overnight at the hospital.

If you must transport your cat during a heat wave, leave all the ventilation holes wide open and use ice water in the shampoo bottle—or, better yet, use a "dry ice pillow." Available in drugstores, this is a heavy plastic pillow filled with a liquid that freezes easily and is kept in the freezer for use on swellings or headaches—or to air condition pussycat carry cases. Be sure to wrap the ice bag or cold water bottle in a sock or towel so it doesn't come into direct contact with the cat.

Putting the Cat into the Case

If you find yourself in the middle of some emergency such as illness or an accident, before even looking at the cat, take three slow, deep breaths through your nose and remind yourself that your cat picks up your emotional vibrations. The three breaths will calm your mind. Just as your cat comforted you when your migraine lasted two days, you must now control your fears and nervousness sufficiently to provide truly honest reassurance. You can do this by focusing on the many positive aspects of the trip. Let your mind dwell on the help and relief in store and how good it will be to find out exactly what's wrong and be able to do something about it. Just before picking up the cat, put your hand into the box so that you feel how nice and warm (or cool) it is in there. As you pick your cat up and put him in, talk about that warmth. Say how you wish *you* were in a nice, warm box instead of having to walk out into that cold weather.

The proper way to put the cat in the carry case is basically the same way you always put a cat down—front feet first. If you've been playing Pick up/Put down (page 18) you should have no problems. The second the cat's front feet touch the bottom of the box, quickly close the lid *on your own hand*. This accomplishes two

23

things: speed and safety. You will be able to shut it rapidly and successfully because you will be secure in the knowledge that there is no possible chance of pinching the cat's tail. Your hand gives that protection. Gently extricate your finger as you tuck the tail, ear, or what-have-you inside. Grab the paper bag and cans of food, and off you go.

Communicating "Good-bye"—and "I'll Be Back"

Many of the loving owners I know have wished fervently again and again that they could somehow communicate to their cat the reassurance that they would be back before the day was over. But the owners don't think the cat can understand these things. They say, "He gets so upset when I leave, if only I could make him understand that it's all right—I'll be back soon." Cheer up, you *can* make your cat understand. I had exactly the same thoughts and the same problem. I simply made my leave-taking into a ritual. This dovetailed nicely, incidentally, with my desire to shape Big Purr's behavior along more adventurous lines—he was inclined to experience undue alarm any time he was outside the apartment door.

On a normal working day, when I'm going to be home again to feed the cats' dinner sometime before midnight, our ritual is this: I throw my purse and grooming kit into the basket of my bike and wheel it into position facing the door. Because Purr now knows that he has the leading role in this good-bye ritual, he comes prancing along and leaps up onto the bike seat. "Are you going to walk me to the elevator?" I ask. I always use the same words and say them in the same tone as I lift him off the seat and place him in the bike basket on top of my things. I wait for him to settle himself comfortably, then open the door and wheel him on the bike out of the apartment and down the hall to the elevator, where I park. Then, while assuring him that he is the most courageous and adventurous cat I have ever met, I pick him up and carry him back to the apartment, giving lots of kisses and nuzzlings and thanking him profusely for his protection. We have never had a problem with lions or tigers or bears in our hall since Big Purr has been on the job. I put him down inside, and now begins the most important part of the ritual: communicating that I am coming back.

Communicating clearly with your cats is mostly a matter of simplifying your own thinking and looking at the situation from the cat's point of view. It will be helpful for you also to read the sections "Therapeutic Communication" (page 204) and "Affirmation and Visualization" (page 262). Cats perceive our thoughts in terms of mental pictures, sense memories (see, hear, taste, feel, and smell), and accompanying emotions. This last is the most important. Cats are very emotionally oriented.

My simple "Good-bye, I'll be back tonight" communication is transmitted with accompanying thoughts that go something like this: "We'll see-touch each other with gladness when it's black dark night outside the window." I picture and feel myself seeing and touching Purr. Then I add the emotion of gladness and picture the dark window in the background to give a time reference.

Later that night when it all comes true, it is always a sort of supernatural feeling as I mentally watch while Purr and I live out the picture I promised him that morning.

The more I practiced what I came to think of as assurance of my homecoming, the easier it became for me to feel it and perceive it from the cat's point of view. Cats are very sense-oriented, so I kept adding sensory details until my assurance of homecoming went something like this:

See: Window, black, dark
Hear: Elevator door opens, footsteps, bicycle, key in lock
See: Front door opens, Anitra and bike come in
Smell: Cold on boots and bicycle tires
Feel: Gladness
Touch: Nuzzle, cold gloves, warm neck of Anitra
Hear: Voice, purrs

Then we go to the kitchen and make a delicious dinner.

I started out speaking these words out loud, trying my best to visualize the scene and recall the appropriate senses and emotions. As we repeated the ritual day after day, I found that the sense memories were sharpening and the pictures were becoming more complete and clearer. Big Purr was coaching me in interspecies

25

communication. I felt no pressure or anxiety about succeeding; I practiced with him because it was fun. I knew he loved me whether I could speak "Cat" or not.

At first I practiced the technique with little faith in myself. "I know he'll pick up some of what I'm trying to send," I told myself, "and it certainly can't do any harm to try." It wasn't until weeks later when I was doing the ritual one morning that I felt my sense memories suddenly clearing and sharpening beyond anything that I had ever experienced in my whole life. I realized with a feeling of total awe that I was *receiving* impressions from Big Purr. There he sat, blue eyes alight, smiling up at me. He had been joyfully joining in the ritual for all those weeks, sending me his communication, until finally, at long last, my rusty human mind opened up and I became consciously aware of his participation and of the wonder that was taking place between us. The emotion that engulfed me then was similar to a feeling I had only one time before— it was years ago in college, the very first time I ever sang with a full orchestra.

If I'm going away for the weekend or off on vacation, I must communicate that more time will pass before I come home. I do this by picturing day and then night, day and then night several times outside the window and visualizing who it is that will be coming in to feed and care for them in my stead.

I have observed that my "good-bye for a long time" ritual is almost superfluous. The appearance of my suitcase tells them all they need to know. In fact, when the suitcase comes out the first thing Purr does is to leap inside it and refuse to budge, perhaps hoping that if he can prevent the suitcase from going anywhere, then I'll stay too. Then, when I try to make my exit, instead of sitting quietly on the floor, looking up at me soulfully and tapping me politely with his mitten, Purr imposes his body between me and the door, grabs my pants with his claws, and rolls about on his back. He refuses to let go, trying to convince me that now is the time for play. Nevertheless, here again I push on with the communication, and right before I pick up the suitcase, I use the ritual phrase "Okay, Purr, I'm leaving you in charge." Then I grab the suitcase, slip through the door, throw him a last blink, and lock up.

It is clear from his behavior that he knows full well I'm not coming home that night. Purr, being the dominant male, will communicate this information to the other cats by his attitude when my usual coming-home time rolls around. And anyway, I remind myself as I descend in the elevator, my assistant Alicia will be in to feed them. She has her own special games with the cats that they all enjoy.

Introducing a New Cat into the Household

Cats who live with a cat friend (or friends) live longer and healthier lives. When choosing a second cat, aim for one that will compliment your own cat's personality and will not threaten his position as first in your heart and master (or mistress) of the territory.

If your cat is	*Look for a cat who is*
A floor cat who perches under things	A high jumper who perches on shelves
A snuggler who loves to be with people	A playful clown who focuses on other cats as well as people
Elderly or sick	A cat's cat; mature and calm; loving to other cats—no rambunctious kittens please
Healthy but overweight	Rambunctious and jolly; a kitten of two months or more would do very nicely here
Too energetic and running you ragged	Young and playful and jolly; a kitten could work but it should be more than five months old; a youngster between one and three years who would take your friend in paw and direct his energy would be ideal
The cat you adore, but you are worried that he is left alone too much	A cat's cat who enjoys the company of cats as much as, if not more than, the company of people

Often there is no question of a choice. The new cat is suddenly there, presented by fate, and the kindly human makes the decision to accept, protect, nurture, and do whatever else is needed for this gift from the cat goddess.

Whether you choose a second cat or have one thrust upon you, your first move is the same: *don't* take the new cat home; take it to your own trusted veterinarian and have it examined for parasites and tested for feline leukemia. You owe it to yourself and your trusting feline friend at home not to bring in anything contagious with the new cat friend. Besides, this will give you the very necessary time to prepare your beloved feline at home.

Before the New Cat Arrives

Demonstrate to your cat how much you love him and need him. If possible, for at least a week before the new cat arrives, give him extra attention. Lavish him with affection, giving physical and eye and voice contact. If you make a bit of a pest of yourself, that's all the better; it will help him to feel even more secure.

Communicate the advantages of having a cat friend. During that week and again the day before the new cat arrives, explain to him that many cats have a cat friend to sleep with and to play with and to generally help take care of the household. Picture these things and communicate the emotions as you did when you communicated "Good-bye" and "I'll be back." Remind him how nice it was back in the old days when, as a tiny kitten, he used to snuggle down with his litter mates and romp with them and get into trouble together.

When the big day arrives *do not bring the new cat into the house yourself*! Find someone who is not well known to your cat who will bring the new cat into the house for the first time and play the part of the new cat's owner. Have that person pet the cat all over to get his scent on the cat and the cat's scent all over him. The ideal person is someone your cat has never met, but who would enjoy participating in the charade that follows. Cats are naturally territorial, and you and your family are the most cherished components of your cat's territory. The entire introduction procedure that follows has been formulated to demonstrate clearly to your cat that he is your cherished family member. He is your first love; he is yours and you are his and you have no interest whatsoever in any other animal.

Remember, we already know that you and the family will accept the new cat. The introduction is designed to ensure that *your cat* will accept him as well so that the newcomer can slide smoothly into everyone's life without experiencing undue trauma. Convey this concept clearly to each person in the household. If you want to make life easy for the newcomer, you'll have to ignore him at first.

Last, but definitely not least, to insure a lethargic attitude, make sure both cats have had a delicious meal about one hour before the introduction begins and be sure all claws are clipped.

Steps for Introducing a New Cat[1]

1. Have the person your cat doesn't know, the "visitor," arrive with the new cat in a carry case that has plenty of air holes so your cat can easily smell that the visitor has a cat with him. There should be torn strips of newspaper in the bottom of the carrier for later use (which I'll get to in step 4).

2. All family members should be *completely oblivious* to the new cat in the carry case. Let the visitor sit with the carry case on his lap for ten or twenty minutes to establish his sole ownership of and interest in the new cat. During this time indulge in a casual conversation about other matters: the weather, vacation plans, or your favorite restaurant—in short, anything *except* cats. Your attitude toward that carry case and its contents should be exactly the same as it would be if your visitor had walked in with an umbrella or an attaché case.

3. After twenty minutes or so the visitor should shift the carry case to the floor next to his feet, making it convenient for your cat to get a better sniff. Continue your pleasant and interesting conversation about sports, the end-of-season sales, and so on. If your cat comes over and sniffs the case and then walks away, ignore him, continue chatting and proceed to step 5. If your cat stays away from the case, include step 4.

---

[1] Parts of this procedure were first introduced in *The Inner Cat* by Carole C. Wilbourn. See Bibliography, p. 431.

4. To help your cat become more familiar with the new cat's scent, the visitor can open the carrier a crack and take a handful of the torn newspaper strips from the bottom, which are impregnated with the new cat's odor. The visitor should then make a trip to the bathroom carrying the strips with him and just happen accidentally to drop several of the paper strips along the way, giving your cat the opportunity to become familiar with the newcomer's scent from a safe distance. Continue your fascinating discussion of the current presidental policies or the Oscar nominations, projecting feelings of calm contentment.

5. Let the visitor continue to sit and talk for a while longer, the carry case at his feet. When your cat sits calmly in the room without staring continually at the carry case, you may safely proceed.

6. Invite your cat out to the kitchen for a snack. Have all family members join you, leaving the visitor and "his" cat alone. During this time the visitor should open the carry case and let the new cat out. This accomplishes two things: (a) as you're all together in the kitchen, your cat won't blame any of the family for allowing a new cat out in his territory; and (b) this gives the new cat a few minutes to explore the strange territory alone so he won't be quite so tense and frightened.

7. When your cat finishes his snack and decides to go back to keep an eye on events in the living room, *the family should stay in the kitchen*. Demonstrate your lack of concern by discussing the feasibility of a trip to Yugoslavia next year.

8. The minute your cat enters the living room, the visiting person should announce clearly his intent to join you in the kitchen and do so, adding his vibes of blissful lack of concern to yours.

9. At no time should anyone offer any expressions of encouragement to the cats. You must all maintain your position of disinterested detachment. The minute you express any interest at all, your cat will become possessive and react with hostility toward the intruder. If you cannot resist an impulse to "peek," one person may do so but only if he can give the impression that he is really doing something else. For example, someone might stroll casually into the living room to collect a magazine or to change the channel on the television and then return to the kitchen.

Hissing is perfectly normal. Hissing is not aggressive, it is

30

defensive, asking one cat to back off and give the other more time to adjust. Disgruntled muttering is less desirable but still to be ignored. As long as there are no humans around to be claimed as territory and defended, the relationship should develop slowly and peacefully.

However, loud growling or screaming is a sure sign that serious trouble is about to develop. To distract the cats in the living room from their focus on each other, accidentally drop a metal pan and two lids onto the kitchen floor. If the loud growling and screaming resumes, you may need to separate the cats. This is almost always a sign that one of the previous steps was not carried out properly.

10. When the two cats reach the stage where they are not pacing around but are sitting down in the same room either watching each other or not, it is time for the humans to demonstrate further their attitude of blissful unconcern by going out for a walk. Leave the cats alone for thirty minutes or so. Be sure to continue to talk about unrelated subjects. Scientific studies have confirmed that cats can pick up your emotions even at long distances.

11. When you return, greet your cat casually; then settle into the living room for another ten-minute conversation. If there is still nothing worse than hissing going on, the visitor can leave at any time. He will just happen accidentally to forget his cat.

12. The final stages of the introduction will continue at the cats' own pace over the next few days or weeks. Remember, the slower the better. You and your family must continue to ignore the new cat. You place food on the floor for him but don't call him or talk to him. Try not to get caught looking at him and, for heaven's sakes, don't touch him if you can avoid it. The cats will explore what it's like to be together in each room of your home. Territories will be identified and claimed.

If hissing or chasing occurs, such interaction is usual in cat society and is best ignored by humans, who seldom understand fully the complexities of cat relationships. In truth, chasing can be a good sign, especially if the chaser and the chasee reverse roles periodically. Another sign of progress is sitting in the same room, no matter how far apart, and *not* staring at each other. When that happens, you're almost home—but not quite. You still mustn't touch the new cat or talk to him or give any sign that you care a hoot about him. Refer to the new cat as the visitor's cat and project no more emotional involvement with him than you would if your visitor had left behind an umbrella. If the new cat jumps up on your lap, put him gently on the floor and say something like "I wish George would come back and take his cat out of our way" and request your own cat's help in dealing with this "problem." At the same time leave them alone together as much as possible and encourage togetherness by providing new experiences that the two cats can share while you're not around. Leave the stepladder up in the middle of the floor while you're gone one day; another time you can bring home two cardboard boxes and leave them side-by-side in the corner of the living room.

When you have the urge to love and nurture the new cat, stay your hand! Be strong for his sake. The success of the relationship between the two cats depends on it. Don't think you can sneak in a stroke or a snuggle when your first cat's back is turned. He'll smell your scent on the newcomer, and the cats' relationship will take a violent giant step backward. The better you play your part, the quicker friendship will flower between the two cats. A really skillful owner can engineer the situation so the first cat will ask to have the new cat included in the games, and then in the petting and other activities. The owner should appear to grant these requests with a tiny bit of reluctance at first, giving in at last only because his first cat is so adorable he can refuse him nothing. Now that you have "agreed" to let the new cat stay, this is the time to assure your first cat that the new cat belongs to him, rather than to you. When you arrive home, call for your first cat first. Pet him first, even if the new cat is waiting at the door and clamoring for your attention. For the next few weeks continue to pet your first cat first and play with him more than the new cat, making it very clear that it is his society you prefer above all others.

The goal of the loving owner is a strong bond of affection and communion between the two cats. When that goal is achieved and the bond first begins to form and strengthen, the cats often go through a stage of intense interaction that seems almost to exclude the human members of the family. Don't worry. Watch your drama unfold; enjoy the spectacle and be proud of your success, secure in the knowledge that very soon you will have not one but two furry-purries to greet you at the door, supervise your household activities, and snuggle you to sleep at night.

Dangers in the Home

Cats who belong to a loving owner just naturally assume that the owner will never hurt them. They will stick their noses into the oven, not realizing you are about to light it; they will leave their tails trailing behind in the door, not realizing you are about to slam it. Our beloved pets are not frightened, and so they are not cautious. If we try a little bit to think like a cat, we have a better chance of protecting them.

For us, the sense of sight is Number One; to a cat, *smell* and *hearing* are much more important. Think of the times that you have seen a cat looking in the mirror at himself. You probably wondered why he seemed disinterested. Didn't his eyes tell him that another cat was there? Yes, they *did*. But his nose and ears told him that he was alone, and his nose and ears are what he believes.

Cats go places that we wouldn't think of going because their noses tell them these are nice places—they're interesting and smell delicious. Cats have been locked in refrigerators because the owner turns away and, without looking, slams the door closed. The owner would never think of crawling into a refrigerator, so it does not occur to him that a cat might find it fascinating. Insulation muffles the cat's cries, and by the time the cat is missed it is often too late. With a cat loose in the house, you can never again open or close any door or drawer with automatic mindlessness. For the rest of your life with a cat, you must always *look as you close*.

We all tend to forget that for cats the home is not a natural environment. We have taken the cats out of their natural environment for our own pleasure, so it behooves us to protect them from dangers that they do not automatically recognize as such. Most cats are curious. Don't ever leave your window or the door to the balcony open; the scents that blow in are absolutely fascinating. Almost all cats find cooking odors from other homes and body odors from other people's animals and birds positively irresistible. Sooner or later your cat will explore them. Chances are he will explore them repeatedly day after day, going back again and again to the open window or balcony. Sooner or later there will be a little stray piece of fluff blowing by or a tiny insect on the wing that will capture his attention completely for the moment. As he lunges to capture that elusive object, one second is all it takes for him to fall. I have come to dread the springtime in New York City because it ushers in the season of death and mutilation from falls. The late Dr. Leo Camuti, the famous cat specialist, said that of all the cases he saw in New York, the most frequent calls were for cats falling out of windows and off balconies.

In all my years as a cat groomer in New York, I have observed that all the cats who fall have one thing in common—each one is a cat to whom "it could not possibly happen." This group of cats is divided into two categories—either "He's been sitting there for eight years, he's certainly not going to fall out now" or "She's terrified of the balcony—how is she going to fall if she never goes out there?" These cats are crippled or die because they are not protected. The cats who are likely to fall out, the ones who are lively, who would obviously leap to the rail of the balcony if allowed to do so, are the ones who are protected because their danger is obvious. So they never fall.

I have twice heard of cats falling from a window that was open "only an inch." In one of these cases, I know for a fact that the owner spoke the truth—but if cats want to explore the outside world they begin by thrusting their noses through even the smallest opening. They work and pry until the whole head gets through. Then pressing their shoulder under is easiest of all, and there they are—trapped on a narrow ledge.

Females in heat and unneutered males are especially prone to this maneuver. They know that there is no mate inside the apartment or home, and if they get the merest whiff of one from outdoors it's all over. Declawed cats, of course, have notoriously poor balance.

Even if you could swear that your cats are fully aware of the dangerous distance between the ledge and the street, you must remember that pussycats' minds are different from ours. They do not automatically assume that that distance is always going to be that way. Sure, you held Samantha up to the railing, and she looked over, and she was scared. But that doesn't mean that tomorrow she won't forget and assume that the floor height on this side of the railing must be the same on the other side too.

Cats perceive the world differently from the way we do. They live almost exclusively in the present, with a very limited and hazy memory of the past and almost no concept of the future. Their concept of space and depth differs from ours, too. Remember also that cats frequently fall out of windows that are open from the top. Window screens are not expensive.

Once you've screened the windows, the average home is still booby-trapped with objects harmful to a pussycat. For example, many simple cleaning compounds such as Lysol, as well as dish-washing compounds, are fatal if the cat gets even one lick of them. That is why I wash the litter box with plain chlorine-based cleanser or a cleaning solution I make myself (see page 83). Because anything cats step in is going to go into their mouths, I always rinse to a fare-thee-well. Cats are always licking their paws, especially if they smell something disagreeable on them. So think twice about any-thing you use to clean any surface in the home or any spray, like room deodorizer. That spray eventually settles down on the floor where your cat walks. Any product containing phenol is particularly deadly. If I use any compound about which I am in doubt, and I must admit I'm in doubt about most of them, I just rinse like crazy. Of course, you must store any cleaning fluids or medicines in a safe catproof place.

The fumes from mothballs destroy the cat's liver cells. A cat accidentally locked in a closet (or sleeping by choice in a closet) where moth crystals or balls are used can inhale enough fumes in a few hours to destroy the liver beyond repair. Such cats with irreversible liver damage are usually put to sleep by the veterinarian rather than being allowed to endure a slow, lingering death. A delightful alternative to moth crystals is cedar. Remember your grandmother's cedar chest? You can turn any drawer into a cedar chest by placing three or four small cedar blocks in among your sweaters. They're available from several mail-order companies in-cluding L. L. Bean. There is also a pleasant cedar spray available from the Eco Safe Company (P.O. Box 1177, St. Augustine, FL 30285).

If your cat lies on a towel, give him one without fabric softener. Fabric softener coats the fibers (making them almost waterproof), and some of this chemical will adhere to your cat's fur and be licked off later. Incidentally, commercial room deodorizers are made of volatile chemicals. I don't pretend to understand why anyone would pay money to add more chemicals to the air we breathe. Most of these products are downright painful to the cat's sensitive nose.

You should never have occasion to use mouse and rat poisons—for obvious reasons. But city people, like it or not, must be prepared to face the cockroach problem. Roach sprays and powders are deadly to small animals and extremely debilitating and dangerous to us big ones. My own alternative is roach traps. Although I have found their effectiveness to be far below satisfactory when used as directed, I have added a refinement of my own that renders them diabolically successful. Every morning and every evening when I feed the cats, I simply take a tiny dot of cat food and place it in the middle of a sticky roach trap. The roaches can't resist it. This trap baiting must be done twice a day, and I find it's best to use only one trap at a time so as not to confuse the little horrors.

A staggering number of plants are poisonous. Poinsettias head the list, with azaleas and dieffenbachia running a close second. Here is a list of some others: philodendron, ivy, chrysanthemums, mistletoe berries, rhubarb leaves, cherry (fruit, bark, stones, and leaves), iris leaves and roots, most bulbs (such as daffodil, jonquil, narcissus, and Star of Bethlehem), poison ivy, privet, oak (acorns, shoots, and leaves), mushrooms, oleander, sumac, sweet pea, and rosary pea (seeds and pods), uncooked potatoes (eye and sprouts), and apricot and peach pits. Even if you decide to play it safe and have only hanging plants of the most innocent variety, there are still plant-related dangers at Christmastime. Angel hair cuts and can be lethal if swallowed or if a tiny piece is inhaled into the cat's lungs. Tinsel is just as dangerous as any string or rubber band. But most dangerous of all is the water that the Christmas tree stands in. The piney fragrance may invite your cats to drink but if they do they could die from it. So be sure to cover the Christmas tree stand in such a way that even the most determined pussycats could never get their tongues into the water.

In the garage, be careful to clean up any spilled antifreeze. Most cats adore its sweet taste and even a few drops can cause irreversible kidney failure if swallowed. In the winter be careful to check under the hood and fender of your car before you start it. Outdoor cats will seek the warmth of the recently used engine and then fall asleep there.

Many commonly used cat toys are quite dangerous. Strings, yarn, and rubber bands have caused many cat deaths. Cat's tongues are constructed so that it is almost impossible for them to spit anything out. The stereotyped picture of kittens playing with a ball of yarn can easily become a horror story. Once they start to swallow a string, they can't stop—they can only swallow more. Strangulation can occur from yarns and string. In addition, yarns, string, and rubber bands can become wrapped around the intestine. Surgery can sometimes save such an animal, but all too often the tangle is too complex to undo before the pet expires. Let your cat chase a sash instead of yarn or string. Be safe.

It's the same with tin-foil balls, corks, and cellophane balls. These articles make stimulating cat toys that crackle and skitter across the floor, tempting even the most lethargic or overweight felines to have a go at the game. But when play time is over, store such toys in an inaccessible container. A piece of cork can cause choking; a piece of aluminum foil is not digestible and can block the intestine. Cellophane cigarette wrappers turn "glassy" when they come into contact with the digestive juices in the cat's stomach. Death by internal hemorrhage follows cuts from such cellophane.

Many toys sold in pet shops and supermarkets are actually quite dangerous because the decorations and trim are only glued on, and when they fall off they are easily swallowed by the cat. Choose toys that are crocheted or sewn together. Don't allow the cat to play with any object that could possibly be swallowed—to be on the safe side nothing smaller than a ping-pong ball. Incidentally, a ping-pong ball makes a great cat toy and an absolutely safe one. Another winner is the plastic lid from bottled water, the cap from a ballpoint pen, or the leaves at the top of the celery stalk.

The Tree House Animal Foundation hits the nail on the head with their slogan, "Remember, your cat cannot judge safety for himself, he needs your help."

Game Time and Encouraging Exercise

Now that you're thinking like a cat to keep your cat safe, let's think like a cat to encourage exercise and have some fun. All cats need exercise. If your cats do not seem to exercise much, you'll have to figure out ways to make them want to do so without letting them know that you want them to. The secret is to structure situations that will tempt them to chase or jump or run. Cats are very imaginative and creative. When they play with a piece of paper or a ball, they really make themselves believe that that thing is some living creature that they are actually going to catch and kill. They endow that toy with all sorts of wonderful qualities such as juiciness, delectable smell, and wilyness; they unsheathe their claws, slash with their fangs, growl, and sometimes even salivate. It therefore behooves us, their partners in play, if we wish to come up to their highly imaginative standards, to throw ourselves enthusiastically into the job of creating the startled, fluttering bird, the terrified chipmunk, or the innocent, tender fieldmouse.

There is one time in nature when activity is a necessity—before meals. If cats living in the wild are going to eat, they must first "catch and kill." Because cats love ritual, a good before-meal ritual could involve a "catch and kill" game.

What should you use to tempt them? Different cats have different tastes in toys. What frightens one cat will fascinate another. There are several elements to consider: size, weight, texture, sound, and smell. An interesting crinkly sound or a scratchy scrapy sound when something is dragged across the floor is fascinating to a cat. Crumpled paper thrown across a bare floor or a tissue or wax paper ball might do the trick, because cats usually prefer lightweight toys. Just remember—things a cat catches and kills in the wild are all lightweight. Have you ever held a bird or a mouse? They weigh practically nothing.

Texture is another interesting aspect to consider. Cats are much more aware of texture than we are. Big Purr's favorite toy, which he brings to me to have me throw for him, is a large-size pipe cleaner twisted into the outline of a butterfly. This particular kind of pipe cleaner has little sharp prickly things twisted into the usual chenille. I should think they would prick his sensitive lips and nose, but I've tried other pipe cleaners and he always goes looking for his old favorite, the worn old prickly one.

If you want the cat to chase a ball or sash or pipe cleaner, you're going to have to do your best to make the toy behave as much like "prey" as possible. For example, don't throw the ball *to* the cat—the mouse doesn't run into the cat's arms. The mouse runs *away* from the cat or scampers innocently by where the cat lies crouched and waiting. Draw the string *across* in front of the cat, preferably almost out of reach, and make the motion jumpy and erratic, like a living creature scurrying along unaware of the fierce and lurking predator. Throw the ball from *behind* the cat so that it rolls past him and away like a little creature who has been alarmed and is streaking for its hole.

When Purr and I play with his pipe cleaner, I throw it up in an arc in front of him so that the apex is three or four feet above the ground. His part is to take one or two steps and then leap, capturing the helpless pipe cleaner in mid-air. Obviously the pipe cleaner is a little bird who has been frightened by Purr's presence—and I assume that I'm the bush where the bird has been sitting. He also has a variation where, instead of "capturing" it, he bats it viciously into the bedroom, runs after it, and pounces. I always wish at these times that a photographer were standing by to capture forever that lithe body stretched out in mid-air, head back, fangs bared, and the look of fierce concentration in the eyes. He looks so ferocious and becomes so emotionally involved in the game that I'm sure he salivates, preparatory to eating what he catches. For that reason, I try to play this game right before meals. After each catch, I always praise him effusively. It took me longer to learn how to throw the pipe cleaners correctly than it took Purr to learn to catch them. He was a natural—I wasn't.

Success is an important part of game playing. Remember that a game, to be a game, must be fun—and failure is no fun. So don't roll the ball so fast that the scurrying creature that it represents makes it safely to its hole every time. Your cat will soon begin to feel that it's hopeless to try and will just give up. Instead, endow the fieldmouse with a thorn in its toe so that it cannot scurry fast enough to escape the fierce predator. Make the winging bird a fledgling whose little feathers cannot lift it far enough to escape your cat's sharp claws. Then, when your cat achieves success, enjoy it with him. Express delight, give praise, and pet him.

Even though Purr is a large cat, he prefers his ultralightweight, small, delicate toy. Once a month or so I dip it in catnip powder to enhance the dimension of smell and taste. He enjoys that a lot, I can tell you.

Little Karunaji, who is a half-grown kitten, doesn't care a rap for Purr's favorite toy. Karunaji stole the metal replica of the Eiffel Tower with a tiny thermometer set into it that sits on my bedroom windowsill. Because it is three inches long, and solid brass, it appears too large and heavy for a cat's taste. The texture of cold metal would seem unappealing to a cat. But Karunaji loves it. It makes a satisfying clatter when she bats it across the bare floor-boards. Karunaji also loves a long, heavy seashell and a clattery walnut shell.

A crumpled-up paper tied to the end of a long string is very hard to resist. Many cats respond better to something that seems to leap up—for example, something tied to a string can be made to leap up suddenly. A Toughie Mouse from the Felix Katnip Tree Company (which can be ordered by mail—see "Product Suppliers," in the Appendix) is smaller and heavier, while a sheet of tablet paper crumpled into a ball is larger and lighter, with the added advantage of going "klittery-scrape" as you drag it along the floor. The following are all supersuccessful toys: peacock feather, ping-pong ball, Super Ball, pipe cleaner, seashell, walnut shell, green bean, toilet paper cylinder, cat dancer.

I divide cats into two categories—the mousers and the bird catchers. The mousers love to chase things along the floor and pounce on them; the bird catchers like my Big Purr execute breath-taking leaps into the air to trap flying pipe cleaners. Try it both ways to find out which hunting method your cat prefers.

There is a great advantage to having a favorite game in which the *same* toy is always used in pretty much the *same* way, in the *same* area of the home, and always at the *same* time of day, because this sameness constitutes a ritual—and you know how cats love rituals. When you go away, this ritual can easily be taught to the cat sitter and will make the sitter seem more like a member of the family to your cat.

Catnip is a powerful tool that can be used for positive reinforcement. Catnip is a stimulant—a mild aphrodisiac. When powdered, it has a snufflike effect that elicits a good sneeze. And it's
just a heck of a lot of fun. Owners really should keep a supply on
hand. Sometimes it's packaged poorly. Treat catnip like any herb;
after you open it store it in a tightly covered glass jar. My cats have
three favorite brands: Felix Fine Ground Catnip, which I get from
the Felix Katnip Tree Company; Noah's Park organic catnip; and
PetGuard organic catnip. (see "Product Suppliers" in the Appendix).

One word of advice: You must keep control of the catnip source
because cats will open things you thought they couldn't open and
will go places you thought they couldn't get to in order to get at
the catnip. One day you'll come home to find your cats rolling
drunkenly on the rug, catnip littered all about. I'm not saying there
is anything really wrong with this—the catnip won't hurt them.
One good binge a year will brighten any cat's life. But cats become
immune to the effect of catnip if it is used too frequently.

Dr. Rowan, the cat specialist for whom I worked, used to give
catnip to every cat on the examining table. He used Felix Fine
Ground Catnip, too. It was a wonderful way to distract the cats
and help them to enjoy his gentle and thorough examination. Then
he'd also throw a little catnip into the cat's carrying case so that
the whole experience of going to the veterinarian, being examined,
and having the teeth cleaned was sort of enveloped in a heavenly
cloud of catnip. Out of the whole experience, that fabulous catnip
is what the cats remembered—especially those cats whose owners
never bothered to have catnip at home. Boy, did they love going
to see Dr. Rowan!

The office cats, however, were quite another story. There were
always two or three of these cats in residence running around.
They were strays found injured in the street, cats whose owners
brought them in and then deserted them, or cats with terminal
illnesses being kept alive with carefully regulated doses of powerful
medication because they were not suffering and they had indicated
that they didn't want to pass on just yet. They worked their way—
acting as hostesses and nurse's aides, calming the patients and
their owners. These office cats were constantly exposed to catnip.
It was wafted in the air, bits and pieces fell to the floor several

times a day—they could have it whenever they chose. I was surprised to learn soon after I started to work there that of all the resident cats there wasn't one who cared a rap about catnip. They were all overexposed. That really saddened me—all the others were having such a lot of fun. So ever since then I've always been very careful to give my cats catnip in any form only once a week. Then we have a party. I put both Felix Katnip Trees (scratching posts) over on their sides and sprinkle them with catnip. I also sprinkle catnip on the floor around the posts. All my cats sniff and sneeze, roll and lick and growl, and thrash around to their hearts' content. After an hour, I vacuum the whole mess up because by that time the entire group is stretched out sleeping the sleep of the sated. What a bash! Of course, when I'm going away I make sure that they have not had a catnip party for at least two weeks before I leave so that that happy ritual can then be performed by the sitter as a nice distraction.

2
Diet

Diet is a tool that any pet owner can use to build health, long life, resistance to disease, and joyous and even temperament. It is a tool so powerful that it is almost a magic wand. *What* you feed your cats and, of equal importance, *how often* you feed them is something you, the owner, and no one else, can control. The magic wand is yours alone.

When I started grooming, I was still working part time for Dr. Paul Rowan. I realized that I had a unique opportunity to reinforce details of home care, because I was spending a full hour with each owner during the grooming session. So I asked Dr. Rowan if there was any information that he wanted me to pass along during the groomings. He thought for a split second and replied that I should try to get all the owners to remove food between meals and to have them add yeast and bran to the food. He explained that removing the leftover food after a half hour or so is more like the natural state, because wild animals don't smell food and nibble all day long. And, he said, the added yeast and bran would raise the protein quality of the whole meal and keep the cat's resistance to disease high. So I dutifully passed these two bits of information along to every client I saw.

When I returned to my clients the next month for the usual grooming session, I found that these simple dietary changes had caused startling improvements in the cats' coats. In fact, the changes were incredible. Persians who always had some matting now had almost none. Oily coats were less oily. Dull, harsh coats began to feel silky and look fluffier and brighter. Of course, I should have expected these results: "You are what you eat." It only makes

43

sense that better-quality food will result in better overall health and therefore a better quality of fur. It's obvious now, as I look back. But at that time it was a big bonus. That was the beginning.

Then I begin to notice that cats whose health was below par did not show the change in coat quality as dramatically. Therefore, I reasoned, coat quality seems to be a barometer of the internal health of the cat. I began nutritional research into helping the cat's body overcome various physical ailments. Through nutrition I had seen the promise in those improved coats, so I knew that if I could upgrade the cat's general health, the shiny, plushy coat would just naturally follow, like the night the day. Sixteen years and several hundred cats later, I can honestly say that I was right.

The Primary Feeding Rule: Remove Food Between Meals

Dr. Rowan's advice, "Stick as close as you can to nature; that way you can never go too far wrong," has helped me out many a time. Let us examine how Mother Nature takes care of her children and arranges to keep them happy, healthy, and strong.

Cats in the wild eat once a day—*if* they are young and strong and lucky. For a wild cat, being served food twice a day would be a luxury bordering on decadence. In the wild, times of fast occur naturally because of scarcity of game or inclement weather, or because the animal is feeling sick and chooses to fast. A day or two or even a week may go by without the taking of a meal. Nature provides these fasting times for a very good reason. During a fast, the blood and energy that are usually used for digestion and assimilation are now available for use in other parts of the body. Healing and repair are accelerated during a fast. Waste disposal becomes more complete, and the body is able to deep-clean itself. Backed-up wastes in the system putrefy—and germs breed in putrefaction. So Mother Nature keeps her children free from disease by providing periodic fasts during which the intestines, urinary tract, lungs, and the pores of the skin can get a good housecleaning. The short fast we provide for our animals between their two regular meals a day is precious little time to give the body to process the food eaten and accomplish the necessary waste disposal. Let us not take away even this little time by leaving food in the dish between meals.

There is also a second reason for removing food between meals. It is the *smell* of food (not the taste) that triggers the brain to prepare the body for digestion. When food is smelled, the olfactory center in the brain sends out the message to slow down the whole metabolism so the body can concentrate on digesting the food. Saliva and digestive juices begin to flow while blood flow and waste disposal slow down. All the organs except the stomach are undersupplied with blood during this process. While all this is a perfect setup for digesting food efficiently, it is not a state of affairs we would want to continue twenty-four hours a day. Moreover, if cats are constantly smelling food, the trigger mechanism in the brain that starts the whole digestive process will soon wear out and fail to respond. Even the odor from a dirty food bowl can cause that trigger mechanism to keep the cat's body in constant preparation for digesting food. Because of the resultant undersupply of blood to all organs (except the stomach) such cats age faster than those whose food area is kept scrupulously clean.

Yet a third reason not to leave food available between meals will be of interest to all those owners who have ever worried about feline urologic syndrome (FUS). Veterinarians usually prescribe acidifier pills for FUS patients to ensure that the urine stays nicely acid because FUS germs thrive in an alkaline urine. Recent studies have revealed that every time the cat smells food his urine becomes more alkaline. Cats who fall ill with urinary blockage almost always come from homes where food of some kind was left available all day long.

Leaving food available all day is also the primary cause of the finicky eater syndrome. Slowed metabolism is a cause of several health problems—among them dandruff, obesity, and skinniness. If a cat has a poor appetite, the answer is not to leave more food available for longer periods but just the opposite—remove all food after one-half hour to give that trigger response a chance to rest.

You will be in harmony with nature's rhythms if you remember that your domestic cat's food equals the wild cat's mouse. The mice do not lounge around all day under the cat's nose waiting to be eaten. Meals are an important, but separate, part of the animal's day.

By all means, feed your cats twice a day—morning and evening. But be sure to leave the food available for only one-half hour—certainly no longer than forty-five minutes. Then remove it and wash everything nice and clean so that no smell remains. Leave fresh water for them to drink at all times.

Although not a psychologist, I have observed that leaving food available is with some people a deep psychological need. Removing the food is indeed a very real sacrifice on the owner's part that they make out of a deep love. I know in advance that these people may cheat a little, and if they do and if the cat is hooked on something, I expect them to call and say, "She's not eating the new food—she has eaten nothing in five days." I will tell you now what I always tell them—if you leave any food around between meals I cannot help you because the cat will not be hungry at mealtime. "But I'm away all day," they say. Never mind—go back and read the very beginning of this chapter and, if you still want to leave food around while you're gone, you're defeated before you start. You might as well skip the rest of the chapter. Such behavior on the part of the owner is selfish and childish. I have my own term to describe the position of a cat belonging to such a person—I call them "working cats."

Some people feel they must leave food available because of their own erratic schedules, which may mean being out from early morning to late in the evening on occasion. My answer to them is to feed the second meal *whenever* they arrive home. The cat will not starve if dinner is a few hours later than usual. And, again, remember that in the wild a cat's mealtimes are highly irregular. To those who still can't bear the idea that Muffy will go unfed for a few hours, I remind them that we humans don't always eat our meals at the same time either.

To the owners who confess their weakness and vow to turn over a new leaf, I give the following advice: All six veterinarians with whom I've worked agree on this—no one has ever heard of a cat who starved to death while something edible was available twice a day. Some cats will hold out for five days before taking a nibble. They may cry and complain. A few creative types that I've known walk over to the dish, very obviously sniff it, then turn around and proceed to scratch the floor as if they were trying to cover excrement. Such behavior may be hard to resist if you do not have the thought firmly in your conscious mind that you love your animals dearly and want them to stay with you alive and well for as many years as possible.

Special treats of food are fun and can also be useful for hiding medication or for reinforcing a desirable behavior pattern. The best time to offer a treat is about fifteen minutes after the regular meal, as if, on their way back to the lair, your cats had chanced on an unwary mouse. But certainly treats should not be a daily habit— otherwise, they are no longer treats but become old hat.

The No-Nos: Foods to Avoid

Early in my search for a high-quality food—one with a minimum of preservatives, colorings, and other nonfood ingredients—it became obvious to me that most cat food stocked on grocery shelves did not fulfill the primary purpose of building health. Most simply sustains life, at least for a moderate amount of time, before it endangers the cat's health with chemical additives, imbalances, and/or general low quality.

Ingredients such as tuna, salt, sugar, and artificial flavors and scents tend to attract the cats and "hook" them. Artificial colors are there to attract the owners (cats don't care about the color of their food). Artificial flavors and colors are not food but chemicals that undermine health.

In researching the foods available, I was surprised to find that every manufacturer of every single cat food available in the grocery store could produce the results of one or more scientific tests proving beyond all doubt that their food was absolutely wonderful— the very best. Also, I viewed an "unbiased" report on pet foods on the television news, and it, too, stated in effect that everything on the shelf was perfectly fine because government regulations were very strict.

Evidently my standards are quite a bit different from those of the government. Preservatives such as BHA, BHT, propyl gallate, nitrates, benzoate of soda, and other additives such as colorings, artificial flavorings, and scents are chemicals that, in sufficient amount, are deadly poisons. In lesser amounts, they produce illness—but in really minute quantities any damage done builds up so slowly that it is hard to measure. These smaller amounts have been declared "safe" despite the fact that several of these substances cannot be excreted. They are stored in the fat and build up over the weeks and months that they are continually ingested. My feeling is simply that, if you do not have to include these nonfood chemical substances in a diet at all, then don't. If a substance in a package marked "cat food" can be considered harmful in any way— in whatever quantity—I avoid that cat food completely. In most cases, research has never been done to discover the dangers encountered when different chemicals, some from one product and some from another, combine within the cat's body. I won't take a chance. I prefer safety and only the highest-quality nutrition.

If you pick up any canned cat food in your supermarket and read the tiny print under the heading "ingredients," you will undoubtedly see the words *meat by-products* or *beef by-products*. Dr. P. F. McGargle, a veterinarian who has also been a federal meat inspector, says by-products "can include moldy, rancid or spoiled processed meats as well as tissue too severely riddled with cancer to be eaten by people."[1] Dr. Alfred Plechner gives a more comprehensive list: "Diseased tissue, pus, hair, assorted slaughterhouse rejects, and carcasses in varying stages of decomposition are sterilized with chemicals, heat and pressure procedures."[2]

Many by-products come from so-called "4-D" animals—dead, dying, diseased, and disabled—which the federal government actually allows in pet food. The theory is that all harmful bacteria and viruses are destroyed by heat processing at high temperatures, which "sterilizes" the meat by-products. How would you feel if you knew that the food you ate every day was composed of diseased meat? Even if the government is right and all the bacteria and viruses have been killed by the processing, would you consider the resulting "food" to be *good* for you?

Be sure to read the ingredients even when you buy in the

---

[1] Richard H. Pitcairn, D.V.M., Ph.D., and Susan Hubble Pitcairn, *Dr. Pitcairn's Complete Guide to Natural Health for Dogs and Cats* (Emmaus, PA: Rodale Press, 1982), p. 13.

[2] Alfred J. Plechner, D.V.M., and Martin Zucker, *Pet Allergies: Remedies for an Epidemic* (Inglewood, CA: Very Healthy Enterprises, 1986), p. 13.

health-food store or from your veterinarian. There is a well-known health-food brand available all over the country that contains lots of tuna and by-products. In addition, many veterinarians I know routinely endorse a brand of food that is made mostly of beef by-products or chicken by-products and contains ethoxyquin, a fat preservative that was originally invented and used as a successful pesticide. Remember, most veterinarians are not nutritionists; that's not their field.

In addition to the by-products and additives in commercial pet foods, there are some additional problems. From the standpoint of the finicky owner who seeks to bolster the health of the cat through a natural approach, we need to consider the quality of the proteins and their assimilability (can they be easily used by the cat's body?).

The *protein quality* in most commercial cat foods is very low. Protein is made up of amino acids. They occur in different ratios in different types of meat tissue. Some amino acids are found more in muscle meat, some predominate in the organs, while others are dominant in meat parts such as blood vessels and intestines. Feet, eyes, feathers and tumors are also made up of protein. Muscle meat and most organs are called "high quality protein" because the ratio in which the amino acids occur in these meats is the best ratio for maintaining a normal standard of health in cats. When a cat kills an animal or bird for food in the wild, Mother Nature provides a nice balance: mostly muscle meat, about one-sixth organ meats, and some intestines and blood vessels.

Lungs, intestines and other meat by-products such as tumors which have been removed from those parts of the meat sold for human consumption are cheaper for cat food manufacturers to buy. The government regulates how much protein must be present in each can of food; however, just which type of protein (the quality and balance of amino acids) is loosely defined.

The second problem, that of *assimilability*, is affected by the processing of the food. As a rule, the lower the quality of the protein, the more processing it will need before it will pass government standards. The cat's body is designed to assimilate raw food. Tumors and partially decayed meats (which are permitted by the federal government as well as many state governments) are processed not only with high heat but, in some cases, also with chemical sprays.

It is very difficult for a cat's body to sustain itself efficiently on the lungs, tumors, intestines, and decayed matter processed with chemicals and extreme heat.

Dry Cat Food

Dry food is a prime suspect in causing feline urologic syndrome (FUS) and bladder stones. Dry food is almost always processed more than canned food, and the protein quality in most dry food is low. Low-quality protein causes the urine to be *alkaline*, whereas a cat fed on high-quality, easily assimilated protein tends to have an *acidic* urine. An acidic urine prevents the growth of germs that cause FUS and helps dissolve bladder stones and gravel.

One brand of dry cat food carries the slogan "Lowest in ash of all dry food." A clever piece of advertising: it is perfectly true. However, this is like saying that grapefruit is the lowest in acid of all citrus fruits. This statement is also perfectly true, but grapefruit, after all, is still a very acid fruit compared to all those outside the citrus family—just as all dry food is still higher in ash than canned foods.

All the veterinarians I've worked with caution against a dry food diet and expressly forbid it if FUS has been diagnosed. Conversely, dry food manufacturers can produce test results proving that a connection between dry food and FUS is, if not actually nonexistent, then at least inconclusive. Recent research has shown that the cat's urine alkalizes every time he smells or eats anything at all. Since owners who feed dry food are the ones most likely to leave food available all day long, this is yet another reason why dry-food cats tend to suffer from FUS and bladder stones.

Dry food does not clean the teeth. It never has and it never will. No one claims that—not even the dry-food manufacturers. I have met numerous cats formerly on an all-dry-food diet with the worst tartar in the world. There are three or four "health food" pet food companies that have carefully developed some very high-quality dry foods to go with their canned food lines. Because dry food is processed more than canned food, I do not feed these products as a meal. However, I do use them as high-quality treats. I recommend them to my clients but suggest that they refer to them as "cookies" or "treats" to help them remember not to feed more than a tablespoonful or so at a time. For acceptable crunchies and treats, see "Acceptable Crunchies" later in this chapter.

Semimoist Food in Packets

Almost every brand of semimoist cat food can be said to be "complete nutrition." Keep in mind that the words *complete nutrition* mean only that the minimum daily requirement of all known vitamins and minerals are in there. It does not mean that these nutrients are necessarily present in a form that can be digested by your cat or assimilated into the cat's system. There's no guarantee of that. And, while we're on the subject, why don't we just take a look at the label and see what else is contained in that convenient little package of complete nutrition?

If a manufacturer wants to make a lot of money on a food product for human or animal consumption, a major criterion is to make something with the longest possible shelf life. The amount of preservatives used in semimoist food is so great that its shelf life approaches infinity. In his book *Pet Allergies: Remedies for an Epidemic*, Dr. Alfred J. Plechner writes: "Semi-moist [food] is a horror story . . . tinted, flavored and processed with a genuine Hollywood flair for special effects. They use artificial colors and flavors, emulsifiers, preservatives, salt, sugar and whatever else most humans avoid who are interested in good health. In my opinion, semi-moist should be placed in a time capsule to serve as a record of modern food technology gone mad."[3]

If you still have any doubt why I would not use semimoist food, I suggest you look at the stool excreted by a cat or dog fed on these substances. The stool looks like Technicolor plastic.

Tuna and Other Fish

Even before we had dry food and semimoist food, there was tuna. "Tuna junkie" is an expression used by veterinarians to describe a cat "hooked" on tuna. The flavor is so strong that cats who eat a lot of tuna come to believe that tuna is the only thing that constitutes food—nothing else fits into that category for them. Tuna is used

[3] Plechner and Zucker, p. 31.

as an ingredient in a large majority of canned cat foods precisely because of its strong addictive properties.

Canned tuna in the cat's diet has two drawbacks. First, the vegetable oil it is packed in tends to rob the cat's body of vitamin E. When the stored vitamin E is sufficiently depleted, a condition called *steatitis* results. Steatitis causes the cat first to become extremely nervous and then to become supersensitive in all the nerve endings in the skin; it is very painful for such a cat to be touched in any way. If an autopsy is done on these cats, the fat is buttercup yellow instead of white. The disease can be cured by giving megadoses of vitamin E carefully supervised by a veterinarian and, of course, by discontinuing any food containing vegetable oil or mineral oil because this will deplete the body's stores of vitamin E even more.

On mentioning to one veterinarian that I had noticed some cat-food companies were adding vitamin E to the tuna fish, the doctor replied that its effectiveness would be like putting a little chemotherapy pill into each pack of cigarettes. Besides the fact that the oil used with tuna depletes the system of vitamin E, tuna, as well as swordfish, salmon, and other carnivorous fish are at the top of the food chain and therefore contain larger amounts of mercury than do the bottom feeders like cod, scrod, haddock, halibut, and sole. All fish bones, no matter how well cooked or how soft and crumbly, contain insoluble mineral salts that can form stones and gravel in the bladder and urinary tract. Tuna has the highest concentration of these salts.

In addition, one recent study at Cornell University showed that tuna cat food had unusually high levels of the toxic metal methylmercury. The Cornell researchers pointed out that the tuna used in cat food comes from the red meat part of the fish, which apparently contains more toxins than the white meat tuna sold for human consumption. The white tuna meat contains less, but mercury is still present there, too.

Ham and Pork

Ham and pork contain fat globules so large that they clog the cat's blood vessels. Just think of your own tiniest capillary and then think what those globules must do in the capillaries and veins of a cat fifteen times smaller than yourself. The preservatives and colorings used in bacon, hot dogs, sausages, and lunch meats are, frankly, lethal in sufficient quantity—even for us big animals. Also, I don't believe in polluting a cat's system with the nitrates and nitrites that are used to preserve most of these meats.

The High-Quality Diet: Fluff City in Thirty Days

Canned foods, although not the best choice, can be a nice, easy, middle-of-the-road diet if you beef them up with supplements and if you choose from the pure-food varieties made without by-products and preservatives; these are now available from pet-food distributors and your health-food store. Freeze-dried and frozen cat foods are also available from natural pet-food companies. See "Product Suppliers," in the Appendix, for brands. Try several to see what your cat likes; then try to settle on at least three or four flavors; variety in the diet is best.

Surprisingly, the price of the "health-food brands" without preservatives or by-products is about the same as the price of the so-called prescription canned foods sometimes sold by veterinarians and the "gourmet" canned foods in supermarkets. One reason the pure-food brands can give better quality at about the same price is that they don't do major advertising. They put the money into the food and let the results of feeding their higher quality food speak for itself. As long as we're talking about expense, consider also how much a finicky owner saves on veterinary bills.

I prefer to save money by buying by the case from a wholesale pet-food distributor. Be sure that organ meat constitutes no more than one-sixth of the weekly diet because, if a cat killed an animal in the wild for dinner, only one-sixth of the prey would be organs. If you can't find any health-food brands in your area (check with both pet-food suppliers and health-food stores) check the Appendix for companies that will ship directly to you.

Baby food meat and vegetable mixes such as Junior High Meat Dinner (vegetables and lamb, turkey and rice, and so on) are also acceptable but only if you add fat and the Vita-Mineral Mix given below to make them suitable for a cat (see page 55). You can use them up to five or six times a week.

Not even the best canned food from the health-food store is perfect, because every canned food is processed by heat, and many vitamins and enzymes are destroyed by heat. Even the newer frozen and freeze-dried natural cat foods don't have all the virtues of fresh food. Cats who hunt and kill in the wild consume the whole mouse, right down to the whiskers. They will eat some hair and probably get a little dirt off the ground in the process. Nature has a purpose in letting the cat ingest these little extras. Hair is roughage, minerals, and protein. Dust is full of minerals. The contents of the mouse's stomach is predigested grain full of B vitamins and enzymes. And the mouse was alive a moment before. The meat is still pulsing with life. (I wonder how long the meat inside of that can has been dead.) How shall we supply the missing elements? Let's think of building a mouse!

To supply the contents of the mouse's stomach, we will use wheat bran. To supply the minerals and roughage of the mouse's hair, we will use bran, again, and either kelp or a mixed trace mineral powder. To supply something living, something still alive when your cat eats it: yeast. The yeast will also raise the quality of the protein in the entire meal and replace some of the amino acids and many of those B vitamins that were destroyed by heat during the processing of the canned food.

I add lecithin granules because they emulsify fatty wastes, help do away with dandruff, and make the coat texture absolutely gorgeous. For longhaired cats, lecithin granules are a must. Because cats' requirements for vitamin E are very high and because vitamin E in food is extremely perishable, I keep a bottle of 400-unit vitamin E capsules available in the refrigerator. Once a week, I puncture one for each of the cats and squeeze its contents into their food. An alternate method is to wipe it onto the cat's wrist and let him lick it off or squeeze the oil onto the finger and then wipe it off on the cat's eyetooth. Once a week I also give each cat the contents of a low-potency capsule, which contains 10,000 units vitamin A and 400 units vitamin D.

At first you may think that you need a full-fledged chemist or a master chef to implement the plan. Take heart. In working with hundreds of very busy New Yorkers, I soon realized that if I wanted all of my cat friends to have the very best it was absolutely necessary to devise a way that was fast and simple for the owners.

Here's what I came up with:

Vita-Mineral Mix

1½ cups yeast powder (any food yeast: brewer's, tarula, or
    nutritional)
¼ cup kelp powder *or* ¼ cup mixed trace mineral powder
1 cup lecithin granules
2 cups wheat bran
2 cups bone meal, calcium lactate, or calcium gluconate

- Mix together and store in a covered container. Be sure to
  refrigerate (everything but the lecithin and minerals perishes
  at room temperature).
- Add 1 teaspoonful of Vita-Mineral Mix to each cat's meal (2
  teaspoonfuls per cat per day).
- Once a week give each cat 400 units vitamin E (alpha tocopherol, not mixed tocopherols) and the contents of a vitamin A and D capsule (10,000 units vitamin A and 400 units
  vitamin D). If your cat dislikes the taste of these supplements in his food, just puncture the capsule with a pin
  and squirt it into the cat's cheek pouch or diagonally across
  the tongue. (Never squirt a liquid down the center of the
  throat. If the cat is inhaling, he could choke.) Or purchase
  from the health-food store an oil supplement for pets
  which contains these vitamins.

This way you can add all these supplements without having
to take five different jars out of the refrigerator twice a day. Store
the leftover food in a covered glass or plastic container and refrigerate. *Do not store in the can.* Cans are usually made of aluminum
and the can's seam is sealed closed with lead. Once you open the
can and break the vacuum, oxygen and moisture are free to mix
with the lead and aluminum. Molecules from these toxic metals
can then get into the food. Avoid lead and aluminum contamination
by removing the food from the can as soon as you open it. I use
a glass container to store the leftover food because so much suspicion has been thrown on plastic dishes and containers that finicky
owners avoid them, just to be on the safe side. A peanut butter

jar is good; a pickled-artichoke jar is perfect. Some imported jams come in jars that are especially pleasing to the eye and hand. Here's a perfect excuse to splurge on one of them and then keep the jar as your permanent cat-food storage jar for the refrigerator.

You can buy all the ingredients for the Vita-Mineral Mix at a health-food store or you can order it already mixed up (see "Product Suppliers," in the Appendix). After implementing this regime for one month, approximately 85 percent of my clients noticed the following changes: dandruff gone; oiliness diminishing and disappearing; matting diminishing and disappearing; shine appearing; texture becoming thick, rich, and plushy. Of the other 15 percent, most noticed the changes after two, three, or six months because the cats were older and had slower metabolisms, or because the owners were slower to make a complete change in diet. For example, some owners, instead of removing the food after a half-hour, would leave the food for as much as an hour and a half for the first couple of weeks. Other owners, whose cats were "hooked" on one of the really low-quality foods, spent the first couple of weeks mixing the old food with the new food, gradually diminishing the former low-quality food until the cat was eating only the high-quality food. Remember that speed is unimportant as long as you and your cat are going in the right direction.

Many of my clients, on seeing the spectacular results in their cats' furs, decided to include the ingredients in the Vita-Mineral Mix in their own diets—as I myself do. If you're one of those people who wash your hair not because it's dirty but because it's lank or oily or if you use some sort of conditioner or styling gel to give it shine or body, I suggest you give these supplements a try. You will also appreciate the effect on your fingernails and the whites of your eyes.

Many of my clients who also own dogs have applied the same diet to their cat's canine friends. All have experienced the same happy results. I am not surprised. A high-quality diet will benefit any animal. The dog's basic requirements do differ slightly from the cat's. Dogs are a bit more like us humans in that they can be vegetarians if all their essential amino acids are supplied; also, they need less fat than cats. The better cat food companies listed in the Appendix also sell dog food and one even offers a vegetarian variety for dogs and a hypoallergenic variety for dogs.

With any animal, it's very important to remove food after a half-hour, leaving only water available between meals. This way the internal organs will all be well supplied with blood and the metabolism will be rapid. Removing food between meals keeps your pet youthful and spry. My Priscilla, at fifteen, was still the champion soccer player with our dented ping-pong ball. Her haunches were so shapely they drove Big Purr crazy. He'd try to nibble them at every opportunity. Priscilla, being a lady, would respond by giving him a good swat. And Priscilla only weighs four and a half pounds, to Purr's twelve.

The Superfinicky Owner's I'll-Do-Anything-for-My-Cat Diet

The superfinicky owner who prepares his or her own cat food from scratch really has a firm grip with both hands on that health-bestowing magic wand. It's simple to do; the time you spend making up food will be saved later because it's faster to open a self-sealing plastic bag than to open a can. Also, your cats will be healthier on their tailor-made diet and you will be required to spend less time on nursing care, pilling, and ferrying to the veterinarian in later years. And—surprise!—the cost is the same or even less than the cost of canned cat food. I suggest you first try it for a month, because that gives you time to get it down to a quick, easy routine, and it gives your cats time to show evidence of the up-graded diet and upgraded coat, temperament, and general health.

Because you are making up your own formula, you can tailor the texture as well as the taste and nutritional content of your cats' meals. It's wise to blend or mash most of it well at first in order to mix the vegetables with the meat; otherwise some cats will pick out the meat pieces and leave the rest. Most cats like a smooth, creamy consistency like a baby food. You can always hold out a few chunks of cooked meat and baked carrot to mix in at the end. Many cats find chomping on lumps exciting. You'll have to ask your own cats' opinion on that.

If you can manage to get all organically grown, unsprayed products, that, of course, is best. Commercial pesticides used on vegetables are poisonous, and chemical fertilizers lower vitamin content considerably. The hormones and antibiotics injected as a matter of course into all the meat and poultry available on the open market are better left right where they are—on the open market, not in your cat's stomach.

Remember, you won't be paying more for the food because you will be serving quality proteins instead of quantity. One organic chicken will last two cats for several days when used in the proper ratio with grain, bean, egg, and vegetables. The proteins you will use are so nicely balanced that not as much animal protein is needed. This careful protein balance yields the added dividend of saving the cats' kidneys and keeping them functioning efficiently into old age.

If you have no blender, just chop and mash—or, as a second choice, you can use the organic baby foods (meat, vegetables, and cereals) available at health-food stores. If you don't have such a store in your area, you'll have to fall back on what the standard grocery store can supply. It's a bit overcooked, but you will still be serving meals far, far above the canned cat foods in nutritional quality and freshness.

When you first begin making your own cat food, use a small measure—a tablespoon or one-quarter cup to equal 10 percent. Make up relatively small amounts of the food until you hit on three or four combinations that your cats really enjoy. Then begin making larger amounts, using a cup or even two cups as your 10 percent measure. Store enough food for one meal in a self-sealing plastic bag. If you have one cat, put one serving in a bag; if you have three cats, three servings. Store them in the freezer and thaw as needed by dropping the bag into a bowl of hot tap water. Or, you can store up to two days of food in a plastic container and freeze it. Then unfreeze the food as needed by standing the container in a bowl of hot water.

Raw-Food Diet

Before I give the recipe, I'll let you in on a few facts about feeding a raw-food diet. There are many benefits to be gained by serving raw meat, grain, and vegetables. It is, of course, the most natural diet of all. Cats in the wild don't build a campfire and toast their mouse like a marshmallow. When food is cooked, both vitamins and enzymes are destroyed. Also, the fat and protein molecules can be altered by the heating process, making it more difficult for the cat's system to digest and use them.

Between the years 1932 and 1942 extensive and long-range testing was done on animals by Dr. Francis M. Pottenger. The results showed that animals fed only cooked food, even though the diet was perfectly balanced, showed markedly reduced immune response. Furthermore, the damaged immune system was inherited by the offspring and then weakened further by continued use of a diet of all cooked food. As the study progressed, heart lesions, arthritis, hepatitis, irritable bowel syndrome, feline urologic syndrome, and other illnesses became more and more common. It took only three generations to reduce the immune response to virtually zero. I am reminded of the heartbroken owners I meet every day whose cats are bravely fighting feline leukemia and the other numerous immune deficiency diseases we are hearing so much about in recent years. Dr. Pottenger's experiments went on to show that the health of these unfortunate animals could be improved simply by returning them to a raw-food diet. However, it took three generations to build the immune system back up to a really optimum level of efficiency.

Whenever I suggest feeding a raw-food diet, which includes raw meat, the concerned owner inevitably asks, "Aren't you afraid of germs and parasites?" My answer is, "Yes, I am. So I take extra precautions with the meat portion." I buy only a small supply that will be eaten up in two days. I buy fresh ground chuck from a store I know has a rapid turnover of merchandise. Or I wait for a sale and buy organic chicken or organic ground beef. Organic meats are more resistant to parasites because the food animals have not been treated with cortisone. I stretch the meat by substituting one organic egg yolk or two tablespoons of tofu for part of the meat portion three times a week for each cat. I store the meat in a covered jar in the refrigerator, taking it out only long enough to remove the portion I need. I don't let it sit at room temperature for even sixty seconds. I take what I need and then I put the rest right back in the refrigerator. The food is left available for thirty to forty-five minutes; then, if there are leftovers, I throw them out (into the alley for the street cats).

Many of my clients are now incorporating a large percentage of raw food into their cat's diets. A few lucky cats are receiving the all-raw-food diet. In every case improvement is obvious. Even cats who are already blooming with health and beauty achieve still higher levels of robust good health within one month.

In 1988 widespread taurine deficiency was causing eye problems in cats all over the country. The problem was reported by a laboratory testing the top commercial and *veterinary prescription* foods. Immediately veterinarians started prescribing taurine pills, and the cat-food brands cited for deficiencies all began adding extra taurine to their formulas. However, as taurine, an amino acid that forms protein, is found mainly in meat and poultry, and as cat food is composed chiefly of meat and poultry, it seems logical that there must have been plenty of taurine in there already. I can think of two possible reasons for the problem:

1. Perhaps the animal parts used in the food were of low quality and didn't contain as much taurine as muscle meat would.

2. Perhaps the meats were extensively processed with chemicals and heat so that the cat's system couldn't assimilate the taurine.

After reaching the above conclusions, I realized that my clients and I had nothing to worry about as far as the taurine-deficiency scare was concerned. All of us were either feeding raw or lightly cooked meat or were using one of the new health-food cat foods that do not include by-products but use human-quality meats processed at the lowest allowable temperatures.

If you decide that you want your feline companion to have all the benefits of a raw-food diet, bravo! But be patient. Start by feeding part raw and part cooked foods and work into it slowly. You can even mix in some canned food at first until your fuzzy gourmet gets accustomed to the finest. Once she's eating a totally raw-food diet with the added supplements you can sit back and enjoy your rewards. Not only the fur but the muscle tone, play patterns, and responsiveness will improve. People who have never met a raw-food cat before will ask if your cat is some wonderful new breed. Raw-food cats are very classy animals.

Please be patient with yourself as well as with your cats. The cats may need time to make the changeover, but they aren't the only ones; you definitely will. You'll need to learn new ways of "fixing" the cats' food. You'll be grating vegetables, soaking oat bran, and separating eggs. These are all simple skills, but nowadays there are many adults who have never practiced them. Before you say "It takes too long" or "I can't," give yourself a week or so to practice grating the zucchini and separating the egg and you'll be pleased to see how quickly you'll pick up speed. And remember, a new skill is more precious than gold. Don't worry if you can't do everything you'd like to do right at first. Speed doesn't matter. As long as you know what you really want for your cats, they'll have it eventually because you've already got what it takes: the patience and perseverance that come with love.

Here's the recipe for The Superfinicky Owner's I'll-Do-Anything-for-My-Cat Diet, with raw-food options listed first:

The Superfinicky Owner's I'll-Do-Anything-for-My-Cat Diet

60 percent protein	Use raw ground chuck, raw organic chicken, raw organic egg yolk; cooked egg white; tofu (only in small amounts); cooked chicken, turkey, lamb, or beef (no cooked poultry bones)
20 percent vegetable	Use finely grated raw zucchini or carrot; finely chopped alfalfa sprouts; lightly steamed broccoli, carrot, or corn; baked winter squash; Chinese broccoli in garlic sauce; a little yam or sweet potato
20 percent grain	Use soaked oat bran (page 262); cooked barley, millet, oak flakes, brown rice, teff, quinoa, amaranth, sweet corn, or mashed potato

- Into each portion add:
  1 teaspoon Vita-Mineral Mix;
  ¼ teaspoon feline enzymes (for the first month only; then they're optional).
- *Once a week* give each cat:
  1 capsule 400 units vitamin E (use alpha tocopherol; cats can-

not digest mixed tocopherols) and 1 capsule vitamin A and D (10,000 units A and 400 units D). Puncture the capsules with a pin and squirt the contents into the cat's food or, if your cat objects to the taste of the vitamins, give as a liquid medication (see page 210).

Since raw foods do not have as strong a taste as cooked foods, you may need to mix them half-and-half with canned food at first or you can enhance the flavor with what I call a "bribe food." Bribe foods are strong-smelling, strong-tasting treats that can be mixed in easily and flavor the entire meal.

Bribe Foods

- ½ jar baby food creamed corn
- 1 lightly cooked chicken liver
- 1 inch piece of sardine in tomato sauce
- Delicious Garlic Condiment (page 256)
- 3 to 4 drops tamari soy sauce
- ¼ teaspoon brewer's yeast sprinkled on top
- 1 teaspoon baby food lamb smeared all over the top

Supplements

First let's clarify the difference between the words *vitamin* and *supplement*. A supplement simply means "something added." A nutritional supplement can be a vitamin or a mineral, like vitamin E or calcium, or more often it is a special food substance that has a very high content of one or more vitamins or minerals, such as using cod liver oil for its vitamin A and D content or using kelp or horsetail tea for its high mineral content. Whenever possible I prefer to recommend a food supplement as opposed to a vitamin, because nature includes many of the elements needed by the body to process and use the vitamins within the food from which they are extracted. For example, it is easier for the body to extract, process, and use the B vitamins when they are given as yeast (a food high in B vitamins), than when they are given in a B-complex pill. Sometimes, however, it may be better to give a vitamin pill—if, for example, the cat needs very large amounts of that particular vitamin, or if there is a possibility that the patient might react adversely to the supplement source. For example, yeast should not be given to cats who are suffering from an attack of feline urologic syndrome. It is to be hoped that the food supplement can be used as the source at a later time after the cat's health has returned to normal. A third reason for giving the isolated vitamins is simply that it's often easier for the owner. It's better for the cats to receive one multiple vitamin a day than for him to be left with nothing but processed food.

Supplements are needed for several reasons. At least two or three of them will apply to any companion cat living today.

1. Cats who have been eating mostly cooked food do not have the normal compliment of enzymes in their digestive juices and so will not be able to extract the vitamins from the food they eat as well as will a wild cat who is killing and eating raw prey.

2. Cats who are ill will not have the standard amounts of enzymes either (see number 1 above).

3. In modern farming methods the use of chemical fertilizers and sprays greatly reduces the nutritional content of foods and/or throws the vitamin and mineral content of foods out of balance, in some cases creating deficiencies.

4. The use of steroids and antibiotics is ubiquitous in commercial meat and poultry. These substances are present in all commercial meat and poultry, and when these products are eaten, they greatly increase the need for certain nutrients to help the body process out the toxic substances. (This is one of the reasons organically grown meat and poultry are far superior.)

5. Certain diseases such as irritable bowel syndrome reduce the cat's ability to absorb nutrients.

6. Certain nutrients, such as vitamins C, E, and the B complex, are used up quickly by the stresses of normal modern life. They are used up even faster when unusual stress is present such as travel, sickness, X rays, loneliness, lack of direct sunlight, or loud music or noise.

7. No two cats are alike. Genes can predispose *any* animal to

have an unusually high requirement for one nutrient or another.

8. Feeding all cooked food throws everything out of whack.

One simple rule will make life easier for the finicky owner determined to do everything possible to keep his furry friend in the best of health. It is this: There are *oil-soluble* nutrients and *water-soluble* nutrients. The oil solubles are vitamins A, D, and E. All the rest, vitamins and minerals, are water soluble. Oil-soluble vitamins (A, D, and E) can be stored by the body and need be given only once a week. All the rest, both vitamins and minerals, should be replenished at every meal because they are continually lost in the urine. This is why the various feeding suggestions allow you to give the vitamins A, D, and E only once a week.

I do not give multiple vitamins every day as a habit. Under normal circumstances, I give them twice a week at irregular intervals. I don't want the cats' systems to become dependent on the vitamin pill, thereby lowering their ability to assimilate the nutrients from the whole food. Also, I feel more secure using food supplements where the vitamins are not isolated. But if your cats get ringworm, fleas, upper respiratory infection, or any infestation or disease, give them a multiple vitamin pill four or five times a week until the battle is over. Double the Vita-Mineral Mix in their food.

If you ever sneak between-meal snacks to your cats, for heaven's sake stop during illness—no matter how nutritious and fabulous they seem to you. To fight an infection or infestation, the body needs that time between meals to cleanse itself of the poisons as much as it needs that supernutritious food you are giving at mealtime. Add 1/16 to 1/8 teaspoon of Delicious Garlic Condiment (page 256) to the food once a day, or give it as you would a pill, but after the meal. Supplements are always given with or after a meal, when the stomach is full. Get a multiple vitamin especially for cats from the health-food store or from the veterinarian and make sure they are pills or liquid. There is a variety of vitamin that comes in a tube and is suspended in a mineral oil. It resembles brown petroleum jelly. This is not good because mineral oil washes vitamins A, D, and E right out of the system. Also, most of these products contain the preservative sodium benzoate, which is dangerous, particularly to cats. (There is also a feline laxative that has the same drawbacks. Mineral oil should be used very, very rarely and only under specific instructions from the veterinarian; benzoate of soda should never be given to a cat.)

My cats adore their vitamin tablets. Natural pet vitamin tablets can be purchased at most health-food stores or from your holistic vet. They're about as big as a nickel and, although they smell perfectly horrible to me, I have to be careful how I present them, because if I place the tablets too close together on the floor my sweet and gregarious cats are not above hissing and swatting each other to try to get the bigger share. They find them truly delicious. It's also acceptable to mix vitamins into the food if your cat indicates this preference.

Acceptable Crunchies

If you would like to feed your cat crunchies and be sure that all the side effects will be beneficial, try two or three yeast tablets or one desiccated liver tablet. There are also several crunchy treats for cats now available in health-food stores and from pet-food suppliers. The new dry foods available from natural pet-food companies also make good occasional treats. Be sure to store them in a tightly closed screw-top container and in a cool place; they contain no preservatives (see Appendix, "Product Suppliers").

To help clean teeth, Dr. Rowan recommends broiled chicken neck vertebrae served as a treat. The vertebrae are the *only* cooked poultry bones that are allowed, because they do not splinter, they crumble. Do not feed any other cooked poultry bones to your cat except the neck vertebrae. Most cats prefer their chicken neck broiled or roasted as opposed to boiled in water. Dr. Richard Pitcairn prefers serving the necks raw because heat destroys the valuable enzymes. Raw birds are closer to the cat's natural diet. If the bird is raw you can feed other bones as well. In fact, Dr. Pitcairn once suggested I serve each cat half of a Rock Cornish game hen. I respectfully declined, explaining that while a half a bird might be devoured in short order by the country cats in his neck of the woods, it might seem a bit overwhelming to our apartment kitties here in New York City. At the time I was thinking particularly of Marfie Lund, a dainty little shaded silver Persian who tips the scales at three and a half pounds.

Whether you cook the necks or serve them raw, I suggest presenting the first serving in the bathroom on the tiles, or better yet, in the tub, because the vast majority of cats become extremely excited on sniffing the poultry and tend to revert to primitive behavior—drooling, growling, and muttering, and dragging the piece away from the rest of the group even if there is no group present, pretending to kill it over and over again. It's fun to watch, and you may see a side of your cat that hasn't come out before.

One word of caution: too much chicken neck tends to make the stool hard, so I never give an entire meal of neck vertebrae. Give one or two vertebrae before or after half of a normal meal to which you have added an extra half-teaspoonful of bran and a teaspoonful of water. This will condition the stool and overcome the hardening effects of the chicken neck. Give only one to three vertebrae per cat two or three times a week.

Additional Acceptable Foods

Owners frequently ask about variety in the cat's diet. Cats in the wild eat sprouting grass and grains; they steal eggs from a nest; they eat a variety of different birds, frogs, lizards, rodents, and who knows what sorts of vegetables and fruits. There are many similar foods you can add to your cat's meal or give as a side dish:

- A teaspoonful of finely chopped alfalfa sprouts (high in nutrients and still full of life when cats eat them)—I use them every day
- Buttered whole wheat toast
- Steamed broccoli tops or Chinese broccoli in garlic sauce
- Peas, corn, squash, or other steamed vegetables
- Baked winter squash
- A soft-boiled egg
- Raw organic egg yolk served in a quarter-cup of half and half
- Cooked meat or poultry (remember, no ham, pork, or poultry bones, and be sure there is some vegetable and whole grain in the same meal)
- An olive
- A cantaloupe ball

- A sliver of pizza
- A string of spaghetti dripping with tomato sauce and cheese (only one, unless it is whole grain)
- A slice of sautéed tofu (bean curd) sprinkled with soy sauce

Note: Never feed chocolate or cocoa.

Ask your cats, even about the most unlikely foods. If they crave something containing sugar, white flour, and so on, this is a symptom of a system out of balance. Upgrade the diet in general. Rare treats can be useful for hiding medication if, heaven forbid, your cat should become ill and have to take a pill (see "Giving Pills," page 208).

As I write this I am enjoying one of my "kitchen sink soups": broccoli, daikon, and aramanth in a thickened broth of tamari, lemon, and garlic. Big black Bartholomew inserts an exploratory paw, pulls out a small broccoli flower, and sends it, plop, onto my manuscript. He sniffs it, then wolfs it down before I can scold, licking up the soupy residue and leaving the manuscript cleaner than it was before Bartie used it for a plate. I'll leave him a nice sample in the bottom of my bowl. After all, it's all good stuff in there.

I mix alfalfa sprouts in with the meal at least once a day. I'm told that alfalfa sprouts tend to satisfy the most incorrigible houseplant nibbler.

How Much to Feed?

When asked about how much to feed, I tell the owner I have to know the cat. Most people overfeed their cats. A cat's stomach, before it expands, is the size of a quarter or a fifty-cent piece. A cat who eats two tablespoonfuls of food at each meal is doing fine. An easy way to regulate the amount is to think of time rather than quantity. In other words, if your cat is healthy and of normal size, neither too fat nor too thin, then the sky's the limit for a half hour or so—twice a day. Also, your cat will not be eating exactly the same amount every day of the year. Appetites vary with temperature, barometric pressure, and so on. It's easy for me to see the patterns because I see so many cats every day.

Owners who previously fed low-quality foods are often alarmed because their cats eat less of the new food. I explain to them that the cats have been overeating because their systems have been reaching for missing nutrients. The poor cats eat and eat the same low-quality food, from which they can never get the nutrients they crave. That is why feeding low-quality food makes for obese cats. The new high-quality food is complete nutrition, so the cats are satisfied. They are getting *quality* as opposed to *quantity*. Flabby cats tend to firm up—they don't necessarily lose a lot of weight—they just get slimmer and more active.

Changing Over to the New Diet

One sacrifice that is the earmark of the true finicky owner is that that owner takes the responsibility and acknowledges the fact that he knows more about nutrition than the cat. I have discussed the various reasons cats can be hooked on an undesirable diet. Just the fact that "Familiarity breeds contentment in a cat" is enough to hook them on almost anything—simply because it is familiar.

When I see new clients and give instructions for an optimum diet, I always take care to explain that these "health-food" cat foods do not contain any sugar, salt, or artificial flavors. Their very purity may make them seem uninteresting to a cat if his palate has been jaded by the stimulating artificial flavors of grocery-store cat foods. If food has always been left available in the past, the owner's job is going to be even more difficult when he tries to make the change-over to a high-quality diet. One thing that will smooth the path is to add about three drops of tamari soy sauce or one of the other bribe foods given on page 62 to each serving. This works to perk up the flavor a bit just at first. Even if you use soy sauce you won't be using as much sodium as most commercial food manufacturers do, and you can gradually do away with it as your cats get used to the taste of normal food. (If your cat is a heart or arthritis patient, he needs a low-sodium diet. You can use potassium chloride [salt substitute] or low-sodium tamari.)

The cat sitters I supply to owners who travel are frequently faced with the assignment of making the dietary changeover while the owner is gone. They have a thorough grounding in the nutritional aspects of cat care, along with everything else. And, because their love is a love of all cats, they're in a good position to remain emotionally detached so they can do what is best for the cat without catering to any psychological needs of their own. Here's the method they use.

First, present the new food—the ideal diet. Keep in your conscious mind the thought of the nutritional soundness of the meal and how delicious it is. (Most cats adore yeast and kelp.) Your own emotions of approval will be communicated to your cats. If you're really handling your conscious thoughts properly, you yourself will be salivating when you put that plate on the floor. Do what is natural then—smack your lips, swallow, say you wish you had a delicious dinner like this; then leave the cats alone. Start your own dinner, wash the dishes, or go read a book. If the cats refuse the food, first of all ascertain whether or not they have eaten anything. Half a teaspoonful per cat is an acceptable amount. Don't put so much food on the plates that you won't be able to tell how much anyone has eaten. Give them only a tablespoon at first; you can always give seconds if they want it. They'll eat more next time— because they won't be eating between meals.

But let's say the cats eat nothing. Not one morsel passes their lips. After forty-five minutes, cheerfully clean away the food and casually forget the whole incident. If they ask for food between meals, given them extra love, cuddling, and play instead. Active play is especially good because it will work up an appetite. Repeat this procedure for a minimum of four meals; after all, that's only two days. A fast of two days is extremely beneficial because many old wastes and toxins will be excreted by the body quickly. That's what a fast is—it cleans the body fast! (*Note*: If your cat is seriously ill, check with your veterinarian. No fasting at all is allowed for cats with diabetes, cancer, or hyperthyroidism unless carefully supervised by the veterinarian. See "Fasting," page 225.)

Some cats, especially those who are used to having food left available all day, will take a nibble of their meal and walk away. Owners of this type are often distressed by the thought of Muffy "going hungry all day." Take heart; there is a compromise. You may feed three or even four meals a day at first as long as you don't break the cardinal rule: Always remove all food after a half-hour.

An owner of a positively obese cat will sometimes ask me in a tremulous voice, full of sincere concern, "But what if she skips a meal—what if she doesn't eat anything at all—what shall I do?" I look at the huge animal sprawled at our feet and then back at the owner, and I reply, very solemnly, "Applaud." The owner usually laughs and relaxes.

After you've done your duty for four meals, you deserve a pat on the back. Ninety-eight percent of the cats will have made the changeover by this time. (Eighty percent of the cats welcome the new food the moment it is set on the floor—they dive into it. This section is only for the benefit of those poor creatures who have no appetite because their food was left available between meals or they were hooked on some undesirable product.)

If your cats are in that small percentage that has not eaten the new food after two days, they will now be hungry—and they will jump at any compromise you offer. So, fine—we'll compromise. I'm not made of stone. Let's try the old "special treats ploy." The technique here is to mix in something that is utterly delicious, something that you would not feed every day, something that is not in itself complete nutrition. For example, something from the list of bribe foods on page 62. The next step is to start gradually increasing the percentage of the new food.

- *First two days.* Three parts special treat food to one part ideal diet. Feed extremely small meals—about half the size of your cat's usual meals. If he wants more, give him only the ideal diet food as a second serving.
- *Next three days.* Fifty-fifty ratio. Again, keep the meals small as before.
- *Next three days.* One part special treat food to three parts ideal diet.
- *From then on.* Only the ideal diet. Your cat can finally have as much as he likes twice a day.

Then you're home free. *Caution*: do not use the food your cat is hooked on. I have seen this method of mixing the old diet with the new ultimately work after fasting a cat two days, but the number of days allowed before making each ratio change must be doubled, and even then there are sometimes setbacks. Try your best not to use any really undesirable food as a bribe. If you're going to stoop to fish, at least make sure it's not tuna, which has been found to be higher in both mercury and magnesium than other fish. To avoid getting your cats hooked on anything ever again, do your best to feed a variety of flavors.

Nature moves slowly. You cannot perceive at first the change that is occurring within the cat—the improved condition of the walls of the veins; the new chemical balance of the blood, which feeds every organ including the brain and the nerves. Then, the resulting youthfulness, the mellowing of the disposition, will creep in like the unfolding of a rose, which can be seen clearly in speeded-up photography but cannot be perceived when you simply stand and look at it. Intellectually, you know the rose is blooming because you've already seen the results many times before. You can assure anyone who has not seen a full-blown rose that yes, truly, that bud will become, in time, a ravishing bloom. It will be like that with the high-quality diet once you see the results for the first time in your own cats. You'll be able to pass it on to others and benefit other cats. In fact, the more trouble you have, the more pitfalls you overcome, the better equipped you will be to help others over the rough and thorny parts. So enjoy your trials and laugh at your errors. Remember, patience and perseverance, like love, always win in the end.

Other Beneficial Side Effects of a High-Quality Diet

One thing I did not expect was the way the diet influenced temperament. The minerals and B vitamins apparently have a favorable effect on the nerves. "She came right out into the living room when company was there" is the sort of comment I hear after a couple of months on the new diet. "He's starting to play again," "She doesn't hiss at the children any more"—in other words, the temperament seems to go toward the golden mean. Nervous cats calm down; lazy cats perk up. Well, why not? Metabolism is speeded up; old waste products are being eliminated; the body is cleaner inside; irritating toxins are disappearing day by day; and health-building nutrients are in plentiful supply. The body of such a cat has a high resistance to both disease and stress.

Another lovely side effect is the perfume exuded by the furs of a healthy cat. To the joys of softness, luster, warmth, and shininess, add also the dimension of a delightful subtle perfume.

Feeding Kittens

If you are so rash as to adopt a young kitten, you must realize that kittens eat much more frequently than do grown cats. Their little stomachs are minute, and their metabolism is fast. The smaller the animal, the more rapid the metabolism. Birds, for example, spend practically every waking hour finding food to fuel their bodies. A kitten between six and ten weeks old requires six to eight meals a day. From ten weeks to four months, five or six meals are required; four meals until six or seven months; then three meals a day up to the age of nine months. Sometime before they're a year old, try to get them down to two meals a day.

Kittens may not be taken from the mother before they are six weeks old. Eight weeks is much wiser and kinder. Otherwise, they get oral fixations and spend their lives sucking buttons and earlobes. Although this may seem cute to some people, it saddens anyone who knows that it is a symptom of maladjustment caused by too-early weaning.

A kitten, once weaned, can eat the same food formula you feed any healthy cat, as discussed earlier in this chapter. A growing kitten needs a high-protein diet, and that's what this is. You might like to add an extra quarter-teaspoonful of butter once a day because kittens can use more fat. Also add some water to make the consistency easier for the kitten to handle. And this is definitely the time for an extra multiple vitamin supplement. Kittens need more of every nutrient to help their bodies manufacture strong muscles and bones.

If, through no fault of yours or the kitten's, you should suddenly find yourself with a kitten of less than six weeks on your hands, then you've got special problems. Many years ago, when I was still working on Broadway, the employees of a printing office called me to say they had discovered a sodden shoebox in the gutter out front with four newborn kittens in it. They had already called the SPCA and a couple of other humane shelters. Each time, they received the same advice: "Kill the kittens quickly and painlessly—kittens that young cannot survive." Then somebody said they knew a lady who liked cats and maybe she would help. At that time I knew next to nothing about feline nutrition. "Fools rush in"—I hopped a subway down there and accepted the four kittens. Three of them were making sounds. The fourth was dead when I arrived. They really were newborn—I doubt if they had ever nursed at all.

I called a vet, who gave me the same advice that the animal shelters had given the office people. When I insisted that I wanted to try to save them, he referred me to a very large pet store that sold powdered queen's milk. (A queen is a female cat.) My friend Mark came over and assisted in keeping the kittens warm. We held them under our sweaters next to our skin. We couldn't find a doll baby bottle so we used a rubber ear syringe made for a baby's ears. We lost two more kittens in twenty-four hours despite feeding every two hours, stroking, warmth, and all our good wishes.

At that time I had two female cats, both neutered. And, although I wasn't sure whether they would accept a kitten or kill it, I was desperate and decided to take a chance. I put the remaining little black male on the carpet in front of Lee-la and Pixie, my two Siamese. That's what I should have done in the first place. Lee-la curled her body around him, and she and Pixie both went to work with those rough Siamese tongues. Lee-la licked and massaged the kitten's lower abdomen with grim determination until, in less than one minute, that little mite had passed a stool. If it's going in one end and it's coming out the other, that's a favorable sign. Pixie cleaned his eyes and his ears to her satisfaction, despite the little one's feeble protests. And, as she began licking his back, the little black male fell asleep. At that point I felt safe in giving him a name, because it looked like the odds in his favor had just risen a good bit. Being newly into yoga, I decided to call him Jai, which means "victory" in Sanskrit. Sanskrit words impart their vibrations to anyone who hears them, and I figured that "Jai" was just what this little squirt needed.

Jai continued to get queen's milk for three weeks. He also continued to get bathed and cuddled and generally mothered by my two prim Siamese ladies. At three weeks of age, I began mixing the baby food mixture given below with the milk. I got him to lick out of a plate by putting some of this food on my finger and dirtying his nose with it. I put just a drop on the tip of his nose, and his little tongue would automatically come out to lick it off. It tasted good. He looked for more and found it on my finger. I kept dipping my finger into the dish and offering it to him. Each time I made him reach closer and closer to the dish by moving my finger down toward it. Being bright, he soon figured out that my finger was a middleman he could do away with by going straight to the source. At five weeks, I had intended to gradually introduce grown-up cat food. However, Jai found it for himself and attacked his foster mothers' plates with such gusto that my problem became one of preventing his overeating.

If you can't get powdered queen's milk, here is Dr. Pitcairn's recipe for nursing kittens:

Mock Nursing Formula

2 cups whole milk
2 raw organic egg yolks
2 tablespoons protein powder
6 drops liquid vitamins for children

Beat with a fork or whisk. Warm the formula first to bath temperature (101 degrees) by standing feeder in a bowl of hot water. Feed kittens in a doll bottle or pet nurser.

Use the following chart to determine a feeding schedule:

Kitten's weight	How much	How often
Under 4 ounces	About 1 teaspoon	Every 2 hours for 2 weeks
4 to 8 ounces	2 to 4 tablespoons per day	Every 3 hours for the 3rd week
8 to 24 ounces	6 to 10 tablespoons per day	Every 4 hours for 4th and 5th weeks

Then begin weaning, mixing queen's milk or the formula with the weaning recipe:

Weaning Recipe

1 jar baby food meat (lamb, beef, or chicken)
3 teaspoons baby food carrot or squash
2 teaspoons baby food creamed corn or barley (comes in a box)
1 raw organic egg yolk *or* ½ teaspoon butter
3 drops children's liquid vitamins
½ teaspoon food yeast
¼ teaspoon calcium lactate or calcium gluconate
Spring or distilled water to desired consistency

Until Jai was six weeks old, I must have fed him six to eight meals a day. Jai remained petite up through six months. He had a mature conformation, but his size was that of an eight-week-old kitten. He looked like a miniature cat. Soon afterward he was adopted by a nice young couple who moved to California. There he had a yard, sunshine, and air—and, before long, a girlfriend (both cats were neutered). I was informed through mutual friends that my tiny Jai was tiny no more. He grew and filled out to become a big, strapping male, the terror of chipmunks.

Feeding the Aging Cat

In the aging cat, the assimilation of nutrients is not as efficient as in younger cats. Attack the problem in three ways.

1. *Feed smaller meals more frequently, as a kitten is fed.* My Priscilla, who is seventeen and a half, gets three or four meals a day depending on my work schedule. I don't make the mistake of giving large meals in hopes of putting more weight on her. The object is to have the stomach less than three-quarters full, because its muscular action is not as strong as it was. And, because digestive juices and enzymes are not as plentifully supplied by her system as before, a small meal will be more efficiently mixed with the digestive juices that are available. Once a week, as usual, I give 400 units of vitamin

E (alpha tocopherol), 10,000 units of vitamin A, and 400 units of vitamin D.

2. *Supply some additional enzymes and bile.* I give Priscilla one-quarter teaspoon of feline digestive enzymes or one-half of a digestive enzyme tablet from the health-food store either in her meal or, more frequently, after the meal crushed up in her favorite dessert of half-and-half and baby food oatmeal. She gets about two teaspoonfuls of this dessert with the half tablet plus one-sixteenth teaspoon of vitamin C crystals (I'd like to give her one-eighth teaspoon but one-sixteenth teaspoon is all she'll accept). I also mix in four drops of cod liver oil, and six drops of a vitamin B and iron tonic called Pet Tinic (which I get from the veterinarian). The enzyme tablet contains bile and enzymes to augment those produced by her own body.

3. *Make sure that the diet is supplied with a much larger amount of vitamins, because the cat won't assimilate them all anyway.* Use more of the high-powered foods such as cod liver oil, wheat germ oil, alfalfa sprouts, organic raw egg yolk, yeast, lecithin—in addition to the Vita-Mineral Mix. And give a multiple vitamin for cats four times a week instead of twice a week. Cats are naturally heavy meat eaters, and because meat is not a perfectly balanced protein it is not unusual to find that cats over fifteen years old have some percentage of kidney failure. I therefore recommend increasing the proportion of complex carbohydrates and vegetables and emphasizing the better-balanced proteins.

The aging cat needs less protein. He's not growing and he's less active. Because too much protein is hard on the kidneys, you will notice the formula below is lower in protein than the basic diet for a cat in his prime. Use the same ingredients in each category as listed in the diet on page 61 but use this ratio:

40 percent protein
30 percent vegetable
30 percent grain

If you're feeding one of the canned foods, you can alter it for the older cat in this way:

1 small can food
2 tablespoons soaked oat bran (page 262) *or* baby food creamed
    corn
2 teaspoons finely grated zucchini
All of the daily and weekly supplements listed on page 61

I have completely eliminated all junk food from Priscilla's diet. A young body can process out and dispose of the sugar in half a teaspoonful of vanilla ice cream. Now that Priscilla is seventeen and a half, half-and-half or light cream is nicer, and much more chic.

3

The Litter Box

There is no area of cat care that is as potentially distressing to both cats and their owners as the litter box. Neither party wants a smelly, dirty litter pan. But, unfortunately, even the most caring owners have found themselves trapped in the old, established litter box system. Well, take heart—there is an alternative.

The Litter-Box Problem

I have seen litter-box setups that must have cost a small fortune. Pet shops have a formidable array—some with plastic domes, plastic liners, even built-in sieves and strainers. For litter, people turn to clay, cedar chips, sawdust, magic sand, and newspaper. Litter boxes are moved about from the kitchen to the bathroom to behind the bed to under the coffee table. Their number can range from one to ten. Because of the random wetting problem, Persian cats are thrown out, given back, given away, or killed. The litter box can be a headache for both the cats and their owners—unless you know how to simplify the system.

In order to devise an acceptable system for both cat and owner, I went back to what Dr. Rowan had once told me, "Stick as close as you can to nature, and you won't go too far wrong." He was discussing food and feeding at the time, but I felt that the same concept should be applied to the litter box. So, how does a wild cat behave in this respect?

The cat's urine is very concentrated, and the smell is strong. Because this smell could attract predators to the nest, cats in the wild always urinate far away from their habitat or any place of activity. They do not urinate where they sleep, eat, hunt, or play. Young kittens are frequently and thoroughly cleaned by the mother, who then swallows any waste matter, passing it through her own system to be neatly disposed of later with her own body wastes. With this kind of training in cleanliness from birth, is it any wonder that cats are fastidious about where they urinate?

Many a random wetting problem begins when the litter box is placed near the food dish or a favorite resting place. That litter box looks great, but the cats would have to be insane to soil near the area where they eat or rest. So the cat simply begins to search for an acceptable place to use. (See "Feline Urologic Syndrome," page 331.)

Cats hide their urine. They are not comfortable or at peace when they have to stand on old, half-wet litter to void again. Cats, in fact, have a universally accepted reputation for neatness. That's one of the attributes we find so very endearing about them.

You might even say they are very much like us. Let us imagine that any one of us should walk into a bathroom and find that the toilet had already been used—but not flushed. What does one automatically do? And even if you could not flush the toilet before you used it, would you then have to stand inside the dirty toilet to use it? And, even if you did, *you* do not have long, silky bloomers to dangle down into the smelly mess—ugh!

Cats cannot flush their own toilet; you have to do it for them. Put the litter pan in the bathroom, and when you flush for yourself flush for them too. Persian cats have especially long, fluffy bloomers, and they are notoriously fastidious about what might get caught in their fur.

Surprisingly, I have found that the people with the smelliest apartments and homes were not those with the random wetting problem but those with the largest, deepest, most complicated, and most expensive litter-box setups. It soon became apparent that the bigger the box and the deeper the bed of litter, the less likely the owner was to clean the box often enough; therefore, the worse the smell and the higher the incidence of random wetting.

The Requirements for a Litter Box

Now let us list the requirements for the litter box, from both the cats' viewpoint and ours.

Cat	Owner
Clean	Clean
Odorless	Odorless
Convenient	Convenient
Out of the way	Out of the way
	Inexpensive
	Simple and quick
	Sanitary

You'll notice that our requirements are the same as the cats' with the addition of inexpensive (because we must maintain the facility), simple and quick, and sanitary (because that is our responsibility—pussycats don't know about germs).

I began my research by simply trying first to satisfy the cats' requirements. The method I ended up with turned out automatically to fulfill all of the owner's requirements as well. Here is one case where the very best is also the easiest, most sanitary, and by far the cheapest.

An Easy, Convenient, and Effective System

Put the litter box near the toilet. This is out of the way and convenient. The cat doesn't eat or sleep near the toilet and you can clean it every time you go into the bathroom. Many owners put the box in the tub because it is then easy to brush up any litter that is kicked out.

If you have a small bathroom, as most New Yorkers do, use a square plastic dishpan as your cat's litter box. It's plenty large enough for any cat and it has the added advantages of being super-light and easy to lift and clean. Also, the sides are nice and high so less litter gets kicked out onto the floor.

Don't buy one of those expensive covered litter boxes—it's not convenient for you or your cat. The dome prevents you from seeing whether it needs cleaning or not. Also, because cats squat upright, a low roof causes hunching and impairs free movement of the bowels and bladder.

Any commercial litter is fine as long as it doesn't contain extra chemicals such as those green and blue "deodorizing" pellets. You and your cat can work that out between you. I find plain clay to be the most efficient. However, I have met one or two rare Persians who prefer newspaper because it doesn't cling to their bloomers. In that case you wouldn't flush; you'd have to incinerate it.

Just keep a giant tablespoon or metal serving spoon, one with *no holes* or slits in it, on a hook or in a glass or mug near the box. Whenever you pass the bathroom, take a quick look at the box. If you see a covered mound or a little wet circle, which is like the tip of an iceberg, pick the litter box up and gently shake all the dry litter to one end exposing the wet clump. Then, take your giant tablespoon and remove every bit of the wet clump and flush it away. The remaining litter is left clean and uncontaminated, so shake it evenly across the pan again, rinse the spoon, and replace the spoon on its hook.

Use only one-quarter to three-quarters of an inch of litter at a time, *no deeper*. You want the wet to hit the bottom and clump, not spread and seep through the other litter to contaminate it and make it smell. If you're going to be gone eight hours or more and you have more than a couple of cats, do as I do. I have one pan for each two cats and clean them on arising, before leaving, when I return, and before bed. It takes about fifteen seconds per pan per cleaning.

Don't buy one of those commercial "litter scoops" full of holes and slits. They must have been invented by someone who wanted you to use up lots and lots of litter. Supposedly they are to be used to lift out "the solid matter." Well, if you just stop to think about it, the solid matter is not the problem. The stool will smell bad for about three minutes, but then it's dry. The cats can easily step around that. It's the wetness that really smells; it's the wet parts that breed germs; and it's the wet parts that make it impossible for a cat to use the box without stepping on old urine.

If you try to remove the wet litter with a commercial litter scoop, you'll have some mess on your hands with half the wet bits of litter filtering merrily down onto the floor, the toilet seat and back into the clean litter to contaminate it and make it smell.

Don't make the mistake of putting too much litter in the box. I have come across great, huge litter pans with ten to fifteen pounds of litter in them. These pans are always the smelliest, because the urine doesn't hit the bottom and clump but continues to permeate the whole ten pounds like a miasmic fog. The rule is "If the litter smells, *use less* and *clean more often.*"

And don't line your nice, smooth plastic pan with anything. Newspaper does not deodorize; it smells. Those messy plastic liners always form little wrinkles where wet litter hides to smell and breed germs. Fifty percent of the time the cat's claw puts a hole in it anyway, and the urine drains through and sits there in a puddle under the liner where there is no litter to absorb the odor.

With my method, you need to change and wash the whole pan only once or twice a week. When they do the complete cleaning, finicky owners will feel as if they are cleaning an already clean litter box. Because they have scooped out the wet clumps so often, there is absolutely no odor about the plastic box. At the most, there might be a little dot of dry stool clinging to the side. With my litter boxes, after dumping out what little litter remains, I swish them out with water, dump that out, sprinkle in a little cleanser, and scrub the boxes inside and out with a vegetable brush that I keep on a hook next to the litter spoon.

I always used a plain chlorine-based cleanser until I got an idea from something my vet was using to disinfect the examining table in between patients—plain chlorine bleach and water. When he told me a 20 to 1 ratio of water and chlorine bleach would kill germs, viruses, and fungus, I got the idea for a litter-box cleaner—cheap, easy, effective, and safe.

Litter-Box Cleaner

Mark off a large spray bottle into twenty-one parts. Fill it with nineteen parts water, one part chlorine bleach, and one part Dr. Bronner's Liquid Soap (available in most health food stores).

Finally, I rinse like crazy. If you think I'm finicky about food, I become absolutely rabid about any kind of chemical a cat might get on his paws or fur and lick off. No residue of soap or cleaner must be left in the box.

There is just no need for those deodorant sprays made especially for "kitty's box." Three of my pussycat clients in one household came down with a stubborn case of foot fungus, the cause of which was finally traced to an aerosol spray for the box. I explained to that owner that if you smell an odor from the box you're doing something wrong—usually using too much litter and not cleaning frequently enough. Using deodorant spray on a dirty box is like spraying perfume on a dirty body—one doesn't. Finicky owners have no need of those things.

I might add that there are some owners who, instead of scooping out the wet with a spoon, prefer to dump the whole thing twice a day. They put even less litter in the box—say an eighth of an inch—and swish the box out with water each time. (If you start the flush before you dump and then dump slowly, there is no danger of stopping up the average toilet.) I call these people "superfinicky," and their cats are absolutely ecstatic about this system. With this new litter-box system, get ready to buy a lot less litter. You will be amazed at how little you will be using.

Even if you have more than one cat, you should be able to identify each cat's stool in order to be sure that each cat puts out a stool once or twice a day. There are many instances when knowing what's going in one end and what's coming out the other is worth its weight in gold. It gives the finicky owner peace of mind. Finicky owners as a group have the highest standards of feline health, fitness, and happiness.

If you notice a change in the consistency of one of the cat's stools, immediately try to figure out what caused the change. Did the cat eat a milk product that made the stool runny? Did the cat eat more than his or her share of chicken neck vertebrae, which turned the stool into a series of hard little balls? If you don't know the cause of the change in stool consistency, then watch the cat carefully for the appearance of any other adverse symptoms such as copious water drinking, loss of appetite, lethargy, and so on. Hopefully the stool will return to normal tomorrow, and you can breathe easy again.

Training Kittens to Use the Litter Box

The mother cat always toilet trains the kittens herself, so you never have to worry—well, hardly ever. On one or two rare occasions, I have received calls for help from people with a litter of kittens who were wetting and dirtying outside the box. Because "everyone knows" that you don't have to housebreak a cat, the amazed owners wondered if these accidents were happening just because the kittens were still too young. The answer is no. Under normal circumstances, at no time will a kitten or cat dirty or wet outside the box. Abnormal circumstances include the loss of the mother before she completes their training, inaccessibility of a litter box, unsanitary conditions in the litter box or use of a strong-smelling chemical or deodorizer around the litter box.

Years ago I ran up against yet another reason for this problem. Triple Champion Purr-du's Lee-la of Mar Wal was a lovely chocolate-point Siamese. To see her was to lose your heart. She was all purrs and cuddling and posing and sweetness—the darling of all who beheld her. Lee-la knew she was a winner, and because the world had always treated her royally she had come to expect the very best at all times. She had never been frightened, so she did not know fear. Lee-la was not the brightest cat I ever met but with all that charm and beauty, who cared?—until her kittens began to use the rugs for a toilet. The family was shocked; Lee-la was unconcerned. Because Lee-la didn't know what fear was, she lacked that basic instinct to protect the young by teaching them to bury their wastes where the smell would never draw dangerous predators to the area. Her six kittens were happy, healthy, and absolutely beautiful, but Lee-la's laissez-faire policy was driving the family to distraction.

The solution to this, as in so many situations, is found on a very primitive level. First let's examine exactly how, in nature, this automatic kitten training actually does occur; then, if necessity arises, a human can duplicate it.

After nursing, newborn kittens pass wastes while lying on their backs when they feel the mother's tongue stroking down their belly and out along the tail. The tiny amount of waste is simply cleaned away by the sweep of the mother's tongue and swallowed by the mother. The procedure is a study in efficiency, cleanliness, and safety. The mother disposes of the wastes a safe distance away from the nest, passing them out of her body with her own excrement.

When the kittens are old enough to walk a little distance and squat without falling over, the mother will lead them to a preferred place (the litter box, in the home situation), and as they stand in the litter she begins to lick the genital area, thus triggering the response of urinating and passing stool.

When the tiny stools and thimblefuls of urine are all lying in the litter box, the mother then rallies her kittens to a jolly group effort of covering up the wastes. The kittens dutifully scratch and sniff and circle around with such vigor that the litter usually flies in all directions, showering the rug and floor for several feet around. Then the proud parent chases them all out of the box and the group runs pell-mell away, putting a safe distance between themselves and the area where lingering smell could attract a predator.

So, if some crucial part of the training is missing, the solution becomes obvious. Someone must supply the missing element—in the case of Lee-la, the mother's tongue that triggers the response to deposit wastes in the litter.

Here's how it's done. After each meal, which is the usual time for the kittens to pass wastes, carry the kitten or kittens into the litter box. Dip your finger into a cup of hot water so it will feel as much as possible like a warm, moist tongue. Then place the finger between the kitten's hindlegs so that the tip of your finger rests against the stomach. Stroke the finger backward against the kitten's tummy and up across the genitals and anus once or twice. Dip your finger in the hot water again and repeat, or go on to the next kitten. When a kitten begins to squat and pass wastes, gently pet its forehead as a sign of encouragement and approval. At the end of the exercise, cover the wastes with your fingertip, lift the kittens out of the box, and lure them away with a toy.

Lee-la used to love to watch the performance from her queenly perch up on the sink. She would purr loudly the whole time. Indeed, I had the feeling that by the time those kittens were finally litter trained, Triple Champion Purr-du's Lee-la of Mar Wal was just as proud of me as she was of them. (The complete story of

Lee-la is found in Chapter 1 of our book *It's a Cat's Life*. Her name was changed to Su-shi to protect her privacy.)

Caution: while you or the mother cat are carrying on litter-box training, you must be sure to keep the box scrupulously clean and, equally important, use even less litter. The kittens' feet are so tiny they sink into the litter. Their little legs are so short that if the litter is too deep you'll have them falling over and swimming through it. Use only one-quarter-inch depth until the babies are eight weeks old.

For more on kittens and the litter box, see Chapter 2 of our book *It's a Cat's Life*.

Special Litter-Box Considerations for the Older or Ailing Cat

My Suzi is twenty years old. When she was nineteen, she began "making mistakes" from time to time, urinating in the kitchen. My veterinarian found no evidence of bladder infection; we reasoned that she just got a little confused. Sometimes she'd wake up and have to urinate, but she'd forget which sleeping area she had been using and in which direction she should proceed to get to the bathroom. So she'd end up in the kitchen and then not be able to hold her urine any longer.

I decided it was time to add an extra litter box for her convenience. It was a plastic dishpan with two pages of newspaper folded flat in the bottom and a paper towel on top for extra quick absorbency so she wouldn't be troubled by getting wet on her paws. I didn't use litter because I don't want anyone kicking litter on my living room floor. I put it near the kitchen door and the problem was solved.

When your feline friend becomes a senior citizen, he or she needs special consideration. If your veterinarian finds no urinary infection, there are several other possible causes for wetting outside the box. Elderly or sick cats may become too weak to walk all the way to the box, or a weakened bladder may release the urine before they can make it. Arthritis may slow them down, make it painful to step over the side into the box, or prevent them from squatting properly as they used to.

Once a cat passes the age of fourteen, there should be a litter box on every floor of the house. If he can't step over the side, cut him an opening in the side of the box, leaving only one or two inches on the bottom to keep the litter from tumbling out. If he can't squat properly and the urine sprays outside the box, put newspaper and paper towel on the floor and/or masking-tape it to the bathroom wall by the box.

The deep love that exists between you and your old friend will inspire you to devise ingenious methods of solving his problem without his ever suspecting that he has one.

4

The Scratching Post

It is a sad fact that many unaware owners have had their cats declawed simply because they thought it was the only way to protect their furniture and carpeting. Fortunately, this is not the case. I hope the declawing operation will become obsolete as owners learn to meet their cats' needs by supplying the scratching post that the cats find irresistible.

The Scratching Post They Love

Cats should be encouraged to scratch because all the musculature, from the claws through the legs and shoulders and down the back, are exercised and toned when the cat scratches to clean and sharpen his claws. A cat who doesn't scratch has underdeveloped muscles. All wild cats love a good claw at a nice rough tree. This tells us that the scratching post should be rough, too.

Unfortunately, most posts in pet shops are made to attract owners instead of cats, as it's the owners who walk in with money to buy the post. Ninety-nine percent of all owners are attracted by a soft-looking, fluffy-wuffy scratching post. The *cat* should be fluffy-wuffy—the *post* should be rough and coarse. We may not find it practical to bring a tree trunk into the home or a small apartment, but there are other alternatives. Cats are attracted to something rough, like the back of a good rug or, heaven forbid, Great-Grandmother's needlepoint footstool. What the cat needs is a post so wonderfully rough and scratchy that Great-Grandmother's needlepoint becomes second-rate by comparison.

Happily, such a post is available. It is called the Felix extra large scratching post, and it is made of sisal. Many local pet stores and pet food suppliers carry them or you can order direct from the company (see Appendix, "Product Suppliers"). Sisal is a harsh, scratchy hemp product. The post stands about three feet high and is fixed in a square base.

I have seen my Big Purr take a flying leap off the table to land on the top of the post. Balancing nicely, he extends the claws of all four feet and blissfully digs in. A far-off look of ecstasy suffuses his countenance as he sways. It is a subtle and sensual dance. As the clawing goes deeper and the dance steps become more pronounced, Purr's post trembles with the violence of his digging and pulling. But it never tips over, because the Felix post has a good firm base.

Many cats are declawed *because of* fluffy scratching posts. Because fluffy scratching posts do not fulfill their purpose from the cats' point of view, they go to your furniture in desperation. Then the owners complain, "I tried a post, and he refuses to use it." It's not the cat's fault—it's the fault of the post. Either it is too fluffy, or too rickety, or too small. The trick is to give your cats a post they can't resist.

If you want to make your own scratching post, use a rug with a rough backing and put the backing side out. Also, make sure the whole thing is secure and won't wobble or fall over. If you meet these two criteria, you're home free. Even the backside of a piece of carpet laid on the floor is better than a fluffy-wuffy post. If you've already been taken in by the fluffy-wuffy variety, why not recover it with carpet turned backside out? This will work fine as long as you have a large, firm base.

As a stopgap measure, the disposable corrugated cardboard posts can also work well and some cats will use the cork variety, but both must be firmly braced so they don't slide around.

In case you decide to purchase a Felix Katnip Tree direct from the company, I am including instructions here on how to set it up because the Felix Company includes none, apparently assuming that the method of assembly is blatantly obvious. After all, there are only three pieces to deal with: the post, the base, and a little metal wedge. However, during the excitement precipitated by the arrival of the post, even the most level-headed and responsible of people can forget themselves and inadvertently toss away the all-important little metal wedge, without which the post has no stability. I have seen so many wobbly, insecure, improperly assembled Felix posts that I must caution you—*don't throw away that little metal wedge!*

There is no need to plan an introduction of the cats to their new post. Here's what usually happens when the Felix Katnip Tree arrives: If you just leave the package lying on the floor inside the door, your cats will soon trot over to have a good sniff. The odor of catnip wafting from that parcel is absolutely fascinating and not to be resisted. If they start clawing at it wrapped as it is, you can help by snipping strings and peeling away the cardboard cover (there are two layers of wrapping).

Now, only the brown paper stands between the cats and their Katnip Tree. They may begin to attack it with violence, ripping and tearing at it with teeth and claws. By now, some of the very potent catnip will have fallen out. The catnip may propel your cats onto Cloud Nine, where they will enter a state of ecstasy, rolling about on their backs from side to side and rubbing their cheeks against the wonderful package. It is not unusual to see cats grab the post with front claws, hugging it to them, while raking it viciously with the hind claws. Their excitement can be felt like the temperature in the room. The catnip may not do much for you, but your cats' wild abandon will tell its own story.

In order to stretch out your cats' pleasure and anticipation of this new toy, leave the post wrapped as it is for an hour or even a day and just let them enjoy ripping at the paper and tape and getting mini-scratches at whatever bit of the post they expose. As a matter of fact, anytime you want your cats to do something, your best bet is to engineer the circumstances so that you keep the cats in the position of asking for it or reaching for it rather than presenting it to them on a silver platter, or even worse, thrusting it on them.

Perhaps the next day, when your cats begin to attack the parcel, you can go ahead and get down on the rug and help them as they rip and tear the wrapping paper away, exposing completely that irresistible scratchiness—the naked post dripping with powdered catnip. Once the post is completely exposed, the cats will probably pull the whole length of their bodies close against its primitive roughness and begin rubbing their cheeks against the sisal fabric and chewing on it. Go ahead—join the party. Scratch it yourself. What an intriguing sound for a pussycat's ears! Then scratch the cats. Really get into it, with your nails and your hands. You'll send them into fresh throes of sensual delight. Cloud Nine will be left far below. Their eyes may glaze over slightly, and they may utter low guttural sounds from deep in their throats. Do not be alarmed, it's normal when cats are totally focused on hitherto-undreamed-of pleasure.

In ten or fifteen minutes, the cats, thoroughly sated, will tumble into a heap somewhere to sleep it off. Now is a good time to assemble the post. Look for some tape around the wooden peg on the bottom of the post. Wrapped in that tape is the all-important little metal wedge. Take it off and save it. After the post is inserted in its base, turn the whole thing upside down. The metal wedge is then hammered into the slit in the center of the bottom of the peg, expanding it to fit snugly into the base. If you throw the tape away and the metal wedge with it, the post will go into the base all right, but when the cats stretch up, extending their eager claws to dig in, the whole contraption wiggles and wobbles and sometimes even falls apart on top of the cats. What a nasty shock! It's enough to put a cat off scratching posts for life. And all because one silly metal wedge was inadvertently thrown away.

Where to Put the Scratching Post

There are several ways to position the post:

- In a corner, with the base touching two right-angle walls so it won't slide around.
- Next to Great-Grandmother's needlepoint footstool, so that when the cats go for the footstool they will see the post and, naturally, prefer the post.
- On its side, like a tilt-board, to make it seem less threatening because many highly bred or nervous cats can be extremely suspicious of anything new or strange.

Once you and your cats decide on the best placement for the post, you can make it even more secure by putting double-face carpet tape on the bottom all around the edge.

If your cats do not immediately leap on the post and begin scratching like mad, you can (1) scratch the post yourself and tell them how much you enjoy the sensation or (2) lay the post on its side, pick the cats up, and stand them on the tilting post. Never grab cats' legs or feet and force them onto the post. Cats hate that, and it will have a very negative effect—just the opposite of what you're trying to achieve. Just stroke firmly down their necks and backs so that you urge their bodies backward. Most cats dig their claws into the post as an expression of ecstasy. Alternate between scratching the post with your fingernails in front of them with the firm, stroking, pulling gesture down their backs. In other words, you are creating a situation where they feel ecstasy, and at the same time you are showing them how to express it.

Encouraging Use of the Scratching Post

To reinforce the association of happiness with the post, work use of the post into other situations that are normally happy occasions, for example, your arrival home, before and after feeding, and/or before and after play time. When I'm caring for cats who are up for adoption, I make sure they are dedicated scratching post users so there is no danger of their ever being declawed by a misinformed future owner.

Every time I come home, the cats are happy and excited. But I don't pet them right away. First I run to the scratching post and begin scratching the top of the post with my nails and tell the cats how glad I am to be back and how much I missed them. In response, they all crowd in and begin clawing the post. As soon as they start clawing the post, I stop scratching it and start scratching them, continuing my verbal assurances of love, interspersed with comments about how strong, lithe, and graceful they look while scratching the post. Because cats adore ritual and sameness, I further reinforce the pleasure of the situation by beginning with a key phrase. I always say, "Let's greet, let's greet" while I run from the door to the post.

Because "catch and kill" with the use of claws precedes eating in nature, you can also scratch the post before you prepare the cat's food, perhaps using a ritualistic phrase such as "Are you hungry?" "Is it time?" or something worked out by you and your cat. After eating, the phrase might be "Was it good?" The same principle can be used before and after play time.

Don't freshen the catnip on the post more than once a week, because otherwise the cats will become immune to its effects and will not react as strongly.

The Physical and Emotional Effects of Declawing

Many veterinarians do not explain the reality of the declawing operation to cat owners. Physically, realistically, it is ten amputations. Moreover, it is ten complex amputations. The cat must remain under an anesthetic quite a long time. Anesthetizing a cat for even a short time is, as everyone knows, chancy. The claw is harder to remove than the tip joint of all ten of your fingers because you do not retract your fingertip. Your fingertip is not set into the joint below in a complex fashion. A cat's claw is. Someone once described declawing to me as "cutting pieces out of animals' bodies for convenience." I was absolutely horrified by the starkness of the way she faced this reality. People prefer not to discuss this so graphically in polite company. I apologize to those who already know the reality for reminding you of it and for bringing into your conscious mind again something so painful. But I have met too many loving owners who were never told, or who had the operation misrepresented to them only to find out, perhaps years after it was done, the truth about what they had actually done to the animal they adored. There are several veterinarians in New York City who refuse to do the operation and are happy to explain why.

The physical effect of declawing is gradual weakening of the muscles of the legs, shoulders, and back. Balance is impaired. The cat is 75 percent defenseless. Cats don't defend themselves with their teeth, they defend themselves with their claws.

The long-range effects are both physical and emotional. A declawed cat is, in reality, a clubfooted animal. He cannot walk normally but must forever after move with his weight back on the rear of his pads. Posture is irrevocably altered, and gone is the easeful grace that is his birthright. Because they are defenseless, declawed cats live in a constant state of stress. This is very draining and, because of the constant stress, these cats are more prone to disease. (See "Stress," page 197.)

Declawed cats bite sooner and more often than cats that have their claws because they are more tense and nervous and because they no longer have their claws to use as a warning. The claws are their first line of defense. With that gone, they must resort to desperate measures—the use of their teeth. For that reason, a declawed cat is not one you would want to have around young children.

Newborn kittens until the age of three weeks or so have not yet learned to retract their claws. But once cats have reached that age, they begin to have control of their claws and can be trained to use them on toys and the post but not on human flesh.

I call the first eight months or so of a cat's life the rambunctious months. During this time kittens are learning to use that wonderful body nature has given them. Just as a little human baby uses his teeth on everything in sight when he is teething, a kitten will try his claws on drapes, furniture, and everything within reach during the rambunctious months. Many cats are mutilated with a declawing operation at this time because owners don't realize that just as human babies eventually outgrow the desire to chew on buttons and fingers, kittens grow out of their desire to claw everything and are easily satisfied with a workout on their scratching post.

Declawed cats are much harder for a groomer or veterinarian to handle because of their nervous state and their proclivity for using teeth. Cats use claws as a mode of expression. We humans have sounds and words and laughter, but cats say, "Mmmm, this feels good" by gently kneading their claws. When I'm grooming cats, frequently they will say to me, "Hey, stop that, wait a minute" by hitting me with their claws when their patience is running out. They do not scratch or harm me in any way. They are simply making a strong statement. I know that "claws out," in this case, means that I have not listened when they tried to warn me with a meow or a wiggle. Cats are polite, they give a warning before they hurt you. If you declaw cats, you have taken away from them this means of being polite and giving warning first. In a way it could be likened to removing a person's larynx. Even if you promise that that person would always be protected, certainly never have to cry for help, even if you promise that that person would always have anything and everything that he might desire (and in real life you can never be sure you can fulfill such promises), still, the larynx is gone. The choice of communicating in the normal way is no longer that person's choice.

Many times I have encountered owners who, after realizing what a declawing operation really means, vow never again to allow a cat of theirs to be declawed. Inevitably when they begin living with a normal cat they are amazed and enchanted by their pet's athletic prowess and grace and they point out to me how very unusual their cat is in this respect. I have to explain to them that their cat is simply normal. All cats leap and bound like super ballet dancers if their feet have not been mutilated.

If you would like more information about claws and declawing, see "Claw and Cuticle Problems" on page 290 and the section "Foot and Claw Problems" in *Dr. Pitcairn's Complete Guide to Natural Health for Dogs and Cats*.

5

The Cat and
Its Human Family

Because my job entails going into people's homes to take care of
their cats, I have a unique opportunity to observe at firsthand that
delightful and complex interaction that takes place between the
human family and its cats. I know so many of these families, and
our relationship has extended now over so many years, that many
common problems have been brought to my attention time and
time again, which I will discuss in this chapter.

The New Baby

There are many old wives' tales about cats, but the two concerning
pregnancy and babies are the ones mentioned by newly pregnant
women. Although they know these old wives' tales sound silly, a
little reassurance is always welcome to an expectant mother.

Several people have asked me if it's true that cleaning the litter
box can cause a miscarriage. It sounds ridiculous, doesn't it? But,
oddly enough, there *can* be a connection. Toxoplasmosis is the
disease to which these people are referring. By far the most common
way to catch toxoplasmosis is by eating raw meat or by touching
raw meat and then touching vegetables that will remain raw. The
contamination is killed when you cook the meat, but it will remain
on the raw foods. For cats to carry the germs they must first have
killed and eaten a rat, mouse, or forest rodent who has the disease.

97

Then, if the cats do indeed contract the disease from this live prey there will be microscopic eggs in the cat's stool. In order to pass it on to a human, the human must in turn ingest these eggs. That is to say—they must eat them. Because they are in the cat's stool, you might think that this is impossible. But wait—what if, while cleaning the litter box, some stool on the side of the box is touched by the owner's hand? If that person does not wash the hand carefully before picking up and eating a piece of food, that food could be contaminated inadvertently. Contamination could also occur after grooming cats or stroking the anal area. Unlikely as it sounds, pregnant women have been known to contract toxoplasmosis, and this disease *can* cause congenital defects or miscarriage. My advice has always been, "Why worry about it?—if the possibility is preying on your mind, simply drop a fresh stool sample off at your veterinarian and he will test it for you and tell you whether or not your cat is carrying toxoplasmosis. You can also get your own blood and urine tested to find out whether or not you have a natural immunity to toxoplasmosis; most adult humans do. And in the meantime, remember to wash your hands after cleaning the litter box."

The second old wives' tale has two variations, the most primitive being that cats like to suck the breath out of babies. The second variation is that the cat will smother the baby. Every time I hear of this slander, I think of little Matthew who was born into a household that already had four large cats. The cats ranged in temperament from lethargic to skittish, from friendly to withdrawn, and from playful to solitary. Both males and females were represented in this group.

From the time Matthew came home from the hospital, the cats loved to sleep with him in the crib. At first, three of the four cats were larger than Matthew. Just imagine what it must feel like to be small enough to snuggle your whole body against a cat's chest and be completely enveloped in that warm, soft fur. Imagine being surrounded by the sound of a cat's purr. I don't know if the cats had anything to do with it, but Matthew was a very mellow and sunny baby. He was always grinning and gurgling.

When Matthew started to crawl, he would sometimes reach for the cats and try to grab hold of them. It was a simple matter for them to slip away from his grasp when they had had enough. They still continued to sleep with him.

During the crawling stage, Matthew and the cats really had a great time because at this point Matthew was almost as smart as the cats. The cats could understand him and play with him safely because Matthew had not yet reached the stage where he posed any sort of threat to the cats. He couldn't yet prevent the cats from leaving when they wanted to.

Matthew's mother knew that the toddler stage begins a time of transition, and the cats had to be protected. The time was approaching when Matthew would be strong enough to inadvertently harm a cat. A toddler may pick up a heavy toy and swing it about and accidentally hit the loving animal sitting close by. Toddlers are not yet capable of understanding that they now have superior strength. More adult supervision was needed now until Matthew learned the rules involved in dealing with a pet.

Teach children the very first rule that will keep them safe for the rest of their lives: Never try to hold a cat if the cat wants to go. If you always let cats go, they will always come back to you. When dealing with strange cats (or dogs), never touch them with more than one hand at a time. That way it's clear to the animals that they are free to leave if they want to, and they won't feel threatened. As long as cats can leave if they want to, they will never have reason to scratch. Cats scratch only as a last resort if they are extremely upset and frightened.

Young Children

Declawed cats are not good to have around children. They are less secure in their own abilities to escape and will be more likely to bite. Cats with all their claws intact are by far the gentlest and safest companions for young children. As children grow up, they will probably find the feeding and litter cleaning fascinating. Many children like to help with these activities, and I know several bright young people who have taken them over completely and have even included grooming in their list of accomplishments. This is one of the lovely contributions that your pets make to your children's welfare and personal growth. Just by their mere presence in the family, cats introduce the youngsters to a sense of responsibility.

However, the wise parent and loving owner never actually

uses a helpless animal as a tool to teach children responsibility. Children may help with pet care—with the adult still in charge and overseeing. But even if the children are given full responsibility and think they are totally in charge, the aware adult will keep a constant, if surreptitious, check to see that each mealtime, each cleanup, each grooming session, and the condition of the litter box continue on the same high standards that prevailed before the younger family members took over. In other words—innocent pets must not be made to pay for children's forgetfulness or carelessness. You, the parent, must maintain an ever-watchful eye.

A word to the wise—little children frequently hurt animals simply because they do not realize what constitutes pain or distress to an animal. Many children love cymbals and drums and cap pistols—however, such things could give a pussycat a heart attack or permanently damage the hearing. Cats are different from people, and it takes quite a while before children are old enough to understand that. (I might add—I've met many adults who still haven't achieved that understanding.)

Children raised in a loving household with pets will usually grow up to be loving owners. When remembering their own childhoods, what a pity it is if they have painful memories of their own cruelty to animals through ignorance or parental indulgence. The memories children will have when they grow up are being made now. Protect your children from painful memories by protecting the cat until the children are old enough to fully understand.

Visitors in the Home

Not everyone owns or understands cats. Many a tragedy has struck because well-meaning friends or relatives or occasional workers come into a home and innocently open a window. If you expect workers to arrive while you are away, lock the cat in one room with litter and water and put a sign on the door that clearly states not to open the door or let the cat out. Many cats are afraid of workers, and a surprisingly large number of workers are afraid of or do not like cats. When friends and relatives come to visit, you can make sure that they know that care must be taken when opening or closing doors or drawers. You can also explain the danger of windows and make sure they know they should not play roughly with the cat with their hands.

Allergic to Cats?

I have frequently had the experience of people coming to visit who didn't know I had cats. Several times those people have told me that they were always allergic to cats and cannot understand why they were not having a reaction to mine. It's nice to be able to help such people understand the reasons by explaining how diet and feeding patterns cut down dander, which is the substance they are allergic to. (See Chapter 2, "Diet.")

I remember Marcie and Lou Gustavson, a nice young couple who moved in down the hall. Lou was highly allergic to cats, as well as to a number of other things. Marcie had always lived with cats and missed them terribly, so one evening they came over to visit me and my cats. I had eleven cats in residence at the time: my own three, a couple of convalescents boarding for nursing care, and six adoptables. Both Marcie and Lou had a great time petting and hugging and playing with all the cats. Lou reasoned that he could always leave if his eyes started to itch or if he had trouble breathing. When Lou had no allergic response, Marcie immediately began to wonder if perhaps all was not lost as far as Lou and cats being able to live together. She asked hopefully if I thought they could try adopting a couple of cats if she kept the cats strictly to the diet I suggested and removed the food between meals. I felt a bit hesitant about committing myself. I'd never tried to solve this particular problem before, and I certainly didn't want to disappoint Marcie. But, because I had so many cats up for adoption, I decided that we should give it the old college try.

I told them that we'd have a much better chance of success if we not only controlled the amount of dander on the cat but also tried to lessen Lou's allergic reaction. They were all for that, of course. Because allergies are evidence of a faulty immunological response, I have found that housecleaning a clogged intestinal tract goes a long way toward alleviating the condition, at least partially. I wanted to give us a wider margin within which to work.

After explaining this, I asked Lou if he would make some

changes in his own diet. Drawing from my experience with yoga and macrobiotics, I told him to eliminate eggs, pork, white sugar, and caffeine from his diet. I also asked him to eat fish instead of red meats, and cut down on butter and other dairy products. I asked him to add one-fourth cup of bran and a tablespoonful of lecithin granules to his diet each day and to eat as many raw vegetables as possible.

He was game to try. When I asked them if they had any special cats in mind, they just looked at each other and smiled. Lou said, "I think we'd like to take 'the married couple.' " I couldn't believe my luck. "The married couple"—Sally and Victor—were two short-haired black cats who had been waiting for adoption for several months.

When I got her, Sally was the smallest cat I ever saw in my life. She was nine years old, and she did not even tip the scale at four pounds. She had arrived when her owner left her, supposedly for boarding, and was never heard from again. I soon found out why. Sally immediately began defecating all over the apartment. She was in sad shape. She had been declawed and was a veritable walking snowdrift of dandruff. She crouched morosely inside an empty cat food carton, hurling threats at any cat who came too close. None of the other cats liked her. So she just sat there frowning, all hunched up in a ball. I wondered how in the world I was ever going to get rid of this one. Who in their right mind would want to adopt an angry pile of dandruff who defecated all over the place?

The veterinarian diagnosed her as having Irritable Bowel Syndrome and I started adjusting and experimenting with her diet until I found that the basic Superfinicky Owner's I'll-Do-Anything-for-My-Cat Diet plus one-half teaspoon bran conditioned her stool so she didn't have to either strain or suddenly let go wherever she was. Of course, this high-quality diet, which was specifically adjusted for her particular intestinal needs, immediately had its effect on the dandruff. Teeny tiny little Sally developed a plushy coat in two months flat. But she still huddled morosely in her box most of the time.

Four-year-old Victor came strolling onto the scene in the company of two other cats, all of whom had been left ownerless when an elderly client had been taken to the hospital with a heart attack and never returned. Victor was as big as Sally was tiny. He was the very picture of shiny black health and vigor. His owner had had the cats on a high-quality diet for over two years. Victor spotted Sally from the doorway when he entered. He just strolled over, jaunty and jolly. "Hi, good looking," he seemed to be saying as he stretched himself out next to Sally's carton. Sally cowered back, muttering swear noises but I noticed she didn't show her fangs and I saw her blink a couple of times, a sure sign that her heart was not entirely made of ice. I think Victor was a gift from the compassionate cat goddess to Sally. He was so mellow and sweet that nobody could resist him—human or animal.

By the second day, Sally and Victor were an item. Victor moved into Sally's carton, and there was a great deal of mutual licking and close cuddling. After Victor's arrival, Sally was seen more and more at large in the room. Victor was the leader, but Sally did follow and leave her cloistered bower. As I watched the romance unfolding, the question was never far from my mind as to how in the world I would ever get them adopted together. It's hard enough to find a home for one cat—opportunities for placing two together are almost nonexistent. I had been steeling myself for the day when I would have to break up Sally and Victor. It was not a happy prospect.

Then into my life walked this nice young couple who announced they'd like to take the two of them. On top of that, from the looks on their faces, I could see that they were already falling in love with my Sally and Victor. Obviously the Gustavsons were a second gift from the cat goddess.

At the end of the month, Marcie called to report that Lou had found his tendency to allergic reactions in general to have lessened. They were anxious to come over and pick up the cats, both of them feeling very positive that all would go well. Lou had lost five pounds during that first month on the new diet and, incidentally, a year later he still declares that he feels better than he has for a long time. Sally does too. There's no longer any evidence that she ever had Irritable Bowel Syndrome. And Lou's allergy to cats seems to be completely controlled. And Apartment 5J down the hall now boasts not one but two married couples.

Taking the Cat Along:
Vacations, Visits, and Moving

Because cats are such territorial animals, loving sameness the way they do, uprooting them and moving them around can be a traumatic event. However, if uprooting them means that they can then be with you, their beloved owner, that is often better than leaving them behind. The thing to do is try it a few times and find out how well it works for you and your cats. For the best chance of success and a smooth transition, start preparing in advance. Tell the cats about the trip you are planning, how happy it will make you to have them with you, and what the trip will be like in every detail from their point of view. Leave the carry case out for at least a few hours a day so they can sniff it and get used to it. Many cats will nap in the carrier. It is a nice size and shape for napping. Throw the weekly catnip party inside the carrier. If your cat has a favorite treat such as olives, cantaloupe, sweet corn, and so on, feed him that particular tidbit inside the carrier once or twice. This way you're creating all sorts of happy associations connected with the carrier.

Review how to choose the case and how to place the cat in the carrier by reading through the pertinent section in Chapter 1.

When the day of the journey arrives, withhold all food and water after midnight of the night before. Skipping breakfast is not one-quarter as traumatic as it would be if the cat dirtied inside the carrier. Whatever your mode or modes of transportation, your safest bet is to leave the carrier closed the whole time, although if traveling by plane they'll probably ask you to open it at the inspection point before you get on the plane. Ask the inspector to allow you to open it inside a room where you can shut the door.

Once comfortably seated in your conveyance, you may consider opening the case so that your furry friend can stretch a little, look around, and get a little more reassurance from you. This sometimes works very well. Again, the only way to find out is to try it. The thing to keep in mind is not to open the case all the way until you have a firm grip on the cat. Make sure you keep your hold on the cat in such a way that at any moment you can easily close the case again. In other words, do not allow the cat to put paws up on the edge of the case. Let the cat sit on your lap *inside* the open case, and you can put your arms into the case and wrap them around him.

As always, when introducing any new activity to the cat, your attitude and mental vibrations are all important. If you are nervous about putting the cat into the case, your cat will be nervous about getting into the case. If you are nervous about flying, your cat will feel apprehensive about flying. Keep your mind centered on the comforts of your cat's situation—how secure the case is and how pleasant it is to be in a case and be carried. Put a nice soft towel in the bottom of the case plus a small piece of your clothing such as a sock or glove to provide additional comfort. Don't allow anyone to rap on the case or call to your cat. When cats are confined in a case and cannot run away, it is in the worst possible taste to confront them with strangers.

I think the watchword is casualness. Try to keep your feelings casual about everything. If you get all upset because the ticket was made out wrong, cats will pick up your emotions, and, because they don't know about tickets, they will assume that some danger threatens.

A word about shipping your cat in the baggage compartment. I understand it's the only way they'll take an animal on the train. Insist on inspecting the baggage car to find out about the temperature factor, making suitable arrangements if need be—hot water bottle in the case if it's winter; cold water bottle if it's summer—and try to secure visiting privileges if the trip lasts more than a couple of hours.

As for sending your pet in the luggage compartment on the airplane, I have never done it because, frankly, I am afraid. I know people who have done it with no ill effects to their pets. On the other hand, I have also heard of pets arriving dead or near death. They were frozen to death from the high altitudes or brain damaged from a lack of oxygen. More than once, heavy baggage has crashed against the carrier, springing it open and releasing hysterical animals to run loose among the baggage until the owner could be summoned to help capture them.

If you know you're going to travel by plane, the easiest way that several of my clients have found is to buy a seat for your pet. Granted, this is quite expensive. So, if you want to avoid this expense, make your reservations very early and secure "pet permission" when you do. Insist that you will only accept a booking that includes pet permission and that you want it *in writing* because you refuse to allow your pet to travel with the baggage.

Pet permission on the airlines is usually available for one pet per compartment per flight. Once you get pet permission, the airline may then insist that you buy a special carrier that fits underneath the seat. I cannot caution you strongly enough—to get that carrier well in advance.

My friend and co-author Norma had to fly with her cat Clarence when she was returning to New York after a season of winter stock at a theatre in Florida. She tried gently putting Clarence into the case just to see if he would fit because it looked so small. She admits that she was having serious doubts and that her mind was not tranquil about it. Clarence became totally hysterical, yowling and ripping at the case, so she let him out at once. Norma then considered sending him in the plane's luggage compartment, but Clarence had been ailing and just the thought of his riding there upset her. Various friends gave conflicting advice, and because Norma had had no direct experience before, she resolved in desperation to ask Clarence one more time. So, the next day, she sat down with him and opened the case on the bed. Very slowly, very clearly, and in great detail, she explained to Clarence the pros and cons of the two alternatives. Then she told him how she felt and how much nicer it would be for her to have him close to her on the trip.

Then she looked into Clarence's eyes and told him very clearly that she wanted to try it just one more time. She picked him up, laid him on his side inside the carrier, and firmly closed the lid. This time Clarence didn't say a word but just lay there waiting for Norma to make the next move, whatever that might be. She opened the case, and Clarence sat up, stretched, and stepped out in a dignified manner. He succeeded in reassuring Norma that the carry case would be okay.

Before the day of the flight friends who saw the case, squat and tiny as it was, and saw Clarence, large and sprawling as he was, gave the opinion that shutting a monster like Clarence in "that little thing" was tantamount to cruelty. Norma had fresh misgivings, vacillating in her mind between the tiny airline carry case and the great unknown luggage compartment. But in the end she stuck by Clarence's decision, as she had promised him she would.

When travel day arrived, sure enough—Clarence kept his side of the bargain. As Norma chatted about the positive aspects of the trip, Clarence curled himself down in that cheap little plastic monstrosity and said not a word when the lid was closed. Norma continued to talk about how nice it would be to be home, mentioning Clarence's favorite sunny windowsill where he had his own special view of New York's pigeons. On the way to the airport, Norma was sharing a cab with her friend Jennie, and guilt feelings kept creeping into her mind about Clarence's cramped accommodations. Jennie, a cat owner herself, said she thought Clarence looked quite smug and content. "You know how cats like to crawl into tight little places," she said. "It makes them feel safe." Of course, Jennie was perfectly right, and a great load of guilt and apprehension lifted from Norma's mind. Norma and Clarence were free to enjoy the fun parts of the trip. About 98 percent of the time, with about 98 percent of the cats, if you feel happy and secure and satisfied about the way your pets are traveling, they will too.

Try traveling without giving your cat tranquilizers before you resort to them. Tranquilizers are debilitating to the cat's system—they are just not very good for cats. They lower resistance to disease. If you decide you must use one, get them from a veterinarian who knows your cats and allow enough time to try out the dosage at least once before the actual travel day arrives. Give it to him on an empty stomach, just as you would when you travel. Food in the stomach changes your cat's body chemistry and alters the way the dosage works. Every cat is different, and if the dosage is not just right a cat may have a hyperreaction: The tranquilizer, instead of calming, can render the cat quite hysterical. So you must work out the dose in advance.

Visiting a New Place

When you arrive, remember how territorially conscious cats are and how uneasy they are with new people and places. You can cushion an otherwise stressful situation by limiting the number of new things they must deal with. First of all, confine the cats to a small space such as the bedroom and bathroom. Even if you're visiting your great grandmother in her three-story farmhouse, don't let them explore until they have spent at least one night in the restricted territory and have become familiar with it. Before you open their cases, set up the old, familiar litter box and their own food and water dish so they will see that their personal necessities are there for them. Try to spend at least a half hour in that territory with them, and leave some of your personal belongings with your smell on them lying about before you leave them. In this way, you reassure them that you're coming back. Hopefully you will have brought their favorite toys, and before you leave you can reassure them even further if you run through their favorite games a couple of times, just as you always do at home.

So, after you have given them their own familiar things and strewn a few of your own familiar possessions about the room, and played their old, familiar games, you can leave with a light heart, knowing that they will probably spend a fascinating hour exploring the new territory and then fall asleep.

The next day, if you decide to let them increase their territory, make sure that you explore it first for dangers such as unscreened windows and poisonous plants or chemicals. Then you may wish to increase the territory gradually, a few rooms at a time. Be sure that everyone who enters and leaves the house knows that your cats are running around loose and that people must be careful about closet doors, drawers, and certainly the door to the outside. You and your host may well decide on certain areas to which they will not be admitted, such as a damp cellar, a dusty attic, or certainly not an unscreened balcony.

If you stay in a hotel, you must put a sign on the door cautioning all who enter not to let the cats out. It's always good to speak to your maid personally, making sure that she understands the situation clearly and that she's not afraid of cats. In some instances, it's wiser to arrange to pick up your own clean linens at the desk rather than chance a maid or bellman unthinkingly opening a window or door.

If you're moving into a new home, the thing to do to keep stress to a minimum is to surround the cats with familiarity and keep them away from the area of upheaval as much as possible. In other words, on the last couple of days before the move, when packing and bustle reaches its height and when you are the busiest, confine them to your bedroom and have the packing boxes in the living room and the kitchen. Leave a few pieces of clothing that you have worn lying around in there so that they have the comfort of your scent even while you're busy elsewhere. If the premoving bustle outside the bedroom becomes noisy, turn on the radio or television in the bedroom and let it play softly. Put in a short appearance every hour or so, letting them feel that you are calm and satisfied and pleased that they are there in the bedroom.

On the actual moving day, the best plan is to confine the cats to some room that the movers will not enter. This may be a bathroom. Give them their litter and water, their favorite toys, a piece of your clothing, and perhaps a cardboard box or brown paper bag to hide in or play in as a special treat. Put a sign on the bathroom door, and have it locked, if possible, or stretch a piece of masking tape across the knob to remind everyone of your instructions. Here again, keep your attitude casual. Emphasize to them the fun they'll have playing in the paper bag. Don't think about the fact that they're closed off in the bathroom. Tell them how lucky they are to be able to rest quietly here while you deal with those noisy movers.

The cats should arrive at the new home only after you have at least one room pretty well settled where you can confine them. They'll see the old, familiar furniture and feel reassured. Just as when you are visiting someone else's house, let them get used to one or two rooms first and then add to their territory a couple of rooms each day. Don't forget to check your new home carefully before you let the cats explore it. Be sure that it is just as safe and cat-proof as their old home was.

While You're Away

Sara and Dan were going to be away for two weeks. They were worried about what to do with their beloved Midnight while they were gone—hire a daily sitter; take him to stay with Norma, who already had a cat; ask Aunt Dot, who doesn't have a cat, to keep him; or board him with a veterinarian or at a pet motel? I heard nothing about it until two days before they were scheduled to leave.

I said, right off, that boarding was not a good idea. Even if they board Midnight at a facility that lets the cats out for a walk twice a day up and down the halls, it's still a small cage. And Midnight would still be exposed to viruses and germs. If the boarding facility is also a pet hospital, there would also be the additional stress of being around cats who are in trouble, in pain, and frightened.

Aunt Dot might be okay because she has no other animals, especially if she already knows and loves Midnight. You'd have to be certain, though, that her windows were screened and that she wouldn't let him out. And you'd have to be sure to supply her with the correct food and the Vita-Mineral Mix. Then you wouldn't have to give a lecture on feline nutrition but only a five-minute talk on the evils of leaving food available between meals.

The absence of the two owners is the first stress factor. And being placed in a new environment is Stress Number Two. Therefore, Sara and Dan should give Midnight additional vitamins—double the Vita-Mineral Mix and add $\frac{1}{16}$ teaspoon ascorbic acid crystals (250 units of vitamin C) twice daily for two days before leaving. If Aunt Dot is amenable, she can also mix $\frac{1}{16}$ teaspoon ascorbic acid crystals into the food twice a day. It would be helpful for him to have the vitamin C for the first five days of his stay. There are new germs at Aunt Dot's that he didn't have in his own environment—a different ratio of germs and viruses for him to deal with. And the stress will lower his resistance; the Vita-Mineral Mix and vitamin C will help bolster it a little.

Norma's cat, Clarence, is an old sweetie pie. I personally would love to spend two weeks with Clarence. But Midnight will not be aware that Clarence is an old sweetie pie. To him, Clarence will simply constitute a great big Stress Number Three—a strange cat. Midnight will feel he is invading "strange cat's" territory. Moreover, instead of the strange new germs he would encounter in a no-cat household, he will encounter a different balance of cat germs at Clarence's house.

Of course, if Midnight is a physically strong robust cat, the pros could outweigh the cons as far as leaving him with Norma and Clarence. Norma is a cat care expert, and Midnight would have the comfort of her companionship as opposed to being left alone. Then, too, Midnight and Clarence might just form such a warm and wonderful friendship that his stay might very well be like sending a child to summer camp. There are always a lot of unknown variables to deal with when working with living creatures.

The safest and most usual way to deal with the situation is hiring a sitter. The only sitters I trust are my own, but it can become expensive if you have to hire a professional cat sitter for an extended length of time. By hiring a sitter, Stress Number Three (strange new territory) is not encountered, but Stress Number Four is—and that's the growing loneliness. I feel very sorry for single cats. Every time a cat is left alone, after a certain amount of time, he begins to expect you. If you usually come home at 5 P.M., then at 5:30 your cat begins to worry. By 6, your cat will assume that you have been killed and eaten by predators and will begin to mourn. It is quite a strain for a pussycat to be left alone for two weeks with a sitter appearing only one hour a day. (See Communicating "Good-bye"—and "I'll Be Back," page 24.)

If only Midnight had a friend, he would never again have to face the horror of being alone. Cats are group animals. They live in prides. When they are together, the worst of terrors are lessened. "Our humans may have met with an accident but together we'll work it out—we'll muddle through somehow, together"; "At least we'll be warm, together"; "Together we can play." Hopefully, by the second day they will begin to expect the sitter, who cleans the litter, supplies the food, and spends the remainder of the hour cuddling, grooming, and/or playing.

So if Midnight is to be left alone in the apartment, extra care must be taken to give him reassurance and to distract and entertain him. The first two days, the sitter should come twice a day instead of once. This will hasten Midnight's acceptance of the sitter and quickly build the new pattern of sitter, food, and fun. Dan and Sara should arrange for the sitter to come twice on two or three other days if he or she deems it advisable. They should be sure to leave the carry case out, leave the food and can opener in plain sight, and leave a note listing:

- The telephone number where they are staying
- The telephone number of a close friend or relative in the immediate neighborhood who also has a key
- The veterinarian's phone number

111

- Instructions for feeding
- Any instructions for medication
- Where to find toys, grooming tools, and catnip

Midnight must be distracted from his loneliness. A toy left lying around all the time is no longer exciting. Catnip, if given every day, becomes a bore. So Sara and Dan should not give catnip for two weeks before they leave. And they should gather up all the toys the day before they go, leaving only one toy on the floor.

Dan and Sara should instruct the sitter to rotate the toys, giving Midnight a different one each day so that each toy is taken away from him before it becomes boring. They should leave one large brown paper bag for each week they will be gone. Then one day a week, instead of the toy, the brown paper bag can be opened and thrown on the floor for Midnight to play with. The next day can be catnip day, putting the catnip inside of or on top of the brown paper bag—excitement upon excitement. The following day the sitter can take it away and rotate a different toy.

To give Midnight the feeling that the apartment is not deserted, the sitter should leave a different light on each night and alternate days with the radio on and the radio off (this also discourages burglars). A small pile of dirty laundry can be left in the corner of the bedroom, and Midnight should be able to get into the bedroom closet and sit on the shoes.

I have several thoughtful clients who leave special food treats for their cats, to assuage their own guilt about leaving for vacation or business trips. Constance leaves barbecued chicken. Caroline leaves sliced turkey; Mrs. Aparicio, miniature shrimp. If I were leaving any of my cats all alone, I'd leave a couple of broiled chicken thighs and, for Priscilla, some baby food oatmeal and half-and-half.

All these things can be fed along with the other food, not exclusively. You don't want to throw the nutrition out of balance along with all the other stress factors.

I have several clients who like to call once a week to assure themselves that all is going well. Usually there is some little thing you want to check on. Is he having a stool every day? If not, the ground psyllium husks are in the cabinet. Is he eating? If not, there's baby food in the small cabinet over the refrigerator.

Remember, there are much worse things that can happen to a

cat than your going away for two weeks. Granted, it's hard, but at least he has shelter and food.

But what if you could cut the stress factor by 50 percent? What if you could really relax, secure in the knowledge that your Midnight is having a ball? It's easy. Get him a friend. Someone to train in his own pawprints. Someone to get into trouble with when your back is turned. Even if you work at home and you're home twenty-four hours a day, and you adore your cat, and your cat adores you, think of it this way: What if you were owned by two of the most wonderful elephants in the world? You love them dearly, and they dote on your every move. They give you the very best food, they give you everything that you want plus a few extra things you never thought of to surprise and delight you. In short, they give you everything your heart could possibly desire except . . . another human. . . . Need I say more. . . .

6

"Neuter and Spay, It's the Kindest Way"

"Neuter and spay, it's the kindest way" is the slogan of one of our finest humane animal organizations—Pet Pride. It is the kindest and the easiest path to take for both the cat and the owners as well as for society at large. I've heard many myths about the disadvantages of neutering and spaying. People think their cats will become fat or lethargic, or will miss having a sexual life, or the female will miss mothering kittens. None of these things are true. Cats become obese and/or lethargic because of faulty feeding whether they are neutered or not. Cats live in the present—in the absolute "now"—and they become sexually stimulated and crave a mate only if their glands tell them to. Sexual thoughts or the need to mother never occur to a neutered cat. However, there *are* drawbacks for both the male and the female if they are *not* neutered.

Undesirable Behavior of the Unneutered Male Cat

Unaltered males are not kept as pets. Catteries who maintain an unaltered tom to sire kittens keep him confined to a space where it will be easy to clean up the urine he will spray about. The cattery will have anywhere from six to twenty females for him to service plus a book of outside females who come to him regularly for stud service. A male who is not used for stud regularly becomes very tense, nervous, and out of sorts, because he is uncomfortable.

115

Unaltered males spray. Their urine smells very strong and quite different from the urine of a neutered male. A full tom will spray in various places all around his territory to mark it as his own. This is as natural as sneezing and not something he can be trained away from. Once you've smelled the urine or spray of an unaltered tom, it's not something you'll easily forget. I can tell the minute I walk into a home if somebody is keeping an unaltered tom. No litter can absorb that smell.

If an owner lets the tom wander about the neighborhood, wander is just what he does, ranging far and wide searching for a female in heat. And when he finds one there are bound to be other toms on the spot waiting to contest his right to mate with her. There are always fights before mating. And these fights are brutal and deadly serious. A fight to the death is common. The unaltered tom, allowed to roam free, leads a short and violent life. And if there are no females in season available for a couple of weeks, his aggression will be easily triggered at home. If he becomes unaccountably rough in play, the lack of a female is usually the reason.

Undesirable Behavior of the Unspayed Female Cat

A female in heat does not spray—she calls. You can tell if a female is in season even if she doesn't call very much by stroking down her back. She will push her hindquarters up into the air with her tail looped over to the side in the invitation to mate position. Unspayed female cats generally become high-strung, nervous, and jumpy. They are usually thin and debilitated. Going through heat after heat drains their body. They easily fall victim to any disease germ that happens to be around—their resistance is very low.

The female's ovaries manufacture eggs with each heat. Unlike humans, these eggs are not released and passed out of the body, but remain in the ovary unless the cat is fertilized. If the cat goes through heat after heat and is not fertilized, these unused eggs are encysted. Cystic ovaries are a sign of a female who has gone through several heats before she's spayed. If a cat comes into heat more than twice a year, you can be pretty sure she has cystic ovaries. Unspayed female cats almost always develop cancerous tumors. Oddly enough, these tumors usually form on the mammary glands rather than on the cystic ovaries and the uterus.

I've met a few owners who've bought male and female cats, planning to breed them. Besides all the potential problems that can be encountered in the course of the mating and birth process, having kittens is a lot of work and costs money too. The mother needs special food and extra vitamins at frequent intervals. And the kittens need constant supervision and feedings six times a day from four weeks on. Both the mother and the kittens can fall prey to a number of diseases along the way. I have warned several owners who had this idea in mind that a female can have her neck broken during mating—it is a rough and violent ritual. Also, if the mother is at all small, you could easily lose her during the birth of the kittens. Veterinarians are finding that the need for cesarean-section births is becoming more and more frequent. This is especially true with Persians and American shorthairs, who are bred with small hips and large heads. But even a seemingly robust domestic shorthaired cat can have a problem giving birth. I clearly remember my shock on seeing not one but three females in a single clinic one day, all cesarean cases. They would have died if the owners hadn't acted quickly and brought them in. And they were all supposedly healthy domestic shorthairs.

Another potential problem after the birth is that during the nursing weeks the mother may experience calcium-deficiency convulsions. She needs lots of calcium-rich foods. In addition, her body needs vitamin D to assimilate the calcium and plenty of fats and high-quality protein.

The Nightmare of Unwanted Kittens

The wandering tom is capable of siring hundreds of kittens every year. The horror of the situation in New York City alone is something that I would rather not bring into my conscious mind. But here again, like the true facts about declawing, I think this is something that responsible people must be made aware of before they can make an intelligent decision concerning neutering, spaying, and allowing cats to have kittens.

Every single day in New York City, hundreds of cats are destroyed. The overpopulation makes cats into trash—refuse. Cats for laboratory use are in such plentiful supply that the going rate is $5 a head. There are too many kittens. Sometimes I hear, "Oh, I have homes already for my cat's kittens, even if she has ten kittens there are people just waiting to take them." I explain to these people that this means there are ten homes that could have saved the lives of ten other kittens who are already alive and otherwise will probably die horribly. Or I hear, "I just want her to have one litter." Well, let's suppose one litter results in five kittens. And let's suppose that each kitten lives an average of even fifteen years. Because you have made the decision to allow your cat to have these little mites, it behooves you to realize that each little mite represents not only six weeks of cuteness romping around your kitchen but fifteen or twenty years of life for which you are responsible.

You may blithely state that you already have five homes—five people panting to sweep a kitten up in their arms and cherish it forever. I assure you that you cannot take for granted that "forever" really *means* forever or that the new owners won't feed a poor-quality diet or leave a window open or allow the cats to run outside unsupervised. Can you be sure the cats will have a yearly exam? Will their teeth be kept clean for fifteen years? And suppose, just suppose, that even one of those five kittens is not neutered and brings forth five more kittens. You must share that responsibility too, you know. If not for your original litter, the second litter would never have been born. And how would you feel if one day you found out that one of those little kittens of yours had been cruelly mutilated by a declawing operation?

Neuter and spay, it's the kindest way. Suggest to your friends who want kittens that they save a cat from possible death at one of the shelters.

The Proper Time to Get Your Cat Neutered or Spayed

The very best time to have the cat neutered is, for a female, after she goes through her first heat; for a male, when the urine changes odor and becomes very pungent. These are the signs in the male and female that the sexual center has transferred from the organs to the base of the brain. You can then remove the organs and yet not disturb the basic sexuality of the cat. Insist that your cat pass through these physical changes before the operation is done. A little care and patience now will pay off in a higher standard of health for the next fifteen or twenty years. The age range for sexual maturity can vary. I've known females to go into heat as early as five months, and I've met Persians who have shown no sign of maturity until a year and a half. The age is somewhere within that range for males also.

The operation for females is simple surgery. Because it's one of the most frequently done operations, almost any veterinarian is competent to perform it. Since anesthetic is used, you'll want to bolster your feline friend's resistance with the appropriate supplements (see page 269).

The female stays overnight in the hospital, and when you pick her up the next day, you will be told to keep her quiet for a day or two. However, I remember when I was working for Dr. Rowan we frequently had owners telephoning, all upset because their cat didn't *want* to be quiet—she didn't realize that she'd just had an operation. She felt perfectly fine and was leaping off the top of the bookcase and bounding from sofas to chairs as usual. When this operation is done by any competent veterinarian, it's a piece of cake.

Neutering a male is even simpler. They usually don't even stay overnight. When Big Purr was neutered, I took him in in the morning and picked him up that evening. He didn't look any different at all, because most vets remove the testes but leave the scrotum. He certainly didn't act any different, either. Except, thank heavens, he was no longer interested in spraying the drapes. I remember at one point I scooped him up in my arms for some reason and suddenly realized that I had lifted him with my hand under his testicles. All his weight was sitting on that recent surgery. But Purr did not have the slightest reaction; he hadn't thought a thing about it. I was all upset over nothing.

Purr still enjoys sexual play. Once I was cat sitting for a kitten who came into season while her owner was gone. She had a torrid affair with Purr day and night for a week. Purr wasn't too sure at first what he was supposed to do but after a day of experimentation, trial and error, the two of them worked it out very nicely. By the time her owner returned she was out of heat and her owner took her in to her veterinarian to be spayed. My friend Phyllis's cats Barnaby and Tulip were neutered in their youth but are a completely devoted couple and enjoy sexual play on a regular basis.

Neutered cats do not suffer the terrific stress of unneutered cats. Their resistance to disease is higher; they're more mellow and happier because life is easier. They indulge in sex play because they want to, not because they are driven to it by their glands. According to statistics, neutered cats live longer, healthier lives than unneutered cats.

7

Grooming

Grooming not only is a necessity for our loving feline friends who live indoors, but also establishes a wonderful and lasting bond between you and your cat. In addition to serving an important function, it is your way of expressing affection—and the purrs that greet your ears will confirm your cat's delight.

Among cats mutual grooming is a form of communication—sometimes an expression of love and companionship. Grooming is a very natural thing to the cat and something they readily understand if properly approached and properly done.

Grooming is also a necessary part of cat care. Dry, artificial heat in winter causes cats to shed excessively. Cats also shed naturally in the spring and, to a lesser degree, again in the autumn.

Cats also shed during the slightest stress situation. If you're away for a while, if you take cats to the vet, if you take them visiting, if workers come to the house, if the cats fall ill—all these are stress situations that will produce excess shedding. If the cats are not groomed regularly, with a bit of special attention during these stress times, cats will attempt to groom themselves, with the result that they will swallow a great deal of hair. Living in the wild, they would not have had to deal with many of those stress situations or with the unnatural heat. The spring and autumn sheds would be the only bad times.

Swallowing a lot of excess hair can affect cats in two ways—either they will form hair balls, which they will then vomit (like miniature wet hot dogs on the carpet), or they will try to pass the hair through the intestines. Because this latter method of disposal is not the most efficient, these hair masses are frequently not passed out of the cats' bodies but lodge in curves and bends of the intestinal tract, causing blockage. Cats with this problem then stop eating— or sometimes vomit an innocuous foamy substance instead of the hair they are trying to get rid of because the hair has passed beyond the stomach into the intestines and can no longer be vomited up. A veterinarian sometimes gives feline laxative in a tube, in the hope of dislodging these lower-intestinal hair masses. If that doesn't work, the doctor can try an enema and, in extreme cases, surgery. What a pity this is, when just sixty seconds of grooming a day will prevent the necessity for even the laxative.

High-Quality Diet = High-Quality Coat

If you remember why we remove food between meals (see Chapter 2, "Diet"), you'll recall that leaving it available slows down the metabolism so that wastes build up and back up. The body will then try to deal with the situation by pushing some of these waste products out through the pores of the skin, resulting in oiliness and dandruff. On a low-quality diet, the cat will have more waste products to deal with. Also, the hair vitamins, mostly found in the vitamin B family, have either been destroyed in the heat processing of the cat food or are simply missing because they tend to be the more expensive ones. These quality and texture vitamins are the very ones that you are now supplying by adding Vita-Mineral Mix (see page 55).

Good-quality hair allows shed hair to slip out of the coat easily. Dead hair is retained in the coat for two reasons: (1) excessive oiliness and (2) a poor-quality coat. Oiliness is caused by a diet too high in organ meats or other rich food or simply by not removing all food between meals. The lecithin in the Vita-Mineral Mix emulsifies the oil and fat and turns it into a water-soluble substance that the blood can carry off and dispose of in the urine. Oiliness turns your cats into little walking dust mops, attracting and holding not only their own hair but any dust and debris from the floor. Unwholesome hair texture works in exactly the same way. Each hair has many microscopic hairs growing out from it. On good-quality hair, these microscopic secondary hairs all grow down, pointing toward the tip of the hair and allowing dust, oil, water, and shed hair to slip right off. On poor-quality hair, they protrude out and up and every which way so they hold the dust and shed hair in the coat. You can imagine how a cat with a good-quality coat would be much easier to groom, because dust would not cling and old shed hair would come right out and not stay behind to build up into a mat in the cat's coat. The yeast and kelp or trace mineral powder in the Vita-Mineral Mix are specifically for the improvement of hair quality.

The first two or three years that I was grooming, I made it a point once a year to go to a cat show. I didn't look just at the cats. Because I was eager to learn anything I could from any source available, I took note of what kind of carry cases were used, what grooming tools, and what was in the bottles and boxes lined up on the shelf near each cat's cage. The first thing I noticed was that about 90 percent of the owners showing cats were using exactly the same bottles and boxes as all the rest. And what was in them? They were marked "Hair thickener," "Baldness preventative," "Texturizing lotion," and "Whitening powder" (or "Darkening powder"). Next to these preparations, I always saw a supply of dry or semimoist cat food.

There must have been hundreds of owners there, and it amazes me to this day that evidently none of them ever made a connection between what they were feeding the cats and the need for all of those artificial cosmetics to cover up the faults and the less-than-perfect coats that the low-quality food was producing. I have never used any sort of cosmetic powder or spray on a cat to change the existing texture of the natural coat. Such things coat the hair and always make the coat more prone to pick up dirt, and therefore the cat needs bathing all the more frequently. Besides, all of these preparations contain chemicals, perfumes, and the like. I will not be a party to putting such preparations on the cat when I know the cat is going to lick them off and ingest them. Virgin hair stays clean the longest. Even if the texture and thickness has not yet reached the optimum, you can't improve on nature. Hair in its natural, virgin state is uncoated, unconditioned, uncolored, and untreated. It provides the best insulation against both heat and cold. And nothing is easier for an owner to groom than virgin hair.

Improve the texture, thickness, and quality of the hair by feeding the diet discussed in Chapter 2, not by spraying or smearing something over the surface.

Finding a Groomer

New clients frequently tell me how they searched for months trying to find someone reputable and gentle to groom their cat. I must say I had the same problem, searching in vain for someone whom I could recommend to take my overload during the busy season. Even in a major metropolis like New York, I have not been able to find anyone whom I would trust to groom a cat except myself and the people I train. I've looked everywhere—in pet shops, dog-grooming salons (even the most expensive), kennels, and several veterinarians' offices. What I found was that in all of those categories people with the highest standards were unwilling to groom cats because they did not feel at home doing it. They were comfortable with dogs but not with cats. People with lower standards would give it a try but were both slipshod and rough. Veterinarians would rather spend their time curing disease than grooming, and the good ones are generally already overbooked with more serious problems.

Most veterinarians use anesthetic and/or tranquilizers before grooming. Anesthetics and tranquilizers constitute a serious stress. I found without exception that reputable veterinarians try to avoid anesthetizing and shaving a cat whenever they can. Several veterinarians I know refer all grooming problems to me.

If the local dog groomer agrees to groom your cat, I strongly advise that you arrange to be present the entire time for at least the first few visits. It is illegal for anyone but a veterinarian to dispense tranquilizers to an animal, yet I know of several groomers who slip them to cats. I have also heard all too frequently of how cats are "subdued" by dog groomers—by trusses, straps, and harnesses, or "It took three of us to hold her down." Cats can die of shock or heart attack under such brutal handling. You must be sure that anyone who grooms your cat is working *with* the cat, not against him.

If there's a problem finding someone to groom a badly matted cat or a cat with fleas or what-have-you here in the middle of New York City, I can well imagine the plight of someone living in a small town or rural area where even a dog groomer is not to be found and the only veterinarians available are those specializing in dairy herds. I decided to write this chapter in as much detail as possible for those owners who have no choice but to try their best by themselves. It is much easier if you have someone to assist you. Your assistant can distract the cat with pleasurable sensations such as throat stroking, back scratching, and murmured praise. I use the owner for this but you can get your cat's second most favorite person after yourself to help you.

I will try to give you all the help I can. Just remember that patience is the watchword. I was the slowest groomer on God's green earth when I started, but I was also the most careful.

Please be aware that just because I am telling you *how* to handle these problems does not mean that I am advising you to do so. If there's no one else, then you can give it a try. But there are many instances where I would strongly advise having the veterinarian anesthetize the cat and shave the mats out just one time. Then you can take over and maintain the coat so that it never gets matted again. Using scissors to cut through mats is dangerous business. The cat's skin texture is like the finest silk. The fact that it is loose, coupled with the bone structure and intricate musculature of the body, makes it very difficult for an untutored person to clip mats safely. And, yes, they must be clipped. Using a comb on a mat is hopeless. It doesn't do any good at all and it does do a lot of harm because you'll hurt the cat and teach him to hate being groomed.

If you elect to have the veterinarian shave the mats out, the perfect time would be when the teeth are cleaned. In fact, any time the cat has to be anesthetized for any reason be sure to check for tartar on the teeth and matting in the furs so these two things can get a free ride, as it were, and be taken care of then. Ear flushing is also a good thing to slip in at that time if the cat has a lot of wax in the ears.

Daily Grooming

Once the cat is in good shape, you can do a complete daily grooming in sixty seconds. And daily is what it should be if you own a longhaired cat and if you're going to keep a couple of jumps ahead of the mats so that never again will your cat have to be anesthetized and shaved.

Grooming should be a pleasure for all concerned. Because you know how much cats like ritual and sameness, make grooming into a ritual. Use the same place, the same tools, and groom the cat's body parts in the same order. If possible, do the grooming at the same hour of the day. Invite the cat to the grooming area with the same signal, and always follow grooming with the same treat.

First we'll cover the grooming area. You know how sensitive your cats are to your thoughts and emotions. They sympathize when you're sick or upset. They sense your calmness when they are upset, and thus they can be calmed. Likewise, they will sense your pleasure in grooming them. So you must choose a grooming area that is pleasing to you.

I'm rather tall, so when I go into someone's home to groom their cat I always work on the kitchen counter. Also, kitchens are usually well lit, and that's important for the grooming area. Some of my shorter clients prefer to use something like a card table, which is a lot lower than the kitchen counter.

I do not spread a towel or anything else under the cat, because the hair sticks to it and it gets all messed up and it wrinkles the minute the cat moves around, creating an uncomfortable, lumpy surface for the cat to stand on—and we want the cat to be comfortable. The surface should be clean—no sense in getting jelly on the cat's tail. After washing the surface with a sponge, be sure to dry it thoroughly with a paper towel. Standing on a damp, cold surface is not your cat's idea of comfort.

Lay out all the grooming tools. (Grooming tools will be covered later in this chapter.) When everything is set up to your satisfaction, invite your cat to the grooming.

Now, in the beginning you will be lifting the cat onto the grooming area. As time goes on and the ritual is repeated, a surprisingly large number of cats will jump the gun and leap spontaneously onto the table themselves. I've had this experience with clients that I see regularly once a month. Especially in multiple-cat households, I frequently have to deal with a "me first" problem.

It's even more important, though, that you be the one to put the cat back on the floor when you're finished. Never, never let the cat jump down. You must establish as an integral part of this ritual that you are the one who says when it is over. Telling him, "Okay, you're done" and letting him jump down is simply not clear enough. You must physically pick him up and place him on the floor yourself, with words of praise and admiration.

If you are just beginning to condition the cat to the joy and comfort of being groomed, you may find it best to spend the first four or five sessions going no further than the first step or two in the grooming procedure. If all you do is establish in his mind that being up on that table brings pleasure, you've already done a great deal. In the beginning, keep the sessions short. One minute is enough. Remember, sixty seconds a day accomplishes much more than a half-hour on Saturday. If at all possible, be sure that you put the cat down on the floor *before* he wants to go down. Try to leave him wanting more. If you must cut out a difficult mat or clean soil off the bloomers or perform some other task that is not altogether pleasurable, always finish the grooming with some type of combing that he does like, such as going back and recombing the head and neck or the cheeks and throat. Your cat will teach you about his special, favorite places. Groomings always begin and end with your cat's special favorite places.

As soon as I get to know a cat—sometimes after five minutes, sometimes after five months—I use my face and mouth a lot while grooming. Because cats groom with their mouths, they seem to understand and enjoy having me kiss them on top of their heads and murmur; take their ears between my lips and, as it were, "hug them with my lips"; and breathe warm air against the skin at the back of the neck or the shoulders. With a nervous cat, putting your face close to the cat's head or body gives him confidence, because subconsciously he knows that your face and eyes are vulnerable and that you would not expose them so if there were any reason to get upset. Because you do expose your face and eyes so casually, the cat thinks that everything must be all right.

A word of caution: Be careful not to puff air into the ears, eyes, nose, or onto the bare anal area. Cats won't like that a bit. And, instead of the calming effect you're trying for, they'll struggle to get away from that unpleasant sensation. Also, do not accompany your kisses with a loud kissing sound, especially not near the cat's ear. This sound is extremely piercing, even for a human. And for a cat, a kissing sound at the ear opening is quite painful.

You can use classical music while you groom for its calming influence. A record, tape, or CD is best, because then you have control of what is being played. It should be played rather softly and be either soothing or happy. The main requirement is that you personally enjoy it. Steer clear of jazz, rock, or pop music. The latest scientific experiments indicate that plants and animals respond best to classical or religious music, with Bach and Ravi Shankar having the most positive effect.

When you use a shaver, the cat must be anesthetized because a shaver can be painful. There are several grooming tools for sale to the professional groomer that make one think of a medieval torture chamber. One is called "the mat splitter." Having a mat splitter sounded like such a terrific idea that I ordered one. When the thing came, I was absolutely aghast at its design. It was something like a rake with curved teeth sharpened like little razors. I assume one is expected to drag it through the mats, incorporating some sort of sawing motion in the process. I could see at once that it was totally impractical and so badly designed as to be dangerous. I tried very gently running it through the silky fur of a freshly groomed cat. Even those lovely unmatted hairs were caught and pulled on the curved blades. I didn't even finish the stroke but threw the sadistic tool into the wastebasket. Over the years, I've run into many strange grooming tools that owners pull out of drawers to show me what they have been using to groom their cats. Any time an owner tells me his or her cat "hates being groomed," I always ask to see the grooming tool. There's one sure way to make it clear to owners that a tool hurts: I hand them the tool and ask them to run it through their own hair.

The Grooming Tools

You will have to be the judge of what tool a cat's coat needs. Here is a list of the tools I carry around with me and their purpose (Figure 1):

- Nail clipper (the best kind are people toenail clippers), to clip the claws
- Cotton swabs, for cleaning ears
- Vitamin E capsules (100-unit) or wheat-germ oil capsules, for oiling cotton swabs
- Resco professional combs, fine, medium, and coarse
- Spratt superfine comb, for "crew-cut" on Persians or all over for some shorthaired cats
- Blunt-nosed surgical scissors (available from surgical supply house), for cutting through mats
- Slicker brush (size small), *for shorthaired cats only*
- Mini slicker brush for between the ears and on cheeks, chin, and throat

Most combs available in pet shops look like a human comb made out of metal, with a thicker tooth at each end. They don't work well because those end teeth catch and pull the cat's fur. They are also usually poor-quality metal, which again causes the comb to catch in the fur. The Resco professional combs are good-quality metal and are medium priced. You can try calling pet shops to see if they stock them, or perhaps they can order them for you. I order them through the mail.

The preceding list is almost a full grooming kit for a professional cat groomer. For everyday grooming on a shorthaired cat who is in good condition, all you need are the nail clippers, cotton swabs, vitamin E capsules, and slicker brush. An outlay of about $20 will probably cover the lot. If you have a Persian cat in perfect condition, all you will need is the nail clippers, cotton swabs, vitamin E capsules, and the Resco coarse comb. If you really want to be thorough, add the Resco medium comb to the list. A finicky owner will enjoy the difference it makes.

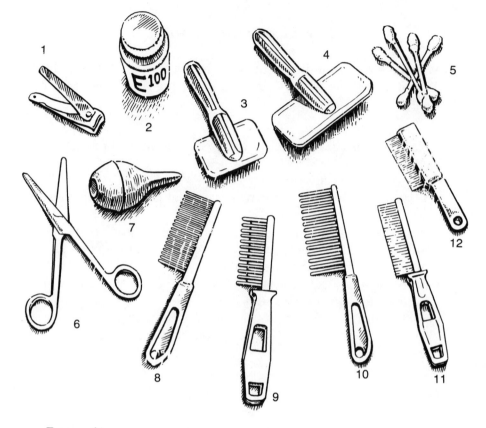

FIGURE 1
Grooming Tools

1. Clippers
2. Vitamin E capsules (100 units)
3. Slicker brush (mini)
4. Slicker brush (small)
5. Cotton swabs
6. 8″ round nose scissors
7. Rubber ear syringe
8. Resco comb (medium)
9. British shorthair shedding comb
10. Resco comb (coarse)
11. British comb (fine)
12. British superfine flea comb

The Grooming Procedure

Just as you won't have to use every tool every day, there will be several techniques that I describe here, such as mat removal, that I hope you will never need to be concerned about. If your cat never has mats or doesn't get ear wax, simply skip those steps in the grooming procedure. Just as I did, you'll probably start slow for the first few weeks and then later find that you and your cat are just gliding through the steps. You and your cats together will decide which techniques you want to spend extra time on because either they adore it or you judge that their particular coats need it.

Step 1: Finger Grooming

No matter what you're going to do in the grooming, always begin every grooming with your hands. After you place the cat on the grooming table, facing away from you, stroke his head, neck, throat, chest, back, outer thighs, stomach, inner thighs, and bloomers. The reason for this "finger grooming" is that you are communicating to the cat what it is you are about to do and also what a pleasant, exciting feeling it is going to be. As you stroke, think in your mind, "I'm going to make you feel good here, and I'm going to make your furs nice there. I'm going to clean out that nasty loose hair." Think of massaging the cat's muscles with your fingertips, stimulating circulation ever so lightly. (Figure 2)

The second purpose for the "finger grooming" is to familiarize yourself with the condition of your cat's body and coat for today. Any little mats? How's the texture? Any soil on the bloomers? Has anything been dribbled onto that lovely ruff? You don't want the comb to catch in something and pull and hurt. Long before you finish your "finger grooming," you should be rewarded with a resonant purr.

Then, when you introduce the grooming tool, it will simply be an extension of what you've already done. The grooming tool will help you express the love more efficiently. Properly used, it should make your cat feel even better than your fingers did. His purr may increase in volume or be augmented by kneading with front paws.

FIGURE 2

Ruff, skirts, and bloomers

Step 2: Light Combing

If your cat is shorthaired, step 2 applies *only* if there is a buildup of loose hair in the coat as found during the shedding seasons. Usually for a shorthaired cat you can skip this step and simply use the slicker brush, described later.

If you're working with a longhaired cat and at some point on the body you encounter resistance indicating tangles or mats, go no further on that particular body area. Mats and tangles are dealt with later in step 4, after clipping the nails.

If cats are matted, they know it, and they also know just where the mats are. They will be afraid to have you comb through the mats because they know that such combing hurts. So don't even try to comb a resistant area; instead, follow the directions given in step 4 of the grooming procedure. On most days of the year, the whole combing procedure will be a "light combing" because you will not encounter resistance at any point—no mats and no tangles.

The first time that you decide to groom your cat seriously, by far the best plan is to begin with a comb that you think is sure to be too coarse (wide-toothed) and begin by using a stroke that you think is sure to be too light. You don't want to pull or make the cat uncomfortable in any way. If the comb goes sailing through without bringing very much hair with it, you can always graduate to the medium comb, then the fine. If you begin with a fine-toothed comb, you could end up pulling the hairs, which is uncomfortable. Or, as frequently happens, because the teeth of the comb are so close together, the comb may go slipping across the tops of the hairs, grooming them only about a quarter of the way down and leaving all the old, loose hair still lodged untouched near the roots to form mats.

Each time you begin grooming, remember to think of using the comb as a method of exploration. Don't automatically assume that the tips of the teeth are going to reach the cat's skin on the first stroke. Mentally divide the length of the cat's hair into quarters. On the first round over the cat's body, let the comb lightly explore the top quarter—the tips of the hair. If all is smooth sailing, go back over the cat again and include the next layer down, combing the outer *half* of the hairs. If you begin to encounter any resistance as the comb goes through, stop and comb that particular area even more lightly at first so that you gradually work the old hair out. Do the same on the third round, when you are combing through the outer three-quarters of the hairs, and on the fourth round, which ends with nice, firm strokes and the teeth scratching the skin.

You need two hands to comb a cat. Your comb hand grips the comb right up by the teeth, with your thumb actually resting against one side of the teeth, near the shank. You must use slow strokes while you're learning because your thumb must learn to be a sensory organ. It is through your thumb that you first get the message if there is any matting or resistance to the stroke. In other words, the sensitivity of your thumb keeps your cat safe from pulling.

Your other hand is used to smooth the skin flat ahead of the comb stroke. A healthy cat's skin is quite loose and can form rolls or rumples under the fur. So this second hand is the "stroking hand." The reason for using the stroking hand will be easier to understand if you realize that, although we want to comb all the cat's fur, some of that fur is located over protruding bones such as those found by the armpit or just in front of the tail.

As I said before, a healthy cat has loose skin. So the stroking hand is used to shift that loose skin about so that you can move the fur away from the bone or hollow and comb through it easily— then let it go back in place. You will probably find it helpful to practice sliding your cat's skin around. It feels awfully good, like any good massage, and can be incorporated into your usual petting and fondling routine.

Explain to the cat what you are doing as you work and be very clear about the reasons for each move you make. "This will get rid of the nasty dirt on your beautiful ruff." Or "You'll feel so much better when all that old, loose hair is gone."

If, during the course of the grooming your cat makes a complaint or gives an alarm, *don't ignore it! Stop.* Nothing makes a cat more nervous than to think that he has no control over the situation. If he tells you to stop, stop. Acknowledge that you have heard. Try to find out what the problem is. Carefully solve the problem, explaining all the while how you intend to do it without hurting. Then continue on. Remember that the whole grooming is one big expression of affection.

Here is the order in which you do the combing:

First, start with the back of the neck—they all love that.

Second, then go on to the throat and chest. The cat should be seated, facing away from you. Reach the comb hand around one side of him and the stroking hand around the other side. Tip the cat's head back slightly and, starting at the top, on the cheeks, stroke the comb downward (Figure 3), using slow and short strokes. Work your way down gradually. No stroke should be longer than three or four inches. Remember, you're still exploring. Overlap your strokes so that each stroke is *begun* in an area that has already been combed and ends by stroking through uncombed hair. Work your way down from the cheeks through the throat, upper chest, and lower chest, reaching between the legs. Your "finger grooming" will have revealed to you the bone structure under that chest fur so that you can avoid bumping the hard comb teeth against any protruding bones.

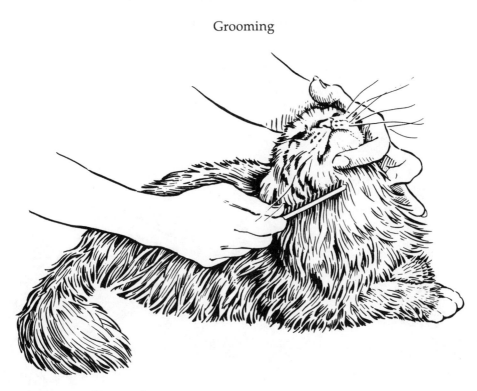

FIGURE 3

To comb the ruff, tip the cat's head back slightly.

Third, comb the neck and throat again—not because it needs it, but because cats love it and you want to reinforce the feeling of pleasure at being groomed. For this reason, you'll be going back to the neck and throat after finishing each section of the cat's body.

Fourth, do the back. Remember the little bumpy bones you found in the chest area? Well, you now have a whole long spine of bones running down the back. A good way to keep an area safe from the comb is to put your finger over the area. So put a finger over the upper spine and think of your cat's back as being shaped like the roof of a house with the spine on top. Comb one side and then the other, stroking parallel to the spine but never allowing the comb to go bumping down the vertebrae. The back is where you will learn how to use the stroking hand. There are three ways to use the stroking hand, depending upon which area you are working on and/or the texture of your cat's hair and skin. The first

FIGURE 4

First stroking hand method:
The skin is stretched by applying pressure with the
hand *ahead* of the direction of the comb.

method is to move the stroking hand ahead of the comb, pulling
the skin forward and making sure there are no protruding bones
or muscles for the comb to hit against (Figure 4) that might hurt
the cat. The second method is to use the stroking hand to hold the
skin taut *behind* the comb, using the thumb to press the skin backward (Figure 5). A variation of this is using the thumb of the
stroking hand to press or pull the skin to one side or the other in
order to move it off a protruding bone or inaccessible depression
in the cat's body. If all this sounds complicated, just remember the
purpose of the stroking hand, which is to keep the comb or brush

136

FIGURE 5

Second stroking hand method:
The skin is held taut *behind* the comb.

from hitting against the cat's sensitive bones and to smooth out skin rumples.

When combing the back, as in combing the throat, use short strokes. Once you've become thoroughly familiar with your cat's body structure, you will know how many bumps and depressions lurk between the neck and the tail. Comb the back hair a little at a time, and use the same overlap technique that you used on the neck. Also, remember that the stroking hand is being used to control the tautness of the skin, and you will soon discover that that control cannot extend for more than three or four inches from the hand's position.

A word about the comb angle: The comb should be held with

the tines pointing straight down at the cat's body. The points of the comb teeth should be directed against the skin. Don't think of combing hair, think of scratching skin.

In training a new client to comb his or her cat between groomings, I find that the most frequent mistake is to angle the teeth of the comb forward so that you are pushing the pointy teeth through the hair. This way your thumb cannot feel any sudden tangling, nor are you getting the teeth down to the skin. The second most frequent, and by far the worst, mistake is what I call the "egg-beater technique." Here, not only is the comb angled with the teeth pointing forward but the wrist is flipped at the end of each stroke causing the comb to lift or pull the hair out away from the body. Instead of starting at the tip of the hair and working down to the root layer by layer, egg-beater aficionados dig in as close to the root as possible and attempt to lift or pull *all* the loose hair off the cat at once. The thought in their minds seems to be that they are trying to comb and fluff the cat at the same time. They usually compound the error by using quick, flipping strokes, which reminds me of someone beating an egg with a fork—hence my label, "egg-beater technique." (Obviously, this mistake is almost never made by owners of shorthaired cats.) I explain to them that no one can fluff the cats' coats better than the cats themselves, when they shake vigorously after the grooming is over. And the very best way to ensure that your cats will want to have a good shake is to slick their hair down, then just let them go.

Fifth, do the thighs. By now it has become obvious that skin that is stretched taut is easiest to comb over. You've used the stroking hand to accomplish this on the back. For the thigh, there is a third stroking hand technique you can use. Slide your stroking hand in between the cat's hind legs and reach forward until it is between the front legs with your palm under the cat's chest and your forearm under the belly. Now slowly begin lifting up a little with your forearm. (This can also work if you lift with the hand, disengaging the front feet from the table.) Watch the thigh, leg, and foot. As you lift, the cat will automatically stretch the leg out, reaching for the table (Figure 6). While the leg is stretched thus, take advantage. Now it's a simple matter to do your light, medium, and heavy stroke combing, stroking from the top of the thigh down. When I do this area, I always have the cat facing sideways. I reach

FIGURE 6

Lift up the cat's abdomen to stretch
the outer thigh for combing.

in from the back and lift up. This is a perfect position for combing
the bloomers, too, because the back of the leg is stretched out as
well as the side.

Now, instead of turning the cat around at this point to do the
other outer thigh, leave the cat where he or she is and do the inner
thigh of the *opposite* leg. Again, using the stroking hand, slip the
hand underneath the foot of the leg you were just stretching and
gently press up so that the foot and leg fold up against the side of
the abdomen. The cat is now standing on three legs (Figure 7).

FIGURE 7

To comb the inner thigh, slip the stroking hand under the
ouside foot and gently lift up. *Don't lift too high,*
because your cat must balance on three legs.

Bend over the cat, look underneath, past the abdomen, and you
will see the inner thigh of the opposite leg. Reach under with the
comb past the leg you are holding up, and comb out that inner
thigh. (At this point, you will find yourself in a position that looks
a lot more difficult and impressive than it really is.)

Here I'd better say a word about the tail. In order for cats to
stand still and cooperate with you, they must control an awful lot
of energy and nervous impulses. Most cats really do a terrific job.
They are awe-inspiring. One thing that enables them to accomplish
this is that they can vent a lot of energy and nervousness with
their tails: They can flick them, lash them from side to side, and

generally express all the feelings they would otherwise have to bottle up. Owners frequently have the impulse to confine the tail or hold it still while working on bloomers, anal area, inner thigh, and so on. I tried the same thing in the beginning while I was learning. The cats soon made it very clear that if their tails are held still, then the movement will have to come out somewhere else. So, if you don't want dancing feet, you should as much as possible leave the tail free and try to work around it.

Now, turn the cat around facing the opposite direction to do the other thigh. Once again, lift up on the tummy to do that outer thigh and bloomers. This time, slip the arm and hand under the cat from the front; then fold up the leg and reach under the leg to do the other inner thigh.

Sixth, the long, silky hair that forms the border between the sides of the cat and the belly is what I refer to as the "skirts." The skirts near the front of the thigh and near the armpit are areas where frequent matting occurs. Bloomers, skirts, and chest are the three areas that must be done every day.

To groom the skirts, you use somewhat the same technique as you do on the outer thigh. Stretch out the area by lifting the cat. Face the cat away from you, open the stroking hand, and slip it under the cat's armpits and chest so that one armpit is resting on your middle finger and the other armpit is resting on your thumb. The index finger is against the cat's chest pointed up, toward his throat. Once again you are going to lift the cat, but don't lift the cat to a perpendicular position. This would make him afraid of falling backward, and he will probably start scrabbling with his back feet. Instead, this is a subtle move. Lift up just enough to disengage the front feet from the table by about two or three inches. The cat will be on a gentle diagonal, the chest resting heavily on your hand (Figure 8). Now, instead of lifting any farther, stretch the cat a tiny bit more forward, away from you, so that the skin under the skirts is nicely stretched out and you can do light, medium, and heavy combing of the skirts. Do the chest and abdomen at the same time as you reach under the cat and around to the skirts on the other side. You can even do fronts of thighs in this position, and that very tricky place where skirts join fronts of thighs.

In the beginning, before you and your cat get used to this little

FIGURE 8

To comb the skirts, place one hand under the chest between the
legs and lift up, stretching the cat slightly forward.

piece of choreography, you will almost certainly have to put the cat down, reposition your grip, and lift again for a few more strokes. You may find it helpful to go back and comb the neck a few times between tries to reinforce positive feelings, especially when you're first learning this maneuver.

Seventh, the chest between the front legs is mostly done by what I call the *Braille method*—you can't see what you're doing. Stand the cat facing away from you on all fours and bring the stroking hand in from one side, the comb in from the other. Reaching up between the front legs as high up on the chest as you can, stroke with one hand and follow with the comb. Coming at it from the other angle, tilt the cat's chin up and comb down on the upper chest, trying to overlap with what you did on the lower chest by reaching between the legs.

Eighth, grooming the tail is left for the final comb-out. Remember to finish by going back and combing the pleasure area again—neck, throat, or lower spine. A special word about the tail— use only the coarse comb on the tail no matter how sparse you think your cat's coat is. You didn't allow the comb to bump against the spinal vertebrae, and you apply the same principle here. The tail is an extension of the spine and very sensitive. Comb it in sections, just as you did the body of the cat. Don't try to cover the entire tail, base to tip, in one stroke. Work down in layers as you did with the combing of the body, and be supercareful not to pull and not to dig in. Tails are delicate and sensitive.

Step 3: Clipping the Claws

Claw clipping can be made very easy if the owner remembers always to include stroking the paws whenever he or she is petting the cat. Make it a practice to massage the cat's pads and toes, massage the claws out and in, out and in, as a part of your everyday ritual of affection. That way, when it comes to claw-clipping time, the cat will not find it in any way odd or alarming that you are picking up a paw and extruding the claws. Moreover, you must be familiar with the anatomy of your cat's claws before you try cutting them. This everyday fondling of the paws and claws gives you the opportunity you need to examine just how the claw slides in and out of the sheath. You will notice the downward curve of the claw as well as two other important features—the claw is flat (not round like a dog's claw), and there is a little pink membrane inside the claw reaching about halfway down the curve.

If, during your examination, you have noticed some waxy brown dirt around the cuticle area, you will need to clean it away in order to prevent irritation, swelling, and infection. This is done right after claw clipping.

When I first started grooming, I experimented with every type of claw clipper I could get my hands on. I came to the conclusion that every single one I tried was designed for a small dog with a round claw. My pussycats did not have round claws; their claws are flat like my nail but turned on the side and thicker. A people toenail clipper was the answer. A great big clipper for flat nails. It works, and it's easy to use because when you squeeze the clipper shut your fingers are right up close to the claw you're working on.

The most dangerous types of clippers I've found are those where the fingers must grasp the end of a handle two or three inches distant from the claw. With a people toenail clipper, you're really working in close. It's even easy to brace the little finger of your working hand against your other hand for steadiness when you clip. When you clip the claw, don't think of cutting it short but rather of blunting the tip. Locate that pink nerve inside the claw, and notice the distance between that and the tip. If you cut off only half of that distance, you'll always be safe. Never cut anywhere near the pink part because that's the nerve; that would hurt and teach the cat that claw clipping is painful. Incidentally, it is polite to clip your cats' claws before taking them to the veterinarian. This is also the best plan because more than once I have seen claws clipped by a veterinarian that were clipped far too short, right into the nerve. With such cats, it takes five or six sessions of careful and patient conditioning before I can convince them that Anitra does not hurt when she clips claws.

In order to maintain a clear memory of easy and pleasant claw clippings, it's nice if the owner does it every one or two weeks. Now, don't expect to clip every claw every time. Some will certainly not need it. When you come to a claw that is already short enough, extrude it from the sheath as usual and just touch it gently with the metal clipper so that the cat has the impression that you have done something to each claw.

A word about extruding the claws: On the first try, most people try to squeeze the claw out. This will work, but it is not efficient and certainly doesn't make the cat feel good. Instead, put your finger on the pad under the claw, press up, and watch the claw come out automatically. Use your thumb above the claw to hold the hair out of the way and keep the claw from sliding back into its sheath. Look at the curve of the claw, and, as you position your clipper, think of making the clip so that the flattened end of the claw will end up parallel to the ground when the cat steps on it—not up and down and parallel to the wall in front of the cat.

Before you actually squeeze the clipper shut, make sure of two things. First and foremost, there must be no chance of catching a part of the pad in the clipper; second, hold the clipper still as you squeeze it—don't move it from side to side, or change position in any way, and don't pull (Figure 9).

If, after clipping the claw, any dirt is left around the cuticles, now is the time to clean the cuticles. See "Soaking Feet and Cleaning Cuticles," page 221.

After you've finished grooming, the cat will probably run to the scratching post and start scratching like crazy to get his claws back in shape again the way he likes them.

Step 4: Getting Rid of the Mats

I feel a tremendous amount of hesitation in including instructions on the use of scissors for cutting out mats. It's such a dangerous business. And it's so hard to describe to someone secondhand, without having them actually present with the cat and the scissors.

I found that the very hardest cats to cut mats out of were elderly cats, because the skin is loose and flaccid as opposed to being loose and elastic; and black cats with dark skins, because it's hard to see where the hair ends and the skin begins. I remember the first matted cat I ever had to groom. It was quite an initiation. The cat was so matted that he was crippled. Any place a cat could get mats, he had them. The mats around the anus were mixed with excrement. He even had little minimats formed in the crew-cut between his ears. The rest of the body looked as if it were in a plaster cast between an inch and two inches thick. My first impulse when I saw him was to cry. I had never seen a cat in such a pitiful

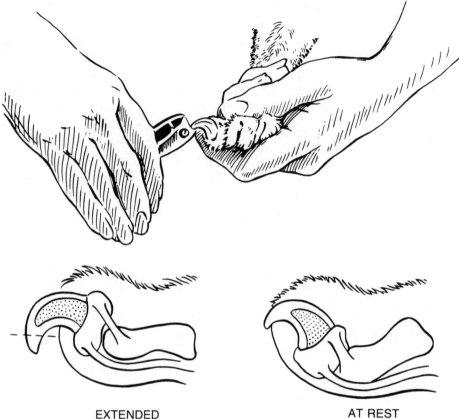

EXTENDED   AT REST

FIGURE 9

Clip the claw parallel to the ground.
Clip only the area below the dotted line.

condition in all my life. I don't remember now what the owner's excuse was for allowing the cat to get like that, but I do remember that the first grooming of my entire life lasted five hours. I didn't know enough then to insist on stopping after two hours and coming back another day, giving the cat a rest. I know I worked slowly— I remember the owner complained about how slowly it was going. But my feelings about a human being who could allow a cat to get into that condition were such that I didn't give a damn about what the owner thought about anything. My sole concern was to help the cat.

Here are a few tried-and-true general rules that will help you:

1. Use *only* a scissors with a rounded tip. *No points.*
2. *Don't bathe the cat while mats are still in the coat* or you'll have some mess on your hands.
3. Before you cut and as you cut, be very sure that the whole time you can see where the skin is and where the hair is. If you lose sight of the skin, don't cut—stop.
4. With every single cut you do, cut slowly. Be aware of every single millimeter of the cutting motion.
5. You don't have to finish an area before going on to the next area. Work a little here, a little there. It's easier on the cat's nerves to go back again and again to a difficult spot, doing it in short tries.
6. When working on one mat, don't hesitate to switch angles of approach—working at it from the right, from the left, from the bottom, from all angles.
7. Give frequent rest breaks. Especially when removing mats, you must remember to put the cat down off the table *before* he starts wiggling and demanding it. If you're working with scissors, the cat must be still, not wiggly. You can spread out the mat removal process over days and weeks, doing a few mats a day. Simply say to yourself that the coat is no longer getting worse and worse—it is now improving, however slowly. Safety comes first.
8. Whenever you are working near any delicate area where you are afraid of cutting something such as a nipple or penis, just remember—if you know where it is, you won't cut it. So cover such areas with your finger while you're working nearby.
9. If the cat is moving, don't cut. Stop.

Splitting the Mats: Mats pull the skin terribly, especially on areas of articulation such as knees, thighs, and armpits—they hurt. Don't pet your cat on the mats. The less you touch them or move them around, the better. As I said, they hurt.

The very first thing I do for a matted cat is to split each mat

FIGURE 10

To split a mat hold the scissors at a right angle
to the skin.

apart into smaller pieces. This accomplishes three things. First and
foremost, it gives the cat relief from the constant terrible pulling.
Second, it demonstrates just what it is you are about to do to make
him or her feel better. Third, it lets you see where the skin is. A
mat is easier to remove in pieces than left whole. When I first began
training assistants to remove mats, I advised them that if they split
the mat into enough segments there would be very little else left
to do.

To split a mat, insert the rounded nose of the lower blade of
the scissors between the skin and the mat so that the blunt side of
the blade is against the skin, and the sharp cutting edge is pushing
up against the mat (Figure 10). *Caution*—do not use the scissors
blade to pull the mat up or away from the skin. You want the skin
to stay flat and smooth, moving it as little as possible. So leave the

blunt side of the blade resting firmly on the skin and begin to *slowly* cut the mat in half.

Notice how, when the cutting in half is complete, the two halves of the mat spring apart. This is evidence that you have just released a great deal of tension from the skin.

Split the same mat again and again. Try inserting the scissors between skin and mat from various angles. You will notice that with each mat certain angles are fairly easy, while other angles of entry are all but impossible. You'll only hurt the cat if you insist on fighting the lay of the hair. This splitting procedure so far is fairly safe as long as you never pull the mat up away from the body. Simply keep the cutting edge facing up away from the cat and cut through the mat. In other words, you are not removing the mat, you are splitting it into many small pieces. Do this with several, if not all, of the mats wherever they occur. Split them up to give the cat relief.

Some mats do not lend themselves well to this type of splitting. With armpit mats, where the anatomy is so convoluted, it is extremely difficult to slip the scissors between skin and mat. Also, mats around the anus and the bloomers are sometimes cement hard because they have been repeatedly soiled and wet.

Cutting Out the Pieces of the Mat: Just as you slipped the scissors between skin and mat and tilted the cutting edge up away from the cat to split the mat, to cut out pieces of the mat you must slip the blade in between the cat and the mat and tilt the blade before cutting.

Choose a piece of mat. Note where the mat is, where the skin is, and the little bit of straight hair holding the mat to the skin. Slip the scissors blade between the mat and skin *close to the edge of the mat*. In other words, instead of inserting the blade near the middle of the mat to split it, insert the blade as *close as possible* to the edge of the mat. Begin tilting the cutting edge of the blade up, away from the cat, just as you did when you were going to split the mat. This time, however, don't tilt it all the way up. Bring it almost all the way so that the flat side of the blade is on an angle. Then again slowly cut through the hair between mat and skin at that angle, cutting the few hairs at the edge of the piece of mat. Then insert the blade again, close to the edge of the piece, tilt the cutting edge of the blade up away from the cat (but not to a full ninety degrees) and cut through a few more hairs, separating even more of the piece of mat from the cat. Repeat this process until you have severed all the hairs that are holding the piece of mat to the body. This technique is also used on mats that are too thick or hard to split or mats that are in difficult anatomical areas where it would be dangerous to try to split them (armpits, elbows, ankles, and anus).

I cannot say it often enough—go slowly. The slower you go in the beginning, the better a groomer you will be in the end. The cat must be standing still, for his or her own safety, so here's a prime place to use an assistant to help keep the cat from wiggling around. A general suggestion: When you are inserting the scissors blade near the edge of the mat, the closer to the edge the better. In other words, the fewer hairs you try to snip through at one time, the safer you will be. Once again, it's a question of patience on your part. If the matting is extensive, it's far better to have the cat anesthetized and shaved that one time if you can trust the veterinarian.

Breaking Up Soft Mats: A soft mat is a mat that is not really a mat yet. Think of a cotton ball. It's nice and soft; it's not a bit lumpy—yet you could not comb through a cotton ball. If, during the light combing, you encounter any areas on the cat's coat where the comb will not go through but you can't feel a lump, treat it as a soft mat. If you do nothing about it, it will soon become a classic hard mat. Treat the soft mat exactly the same as when splitting a mat, except that in this case, to save as much hair as possible, you should slip in your scissors parallel to the lay of the hair. Don't cut across the lay, thus cutting off a lot of hair. Only cut through the tangles and debris that crisscross back and forth across the growing hair. The effect will be as if you were thinning. Cut parallel to the lay of the hair again and again and again, always keeping the cutting edge facing out away from the cat, just as you did in splitting the mat. Then take the coarse (wide-toothed) comb and, beginning with a very light touch, gradually work deeper and deeper toward the skin, removing the hair debris you have freed. If the comb encounters resistance, go back and split some more. The more you split, the easier the combing will be and the better your cat will like it.

Step 5A: For Longhaired Cats: The Final Comb-Out

This step is simply a repetition of step 2—light combing. It is always done after removing mats or splitting soft mats. This step ends when you're combing through the entire cat with the points of the comb tines stroking directly against the skin of the cat and when you are encountering no resistance whatsoever in any part of the cat's fur.

Use a coarse comb for this step. Then, if your cat's fur is not very thick, you can repeat with the medium comb and maybe even follow that with the fine comb, but only on crew-cut, cheeks, neck, and throat—shorthair places where it doesn't pull at all. The work with the medium and fine combs is for the pleasure of finicky owners and their fortunate cats. The purr crescendos to fortissimo during this step.

Step 5B: For Shorthaired Cats: The Slicker Brush

The slicker brush is a delightful tool that shorthaired cats become very fond of. Because it only reaches from one-half to three-quarters of an inch of hair, it is unsuitable for longhaired cats. If your cat has long hair, a slicker brush would groom only the tips of the hair. The slicker brush must be used properly, because it can prick and scratch if improperly handled. Use the slicker brush only on the back, the sides, outer thighs, throat, and chest. Do not use it on the stomach—it could scratch the nipples. (If the coat is in very poor condition you may need to begin by first combing with a coarse or medium comb as in step 2.)

Hold the slicker brush very loosely by the handle and stroke it ever so lightly down the cat's coat. The cats often press up against the slicker brush, urging you on to a firmer stroke. Let your cat guide you. In order to avoid pricking the cat with those sharp little needles of metal, be sure that you always *keep the handle low and close to the cat's body*. When learning to use a slicker brush, beginners always make the same two mistakes: They try to stroke too rapidly and, worse, they flick their wrist at the end of the stroke, thus raising the handle up and digging the little pointy wires into the cat's skin. The first two or three days that you try it, make each stroke an individual activity (Figure 11).

FIGURE 11

Use a slicker brush for shorthaired cats only.
Stroke down the back parallel to (but not on) the spine, keeping
the handle low and close to the body.

It's helpful to stroke the slicker brush a couple of times down
your own forearm. Try it very lightly—a feather touch. Then add
a little steady pressure. This will go a long way toward helping
you to know your tool. Now try this: Stroking in slow motion,
begin to raise the handle up away from your arm at the end of the
stroke. Do it slowly, because you will feel how those little prickles
dig in to the skin. A good way to keep the wire bristles at the
correct angle is to think of keeping the knuckles of the brush hand
down on the fur.

Some groomers hesitate to recommend the slicker brush for fear the client will use it carelessly and condition the cat to dislike being groomed because of the pain experienced from tipping the brush at an improper angle at the end of the stroke. But nothing works as well as a small slicker brush for shorthaired cats. Nothing removes the loose hair quite so efficiently and in such great volumes. Nothing scratches and stimulates the cat's skin in quite so delightful a fashion. Cats have told me with their purrs and by pressing their bodies up against the brush that they adore it when it's used right.

If your cat has a coarse coat the Twinco slicker brush, size small, will probably do the best job. For a finer textured coat, I use either a Warners or the new Evergentle, again size small. Warners has an interesting new mini version that fits exactly between a cat's ears to groom the forehead and also does a nice stroking down cheeks and throat.

Because you can't use the slicker brush on the abdomen or any bony place, such as the forelegs or tail, use the fine-toothed comb for those areas. Never press hard against the bones or the tail. Remember, the tail is an extension of the spine.

Step 6: Washing the Eyes

Note: This step in the grooming procedure is only for those cats who have runny eyes or who tend to build up dirt in the corner of the eyes. If your cat's eyes are bright and shiny and clean, skip this step.

I have seen eye exudations on cats of all breeds. Runny-eye syndrome often markedly improves and in some cases clears up completely after a holistic regimen is begun. But in cases of eye infection or where careless breeding has rendered the tear ducts all but nonexistent, you do have to clean the cat's eyes every day, and sometimes twice a day.

Wiping away the dried tears and the brown stain will help only temporarily because the cause of the problem persists in the tear ducts. It is there and to the general health that we must address ourselves if we hope to effect a real and long-term improvement. Irrigation of the tear ducts is simple, soothing, and remarkably effective. As in any physical complaint, it would be foolhardy to expect any single therapy used alone to result in complete and permanent elimination of the problem. Attention must be given to diet, nutritional supplements, efficiency of the entire waste disposal system, and stress reduction. I see a lot of Persians with this problem, and I am happy to report that regular irrigation of the tear ducts used as part of a holistic health program *always* reduces the problems and usually eliminates it altogether. Since the procedure actually feels good to the cat and has no negative side effects, I use it freely.

The purpose of washing the eyes and irrigating the tear ducts is to cleanse and disinfect the ducts and to sooth and shrink swollen tissues so that closed or clogged ducts will open and allow fluid to run freely from the eye into the throat. This procedure can be used in addition to nose drops if your cat is suffering from upper respiratory problems. (See also "Eye Problems," page 315.)

Washing the eyes is easy, pleasant and soothing. Follow the instructions for giving eye drops on page 212, using one of the eye and nose drop formulas.

Step 7: Examining Teeth and Gums

Just as you should be aware of the condition of the cat's stool and urine for your own peace of mind, you will want to keep abreast of the condition of the teeth and gums. Tartar builds up on the teeth of most cats sooner or later, and it must be removed before it compromises the health of the gums, then the upper respiratory system, and finally the entire organism. If you notice that the gums have a line of bright red near the teeth, this indicates that something is amiss in the cat's system. Begin the acid-alkaline diet swing, as described in Chapter 8, for two weeks if you find inflamed gums. Also, be sure the teeth are clean.

So, how are you going to look at the cat's gums? Take the pill-giving and ear- and eye-medicating position: Kneel on the floor with your knees apart and feet together behind you, and then back the cat in toward you and have him sit. With your left hand, bring your thumb and forefinger under the cat's cheekbones and lift the head up, tilting it back as if to give a pill. With the right hand, lift the upper lip enough to peek at the gums and see if there's any tartar on the teeth. Then pull the lower lip down to check out the lower teeth. Also, insert the nail of your middle finger between the upper and lower front teeth and pull the lower jaw down so you can get a better look at the molars and the inside wall of the upper and lower teeth.

On your first examination, become consciously aware of the difference in color between teeth and tartar. If I find anything amiss with a cat's teeth or gums, I always show the owner. I have found that most owners can easily see the line of red on the gums near the teeth but most are not able to distinguish between tooth and tartar because tartar can be light yellow as well as dark tan.

So, in the beginning, examine the cat's teeth as a part of each grooming just so you can learn what the tartar looks like. Then, after it becomes obvious to you, you need only examine the teeth once a week. If you become aware that there's an awful lot of tartar buildup, plus inflamed gums, let the veterinarian clean the teeth. (See Chapter 9, "Seeking Professional Help.") The gums will probably not improve until you clean the filthy tartar away from them. Incidentally, an unpleasant smell to the cat's fur usually indicates a tartar problem because the cat will be washing himself with saliva that is loaded with smelly germs from the tartar.

Because teeth cleaning sometimes involves the use of anesthetic, it is to be hoped that this will not have to be done more than once a year at the most. Priscilla needs to have her teeth done every year, while Big Purr is eight years old and his teeth have never needed cleaning. If you see tartar forming in between cleanings, you can sometimes flick it off with a fingernail. This is easiest done if you let the tartar build up to a good-sized chunk first (a layer or two is too hard to deal with). Then one day while you're examining, instead of simply pulling the lip back and looking, insert your right thumbnail between the tartar and the gum. Place your right index finger on the point of that tooth and attempt to scrape that tartar down with the thumbnail toward the waiting index finger. This procedure is easier to practice on some cats than on others because of the cat's temperament, the owner's skill, and the density of the tartar. My Priscilla's tartar resembles granite, and the veterinarian advised me that my efforts with a thumbnail were worse than hopeless. However, I frequently use this method on cats that I'm grooming. The best approach is not to force the issue. Make a gentle attempt, each time you examine the teeth, to flick

155

off some tartar. If the cat protests, respond politely with "Okay, never mind, we'll try it again tomorrow." The cat will soon begin to smooth out your technique if you persist with patience.

However, don't try flicking tartar off the teeth if the gums are too inflamed. Inflamed gums hurt. Let the veterinarian take care of it under anesthetic. After dentistry has been completed, soothe and clean the gums using the Healthy Mouth Formula once a week (see page 257).

Step 8: Cleaning the Ears

I like to do the ears last. Many cats find ear cleaning itchy and tickly, because there are many little hairs in the ear that get moved around by the cotton swab. Many cats' ears are just not dirty, and in such cases I skip the ear cleaning. But, if you see a couple of black specks of wax, just take the cotton swab and clean *any part of the ear that you can actually see.* Don't try cleaning down into the ear canal, because you need a refined technique for that. It's not uncommon for a well-meaning owner to inadvertently tamp the wax down farther into the ear canal and against the ear drum.

It's nice to put oil on the cotton swab. Mineral oil is acceptable but, because the cat is going to wash the oil off and swallow it as soon as you put him down, I prefer to use the contents of a 100-unit vitamin E capsule or a wheat germ oil capsule. Don't buy vitamin E oil or wheat-germ oil in a bottle. It begins to oxidize and go rancid the minute you break the seal. Even in the refrigerator it is usable for only two weeks. The capsule keeps the oil fresher. Also, I find that the capsules are easy to carry around with me as I go grooming from house to house. I just puncture a capsule, squeeze the contents onto a saucer, and roll the end of the cotton swab in it. That way I feel secure in the knowledge that the oil is sterile, and when the cats wash their ears they will get a tiny but beneficial amount of vitamin E instead of the mineral oil, which washes vitamins E, A, and D out of the system.

Remember, anything you put onto the cat's body will eventually be licked off and swallowed. And oils will also be absorbed through the skin. So, if you're ever in doubt about using some substance on or around a cat, just ask yourself if you would mind if he lapped up a teaspoonful of it.

156

Step 9: The Catnip Party and Admiration

At the end of every grooming, even the daily sixty-second grooming, you must make every effort to convince your cats that in being groomed they have performed the cleverest of feats. Assure them that the grooming has revealed anew all their natural beauty, their wealth of symmetry and grace. Stroke their favorite spots to end the grooming on a high level of sensual pleasure.

You cannot give catnip every day, or the cats will lose their taste for it. But once a week or so present catnip after the grooming. Alternate treats are brewer's yeast tablets, liver tablets, or any one of the treats listed on page 65.

The Bath

Whenever anybody asks, "Can you give a cat a bath?" they always ask it in hushed tones, as if it were almost unthinkable. The bath is easy. Bathing a cat is really quite simple if you know how to go about it. A bath is luxurious and pleasant—warm, gentle, and sweet-smelling. Cats love to be clean, to be massaged, to be crooned over. A bath is all these things. A bath can be a wonderful demonstration of love, physical affection, and sensual pleasure.

Many cats never need a bath. If they're on the proper diet, they may never need one their whole life long. However, there are special circumstances where I would definitely recommend that the cat be bathed: at the beginning and end of a flea treatment, if the cat has soiled himself with diarrhea, if the cat gets into something, or if something is spilled on him.

It doesn't hurt a cat to be bathed any more than it hurts you to have your hair washed. But it's much better if the cat's general health is on such a plane of perfection that bathing becomes superfluous. A cat who needs to be bathed every month because he's greasy has a health problem. A cat with kidney failure will require frequent bathing: a cat with pancreas malfunction will also have a greasy coat. The bath doesn't solve the health problem—it just gets rid of the symptoms for a couple of days.

When new clients present me with a cat that has an oily coat and ask me to give a bath, I always inform them that it is against

157

my policy to bathe any cat until he has been on a proper diet for one month. (I make an exception for a cat that has been soiled in any way.) I explain this rule thus: If I'm going to ask a cat to stand still for bathing and stand still for drying and comb out, I feel that that cat deserves to stay looking clean and terrific for at least a couple of months after the bath. If the cat's coat is greasy and full of dandruff because of a slow metabolism and low-quality diet full of waste products, the cat will still continue to exude old wastes through the pores in the form of oil and dandruff for at least two or three weeks after beginning the high-quality diet. By then the backlog of wastes is gone. So I tell the owner to put the cat on the proper diet, remove food between meals, increase activity, and then in a month I'll come back and bathe the cat. Then, when I do come back, often the cat looks so great that I can say, "Are you sure you want Samantha bathed? I really don't think she needs it." I love to be able to say that, and the owners are always so proud. Young cats respond fast to the dietary change—some old cats do too. You never know until you try.

But if the cat's oily coat has resulted in the dust-mop effect, a bath may be just the thing he needs.

What do you need to give a bath? A cotton ball, some plain eye salve or petroleum jelly, three or four bath towels (you may not need them all), the cat's comb (no slicker brushes are used here), a hand-held hair dryer, a cat shampoo (see "Product Suppliers," in the Appendix) and a hose that will connect to the faucet of either the kitchen sink or the bathtub. The hose should be the type used in barber shops and beauty parlors for rinsing hair. For cat bathing, you must cut off the spray end so the water comes out of the hose in a stream—a wide spray is just what you *don't* want.

In giving the bath, you are aiming for clean, virgin hair because virgin hair sheds dust and dirt. Do not use any shampoos with additives such as conditioners, lanolin, and so on. Most pet store shampoos have these additives. They are undesirable because they coat the hair follicle and give you the dust-mop effect all over again, which is just what you're trying to get rid of. Don't use a baby shampoo because it is too mild (you wash your hair once a week or more, but the cat gets a bath once or twice a year). If you can't find a pure Castile veterinary shampoo without undesirable additives, look for a pure Castile people shampoo—the strongest possible. Usually a formula for oily hair will be stronger. Try the cosmetic section in a health-food store. Most health-food stores include a pet section. Several natural pet products companies make good shampoos (see "Product Suppliers," in the Appendix).

To prepare for the bath, first groom the cat to a fare-thee-well. *Never wet the cat's coat while there are mats or even loose hair present.* The very best plan is to groom the cat in the morning and bathe in the afternoon. That way you're not asking the cat to hold still for a long period at one time. Do a one-minute combing right before the bath.

Next set up the dryer, the comb, and three or four towels in a comfortable place away from the bath where you can sit with the cat on your lap and dry him. Adjust the dryer setting so that you have a good, strong stream of air but *not too much heat.* The temperature should be warm, never hot or cold. When it's properly set to your satisfaction, turn the dryer off.

Then mix a solution of half shampoo and half warm water into a dish or, better yet, an empty squeeze bottle. Shampoo must be warm and soothing, not cold and shocking. Attach the hose to the spigot and warm the tub or sink that you're going to use by swishing hot water around in it. The cat must be standing on pleasant warmth. Regulate the water temperature so that the stream of water coming through the hose is a bit warmer than baby bath temperature. The cat's body temperature is normally higher than ours. Test the temperature against the inside of your forearm. If you love it, your cat will love it. Let the water continue to run from now until the end of the bath.

While you're letting the water run a bit, put about a quarter of a cotton ball into each of the cat's ears. You don't have to stuff it down, just make sure it is secure. The cotton will absorb any stray droplet that might splash that way. A drop of water in the ear wouldn't hurt, but there's a chance the cat might be startled.

Then take the eye salve or petroleum jelly and apply a drop to the inside of the lower lid of each eye. (See "Giving Eye Medication," page 211.) This will provide a film of oiliness over the eye, protecting the eyes from any stray drops of water or shampoo.

Don't begin to wet the cat until you're sure that the water temperature is going to remain constant throughout the bath. Put one towel within easy reach of the bath area to receive the cat afterward. In the wintertime, many finicky owners like to heat the towel on a radiator or in front of the oven.

Now the sink or tub is warm, the shampoo is warm, the water is warm, and the towel is warming. As you prepare each of these things, think of it as a gift you are going to give your cat. Consciously realize how much you yourself would enjoy each of these facets of the bath. Recent scientific research has established that cats "pick up" our mental attitudes.

Back in the first year that I was grooming, before I had developed my techniques, my biggest concern was that the cats should not be frightened. In my zeal to reassure them, I myself would lie in the tub with the cat on top of me, attempting to demonstrate that it must be perfectly safe, or I would surely be drowned first. Although this did work pretty well as far as calming the cat, I found it was rather difficult to give a thorough shampooing while lying supine with the cat standing on my stomach. Besides, it did not give a professional impression.

Now, after sixteen years of experience, and with my technique developed to a fine art, I still get wet. Oh, it's not that there is ever any wild splashing or thrashing about; the bath is still calm and luxurious. But there is just no substitute for the assurance that close physical proximity can give. You will want to nestle your cat close not only to your face but with your arms as well. I wear a sleeveless cotton smock that dries in a jiffy. Although I prefer to work in the kitchen sink, if I have to use the tub I wear shorts because I will be kneeling in the wet.

Now arrange the hose on the floor of the tub or sink so the water is calmly running down the drain. No splashes or gushes, please. Pick up the cat and say that you're going to make him feel good. Place him in the tub or sink. *If you're using the sink*, start by placing his hind paws in the sink and his front paws on the drainboard. Hold the cat close to you—do a lot of nuzzling with your face near his head and neck. Having your face close to his in a new and unfamiliar situation is very reassuring. *If you're using the tub*, it's best if you get into the tub carrying your cat. With your back to the spigot and drain, take the kneeling position as if to pill the cat (see Chapter 9) by backing the cat in toward you so that both you and the cat are facing the back of the tub. In both these cases, you are playing down the water aspect. The cat hasn't really seen or felt much water yet.

If the cat reacts as if trying to tell you, "Hey, watch out, there's water here—I'm getting all wet!" immediately put your face up next to his and reply that you know about the water. Tell him that it's going to feel good, it's warm, and it will make him nice and clean. You must explain everything you are doing, because the cat will be reading your tone, and your words will carry the desired emotional concept. Continuing to talk and nuzzle, pick up the hose so the end where the water comes out is nestled in your palm. The cat still hasn't seen it. Before you introduce the sight of the hose, introduce the pleasant, warm feeling of it by rubbing your hand containing the hose against his haunch. As you nuzzle him and describe in detail how much you love nice warm water, wet his thighs, lower back, sides, inner thighs, upper back, shoulders, and chest—in that order. Throughout all this, you must tenaciously hang on to the truth of the situation—the water feels fabulous. By this time, he will be standing in a quarter inch or so of water sloshing about in the bottom of the tub or sink. He may find this alarming and assume that you are not aware of this shocking development. Continuing the nuzzling, you must make two things crystal clear to him. First, you are fully aware of his concern and the reason for it and, second, you are doing what you are doing on purpose because it is marvelous and will make him feel wonderful if only he gives it a chance. Remember, that, in this case, if a cat is upset, he's upset because of fear of the *unknown*, not because of any kind of discomfort or *actual* danger. I call it suffering from an attack of the "what ifs." It's easy to understand—we humans do it all the time.

Now touch the hose to the floor in front of him and let him see the water running out. Still nuzzling, go back and redo his thighs, back, and so forth. This will prevent any chill. But this time continue on to include the throat and the back of the neck. Do not bathe the cat's face, forehead, or ears except when specifically soiled or when treating for fungus or fleas. Cats do pretty well in those areas by themselves. You can always wipe those areas off later with a damp cloth.

Now the cat's coat is thoroughly saturated with water. If the coat is greasy, you may have to go over it several times before it will hold the water. Before you apply the shampoo, lay the hose out of the way on the bottom of the sink or tub with the stream of water pointing down the drain so the cat feels he can safely forget about it. If you are working in the tub, you can hold the hose in place with one foot. Now you are going to focus the cat's attention on one of the biggest pleasures of the bath. Apply the fragrant, warm shampoo solution to the neck, throat, shoulders, chest, armpits, upper back, lower back, tail, tummy, and inner thigh—in that order. If there's a problem area, such as lower back or tail greasiness or a soil or stain anywhere, apply the shampoo in that area first. Massage the cat's body, working up a nice foamy lather all over. This step really makes the cat feel fabulous. During this step, reapply warm water every thirty seconds so the cat doesn't feel chilled.

If you're working with a greasy coat and you fail to get a good lather on the first shampooing, don't worry about it. You always do two soapings anyway, so you can save the really fabulous massage for the second soaping when the shampoo is good and foamy. An owner never has a better opportunity than during the bath to explore the incredible musculature of the cat. Keep up a running commentary to your cat in which you exclaim about the quality of his muscles and the delicacy of each bone your fingers encounter. As your fingers explore the cat's symmetry and grace, express delight in audible exclamations of appreciation. In trusting you so far as to submit to such a very odd ritual, your cat is in effect giving you a tremendous gift—his confidence and love.

To rinse, be careful to hold the hose right at its tip. *Never let the cat see water flying at him.* Rinse in the same order that you applied the shampoo, starting high on the neck so that the dirty shampoo runs down and off the legs. Rinse it off the back, off the sides, and so on, leaving the legs, paws, and tail until last.

Be thorough with the rinse. This is the most important part of the bath. Soap left in the coat is sticky and produces the dust-mop effect. It is also itchy and causes matting in Persians. You can get away with a little mistake in any other step, but this one must be perfect. To be sure the coat is soap-free, you can finish with a lemon or vinegar rinse (see page 262). Then rinse again. Give special attention to rinsing the tail, skirts, outer thighs, inner thighs, and lower chest: in other words, all those places where matting tends to occur. During the rinsing, continue to nuzzle your face close to the cat's head as much as possible and call attention to the way the water is making him nice and warm again and how the nasty oiliness and dirt are being washed away down the drain.

When the coat is squeaky clean and free of soap, get rid of some of the water by pressing the coat against the skin and very lightly squeezing his legs, paws, and tail. Remove the cotton from the ears, grab the warm towel from the radiator or stove and bundle the cat up in it, telling him that this warm towel and the forthcoming warm dryer are the rewards for the heroic patience he has displayed. Carry him out to the drying area. Drape another towel across your lap and fold him in another dry towel (the first towel is probably wet by now). The more towels you use, the faster he'll get dry. As you want the towel to absorb water, never use a towel that has been treated with fabric softener. It coats the fibers with a chemical and renders the towel nearly waterproof.

To introduce the dryer, use the same principle you used when introducing the water. Break the dryer up into its component parts—sound, sensation, and sight. As you're toweling the neck, nuzzling the cat's cheek, and telling him how delicious he smells, hold the dryer far away with your other hand well out of his sight. Continue talking to him and casually turn the dryer on, ignoring it completely and continuing to focus on the delicious-smelling cat.

Proceeding on to the feel of the dryer (making sure he cannot see it yet), slowly introduce the stream of comfortably warm air against the thigh or lower back. Try to always have your hand or finger on his body *included* in the path of that warm stream of air, so that you can judge the temperature. Don't allow the dryer to get too close. *The dryer must always be kept slowly moving.* If you hold it still, it will burn. Remember that the cat's skin is extremely delicate and sensitive. Think of the mucous membrane lining the inside of your lower lip. If you treat all the cat's body as if it were that sensitive, you'll always keep him safe.

The cat will probably move and want to get up. Turn the dryer off when this happens, readjust his position, and perhaps take a fresh towel. Drying is much more difficult to do alone. It goes three times faster if you can find someone to hold the cat on a lap and distract him while you apply the dryer in one hand and the towel in the other. Allow the cat to see the dryer at a time when it has already been turned on and directed against the body for a couple of seconds. (Remember to keep the dryer moving.)

After the hair is more than half dry all over, begin combing with a wide-toothed comb as you dry. An assistant is invaluable here, because combing and blow-drying simultaneously speeds the drying about 300 percent. If you're alone, you have to go from one to the other. The comb is in the right hand, and the dryer is in the left hand. Comb ever so lightly, and again be sure to keep the dryer moving. Combing separates the hair so the stream of air can dry it even faster.

When drying the neck or throat, cup one hand over the cat's ears, eyes, and nose so that the stream of air from the dryer is never directed there. The cat can take care of drying those areas himself with his paw and tongue. It's also very easy for him to dry feet and ankles. Although the tail is easy enough for him to reach, the hair there is usually longer and thicker, so it's nice to give him a good headstart by using the dryer on the tail.

You don't have to get him absolutely dry, especially during the summer or in a well-heated apartment. However, the cat must be dry enough so you can easily run the comb through the hair all over the body. Otherwise longhaired cats may mat. Even if you try your best to get a cat completely dry, it's almost impossible. Anyway, cats reach their peak of fluffy beauty the day after a bath. When you decide to call it quits and put the cat down, go all out with positive reinforcement. If you have a brass band available, strike it up now. Tell your cat that he or she is not only the bravest and the most patient but also the softest and most gloriously beautiful creature with the most delectable scent on God's green earth. Repeat your rhapsodic performance at intervals all during the rest of the day. It won't be difficult to do. You'll understand what I mean the first time you experience a freshly bathed cat. Chances are you won't be able to keep your hands off those lovely furs. After the first bath, I always remind owners that after the cat has been on the high-quality diet for a while this is the way he or she will always look and feel.

Two or three times a year, I run into cats who are afraid of the dryer. If you follow all the prescribed steps in introducing the dryer and yet the cat has a reaction verging on hysteria when you turn it on, don't persist. Just turn up the heat in the room, turn on the oven, and towel dry like crazy, using about eight or nine towels and follow that with about fifty paper towels. Keep at it until you can successfully run the comb through all the hair. Your cat will still look beautiful tomorrow, just like a cat that has been blown dry.

I had this problem when I was caring for a big gray male named Apollo who was convalescing from a mouth tumor. The veterinarian wanted him bathed once a week to clean away the discharge from his mouth, which soiled his chest and front legs. Apollo is enormous, gentle and intelligent; but the sound of that dryer threw him into such a state of helpless terror that he was not responsible for his actions.

I had to dry him quickly because I couldn't allow him to become chilled; it was early spring and the radiators were off. I solved the problem this way: every week after Apollo's bath I would dry him as well as I could with several terrycloth towels, then carry him in to the office where I had pulled out the bottom drawer of the desk and fixed two clip-on reflector lamps with one-hundred-watt bulbs. They were focused on a dry bathmat on the floor and were only about two feet away. Apollo would lounge there for an hour or so, turning himself like a sunbather and licking himself dry all over. I would pass by every fifteen minutes or so and hurry his process along by combing through whatever portion His Nibs was then exposing to the two hundred watts of warmth.

If you are bathing cats because they have fleas, refer to "Fleas" in Chapter 10. It is to be hoped that your cat does not have fleas. If not, you have the option of applying the "ounce of prevention" principle. If you think there is the slightest chance of a single flea rearing its ugly head anywhere near your cat, you may want to add an herbal flea repellent or oil of eucalyptus to the second soaping or finish off with a spray of Spritz (now marketed as Natural Animal Coat Enhancer; see Appendix, "Product Suppliers").

One word about dry shampoo—forget it. It coats the hair, and it just doesn't work well. The tiny bit of oil it absorbs could be done away with much more efficiently by using simple cornstarch or fine cornmeal. So don't waste your money, and don't put harmful perfumes and chemicals on your cat's coat.

Grooming for Seasonal and Stress Situations

Most of my new clients come to me either in the middle of the summer, after the big spring shed, or after they have been away, come back, and found their Persian full of mats. The format is almost always the same. The hysterical owners call me and tell me they returned after a few weeks away to find the cat totally matted: "It's never happened before, and the cat won't let me comb him— can you help?" I always reassure the owners that I can put the cat back in shape again. But I ask them not to touch the mats until I get there. "Pretend to the cat that you've forgotten about the mats," I say. I don't want the cat to have a fresh memory of being hurt by someone fooling around with the mats.

Almost always the cats are grateful that I'm working on them once they catch on to what I'm doing. It happens again and again, and yet I'm always awed by how much a cat can understand. I get the owner to talk to the cat about interesting things that happen in the cat's life, and this helps the cat to focus on the beloved owner's voice rather than on the nerve-racking process of Anitra cutting out the mats. The poor owners are always contrite, assuring me over and over again that this could not possibly have happened if they'd been home and it had certainly never happened before.

It doesn't ever have to happen again even if you do go away or some other stress situation occurs such as moving, sickness in the family, or anything that might be stressful to the cat and might keep you from the necessary daily grooming. All you have to do to prevent it is to plan in advance and take "a stitch in time." Half the battle is keeping the nutrition at a high level and doubling the amount of lecithin in the Vita-Mineral Mix during times of stress. This makes the hair easier to groom. If you know already that your cat has a tendency toward either diarrhea or constipation when under stress, double the bran as well. If it is a Persian, trim more widely around the anus and inner thigh.

Be very specific about the feeding instructions you give to whomever is going to take care of the cat. Now is certainly not the time to be lax. I am always surprised when owners do not give detailed instructions for feeding to the person taking care of the cat in their absence. Often they seem to feel that it's enough of an imposition to ask someone to care for the animal even if they're paying the person, and they don't want to inconvenience the sitter even more by asking for any sort of special dietary requirements. I tell these people that they are dead wrong.

First of all, sitters in general are very nice people. Just put yourself in the place of the sitter. What most nice sitters want more than anything else is to be given as *much* information as possible about how best to keep your pet in top physical shape until you get back. Taking care of someone else's cat is a heavy responsibility, even if it is also a great delight.

Even if your sitter declares that he or she will enjoy combing the cat, it's safest to clip the hair short, at least in the armpits, around the anus, and along the inner thigh. How far you extend the clipping depends on whether your cat's coat is easy to groom or long, thick, and difficult to groom. The principle is to clip down to an inch any and all hair that might present a problem to the neophyte groomer. Remember when you began grooming the cat, and recall which areas of the cat's fur tend to mat up first. You will definitely want to clip those areas shorter.

Clarence Eckroate's coat is sparse and silky. It's supereasy to groom, and Clarence's personality falls under the heading of "old sweetie pie." Normally we don't even clip his armpits. However, if Norma were to take a business trip in the middle of the shedding season, I would advise a modest trim in the armpits and around the anus just to be on the safe side.

Pandy Kaufman's coat is quite thick. Besides, she is a high-strung cat who has never learned to enjoy her groomings. Her owner, Diane, and I have decided that it's wise to keep a jump ahead of the mats by clipping Pandy's armpits, leg crease, anus, and inner thigh every single month. Pandy is nervous enough during her normal monthly grooming, which she barely puts up with. If a mat forms anywhere in the furs, Pandy knows it, focuses on it, and imagines all kinds of dire consequences that could befall her during that mat's removal. With Pandy, it's much wiser and kinder to clip too much rather than too little.

When Diane Kaufman, Pandy's owner, goes away, we go all out—stopping just short of the "Cape Cod Clip" (see page 168). We trim down to less than a quarter inch all the hair on Pandy's abdomen, inner thighs, armpits, and chest. I extend the clipping line of the armpits and leg creases right up Pandy's sides toward the shoulder blades and hip bones respectively. When we're finished and place Pandy on the floor, she gives an irate shake, and as she stalks off we can see that she has so much fluffiness left that no one would ever be able to detect our sneaky clipping without turning Pandy upside down. Knowing Pandy, I can't see how that's likely to happen.

Sammy Levy's coat is the longest and thickest that I've ever seen. Sammy is a fabulous brown tabby Persian. His ruff hairs measure about four and half inches from root to tip. Sammy is a darling, but his health is rather delicate, and there have been a couple of times over the years when Sammy's coat became greasy and full of dandruff as a result of a breakdown in his physical health. He enjoys grooming to a certain extent but is supersensitive, and when he falls ill that sensitivity increases.

During his first illness, his owner and I agreed that Sammy's comfort came first. We sacrificed the beautiful, thick, soft hair of his inner thighs, abdomen, chest, and so on. I gave him the same sort of clip I used on Pandy. With Sammy, I also took off part of the skirts and the fronts of the thighs. The clipping was so extensive that one could easily see the difference in Sammy's shape as he walked about. But Sammy loved it. On hot summer days, he'd lay his abdomen against the cool bathroom tiles and sleep with a contented smile on his face. Because the worst areas of potential matting were now eliminated, Sammy could again relax and enjoy the luxury of his biweekly grooming during his convalescence.

One thing I do every month when I see my regular longhaired clients is clip off all the fur in the armpits and about a half-inch of fur around the anus in a circle because these are the prime areas for matting. If the bloomers are full and fluffy, I also clip a "free-fall area" underneath the anus by clipping short some of the hair of the bloomers on the back of the inner thighs.

When I clip armpits and the anal area, I cut the hair down to less than a sixteenth of an inch. No one but you and the pussycat will know that beneath that fluffy exterior the armpits are bare—unless, of course, your cat does a lot of waving.

To satisfy public demand, I have had to devise what I dub the "Cape Cod Clip." This is for owners who are taking their cats on summer vacation to woodsy, weedy, sandy, buggy areas full of briars and brambles. I had to think of a way to protect the cat from the sun from above, leave most of the ruff and tail, to satisfy the cat psychologically and get rid of most of the cat's hair because the owners didn't want to bother with it under the wilderness circumstances. At the same time, my professional eye insisted that I end up with a cat who was still esthetically pleasing.

I dubbed it the "Cape Cod Clip" in honor of the first cat I tried it on. She was, as you may have guessed, bound for Cape Cod. She was an elderly tabby Persian with a medium-thick coat. I did the extensive clipping in the armpits, extending the clipping half way up on both sides of the chest and then clipped the chest fur down to a half inch. Beginning with the lower part of the ruff, I left the hair longer and longer to blend the short chest hair in with her medium-length ruff. When working on a cat with a very long ruff of three or four inches, I usually trim the ruff hair down so it is no longer than two inches. I trim the leg creases, inner thighs, abdomen, and backs of thighs down to an eighth of an inch or less. If the cat has long, silky ankle feathers, I trim them right down, leaving the leg fur about a quarter inch long. I trim the outer thighs down to a quarter or half inch, and about halfway up the thigh I allow the length of hair to increase so that, for about three inches on both sides of the spine, the hair is left at normal length to protect the cat from the sun. That area is very easy to groom, anyway.

From the long hair around the top of the cat's back to the very short hair on the abdomen, I simply taper gradually. For esthetic reasons, you may want to cut off as much as a half inch from the tail, but *only near the anus* in order to taper the tail into the anal clip. Caution: Don't cut the hair on the tail unless it's matted or badly soiled. Tail hair takes many months to grow in again.

On returning from Cape Cod, the tabby Persian's owner informed me that she was frequently asked what kind of a cat she had. People thought her cat was quite lovely and wondered where they could get one like her. She had a hard time convincing them that Mimi was a classic tabby Persian wearing her Cape Cod Clip.

8
Seeking Professional Help

Finicky owners are as choosy about their pet's health needs as they are about their own. You never know when an emergency will come up, so it's important to know the symptoms of illness and to have competent and caring feline health professionals who know your cat's medical history.

When Do You Need the Veterinarian?

"The most common cause of feline death is people bringing the cat to the veterinarian too late." Every veterinarian I know has said these words to me at one time or another. It's not because the owners are careless; it's just that it is often hard to spot the early symptoms of disease in the cat.

Cats accept pain and discomfort in their bodies just as they accept a rainstorm or a cold day. They assume there's nothing to be done, so they make the best of it and try to carry on as usual. Because they don't cry or moan or fall down, the average owners are completely in the dark about their pet's deteriorating health until the condition becomes so acute that the cat is weak from dehydration or gasping for breath because the chest is half full of fluid.

The case of Daphne comes to mind. Daphne, a tortoiseshell Persian, was a perky little number adopted by a client of mine as a friend for her charming female Persian Rags. I placed Daphne with this particular lady partly because I hoped that Daphne's jaunty, devil-may-care attitude might serve as a bit of a tranquilizer for her new, very sweet, but rather highstrung and overprotective owner, Carlota. I had had Daphne examined by the veterinarian just before I introduced her to her new home. At the time, Daphne had an intestinal bug, which was medicated and cleared up in less than a week. I groomed her on two occasions during the next four weeks, and my assistant cat-sat while Carlota went out of town for three days, so Daphne did not lack for expert observers. She was flirty and playful and ate like a horse the whole time.

After Carlota came back, I was surprised when she called to tell me that Daphne hadn't passed a stool for two days and asked me if I thought she should take her to the veterinarian. Ordinarily I would have said no and simply had her add ⅛ teaspoon of finely ground psyllium husks and three tablespoons of water to each of Daphne's meals and then call me again the next day. But I remembered Daphne's recent intestinal virus, and I knew that Carlota would continue to worry and pass that tension on to both her cats. So I told her to make an appointment with the veterinarian and take Daphne in right away.

During the course of the examination, Carlota mentioned to the veterinarian that she noticed that Daphne made a funny little noise when she breathed. The veterinarian listened with the stethoscope, and then he listened again—and again. Then he took an X ray. Sweet, playful, flirty Daphne had pneumonia. Her chest was filling up with fluid, and she had a temperature of 104.5 degrees F (normal cat temperature is about 101 degrees F).

Daphne is feeling fine and healthy now, thanks to the veterinarian's diagnosis and treatment and to Carlota's finicky, overprotective ways and devoted nursing care. The point of this narrative is that Daphne's pneumonia was discovered almost by accident. If she hadn't had constipation, she might have been allowed to continue to "breathe funny" until her chest was so full of fluid that she couldn't breathe at all. After all, the veterinarian had seen her four weeks before, and both my assistant and I had seen her in the intervening time. Because she didn't act sick, we didn't suspect that she was.

The best advice I can give to an owner is this: Any change in your cat's usual behavior patterns should be carefully watched. If it persists or if two or three questionable changes occur, have the veterinarian check it out. Remember, cats don't know that you have the power to make them better, so they are not going to come and tell you if something feels bad. But don't worry and dwell on all the negative possibilities. There is no one better equipped than you, the loving owner, to spot little changes that could spell trouble and correct them long before they become serious.

Of course, the annual visit to the veterinarian for a physical and dental examination and teeth cleaning is wonderfully reassuring and sometimes uncovers a small trouble long before it becomes serious. Over the years, many loving owners have told me stories about taking a beloved animal to the veterinarian for no better reason than "She looked worried to me." In every single case, the owner was right; illness of one sort or another was discovered in the beginning stages and was diagnosed and treated.

If you notice a symptom, don't panic; it could be nothing. Observe whether a symptom persists or if there is more than one symptom present. You can go through the checklist below. It will help you gather information that you can make note of and then convey to your veterinarian by phone so that the two of you can decide whether or not your feline friend needs to go in to the office for a hands-on examination.

Checklist of Symptoms

- *Vomiting* is usually not serious unless repeated. Cats vomit more frequently than humans because of their short intestine. They *should* vomit hair balls if they swallow too much fur. If the vomited matter looks like a small wet hot dog, it is a hair ball. This is *not* a symptom of something wrong; it is normal and natural. Cats can also vomit food if they eat too fast or too much or if it is too hot or too cold. If none of these reasons apply and if food is vomited repeatedly or if food is vomited hours after it is eaten, that is noteworthy and should be reported to the veterinarian. If vomit is not food, then you must note the color, consistency, amount, frequency, and how soon after eating it occurs. Repeated swallowing should also be noted.
- *Loss of appetite* is usually not serious unless prolonged. Cats don't eat the same amount every day. Temperature, stress, a recent snack, a large meal the day before, or leaving food available between meals can ruin the cat's appetite. How-

ever, a low-grade infection, nausea, painful gums, dirty teeth, constipation, dehydration, or any one of several diseases can also cause anorexia. Cats won't eat what they can't smell; a stuffy nose can also cause poor appetite (see "Giving Nose Drops," page 216). Offer a tiny serving so you can see precisely how much your cat is actually eating and keep accurate track of his intake.

- *Claw biting* is a normal part of the cat's grooming procedure, but it could also signal an infection, a split claw with something caught in it, an in-grown claw, or it may be because of dirty cuticles. Check claws, cuticles, and pads.
- *Dirty cuticles* (especially on back claws). A buildup of waxy dirt around the cuticle is a sure sign the cat is scratching at something that itches and is exuding a discharge. The cuticle dirt can infect the toe. Check for waxy ears, skin problems, and tooth and gum problems—any of which could lead to dirty cuticles. (See "Soaking Feet and Cleaning Cuticles," page 221.)
- *Excessive sleeping* happens naturally after a big meal or if the cat is bored. It also happens during the spring and autumn sheds, but it could also mean the cat's body is fighting off an infection. It could also signal a weak heart, liver, or kidneys. Check for other symptoms.
- *Withdrawing, sitting facing the wall, or seeking warmth or coolness* are signs of depression that indicate stress or inner tension and usually mean the cat is in pain or feeling very sick. Hiding, sitting in the litter box, or pressing his forehead against things are also signs of pain. Change of preferred perches and resting places could be caused by a whim or by a change in the weather but could have a more serious significance and the owner should watch for other symptoms.
- *Coughing* could be a temporary irritation or something caught in the throat. If it persists there may be a serious obstruction in the throat or windpipe, upper respiratory infection, pnuemonia, roundworms, heart problem, or other serious disease. Note the frequency and duration of coughing spells, when they started and when they happen (for

example, after exertion or when he wakes up or after eating, and so on).

- *Sneezing* can be caused by any sudden sharp smell or by cold temperature. Environmental causes can be dust, cigarette smoke, room deodorizer, fabric softener, or some of the same things that cause coughing. It might also be caused by an eye infection or tumor or polyps in the nose or sinuses. Keep the same type of notes as for coughing above.

- *Eyes.* The pupils should both be the same size. They should get small when looking into a light. Face your cat toward a lamp; then cover the cat's eyes with your hand for 15 seconds. When you uncover the eyes, the pupils should be large and then get smaller. If the pupils are different sizes, alert your veterinarian immediately. Conjunctive tissue around the eyes should be a pleasant pink. Gently draw the skin away from around the eye and note the color of the conjunctive tissue. If it is too light, the cat may be anemic; too red and/or bloodshot means irritation indicating that an infection or a foreign body is present. Note also if your cat refuses to let you touch the eye. Discharge collecting in the corner of the eye may be chronic in some cats. Note the color of the discharge: brown is usually not serious; white, mucusy, yellow, greenish, or red discharge should be reported to your veterinarian at once. Copious discharge, whether it is clear or colored, could mean blocked tear ducts, upper respiratory infection, or infected gums. (See also "Eye Problems," page 315.)

- *Scratching mouth with claws.* Something may be caught in the teeth or throat, or there may be painful gum infection, rotten teeth, or an abscess.

- *Scratching head with hind feet* could be due to ear discharge, fleas, mange mites, ear mites, ringworm, ear infection, or tumor.

- *Shaking head.* See "Scratching head" above. Could also be an inner ear, semicircular canal problem, or brain problem.

- *Stumbling, staggering, or tilting head* could be serious and should be reported double quick. See "Scratching head" and "Shaking head" above. Also check the pupilary reflex and relative size of both pupils (see "Eyes" above).

- *Licking genitals or "scooting" on rugs,* and the like means irritation and/or itching. Check stool (see below). Have veterinarian check stool sample for parasites or check cat for possible anal gland problems. Also watch urination habits for symptoms of feline urologic syndrome (see "Urine" below and see "Feline Urologic Syndrome," page 331).

- *Urine and urinary habits.* The urine output should wet at least a tablespoon of litter each time the cat goes to the box. If your cat voids a smaller amount or nothing at all and runs frequently to the litter, take him immediately to the veterinarian to check for feline urologic syndrome (FUS) and/or bladder stones. If he voids a normal amount or more than normal and runs frequently to the box this could signal kidney disease or diabetes, especially if the urine is very light yellow or almost colorless and if you also note copious drinking. (Urine should be yellow.) Take him to the veterinarian immediately. To check color, cover the litter with a white paper towel. If the urine turns it pink, there is blood in the urine, which is very serious, and the cat should be taken to the veterinarian at once (even in the middle of the night). Very light yellow or clear usually means kidney problems as mentioned above. If your cat starts his urination in a squatting position but then gradually raises his rear until, sometimes, the stream shoots out over the edge of the box, this could mean arthritic hips, stress in the environment, such as a new cat, or, more seriously, straining because of urinary infection and possible blockage. Report to your veterinarian. Urination outside the box is almost always caused by a physical problem: early FUS or, in aging cats, weak bladder, general debilitation or arthritis. (See "Special Litter-Box Considerations for the Elder or Ailing Cat," page 87.)

- *Stool.* The cat should pass stool once or twice a day. It should be formed (long) in two or three pieces, no more, and it should be softly firm and dark brown. Note any deviation. Diarrhea is sometimes not noticed because the cat covers it and mixes it with the litter. Check the stool once a day, and note the frequency, color, texture, and smell. A too-strong smell can mean intestinal infection or imbalance. Flatulence means imbalance or irritable bowel syndrome (see page 365). Diarrhea can be caused by dairy products in some cats. Many cats get diarrhea when taking oral anti-biotics (see page 266). If stool is not passed every day or is hard or appears in balls, note this and see the section on constipation (page 293). Check for excess shedding (see below), lack of dietary fiber, dehydration, kidney disease, hyperthyroidism, diabetes, or irritable bowel syndrome.

- *Coat.* Except in the shedding seasons (February through April and September and October) shedding should be moderate. Skin should be clean, free of parasites and scabs, hair free of dandruff and oil. Note any deviation and look for further symptoms.
- *Bad smell* can indicate serious problems—find the source of the problem at once. Usually caused by germs and putre-faction, infected or dirty ears, intestinal blockage, impacted anal glands, worms, dirty teeth, licking coat with dirty mouth, or soil on the fur near the anus.
- *Twitching skin* can be caused by dry skin due to indoor heating during the winter months or from lack of fat in diet or vitamin E deficiency. Examine the cat for scabs and parasites. Twitching skin can also happen because of heart disease or brain problem.
- *Temperature* should be 100.5 to 101.5 degrees F. The cat's temperature fluctuates more than ours does. Excitement and stress, as well as infection, can cause it to go up. A low temperature is usually more serious than a high one. (See "Taking the Temperature," on page 229.) If you learn to do this at home, you will be able to give valuable information to your veterinarian.
- *Dehydration* is sometimes difficult to judge. There are several signs you can look for such as lack of appetite, constipation, and/or frequent drinking. Sitting with the head over the water dish, the coat separating into "clumps," a pinched look to the face, or eyes that appear to be sunken are signs of dehydration. This is an indication of serious illness, usually high fever, and is often the last state before

collapse. To test the skin, grab a handful of skin at the neck scruff. Grasp it tightly; then let go suddenly. It should flatten back into place at once. If it stays in a pinched position or if the cat shakes himself to get it to flatten back into place, he may be dehydrated. Dehydration makes a cat feel nauseous and headachy.

- *Breathing* that is shallow and fast often happens when the cat is purring and means nothing. On the other hand, shallow and fast breathing can also be caused by heat, stress, fear, fluid retention, or tumor in the chest or abdomen, pain, or nausea. Breathing with the mouth open is usually a very bad sign.
- *Pale whitish ears, gums, or tongue* can mean anemia or shock or a weak heart. The veterinarian will want to see the cat and will probably suggest some tests.

It is hoped that a real emergency situation will never arise for you and your cats. After all, they are eating high-quality diet, which will keep resistance to disease and stress very high. And your annual visit to the veterinarian for teeth cleaning and checkup will help keep you a jump ahead of any challenge to your furry friend's health.

Repeated Infections

If a cat seems to be forever coming down with something—either the same health problems over and over or different problems—this is a sign that the immune system is weak and that there is something very much amiss in the basic body functions. Deeper diagnosis is required. The veterinarian will probably request that you let him run some blood tests or perhaps take X rays or an EKG. At this point the modern owner might begin to question whether the medications he's been giving his pet are treating the cat or just covering up symptoms temporarily. This is the sort of situation that prompts many owners to seek some sort of natural or holistic health care or advice.

This is exactly what happened to sweet-tempered Apollo Kulp. After four successive and random infections, Apollo became short-tempered. He began growling at his companions and sulking in corners. Apollo's veterinarian suspected feline leukemia or some other blood disease. Happily, the tests came back negative for leukemia but revealed liver inflammation, which explained Apollo's low resistance. After homeopathic treatment was begun and the owner bolstered the immune system by upgrading the diet, skinny, lethargic Apollo gained weight and became his old easygoing self again.

The Therapeutic Environment in the Veterinary Clinic

Now that you have a better idea of when your cats need medical attention, let's examine where you are taking them and take a look at how you, the owner, can lend your support to enhance and augment the veterinarian's treatment.

Ask cat owners what their cats do when they are scared, and every time they'll tell you, "They run under the bed, into the closet, behind the bookshelf, or in back of the couch." *Under, into, behind, in back of*—they hide, they find a safe nook. A high-strung cat will hide out of sight for what seems to us to be the flimsiest of reasons. The mere sound of the doorbell is enough to send some purebred types scurrying. Fear of the unknown is the cat's worst fear. To run and hide when frightened is natural to a cat. A declawed cat develops this instinct to an even greater degree.

Nevertheless, most veterinary clinics lump all small animals together as a group. Those clean, airy, open cages that are heaven for dogs are a nightmare for cats. Far from providing the secluded nook they crave, they are trapped in plain sight; everyone can see in and the cats are forced to see out. They are in a constant state of apprehension because of all those new sounds; those strange people doing strange things; and those frightening, sharp smells. Caged, they cannot run away, and there is no place to hide. Worse still, in the absence of any other alternative, hospitalized cats often seek the limited shelter behind the low sides of their litter box. All day and all night they crouch there, tense and ready, expecting to be attacked, adrenalin pumping, vital energy burning away.

What a shameful waste! After a few hours of this, cats are worn to such a frazzle that any loud noise or unexpected movement is quite enough to cause spontaneous urination or defecation, which immediately adds one more stress to their already wretched state. Think how terrified they must be to hide in the litter box. Then add to that the horror of having to smell excrement or urine on themselves.[1]

Some cats are held like that for days. If you were the doctor, how would you like to try anesthetizing a cat in the morning after the cat had just spent a night like that? How would you like to treat a cat in the clinic over a number of days in this stressful situation? If the cat were ill with some disease, what odds would you give for recovery? If she wasn't ill when she came in, she probably would be before long.

Anesthetic is a stress factor that can be isolated—it's a physical thing. Other stresses are no less potent, but unfortunately they are less solid and more difficult for the doctor to isolate, measure, and control. But suppose we could pinpoint and isolate even a few more of those additional stresses, then turn them around or simply eliminate them? Think what that would mean in terms of saving the patient's vital energy, calories, and adrenalin. It would widen the margin of safety, raise the percentages in the cat's favor, and increase the chances for survival on a borderline case.

Although we cannot change the fact that a hospitalized cat is going to be surrounded by many frightening unknowns, it is a relatively simple matter to cushion the shock and soften the harsh realities. To begin with, lay a large paper bag (no handles, please) open in the cage, providing the cat with a little cave—the means of gratifying his instinct to hide. Dr. Rowan sometimes draped a towel over the front of the cage for high-strung cats. In his clinic, soft classical music was played to mute the other noises a bit, and large, healthy plants were hung in every room to add their oxygen to the air. No smoking was allowed, even in the waiting room, and cage doors were opened and shut with care, never slammed.

If the veterinarian treats both dogs and cats, it is not unusual to see them mixed indiscriminately in adjoining cages. But stop and think—the great majority of city cats have never even met a

[1] See also the chapter "Maizey's Story" in *It's a Cat's Life* by Anitra Frazier with Norma Eckroate (New York: Berkley Publishing, 1990).

dog. Dogs caged at the veterinarian's clinic usually bark and yap —at least some of the time. This is quite normal for a dog. But just imagine poor, terrified Muffy trapped in her small cage. She cannot see the animals who are making those sharp, loud sounds, but they certainly seem close. She doesn't know why the dogs are barking, but she assumes that they are after her and that any minute they will succeed in breaking through and into her cage to kill her. She cowers lower into a corner, trembling, ready to fight and die. If Muffy wasn't ill when she arrived, she certainly will be before she leaves. Her resistance will all be used in fighting stress. To help achieve a therapeutic environment, dogs and cats should be housed in separate rooms or, at least, as far away from each other as possible.

In many veterinary clinics and offices, cats are forcibly restrained while medical procedures are performed. The usual method is to hold the cat firmly by the scruff of the neck and the hind feet and stretch the animal out. I know of one veterinarian who was so afraid of being bitten that he insisted that all cats be held like this even for a simple yearly examination. It is a terrifying experience even to watch such a scene. Think of the trauma the cat undergoes. To put it plainly, the cat expects death. "Why else," the cat reasons, "would they hold me this way—stretched vulnerable, unable even to swallow properly?" Again, what a stupid waste of the cat's vital energy. I advise all my clients to insist on being present during all examinations and nonsurgical procedures. Dr. Rowan could do an entire examination, including shots, palpation of the abdomen and anal glands, listening to the heart, clipping the nails, cleaning the ears, taking the temperature—everything— without the cat ever realizing that the exam had even begun. The assistant who held the cat distracted him or her with loving words and expert petting and scratching. Add to this the catnip they always sprinkled on the table at the end of the exam and you can see why cats did not become tense when visiting his office and hospitalized cats rallied quicker and recovered easier even after complex procedures. Their energy wasn't wasted.

Many veterinarians use anesthetics for such routine procedures as X rays and taking blood. Besides being a major stress, the anesthetic actually changes the chemistry of the blood that you're trying to analyze. For this reason, more holistically oriented veterinarians avoid tranquilizers whenever possible. They employ veterinary technicians and helpers with the knack of gaining the cat's attention and trust as they hold the cat still gently but firmly while the vet does these procedures.

You can spot the holistically aware veterinarian by studying the assistants and technicians in his office. If a therapeutic environment is being maintained, they will be trained to respect the cats' physical bodies even while the cats are under anesthetic. After surgery, anesthetized animals will be carried directly back to the comfort of their quiet cages and the security of their paper bags—never left exposed on the cold table or laid aside on the floor until it is convenient for someone to transport them back. Be sure your veterinarian provides a nice thick pad of newspaper between the patient and the cold metal cage floor or, even better, a towel on top of the newspaper. This prevents hypothermia, a dangerous lowering of the body temperature, which is a serious threat following the use of any anesthetic or tranquilizer.

In a properly run veterinary clinic an animal should never be lifted—awake or asleep—by the scruff of the neck without supporting the hindquarters. Beside the fact that the haunches and pelvis are by far the heaviest part of the animal and therefore must be supported, such action has no part in the attitude of respect we hope to find in a veterinarian and his assistants. Lifting cats by the scruff may be only a minor trauma to the cat's body, but lifting carefully and with respect is, after all, very easy to do.

In a therapeutic environment cats are made to feel that they have a say in what happens to them. A greeting is given before they are picked up and handled. An explanation is given before a procedure is done. The cat will pick up the attitude of respect and love and respond with greater cooperation. Dignity will be preserved, and dignity is very important to a cat. If a liquid medication is accidentally spilled or smeared on the furs of the cat's face or ruff, it should be sponged off at once. I have seen fastidious cats distressed by their soiled condition to such an extent that they ripped chunks of fur out by the roots in a desperate attempt to rid themselves of spilled medication that had hardened on the hair. Choose your veterinarian carefully.

Choosing a Veterinarian

Choosing a veterinarian can be a lot like trying to find a television repairman or a jeweler to fix your watch. You know absolutely nothing about the inner workings of television sets and watches so you feel very much at the mercy of the repairman. Usually all you have to go on is someone else's recommendation. Unfortunately, I have found that most people recommend a veterinarian not because they have any rational method for judging, but simply out of psychological need. Their beloved pet's very life may one day be at stake, and they desperately want reassurance that they have indeed chosen the right veterinarian. So, the more people they can get to agree with them and to use the same veterinarian, the more secure they feel. They go about trying to convince all their friends and neighbors that their veterinarian is the very best and that everyone should use him and no one else. Their judgment of the doctor is actually worth very little as it is based on their own psychological need and not on fact. Your judgment is probably a lot better than theirs, so gather your own evidence and make your own decision.

The time to begin searching for a veterinarian is certainly not during a crisis. Begin making inquiries at your leisure, and when you find a new veterinarian you want to try, take the cat in for an examination.

Over the years I have met many veterinarians. Some were brilliant diagnosticians, some were skilled surgeons, some were gentle and sensitive, some combined many skills. Some were realistically aware of their strong and weak points and were very relaxed about recommending a talented colleague to perform any procedure if they felt the job could be done better by someone other than themselves.

It is important to be consciously aware of what a veterinarian is and what he isn't. Allopathic veterinarians (those who are trained at the average veterinary schools) do not study health; they study disease. They do not study nutrition. Their training is not focused on prevention but, instead, on treating the problems that occur after the cat's health has already broken down. They are trained to effect that treatment with various drugs, chemicals, and surgical procedures. Unless they elected to take a specialty in feline nutrition, most vets' training included only about two hours in that subject during their eight years of study.

If you are holistically oriented, you are used to building health, your own and your pets', through nutrition, supplements, stress management, visualization, exercise, and so on. When humans become sick or injured, we have an ever-increasing range of health-care professionals at our disposal: chiropractors, homeopaths, acupuncturists, nutritionists, stress management experts, and many others.

While many traditionally trained doctors will dismiss these new insights into health and healing, an increasing amount of evidence leads the wise owner to be open to many different healing methods and to use those that feel most comfortable to him. The veterinarians I work with are open to and frequently encourage therapies such as acupuncture, homeopathy, chiropractic, herbs, nutrition, behavior modification, stress reduction techniques, interspecies communications, homeopathy, and the use of visualization.

For people who can't locate a holistic veterinarian nearby, I suggest finding a veterinarian at a distance who practices holistically and is willing to have your cats as "long distance" patients. I have worked with holistic veterinarians on this basis with great success. Then you must secure the services of a local veterinarian to do hands-on examination, diagnosis, and therapies. See "Holistic Professionals" page 187 for guidelines on selecting and consulting with a holistic veterinarian and other holistic professionals. The Appendix gives information on organizations that compile lists of holistic veterinarians.

Your local veterinarian must be a diagnostician and surgeon, a person who likes to handle cats and who has a reputation for getting along with other veterinarians. The facility should be clean, well-equipped, and well-staffed with loving people. Tell the veterinarian that your cat is the patient of the holistic veterinarian who is at a distance and that you would like him to act as the local consulting veterinarian and perform hands-on examination, diagnosis, and therapies. Be clear with him that you and your holistic veterinarian are open to allopathic medicine when it is absolutely necessary but that you will always want to double-check with your holistic veterinarian before giving the go-ahead to give any drugs to your cat. If he is open-minded and willing to work as a consulting veterinarian and you feel good about him, you've found your local veterinarian. If not, persevere until you find someone you feel confident about.

If your cat is ever hospitalized, I suggest you make a list of requests as to how your cat is handled, such as (1) doctor and staff announcing their presence before touching the cat, (2) supporting the cat's hindquarters when lifting him, and (3) keeping the cat warm if he is anesthetized by always providing plenty of padding under him and using a heat lamp or a hot water bottle that you will provide if necessary.

Veterinarians are people, too; they have morals and standards. Simply look your veterinarian in the eye and calmly explain that you are aware that certain practices of which you disapprove are common in some clinics. Say that, because you have no idea whether any of these things is ever done in his hospital, you need to bring these questions out into the open rather than taking anything for granted. That way you won't be shocked or upset just at a time when you need to be giving calm and reassuring vibrations to your cat. If the veterinarian also looks you in the eye and does not get all touchy and insulted but calmly gives you his word that your cat will be treated as you wish—specifically on all the points just mentioned—chances are it will be done so.

To be sure there is no change in the way your cat is handled, I advise owners to double-check and go over these specific requests again each time your cat is left at the clinic and certainly if your veterinarian takes on an associate or employs a new helper. I also spring surprise visits to double-check. Remember that different people have different priorities. Your reminder of what your specific priorities are will ensure your cat's comfort and safety and avoid misunderstandings. I like to have my own requests written out on my cat's cage card. Then there can be no mistakes.

Visiting Rights

For me the veterinarian's policy on visiting hospitalized cats is a crucial question—I could never leave my cats in any facility where I could not personally pop in and check on them as often as possible. When checking out a new veterinarian find out whether or not he recognizes the psychological value of moral support by the owner for a sick cat. Ask if he allows visiting privileges. There may be certain hours on certain days when no visiting is allowed because surgery is going on or some other procedure is in progress, but, other than that, most veterinarians will encourage the owner to visit.

The Second Opinion

You will also have to ascertain the veterinarian's attitude about getting a second opinion. Whenever there is a question of a disease or any malfunction in the cat's body not responding to treatment, do not accept a verdict of "chronic" or "incurable" without seeking a second opinion from someone outside your own vet's office. This could be applied also to any case where surgery is suggested as long as the delay would not be considered dangerous to the cat.

Another instance when a second opinion is a good idea would be if you, the owner, feel that something is not quite right with your cat—perhaps the symptoms are slight and vague. If your own veterinarian can find nothing amiss but your worry persists, seek another opinion. You just might be very glad you did. No one knows your cat better than you and therefore no one is better able to judge when your cat's behavior is abnormal.

I have several times over the years confronted veterinarians with my intention of taking a cat of mine or one of my clients' for a second opinion. Most times the response is the same. The doctor digs out the records of medications given, treatments tried, pulls out any X rays or test results, slips it all into a big envelope, and, as he hands it to me, he usually says, "Let me know what he says, I'd be interested." Most doctors are always ready to learn something new. I've often heard doctors conferring with other veterinarians by phone.

I can't work with a doctor who harbors a sense of competition or defensiveness over my desire to see if two heads might be better than one. More than once I've brought back to a veterinarian a general confirmation of everything he said but with some little helpful suggestion about possible dietary treatment or physical therapy to try. Once you have the second opinion, be sure to give your doctor the information so your cat can benefit from the combined knowledge.

A last word about treatment: If the medicine your veterinarian prescribes doesn't seem to be doing any good, don't hesitate to call him at once and say so. Every living creature is different. There may be allergies and sensitivities to consider, or there may be a second disease lurking behind the primary one. Before you decide to change veterinarians, be sure you have given your present doctor every bit of information you have to help him diagnose accurately. Also, every medicine has some known side effects. If your cat has an adverse reaction such as diarrhea or excessive sleeping or panting, let the doctor know. The veterinarian is not a psychic; you have to call and tell him. He may just say that your cat's reaction is normal in the circumstances and thus put your mind to rest. The veterinarian is best equipped to judge whether or not to continue treatment or change to a different drug.

Holistic Professionals

There are as many definitions of "holistic" as there are holistic health-care givers. Some of the goals your holistic veterinarian and other holistic professionals strive for are:

1. *Treat the cause, not the symptom.* Most of what the traditional veterinarians call disease is thought of as a symptom by the holistic professional. For example, tumors are a symptom of (a) the body chemistry being out of balance; (b) an invasion by environmental or food chemicals; (c) congenital predisposition; (d) an immune system weakened by vaccines and/or steroids and/or poor diet and/or all cooked food; and (e) all or some of the above.

2. *Primum est non nocere: Above all, do no harm.* Not to use drugs, chemotherapy, or anything that will do harm to the system.

3. *Treat the whole animal.* Address body, mind, and spirit using as many complementary therapies as necessary and practical. For example, the *mind* and *spirit* are treated by stress reduction, Bach flower remedies, homeopathy, affirmations and visualization, and demonstrations of love. The *body* is treated with homeopathy,

187

herbs, exercise, shiatsu, acupuncture, nutrition, orthomolecular therapy, and, on rare occasions, even surgery and antibiotics.

Owners who practice holistic health care for themselves are usually the ones who seek the same advantages for their feline friends. Increasing numbers of veterinarians are responding, each in his own way and at his own pace. Owners should keep in mind that we are all on the same team, sharing the same goal of upgrading health care for animals. The aware owner knows that the modern natural therapies encourage a much greater participation and involvement on the part of the patient or, in this case, the owner. The responsibility no longer rests exclusively on the shoulders of the veterinarian, nutritionist, or homeopath, but is shared equally by the owner and whichever health-care practitioners he or she is consulting. (I use the word *practitioners* in the plural because I have found that one of the keys to success is the utilization of more than one source of information.)

This increased owner involvement is as it should be because no one, no matter how skilled, is in a better position than the owner to build the animal's health and to observe and evaluate the patient's response—physical, emotional, and mental—to any therapy being used. The successful resolution of any problem will depend upon teamwork with much give and take on the part of all team members. This attitude of mutual respect and enthusiasm always results in new knowledge for every member of the team. It's a beneficial side effect cherished by all members of the holistic community.

When an owner first begins the journey on this particular path, he will encounter new attitudes and find that emphases are differently placed. These attitudes of respect, openness, encouragement, and mutual support are all predispositions that the health-conscious owner has greatly desired and has long been seeking, but nevertheless, they are unfamiliar and, like the cats, we humans often feel insecure in a situation where there are bound to be many unknowns, puzzles, and surprises. After many years, I still feel insecure, but I have learned that insecurity is not necessarily a negative quality; it keeps me on my toes. However, too much insecurity interferes with efficiency. So, I have found a few ways to cut insecurity down to size:

1. Minimize the need for crisis intervention by practicing prevention. Follow the suggestions in this book, including a homeopathic evaluation. (See "Homeopathy," page 244.) You can raise the level of your cat's health and learn a lot in the process.

2. Keep a weekly health log on each cat. Almost all health problems begin long before the owner realizes that anything is going on. The checklist of symptoms on pages 173–78 will give you some idea of what to include in your log. If you see three or four deviations from the norm in one week, you can call your veterinarian, homeopath, or other holistic practitioner, and together you will have an excellent chance of nipping a potential health problem in the bud.

3. Find experienced advisors. "When the student is ready, the teacher will come" is an ancient yoga aphorism. Make an effort to find advisors and teachers (one of whom is a veterinarian) well established in one or more of the holistic healing arts of homeopathy, herbalism, orthomolecular nutrition, home-nursing care, and/or acupuncture. There are several around the country who will consult by phone. They charge for their time, just as if you were making an office visit, and most cannot take time to answer letters. The standard procedure is to write down your questions until you have several, and then call and request a consultation. You will then be given a time that is mutually convenient when you can call, ask your questions, and receive information and suggestions. Some of these veterinarians will agree to guide the treatment of your cat by long-distance phone consultation. If the advisor you are calling has written a book, it is both sensible and practical to read the book first.

4. Do away with as many unknowns as possible by increasing your knowledge. There are several ways to do this. I can give you some idea of how I go about collecting information and some guidelines I have discovered along the way, but you must make your own evaluation of my sources and of any other information that comes your way. Only you can tell if it feels right for you and the cats you love.

Sources of Information

1. *Bibliographies.* At the end of most "how to" books like this one there is a list of source books where the author found useful information. Consult these books and, in turn, check the bibliographies in them. If you see the same book listed in several bibliographies, that should make you especially curious to read it.

2. *Lectures, workshops, seminars, and classes.* Get acquainted with holistic health periodicals and schools. Your health-food store probably has one or two free magazines in which lectures, classes, and books are advertised. Health-food stores, herb shops, and bookstores that carry holistic health titles often have bulletin boards. Don't limit yourself to courses and books on animals.

3. *Personal observations*

- New knowledge is never a waste of time; no information is "useless."
- Nobody's perfect. No source of information is perfect. Because someone knows a lot and helps you a lot does not mean that he or she knows everything. Conversely, even if you disagree with or dislike a person or book, you can still learn something from them.
- Test and evaluate for yourself and collect other sources of corroboration or disagreement.
- Discover people's strong points. Become aware of the categories in which each of your sources of information is usually the most reliable. For example, ask the surgeon about anesthetics; do not ask the surgeon about nutrition.

Hospitalization

If it turns out that your cat must be hospitalized, prepare his cage in the following manner: If the cage is metal, as most of them are, remember that cold metal will rob your cat's body of heat. This is especially debilitating if the patient is elderly; if he has diabetes, kidney disease, liver disease, or cancer; or if he is to be anesthetized. To prevent hypothermia, be sure there is a nice thick pad of newspaper, at least six sheets of thickness, under your cat. Put his towel on top of this. Then take a brown paper bag, open it, and turn down a cuff all the way around the top. Do it slowly and carefully so that it doesn't tear. The purpose of the cuff is to hold the bag open. Lay it inside the cage, thus providing a nice little cave of darkness and security the cat can crawl into if he wants to hide. The object of this is to prevent a frightened cat from cowering inside the litter box. It's nice to lay a small piece of clothing you have recently worn in the bag for your cat to snuggle with. Your scent will provide reassurance in a situation that is new and strange. Put fresh hot water in a hot water bottle, cover it with a sock, and slip it into the bag too. Your object is to cushion a stressful situation in as many ways as possible. You've provided extra warmth with the hot water bottle; an illusion of security and an option of hiding with the paper bag; and your dear, familiar scent with your sock.

Take your leave casually. Here is an ideal time to use the ritual phrase that you always use when leaving your own home to signal your cat that this will be a short absence on your part. (See "Communicating 'Good-bye'—and 'I'll Be Back,' " in Chapter 1.) For myself, when leaving in the morning for the day's work, my last words are always "See you later, Alligator," as opposed to "Okay, Purr, I'm leaving you in charge," which is what I say if I'm going to be away for the weekend or longer.

If a cat of mine is going to be anesthetized, I always request that the vet order a heating pad to be put under the towel and turned on low until the patient is past the recovery period and fully awake. Always cover the pad with a towel; they all have "hot spots." Anesthetic lowers body temperature and an outside source of heat can mean the difference between a quiet, uneventful recovery and some nasty complications. I advise clients to bring their own heating pad if necessary and to be certain that the vet writes the order for its use on the cage card.

All that is left to do now is to extract an oath signed in blood by the veterinarian and his staff that he will not provide hospital food—which is usually filled with by-products and chemicals—but will use the food that you brought. Chances are either (1) the cat will not be hungry, or (2) the cat will be required to fast preceding some hospital procedure. You may want to provide some special treats when you visit—such as chicken soup or steamed broccoli tops. You know what your cat loves. Discuss it with the veterinarian. Just make sure that, at this time especially, it is top-quality nutrition. No tortilla chips or rum raisin ice cream!

Euthanasia

This part of the book is about courage. It takes a certain kind of courage to adopt an animal knowing as we do that there will come a time when we will have to say good-bye. Our animal friends live shorter lives than we do; it's a fact we all have to deal with.

When first we allow this thought into our conscious mind, it seems a tragedy. While that is partly true, there is another side to this coin. Tragedy can be turned into a triumph. You may lose your friend, but nature has placed you in a position where you can influence and structure the circumstances surrounding your friend's leaving.

Many owners are not aware of the options open to them. Although you cannot stop your friend from going, you can greatly influence the manner in which he goes. There are drugs available that make euthanasia a gentle slide into slumber and then out of the body permanently. The homeopathic patient can be helped through the progression of body changes that precede death by careful prescription by his homeopathic veterinarian (as long as no corticosteroids have been used in the past). Many veterinarians will come to the animal's home to perform euthanasia.

I am a great believer in prolonging life. I will use force feeding, subcutaneous hydration, and all manner of herbs and remedies to help an owner extend a cat's life. As long as the patient seems to be enjoying some sort of comfort or satisfaction, be it eating, sleeping, petting, or warmth, I will continue to help the owner fight for him with everything I know. But when major organs break down there can be pain, inability to breathe, and extreme weakness. The animal experiences not only the pain but also terror because he cannot control his own body. Then there comes a time when the act of prolonging life becomes the act of prolonging death.

My aim in each individual case has been to help the owner judge the time when discomfort begins to outweigh contentment. If the veterinarian and the owner and I see that a time of fear and pain is fast approaching, then we arrange to help our friend escape from the worn-out body before it can cause him any further distress. The key to success lies in gathering information in advance and planning in advance.

Facing this challenge, asking the crucial questions, and making the crucial arrangements all require courage. The courage you need can be found in the love you bear for your furry friend. I can assure you that it is much easier to make as many inquiries and plans as possible well in advance, when your cat is active and healthy, rather than waiting until you are already distraught because of his rapidly failing health.

Smoothing the Path: Planning in Advance

1. Know your veterinarian's euthanasia policies—not every veterinarian has the same procedures. Will he make a house call? Will he allow you or a close friend to be present when the final injection is given?

2. Know your veterinarian's office hours. Discuss with him your preferences and ask his help in finding other veterinarians and/or animal hospitals that will accommodate your wishes and requirements if he should be unavailable when you need him.

Over the years I have tried to improve my ability to judge the correct time. Knowing what signs to look for gives the owner a better opportunity to make the right move at the right time. The better informed you are, the better your judgment will be. If your cat already has a serious illness, you can ask your veterinarian what signs to watch for in that particular illness that will help you recognize that the end is near. Although veterinarians seldom volunteer this information, they will always give it to you willingly if you request it. Below are some general signs that appear during the final stages of many illnesses. If one or two or more of the following symptoms appear, you should inform your veterinarian. The patient may rally, but you should be ready to proceed with the euthanasia at short notice if it is needed.

- *Confusion.* Inability to locate the litter box or inability to get back to his bed.

- *Extreme weakness.* Staggering while trying to walk. Leaning against things. Collapsing to rest before getting to the litter or back to bed.
- *Sitting or lying in the litter box.*
- *Sitting with head over the water dish.*
- *Subcutaneous hydration therapy no longer being absorbed.* Fluids settling in one leg like a thick sock.
- *Body temperature drops below normal (below 100.5 degrees F).* Cold ears and paws; cold legs.
- *Refusing warmth* even though the temperature is below normal.
- *Constant uninterrupted purring* for no apparent reason.
- *Lying or crouching and staring off into space.* Eyes unfocused. Not caring what you do or don't do to care for him.
- *Breathing rapidly through partly open mouth.*
- *Abdomen heaving with each breath.*

The loving owner will remember the death of his pet for the rest of his life. Owners who have the best memories are the ones who make an effort to provide love, approval, and tranquillity during this very important time of transition.

See also "Ginger's Story" in our book, *It's a Cat's Life* (New York: Berkley Publishing, 1990).

9

Home Nursing and Health Care

The Immune System

The immune system is the body's best friend. The natural state of the body is perfect health. We and our cats, in fact all animals alive today, have evolved successfully over the millennia because we have all built up a wonderful defense system to withstand the germs and viruses and other microorganisms that have evolved along with us and are always present. That defense system is called the immune response.

Like any really good friend, the immune response will sometimes make us a bit uncomfortable if it has to do so for our own good. If germs invade the body, the immune system will make us uncomfortably warm, raising the body temperature to make an inhospitable environment for those invading germs. The skin protects us from germs. If the skin is punctured, the immune system will send an extra blood flow to the area, carrying white cells and nutrients to fight the invading germs and repair the broken tissue. This extra blood flow causes swelling and redness. If there were no swelling and redness at the site of the wound, invading bacteria would thrive and multiply unchecked. The pus that sometimes forms at the site of a wound is made up of dead white cells and dead bacteria. It is the proof that the body is waging a fierce battle against infection. Fever, swelling, mucus, pus, diarrhea, coughing, vomiting, or any of those things we have been taught to call disease symptoms are actually, to the holistic doctor, symptoms of health. They are proof that the individual's immune response is strong

195

and alert and is reacting appropriately to a potentially dangerous condition.

Allopathic medicine, that which is practiced by most doctors in first world countries today, tells us that if the cat is coughing up phlegm and sneezing out mucus we should give him an anti-histamine or an antibiotic to "stop the disease." A holistic veteri-narian, especially a homeopath, would explain that what they're really stopping is the cat's immune response, which is doing exactly what it's supposed to do to throw the germs out of the body. He would then prescribe a remedy that would promote the expulsion of toxins. He might also recommend a short fast on chicken broth to speed up the process of detoxification.

Allopathic medicine focuses on the invading germ or virus and tries to kill it with a drug. It is most effective in treating acute conditions, and it can save lives. However, it does nothing to build and strengthen the body's natural immunity; in fact, drugs tend to weaken the immune system while they kill the disease germ so the patient becomes more and more susceptible every time he is treated by a drug.

Holistic medicine, on the other hand, focuses on the many ways of helping the patient's body and mind restore itself to a normal state so the body's own immune system can fight disease as it should. A high-quality diet, herbal preparations, vitamins and supplements, acupuncture, and homeopathy are some of the ways to enhance naturally the body's ability to withstand and fight disease.

All allopathic medications have some undesirable side effects. Some are relatively minor while others can be life threatening. These side effects can range anywhere from destroying bone mar-row or the cells of the liver or kidney to depleting or washing out one or more vitamins or minerals from the body.

Remember when your cat is taking any medication that every cat is different, just as all people are different, and your cat may react badly to one particular type of drug. So if your cat develops some undesirable symptom shortly after beginning a medication, call your veterinarian at once and tell him. It might be a recognized side effect that is not threatening, or it could be a sign that the medication is dangerously toxic to your particular cat. Remember, you are the only one who can monitor your cat's reactions. The veterinarian will appreciate the report of an alert and observant owner.

Here are some of the changes that can signal a dangerous condition that the veterinarian will want to know about at once:

- *Panting, salivating, or swallowing.* Can indicate nausea or poisoning, overload of toxins to the liver or kidneys, or heart problems.
- *Urine changing color, stopping, or becoming copious.* Liver damage or kidney failure.
- *Diarrhea or stool changing color.* Imbalance in intestinal chemistry or liver inflammation.
- *Shallow, rapid breathing.* Pain or internal swelling, possible heart problem.
- *Head tilt, shaking head, stumbling.* Inner ear and/or kidney problem, or possible complications in brain.

I reason that if a cat needs some medication because he is sick, then he must have it. But, once we know what the side effects are, we need not accept them as inevitable. As long as we know *what* they are, we can attempt to control or at least mitigate these negative factors.

When a cat client of mine is given a medication, I always want to know what it is—what family or category it fits into—antibiotics, diuretics, cortisone and other steroids, anesthetics and tranquilizers, or mineral oil. I then tell the doctor what I intend to do in terms of adjusting the diet and adding nutrients or vitamin supplements. I want to be sure that any changes I make do not in any way aggravate the cat's special problem or interfere with the action of the medication prescribed. I'll give more specific information later, both in this chapter and under the specific health problems in Chapter 10.

Stress: A Cat's Natural Enemy

For a good many years now, the role played by stress in diseases of the human body has been a major concern. In cats, the link between stress and illness is even stronger. Cats have a lower threshold of stress than humans have. This means that things not ordinarily stressful to us sometimes can actually be painful to a cat. The cat's sense of smell, for example, is so highly developed as to make ours seem virtually nonexistent by comparison.

Besides the cat's supersensitivity to physical stress such as sharp smells, loud noises, or extremes in temperature, the cat is also extremely sensitive to emotional stress. The loss of a loved one, be it animal or human, often sends the cat's emotions plunging into depression and even beyond, into deep mourning. Such hopeless sadness, if left unchecked, drains the system and leaves the body open to invasion by any germ or virus that happens along.

In the normal course of life, cats can usually handle stress pretty well. But when the cat is faced with multiple stress, extreme stress, or prolonged stress, the body's reserves of energy are drained to a danger point. Cats faced with too much stress over too long a period of time become tense and nervous and then begin to withdraw. I've noticed that families who habitually hold two or three conversations simultaneously and therefore always speak in a shout also have shy, nervous cats who can usually be found huddled away in the darkest corner of a back bedroom closet. Cats cannot feel at ease in a stress-filled environment. It is obvious to them that they are not safe, and they live in a constant state of readiness for the next assault on their senses.

Cats in such situations are faced with prolonged stress that wears on their nerves and eventually leaves them vulnerable to disease. A germ, virus, or fungus that other cats would normally throw off can take hold easily when a cat's resistance has been depleted while dealing with stress.

Stress can also be a trigger that activates any latent disease or lurking pathological condition within the body. When the same condition is repeatedly activated by any stressful situation in a cat's life, it is referred to as that cat's "stress target." When confronted with a feline client who tends to get any particular disease again and again, I always question the owner about what was happening in the household immediately preceding the onset of the disease. Was the family away on a trip and the cat left alone? Did the family have visitors—perhaps young and active visitors? Or perhaps the painters came—moving furniture out of place and causing an excruciating smell?

It's a generally accepted fact that feline urologic syndrome, although caused by an alkaline condition in the urine, is emotionally triggered. However, almost any illness, from upper respiratory infection to foot fungus, can become active if too much stress in the environment lowers resistance to the point where a cat's particular weakness can take hold and thrive.

Granted, there will be many times in the life of the cat and its human family when you must knowingly subject your cat to serious stress. So, to avoid having your cat succumb to an illness, simply recognize stress situations for what they are and then make an extra effort to eliminate or a least cushion all other stress in the environment that you can control.

Our first job is to determine what exactly constitutes stress to a cat, especially a sick or nervous cat, and then cushion or eliminate that stress as best we can. Here's a list of some stresses a cat may encounter, along with suggestions about how to cope with them. In a majority of cases, common sense goes a long way.

- *Any surprise.* Announce your intentions before doing anything—touching the cat, giving medication, and so on.
- *Loud noise.* Caution all visitors to speak in calm and soothing tones. If there is unavoidable noise in another part of the home, put a source of soothing classical music near the cat's resting place.
- *Owner being upset or unhappy.* If you are dealing with a serious problem in your life, accept the fact that you cannot hide your tension from your feline friend, so don't try. Instead, tell your cat how you feel and assure him you're glad he's always there to help you feel calmer. If your source of worry is his illness, bring into your conscious mind positive thoughts of love and constructive plans about how you can make your cat more comfortable and hasten his journey back to health.
- *Change within the cat's environment.* Confine the cat to a small area such as the bathroom where no change is taking place. Or surround your cat with as many familiar things (toys, favorite pillow, one of your sneakers, and so on) as possible.
- *Change to a new environment.* Move the cat into one room

that is already furnished with old, familiar furniture. Have the cat's litter box, food and water dishes, and toys already there. Let him get used to that room before introducing the rest of the new territory.

- *Introduction of visitors.* If your cat is shy, any new person should be seated and should first give eye and voice contact before touching the cat. Then he or she should extend *one* hand only, palm down, *below* the cat's nose level. Allow the cat to sniff the hand before the hand touches the cat. Don't force the issue; let the cat take his own time.
- *Absence of familiar people or being left alone.* See "While You're Away," page 109.
- *Being held down or restrained (during medical procedures such as an EKG).* Keep calm and loving thoughts in your mind. Announce your intentions. Try to feel that what you're doing is an extension of petting. Explain "why" before you begin and again during the procedure.
- *Confinement or caging.* Explain why and tell when you will be back to fetch him. Provide a brown paper bag or small cardboard box in which the cat can hide, as described in Chapter 8, "Seeking Professional Help."
- *X rays, anesthetics, and medications.* For a week before until a week after, add to each meal 250 units vitamin C or 1/16 of a teaspoon ascorbic acid crystals or sodium ascorbate powder.
- *Surgery, catheterization, and wounds.* Give extra supplements (see pages 241 and 271).
- *Preservatives ingested in food, in vitamin preparations, or in hairball remedies.* Preservatives such as sodium benzoate (benzoate of soda), ethoxyquin, BHA, BHT, nitrites, and nitrates affect both the central nervous system and the automatic nervous system. Read labels—even of products prescribed by a veterinarian. Vets can't always keep track of everything.
- *Inhalation of nerve gas given off by some commercial flea collars.* Buy your flea collars in the health-food store. Finicky owners prefer flea collars made from natural ingredients rather than potentially toxic chemicals. See Appendix, "Product Suppliers."

- *Major trauma or fright* such as an accident or being attacked. Give Bach Flower Rescue Remedy (see page 249)—three drops every twenty minutes for four doses; then every two hours for three doses; then three times a day for two days.
- *Noise and drafts.* Create a "snug retreat" (page 240).
- *Extremes of heat and cold.* Use a hot water bottle or an ice pack in the carry case (page 22), and use a snug retreat as described on page 240.
- *Litter-box problems.* Usually, it's not good to have the litter box near the sleeping area, but in the case of a convalescent cat an exception must be made in order to make it easier for the patient. Be extra finicky about keeping it clean—a dirty box is a definite stress. (See Chapter 3, "The Litter Box.")
- *Inactivity.* A sick cat needs rest while recuperating, but the attentive owner will sense the time when a little exercise will not go amiss. The best way to get the circulation going is to encourage the convalescent cat to begin moving about a bit. So, after the patient has gained enough strength, encourage him to walk a bit by carrying him into the next room and letting him walk back to his bed. Easy does it.
- *Sharp smells (tobacco smoke, room deodorizers, or other chemicals).* Try to be aware, and you'll improve your own sense of smell and avoid stress for yourself, too.
- *Obesity.* See "Obesity," page 387.
- *Being soiled by excrement, medication, and so on.* Wipe it off at once before it hardens on the cat's fur. See Chapter 7, "Grooming."
- *Any infection or infestation.* Follow your holistic veterinarian's orders. See suggestions under the appropriate health problem in Chapter 10. Also read the appropriate section in *Dr. Pitcairn's Complete Guide to Natural Health for Dogs and Cats* (Rodale Press).
- *Tooth tartar or cavities.* Dentistry should be done by the veterinarian as soon as the cat is well enough.
- *Pain.* Minimize salt (sodium) in the diet and add one-quarter teaspoon bone meal and one dropperful of cod liver oil to the cat's food. Bone meal is high in calcium, which has proved effective as a relaxant and pain reliever.

The cod liver oil is high in vitamin D, which the body needs to assimilate calcium. Also give homeopathic remedy arnica 6 times twice a day if swelling, incision, wound, or redness is involved. (See "Homeopathy," page 244.)

- *Overfilling the stomach.* It's better to feed too little than too much. See "Fasting" and "Force Feeding" in this chapter.
- *Food too hot or cold.* When in doubt, feel the cat's food with your finger. If you like it, he'll like it.
- *Being unneutered.* Have the cat neutered by a competent veterinarian. See Chapter 6, "Neuter and Spay, It's the Kindest Way."

When caring for a cat who is already ill with a disease—in itself a major stress—minimize other stresses as much as possible in order to save the cat's energy, calories, adrenaline, and vital life force, so that they can be used to fight the disease. It is a gratifying experience for the sensitive owner to be able to raise the odds in a pet's favor in this way, especially when the pet is ill.

To cushion any stress

- Check environment for *all* of the above.
- Provide a snug retreat (see page 240) in a quiet area and give frequent short contacts of attention and love.
- Bolster the cat's system by including antistress supplements (see page 240) in the cat's diet.

Administering Medications

When doing anything to cats—pilling, force feeding, grooming, and so on—it's best to try to indicate to them *beforehand* what you are trying to do. Don't have any secrets; fear of the unknown is the cat's greatest fear. If you can let him know what you want to do, even though he may not like it or may indicate an objection or try to leave, at least he will not become hysterical. If you keep him from leaving and control his objections as you proceed to gently have your way, chances are the whole thing will be over very quickly. He'll come to regard the experience as one of those bizarre acts that owners indulge in from time to time that are, on the one hand, mildly unpleasant and not to be understood, but, on the other hand, neither painful nor threatening. Because there's nothing a cat can do, he puts up with such acts out of the love he bears in his heart for you. After all, you have not been raised as a cat and therefore cannot be expected to be perfect in every way.

I find I can get away with an awful lot and save a great deal of wear and tear on the cat's nerves by making the cat believe that I am "petting" him. If I have to do any touching with the hands— it doesn't matter what the reason really is—if I truly believe in my heart that I am expressing love by doing this thing, then I can convey that feeling to the cat.

Cats do understand that humans are different from cats and have different ways of showing affection. For example, Marshmallow Goodfellow, an abandoned white shorthair, had to take six pills a day during treatment for feline urologic syndrome brought on by bladder stones. Poor Marshmallow had spent his first four years before landing at my place consuming huge quantities of dry food and tuna fish. He was an enormous and fearsome-looking white male whose personality was best described by his name: Marshmallow. His craving for physical affection was so great that he would lift a paw and pat my trousers again and again to get attention and then throw himself on the floor at my feet, roll onto his back, and lick my ankle. When finally picked up and hugged, he liked to wrap his front legs around my neck and hug back, capping the joyful moment by vigorously washing my cheek.

I was very busy during his first weeks with me and never seemed to have enough time to fill completely Marshie's need for affection. Because feline urologic syndrome is well known to be a stress-linked disease, I didn't want him to feel threatened because every time he saw me I started shoving a pill down his throat. I had to condition Marshmallow to believe that petting was petting no matter where he was touched, so I set up a positive association between pilling and petting and love so that he would look forward to the pill rather than fearing it. It wasn't hard. All I did was always assume the kneeling pill-giving position (described later in this chapter) every time I petted him. Then I began to broaden his petting horizons, as it were, by stroking his legs, feet, thighs, and so on, along with all the usual places. Then, because I wanted to give him pills, I even included his teeth, lips, and tongue. He gave me a doubtful look the first time but seemed to accept it philosophically thereafter. When I worked in the actual pilling procedure, that sweet animal accepted it along with all the rest. He looked forward to pilling time with happy anticipation as his own special petting time. And to this day that sweet animal still cherishes the belief that crazy Anitra likes to express affection by petting a pussycat's tongue. You can establish the same petting association with anything you need to do to care for your cat: nail clipping, grooming, and the like. I found it very easy to examine Marshmallow's teeth for tartar after that.

But first, before you begin any procedures, always remember to wash your hands. And, even more important, rinse them. Remember, the cat's sense of smell is many, many times sharper than yours. If someone wanted to pop a small piece of your favorite candy in your mouth, how would you accept it if, just as the hand approached your face, you caught a whiff of chemical or other unpleasant odor. Good grief! Make sure your hand smells only like a hand.

Therapeutic Communication

Cats easily pick up your intentions, feelings, and emotions. So when you're going through all the steps leading up to pilling or wrapping the cat in a towel, or grooming, or whatever, think of each and every step along the way as separate from all the other steps, and fix clearly in your own mind that you are expressing love by doing it. In almost every case, you will be able to find a way to make each separate step feel good to the cat.

As you continue to stroke him, use your own words to convey these ideas:

Tell him the reason for doing the procedure:	"I know how you're feeling . . ." (Describe in detail how his body is feeling.)

and follow with:

Tell him the purpose of what you're doing:	"I'm going to help you feel better . . ." (Describe how you want his body to feel.)

and finally:

Tell him the procedure:	"This is what we're going to do to make you feel better. First, . . ." (Describe each step of the procedure. When you're following suggestions from this book, read them aloud to your cat.)

Using this method of communicating with your cat accomplishes two goals: First, it conveys to the patient some idea of what you're planning. (Remember, cats hate surprises.) Second, describing the procedure to your cat will actually help you to do it better. It's a scientific fact that doing something first in your conscious mind improves your technique.

Wrapping the Cat for Medication

As close as my Priscilla and I are, I always have to wrap her to give her remedies by mouth. Otherwise she reaches up her left paw—Priscilla is left-handed—and keeps pushing my hand away so I'm not able to get the remedy beyond the hump in her tongue and down her throat. I know she really wants to cooperate, and she wishes she could, but she simply can't control herself. Cats are like that. Sometimes, even though they want to cooperate, they need your help.

Wrapping the cat in a towel gives you much more control. Instead of the cat being almost an equal partner in the project, it puts you totally in command. The towel should not be thick, fluffy, or expensive. The easiest towel to work with for wrapping is a bath towel—thin and old.

Here is a suggested breakdown of the steps, but you can break any one of these steps down even further if you like (see Figure 12).

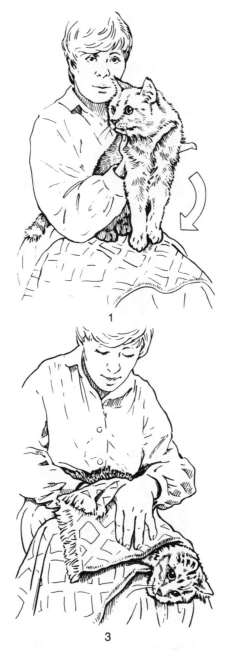

1

2

3

4

FIGURE 12

Wrapping the cat

1. Set up a chair by the table, place the remedy on the table; put the towel folded in half the long way on the back of the chair.
2. Carry the cat to the chair, sit down with your knees together, and drape the towel across your lap. Then stand the cat on the towel facing away from you.
3. Grasp the cat's forelegs up near the chest in your right hand and, with your left hand on the rump, lift the cat up and lay him on his left side on the towel, with feet pointing to the right.
4. Hold the forelegs downward, flat against the cat's chest, fold the left towel flap, then the right *snugly* over the cat's front legs to pin them down securely. Hold the towel flaps secure with the inside of your knee.
5. Medicate the cat; unwrap him, and then give a treat.

Be sure to wrap the cat firmly. You are not doing the cat a favor by leaving the towel loose. Not only is this totally ineffective; but if there's any room for struggle, rest assured that the cat will struggle and thrash and work himself into a much worse state than if the towel were snug. The whole purpose of wrapping is to immobilize the cat.

It's almost a necessity when you wrap a cat to be able to do it swiftly and smoothly so that your motions are a few beats ahead of what your cat anticipates. That way he can't imagine anything dire or terrible; it's already done before he knows it; and it's not terrible at all—it's only snug and secure.

As always, turn the whole thing into a demonstration of love accompanied by much nuzzling and praise. One of my clients asked her black Persian, Binkey, to help her do "a wonderful new trick." Binkey enjoys performing his towel "trick" for visitors. You might like to practice the wrapping ritual once a week to be sure you have the skill whenever you might need it. Start by practicing only steps 1, 2, and 3 until you are at ease with them. Then add one more step at a time. As long as you're doing a lot of head scratching and throat stroking, with a treat afterward, your cat will learn to look forward to a pleasant experience when he sees the special towel come out. This is a perfect occasion to end with a yeast or liver tablet, followed by a nice mutual scratch on the post or a chase after the Toughie Mouse.

Patience is the watchword. Think of each of the steps as a separate accomplishment. Because during practice runs you are not under any pressure to actually get medication into the cat, you can begin by spending the first two or three sessions just stroking him around the armpits and shoulders, which you will later be grasping to lift and turn him over. That way you'll learn how the leg bones feel, where the underarm tendons are, and so on.

I feel sorry for owners who never get beyond stroking their pet's head and back. Cats are very sensual, and finicky owners want to know their pet's whole body—bloomers and inner thigh, foreleg muscles and shins, paws and claws. Explore the bone structure and musculature as if you were giving a massage—your cat will love it.

Giving Pills

Note: This information covers giving supplements or medications in pill form EXCEPT FOR HOMEOPATHIC PILLS. *For methods of giving homeopathic pills, see pages 244 to 249.*

Before you begin, file down the nail on the index finger of your pill-giving hand so you won't scratch the cat's throat when you push the pill past the back of the tongue. The easiest way to give a cat a pill is to kneel down on the floor, with your knees apart, your feet together behind you, and your seat on your heels. Back the cat in toward you. Have the pill ready beside you. With your left hand, palm down, grasp the cat's cheekbones from above and tilt the head back. Hold the pill between the index finger and thumb of the right hand. With your pill-giving hand palm up, use the back of the nail of the middle finger of the pill-giving hand to pry the lower jaw down. Insert the fingernail between the cat's teeth. Then with the index finger push the pill far back down the throat—beyond the hump in the tongue. Let go suddenly, so the cat will swallow with surprise.

Some people like to massage the throat down in a swallowing motion. This is fine, but don't make the mistake of holding the cat's mouth closed. Cats swallow with their teeth ajar, and the tongue must be able to move out through the front of the lips. In fact, you can tell that the cat has swallowed by watching for the appearance of the little pink tongue flicking out and in. Don't hold the head back once the pill is in the mouth. This, too, prevents the cat from swallowing.

Like so many other things, pilling becomes easier the more you do it. Dr. Rowan preferred to throw the pill down the throat in a lovely little arc. He also had a way of lightly blowing into the cat's nostrils to make the cat open his or her mouth. He had developed "pilling" to a fine art.

I found that my own art developed between my trying to teach the cat how to take a pill and the cat trying to teach me how best to give it. I think with this attitude you will definitely progress. With some cats, I use the index finger of my right hand to shove the pill over the tongue hump toward the throat opening. I keep the nail on this finger so short it is practically nonexistent. You cannot use this method if you have anything but the shortest of nails. A nail could scrape against the roof of the cat's mouth, and the mucous membrane is very delicate back there.

Before you try to pill a cat, find out from your vet if it's all right if he takes the pill with food, as some pills must be given before the meal. If it is okay to put the pill in the food, I suggest you use the method I worked out when Ruth Vollbracht was boarded with me while she convalesced from a liver infection. I had to make sure she took all of the medication and didn't just eat around it. I delayed the dinner and then took an unusually long time preparing the meal so Ruth smelled the food but could not get at it. Her hunger became even sharper. I crushed the pill and divided it into two sections. Then I took a quarter teaspoonful of food and hid a part of the pill inside it. I held the bit of food with the pill inside just out of Ruth's reach and asked her if she'd like to have it. When she reached for it, I gratified her. I gave it to her with lots of love and encouragement. This way she wolfed that little bit down, never noticing the piece of pill hidden inside.

Now I pretended that that was all I was going to give Ruth. I started making my own salad. When she asked for more to eat, I appeared surprised that she was still hungry and repeated the process of holding the tidbit concealing the pill, asking her if she was quite, quite sure she still wanted it. Then again I relented and gave it to her with more gushes of love. Once the pill was consumed, I placed the rest of her dinner in the dish on the floor as usual. I didn't mix the pill in with all of the dinner because that might have been just the day that Ruth decided not to finish it. I had to remain in control of those bits of pill until they passed safely down Ruth's gullet.

If this doesn't work for you, you can try the exact same ritual except that, instead of hiding the pill in quarter-teaspoonfuls of your cat's usual dinner, you can mix it with a small amount of some fabulous treat that your cat is sure to gobble up if he gets the slightest chance—baby food lamb, a quarter teaspoon of soft butter, or perhaps a small piece of sardine if you're desperate—but don't stoop to tuna, that's really beyond the pale. Sometimes even this won't work, and you'll have to pill the cat in the classic manner described earlier, or after wrapping the cat in a towel. Or you can mix the crushed pill with baby food meat and bit by bit wipe it off on the pallet just behind the front teeth, as in force feeding (see page 225).

Giving Liquid Medication

When giving liquid medication, you must be careful not to choke the cat by suddenly shooting a stream down the center of the throat. Proceed in exactly the same way that you force-feed a liquid (page 227). Insert the dropper at the corner of the mouth, pointing it down the side between the cheek pouch and teeth and releasing the medication in four or five gentle spurts so the volume of the liquid is small enough each time for the cat to deal with easily. Do not try to give it all at once. Give the cat ample time to swallow each spurt.

Giving Paste or Gel Medications (the Pâté Method)

An example of a paste or gel would be a laxative in a tube. Some vitamin preparations also come in a tube, but I avoid them because most contain benzoate of soda (sodium benzoate or benzoic acid) as a preservative. However, there is a technique for getting unpalatable vitamins or other supplements or some pills down a sick cat's throat that I call the pâté method. You mix the necessary medication or other supplement into about one-half teaspoon baby food meat and vegetables, adding water to thin or baby food barley flakes to thicken. Bring it to a pâté consistency that will hold a pea-size shape and stick to the tip of your index finger. Read the section on force feeding on page 225. Then give the pâté bit by bit the same as when you force-feed.

Giving Eye Medication

Position the cat the same way you do with simple pilling—kneel on the floor and back the cat in between your knees, making sure your feet are together so the cat won't slip out behind you.

Begin stroking the head and the throat—you know your cat's favorite places. Eye medication is usually a salve in a tube. Put a dot of the salve on the tip of your right index finger. (Once again, be sure your nail is short.) Continue stroking the cat's head with your left thumb. Now you want to indicate to the cat that you're going to do something to the right eye. You want him to close his right eye. Stroke ever so lightly near and around the eye. Be soothing. The cat will close the eye. As soon as he does so, stroke lightly and gently over the closed eye from nose to cheek several times, making loving, murmuring sounds.

Position that right index finger against the lower lid so that the dot of salve can be wiped off on the inside of the lower lid by simply rotating the finger inward. Don't do it yet. The eye is still closed—you are still stroking with your thumb and murmuring. On one of those thumb strokes, stop mid-way, place the thumb above the upper lid just above the eye slit, pull the lid a little upward to separate it slightly, exposing the eyeball; rotate your right finger inward, and wipe the salve off on the inside of the lower lid. Then immediately release the thumb, letting the eye close, and stroke the forehead a few times. You repeat with the opposite hand for the other eye—put the salve on the left index finger for the left eye. Dr. Camuti, the famous cat doctor, always medicated both eyes. He reasoned that, because cats will always scratch the eye that was treated, you should treat both to create confusion. If the salve is an antibiotic or some other drug, I feel better if I use a dot of plain petroleum jelly on the healthy eye. The fewer drugs in a cat's system, the better.

Keep all your motions very small. Always move in from the back of the head toward the eye. If your cat sees you poking your finger at him from in front, he will naturally try to avoid it by turning his head and wiggling away. It's a reflex action. Humans have the same reflex.

The whole process is really quite pleasant and tranquil. Smearing the dot of salve inside the lower lid is one of those things that cats can place under the catchall heading of bizarre but harmless human behavior that a loving cat learns to accept and forgive.

Giving Eye Drops

Eye drops are used to cleanse and irrigate the tear ducts, soothing and shrinking swollen tissue. Prepare for giving eye drops by gathering the following equipment:

- Piece of sterile cotton or one-eighth of a paper towel
- Paper towel torn in quarters
- Eye and nose drop formula—see formulas below and indications for which formula to use
- Teacup or small cereal dish
- Medium-size bowl or saucepan

Eye and Nose Drop Formulas

Never try to use human commercial eye or nose drop preparations. Most contain chemicals dangerous to cats. Instead, make your own normal saline solution (see directions below) *or* buy unpreserved unbuffered saline solution for contact lens wearers. (Be sure the saline solution reads *unpreserved* and *unbuffered* on the label.)

212

I. Normal Saline Solution

Use this solution to shrink tissue and open tear ducts:

½ cup boiling water
⅛ teaspoon salt (sodium chloride or sea salt)

- Dissolve salt in water; *cool* and store in covered container in refrigerator. Keeps for a week or so. Before using, heat to warm bath temperature by standing the container of solution in a bowl or pan of hot water.

II. Boric Acid Solution

Use this solution to wash out debris in the eyes:

½ cup boiling water
¼ teaspoon boric acid.

- Combine ingredients in a covered jar. Shake well until powder is dissolved. Cool and store as above with Normal Saline Solution.

III. Herbal Solutions

To shrink swollen tissue and disinfect:

- Add 1 drop golden seal extract to 1 tablespoon Normal Saline Solution.

To soothe red tissue:

- Add 1 drop eye bright extract to 1 tablespoon boric acid solution.

Preparation

1. *Practice the technique.* Cut the cotton ball in half and saturate it with the solution. Squeeze it out a bit so it doesn't drip. Hold it between the thumb and the *second joint* of the index finger. Point the index finger straight down about a half-inch above the sink, and gradually squeeze the cotton so the solution runs down the finger and drops fall off the fingertip one at a time (Figure 13). Practice until you can count three drops and then stop. Then prac-

FIGURE 13

Administering eye drops

tice pointing your finger down at a target that represents the inner corner of the cat's eye (the tip of a teaspoon would be a good target). Practice until you are able to make the three drops land where you want them to land. Have your finger only a half inch above the target; otherwise the drops will hit the eye with too much force.

2. *Warm the solution.* Pour two to three tablespoons of the solution into the cup, and stand the cup in a bowl or pan of hot water. Warm to cat's body temperature (100.5 to 101.5 feels like pleasantly warm bath water). To each tablespoon of solution add one drop of golden seal or eye bright herbal extract.

3. *While the solution is warming, bring the cat to the therapy area.* Take the pilling position (see page 208). Before you give the drops, stroke all around his head, cheeks, forehead, and eyes. As you do this, follow the therapeutic communication technique (page 204). Tell him (a) that you understand his problem (describe how his eyes feel and look); (b) what you're going to do about it (how the drops will cleanse the eyes and nasal passages, shrink swollen tissue, and help him breathe more freely so he can enjoy the smells of his food and his friends again); and (c) in detail all the steps in the procedure below. All of this elaborate explaining beforehand has another very important benefit—it improves your technique tremendously.

4. *Follow the procedure below, explaining everything again as you do it.*

Procedure

Note: *Whenever you do anything involving the cat's eyes, never approach directly from the front because this will cause the cat to turn his head away from the oncoming fingers. Instead, keep all motions close to the head and glide in slowly from the back or the top of the head to whatever position is required.*

Ask your cat to help you by giving you his cooperation.

1. Resaturate the cotton with nice warm saline solution, and, holding the wet cotton between the right thumb and second joint of the index finger, squeeze it out to desired wetness.

2. With your left hand grasp the cat's head from above, placing your thumb and middle finger below the cat's cheekbones.

3. Gently tilt the cat's head back until his eyes are facing up toward the ceiling.

4. Moving the hand around from behind his head, position your right hand holding the wet cotton so the index finger is pointing straight down and the fingertip is about one-half inch away from the inner corner of the cat's eye.

5. Slowly squeeze the cotton until three drops roll one at a time down the index finger and drop into the inner corner of the eye. (If the cat closes his eye, simply keep his head back; put the cotton down and urge the eye open a slit by gently massaging upward on the skin above the eye so the liquid can flow into the eye.)

6. Continue to hold the head back in the tilted position; pick up a piece of paper towel; let the eye close and blot the excess solution with the paper towel before it trickles down the cat's nose or cheek—they greatly appreciate neatness.

7. Release the head. Pet and praise and thank the cat and watch to see if his tongue tip flicks out at the front of his lips. This tongue action indicates the cat has had to swallow because the solution has run down the tear duct from the eye into the back of the throat. The tear duct is open and has been successfully irrigated.

8. If no tongue appears, indicating that no swallowing was necessary because the tear duct is still blocked, repeat the procedure up to three times. Always irrigate both eyes even if only one eye has a problem.

Giving Nose Drops

Read the section above on giving eye drops (page 212) and select the appropriate eye and nose drop formula for your cat's needs. Be sure to practice the procedure first without the cat. Here's the difference in administering nose drops:

To administer nose drops tilt the cat's head so his nostrils are facing up toward the ceiling. Do three or four drops in one nostril; keep the head back for a count of six so the drops will run into the sinuses before trickling down into the throat. Then let the patient relax and swallow. Now do the other nostril. It feels so good I usually do three rounds. Be ready with a tissue. Saline drops break up congestion. If you're lucky, the patient will give a good sneeze. Your cat always appreciates knowing what you're going to do before you do it, so explain the entire procedure to him step by step, making sure to tell him why you do each step and how each step will feel. Explain the results: how the drops will cleanse the eyes and nasal passages, shrink swollen tissue, and help him breathe more freely so he can enjoy the smells of his food and his friends again. As I pointed out, all this elaborate explaining beforehand has another very important benefit—it improves your technique tremendously.

Giving Ear Medication

As a general rule, the less you put into the cat's ears, the better. If your cat's ears are clean, pink, and healthy, a finicky owner can determine on a regular basis that they are indeed staying that way by cleaning only the area that can be seen with the naked eye once a week with a sterile cotton swab moistened with a drop or two of vitamin E oil squeezed from a punctured capsule. Warm olive, almond, or sesame oil will also work. Gently swab all dirt and exudation away from any area you can see; then, holding the swab about one inch from the tip, clean only an inch down into the ear canal. If you see a tiny bit of soft brown wax on the cotton swab, don't panic. All cats—in fact, all creatures including you—secrete wax in the ears. The wax traps the dust. If you didn't secrete wax, dust could blow in and lodge near the eardrum acting as a sort of mute. So don't worry about a little wax. It's when there's a lot of wax or, worse yet, when there's a great deal of hard, blackish-brown wax, that you are allowed a startle reaction and should phone the veterinarian for an appointment. Whatever the diagnosis turns out to be, you will probably be given something—a liquid or salve—to put in the ears. You can also refer to the specific problem in Chapter 10.

You may have to wrap your cat in order to be sure that you get the salve into the ear rather than all over the ruff and whiskers.

I usually medicate ears by simply kneeling on the floor and backing the cat in between my legs (as described in "Giving Pills," page 208). Here again, take the opportunity to make each step feel good, and, before you begin, describe to your cat exactly what you are going to do and how it will help him. Remember that the cat's ear canal is itching and burning. Have the salve or dropper open and ready on the table beside you.

First, make your cat feel a little better by stroking the forehead and behind the ear, thus distracting attention away from the discomfort inside the ear and indicating clearly where you're going to be working so it won't be a surprise. Include the ear itself in your gentle stroking. Next, take hold of the ear down near the base. Don't try to hold the tip—but first stroke through that hold position, letting the ear slip through your fingers. Again, it feels good and distracts your cat from the discomfort. While you stroke, look for the hole down which you will drop the salve. Pick up the dropper or tube of salve, and when you have the medicine ready at the tip of the applicator, take a last stroke, and now gently hold the ear still. Insert the tip of the dropper or applicator tube into the hole, pointing it in and down toward the throat, and press out the prescribed amount of the soothing, healing substance. You are making your cat feel better. Now, withdraw the dropper or tube and swiftly press the hole closed by pressing the ear flap over it from back to front to hold the healing remedy inside. Be consciously aware of that soothing cream or liquid trickling down the itching, irritated tissue. If you can bring these facts to your consciousness and tell the cat in an honest way what is happening, the cat will focus on the relief experienced rather than on the strangeness of your current mode of expressing love. If you very gently massage the area, you can sometimes hear the medicine gurgling around in there, bathing irritated membranes and suffocating the nasty organisms. Tell the cat what you are doing. Finicky owners have very close relationships with their cats and will derive immense satisfaction from the relief they give during an ear treatment.

Now, a word of caution. If you are dealing with mites, the standard medications are always quite harsh. Mitox, for example, which is used only once a week or every ten days (but for six or seven weeks), is quite caustic. So skip the massaging part of the ritual once any mite medication is in the ear. Simply hold the cat's head as still as possible, a little tipped to the side in a position so the liquid can dribble deep into the ear canal and kill the mites. *Don't clean the cat's ears with a cotton swab before or after mite medication— you don't want to irritate the mucous membrane inside the ear in any way.* (See more about ear mites in "Ear Problems," page 315.)

Irrigating Ears or Abscesses

This irrigation technique is used to wash out debris and infection, killing germs and fungus, while soothing and shrinking inflamed tissue.

Irrigation Formula I
(for cleansing)

This formula will cleanse, kill germs and fungus, and reduce swelling.

    1 cup distilled or spring water
    1 teaspoon Betadyne solution *or* 10 drops golden seal extract
    ½ teaspoon sea salt

Irrigation Formula II
(to soothe and heal)

This formula will cleanse, soothe, reduce swelling, and promote healing.

    1 cup distilled or spring water
    ½ teaspooon salt
    1 teaspoon tincture of calendula

Irrigation Procedures

    For ear flush: Use a rubber ear syringe.
    1. Before using, heat the solution to 101 degrees (cat's body temperature) by standing a cup of the solution in a bowl of hot water.
    2. Do therapeutic communication (see page 204), explaining to the cat what you intend to do (steps 8 and 9 below) and what you expect to accomplish. Do this even if you've already irrigated the abscesses or flushed the ears before. The cats love it.

3. Warm the bathtub by running hot water into it and let it stand while you go on to step 4.

4. Prepare one of the irrigation formulas given above. Let the cup of formula stand in a bowl of hot water throughout the procedure to maintain a "warm bath" temperature of 101 degrees.

5. Drain the bathtub and dry it with a hand towel. A warm tub is more pleasant for the cat to stand in than a cold tub.

6. Get the patient and bring her to the nice warm tub. Get into the tub with the cat, take the pill-giving position (page 208), and go through the therapeutic communication procedure again as you proceed step by step.

7. Fill a syringe with the irrigation formula. Stroke the cat's head, neck and body lovingly; then lightly include the area you will irrigate.

8. The possible discomforts that could occur during an ear flush would be if the solution is too hot or cold, if the inside of the ear has been irritated during frequent cleanings with a cotton swab, or if the syringe used is not filled completely and emits a hissing or bubbling sound as air is permitted to rush in or out. This squishing sound so close to the eardrum can be painful to a cat, so make sure the syringe is completely full of solution by holding the syringe with the tip upward and slowly squeezing the ball of the syringe until the liquid starts to come out the tip. Then, holding the ball in the depressed position, quickly plunge the tip back into the solution, release the ball, and allow the syringe to fill all the way.

9. Now, communicating as you go, grasp the ear at the wide part near the bottom. Insert the tip of the rubber syringe into the ear, pointing it downward toward the throat, and express the solution forcefully. Only express about half the fluid. Pull the syringe out and away from the ear *while still expressing fluid*. This prevents the sucking sound of air going into the syringe from happening close to the cat's eardrum.

10. Dry the patient, including wet paw pads. Tell her how well she's done and carry her back to the perch where you found her.

For abscess irrigation: Use a hypodermic type syringe but with a curved tapered plastic tip instead of a needle, or use a baby ear syringe.

1. Follow steps 1 through 7 under Ear Flush above.

2. Communicating as you go, take hold of the drain (rubber tube) if there is one and gently insert the very tip of the syringe into the opening, guiding the tip by pressing it against the rubber. Slowly express the fluid into the abscess pocket. Then gently press the pocket flat, expressing the fluid.

3. Repeat this step two or three times. If there are two openings, alternate from one incision hole to the other. Do not move the tip of the syringe around once you start to express the fluid. You'll be more sure of the cat's comfort if you hold the syringe very still with only the liquid moving. Do not let the stream of fluid be too forceful or it might tickle and cause the patient to wiggle.

4. Follow step 10 under Ear Flush.

Soaking Feet and Cleaning Cuticles

A foot soak is a very handy little therapy to have at your disposal. It can be used to cleanse a wound, take down swelling, help heal a cut, and most important, clean away that waxy brown dirt that can build up around the cuticle.

If a cat has dandruff, feline acne, ear mites, head mites, ringworm, or a mouth problem, he will dig at it with his back claws and the dirt and debris are bound to build up around the cuticle. If you neglect to clean the cuticles, you haven't a hope of getting rid of any of the above problems because the cat will reinfect himself every time he scratches with the dirty claws. That waxy, dirty buildup is very difficult to budge and can cause a nasty toe infection if left where it is.

I have found a practical solution; however, I must caution you to remember that a cat licks his paws more than any other part of his body. *Always wash off thoroughly anything you put on the feet, legs, or claws.*

Equipment to gather:

    2 large heavy ceramic mugs
    Appropriate solution (see below)

Terrycloth towel or two to three dry washcloths
Large bowl of clean warm water

Foot-Soaking Solutions

Ringworm

1 cup warm water
10 drops tincture or extract of echinacea or golden seal

or

1 cup warm golden seal or echinacea infusion (see page 259)

or

1 cup warm water
1 teaspoon Betadyne solution

• Soak each foot four to five minutes in one of above solutions. Do not rinse after golden seal or echinacea soak. If you use Betadyne soak, rinse well and then follow with golden seal or echinacea soak.

Puncture Wounds or Dirty Wounds
(to draw out infection)

1 cup warm water
1 or 2 teaspoons Epsom salts

• For open wound use mildly warm water and only 1 teaspoon Epsom salts. As wound heals you can use warmer water and 2 teaspoons Epsom salts.
• Soak 2 to 5 minutes. Rinse well and follow with soak in 1 cup warm water and 10 drops tincture or extract of golden seal.

Healing Cuts, Punctures, and Abrasions, Swelling, and Irritation

1 cup warm water
10 drops tincture or extract of calendula
⅓ teaspoon sea salt

• Soak 2 to 3 minutes. Do not rinse.

Dissolving Cuticle Dirt

(*Note*: Do not use if foot is injured in any way.)
¾ cup warm water
2 teaspoons dishwashing detergent or Murphy's oil soap
• Soak 5 minutes or more. Rinse extremely well.

Foot-Soaking Procedure

1. Read through the procedure; then bring equipment to therapy area.

2. Bring your cat to the therapy area. The kitchen or bathroom is best since you are using a liquid. I like to stand the patient in the dry kitchen sink, but for a very nervous cat I kneel with him in the bathtub. Kneeling in the tub is easiest if you haven't done the procedure a lot. Take the pill-giving position and stroke your cat all over including the legs and feet. Do the therapeutic communication (page 204), explaining the procedure in detail and what the two of you will accomplish by doing each of the steps. Request his help and cooperation.

3. Fill one mug one-third full of warm soaking solution and place it alongside the foot to be treated.

4. Gently place the flat of your hand against the same side of the cat as the foot to be treated and press, urging his weight onto the foot on the other side.

5. Lift the foot to be treated and place it inside the mug but not necessarily down into the warm fluid.

6. Place the flat of your hand against the cat's opposite side and very gently press, urging him to shift his weight onto the same side as the foot to be soaked. He will naturally lower the foot to support himself and find himself standing in the warm soothing fluid. Tell him he did everything exactly right.

7. Check to make sure the mug's position allows your cat to stand four square, secure and comfortable. If necessary you can shift the mug a bit or allow the patient to adjust slightly the position of his other three feet.

8. If you're doing one of the longer soaks and the solution cools, you can have more soaking solution ready in another mug

that is standing in a bowl of hot water to keep it warm. Every sixty seconds or so, tip the patient's weight away from the soaking foot, lift the foot out of the mug, switch the mugs, and replace the foot in the new mug of warm solution. Shift his weight back over the foot so he will again stand down in the mug. The whole time just continue pointing out how warm and good it feels on his pads and between his toes and what the solution is accomplishing. Now is a perfect time for a visualization (see page 262).

Special Cuticle-Cleaning Technique

1. Read through the following procedure and then do the therapeutic communication (page 204), explaining each step to your cat.

2. Extrude each claw and clip the tip (see "Clipping the Claws," page 146).

3. Extrude each claw again and, using your thumbnail, try to scrape away gently some of the dirt. Be aware of the cuticle; it is very sensitive. Don't scrape the cuticle. Don't try to be thorough; this is only the first stage.

4. Extrude each claw again and soften the waxy dirt by massaging warm olive oil or almond oil into the dirty areas.

5. Wait about three minutes; massage the oil in again; then clean away the softened dirt with cotton swabs. This may be all you'll need to do.

6. If stubborn, hardened dirt still remains, do the foot soak for dissolving cuticle dirt (see page 223). During the five-minute soak, repeatedly extrude the nails and gently massage the solution around in the dirt. Then, once again, clean away the remaining dirt with cotton swabs.

7. *Rinse very well.* No soapy solution may be left on the legs and feet. A final rinse in one cup warm water and one-half teaspoon white vinegar will ensure that all soap is gone. Then rinse a last time in clear water. Or, if the cuticles seem irritated, follow with the soothing calendula foot soak given above.

8. Dry with a fluffy towel or washcloths. Thank your cat for his help and offer a treat followed by a catnip party.

Fasting

Caution: Do not fast kittens, immature cats, pregnant or nursing females, and cats with cancer or diabetes. Do fast an ailing cat but not without consulting your holistic veterinarian. Do not fast the cat while you are away. Do it on a day when you are home and can give extra play and love sessions.

Fasting can be a wonderful tool. Wild animals fast themselves naturally if they become ill. Fasting accomplishes two things. First, it gives the body a chance to "deep-clean" itself and pass off some of the old backlog of wastes that have accumulated and that often show up as dandruff, eye discharge, ear wax, or as arthritis when the wastes lodge in the joints as calcification. Second, the energy that would have been used to digest food can now be put to better use by the body to fight the germs, viruses, or parasites.

Veterinarians say a fully grown cat in good health can fast three to five days without harm. Personally, unless a cat is under a veterinarian's supervision, I don't like to fast more than three days. It's a good health-conscious practice to fast your cat for one day per month.

Fasting does not necessarily mean taking no nourishment at all and drinking only water. I prefer the gentler approach of a liquid fast on High-Calcium Chicken Broth (page 243). Twice a day the cat is allowed all the broth he wants.

Fasting can be used to perk up the appetite for cats who won't eat. If you skip one meal or even two—not even offering food (in other words, don't even let them smell food)—then at the following meal, when you finally do offer food, there is a much better chance that they will eat. That trigger mechanism in the brain that is activated by the smell of food has had a rest.

Force Feeding

Force feeding may become necessary if the cat is very thin and sick and if the veterinarian recommends it. But don't be in too much of a hurry to force-feed a sick cat. Remember, a sick cat just naturally fasts because, during a fast, energy is turned away from digestion and toward healing.

Before resorting to force feeding, you can try a couple of ploys to try to get the cat to eat on his own. Cats won't eat what they can't smell. You may be offering a delicious snack with a very strong aroma, but if your cat's nose is stopped up, she won't be able to smell it. Try giving the saline nose drops (page 216) five minutes before each meal. You can raise the odds in your favor even more if the food you offer is something absolutely stupendous. I always try juicy broiled chicken. It hasn't failed me yet. But be sure to broil the chicken—canned chicken or chicken boiled in water usually won't work. I've also seen excellent results with baby food chicken, lamb, or beef with one teaspoonful of Vita-Mineral Mix (page 55) and one-half teaspoonful of butter added. Never feed baby food meat alone; it can cause constipation.

Understand that these tempting morsels are *not complete nutrition* in themselves. As soon as possible, I mix in one part baby food oatmeal, barley, or creamed corn, and one part vegetable to two or three parts meat. I also slip in a raw organic egg yolk instead of the butter as soon as I can.

The main ingredient needed for force feeding is patience. You must make the experience pleasant for the patient. If the cat is thrashing around or nervous, you can wrap him in a towel first (page 205).

Force Feeding of Solid Food

Prepare a special pâté made up of two parts baby food (High Meat Dinner, beef, chicken, or lamb), one part puréed vegetable, one organic egg yolk or one-half teaspoonful butter, one-eighth teaspoonful feline digestive enzymes (if available), and one part baby food barley. Or prepare a mixture from scratch using broiled chicken and the other ingredients puréed in a blender. Add a teaspoonful of Vita-Mineral Mix (page 55) and an extra teaspoonful of powdered bran, and use just enough water so it will hold together in tiny balls no bigger than a green pea. Pick up a small amount of the food on your index finger. With your left hand palm down, grasp the cat's cheekbones from above and tilt the head upward. Then, holding your right hand palm up, insert the nail of your right middle finger between the front teeth. With the back of the nail press the lower jaw down while you quickly wipe the morsel off your index finger onto the palate *right behind the upper front teeth*. In fact, I use the front teeth to scrape the morsel off my finger. The farther forward you leave the morsel, the easier it is for the cat to swallow it. (This is just the opposite of pilling, where you place the pill halfway down the throat.) Then let go and allow the cat to swallow several times. You must give ample time for swallowing. As long as the cat continues swallowing and licking, don't try to feed the next morsel. This may be all you need to do to get your furry friend started. Sometimes if she has had trouble smelling the food because of a stuffy nose, she will be able to taste the morsel in the mouth and will take over from there. If not, you can gently continue.

It may take ten to fifteen minutes to get a teaspoonful of food down the cat this way, but a teaspoonful is ample for a feeding because a cat sick enough to be force-fed needs to be fed only tiny amounts every four hours. Frequent small meals are easier for the stomach to handle. Feeding too large an amount may throw the patient into a decline because it takes too much energy to digest it—the stomach can't handle it. If the cat vomits it back up, you've lost everything.

Force Feeding of Liquids

> 1. Assemble these items beside where you're going to work:
>   dropper or syringe
>   ¼ cup or so of warm fortified broth in a teacup or custard cup
>   saucer on which to rest the dropper
>   paper towel torn in quarters (cats don't like to have their face or ruff wiped with a big floppy full-size paper towel)
> 2. Become familiar with your equipment:

Dropper: A dropper is always held, carried, and used *tip down, ball up*. If, when you insert the dropper into the cat's mouth, you see that the ball is lower than the tip, STOP. This tells you the cat's head is not tipped back at the correct angle. If you depress the ball now you'll only squirt air into his mouth.

Syringe: Many owners prefer to use a 3 cc syringe (without the needle, of course), which your veterinarian will be glad to give you. To better control the size and speed of the successive squirts, don't press the plunger with the thumb tip. You will gain wonderful control if you place the end of the plunger against the heel of your thumb (the base down in the palm). Try it. Fill your syringe with water and play with it. *Note:* syringes wear out and get "sticky" before long. They are called *disposable* syringes, so keep an extra on hand. To lengthen syringe life, wash only in cold water.

3. Heat the liquid to between room temperature and baby bath temperature.

4. Read through the steps below and while the broth is heating do your therapeutic communication (page 204) with your feline friend, ending by reading the steps below to him and explaining how and why each will be done and asking for his help.

5. Kneel in pill-giving position, with your feet together and knees apart (page 208) and back the cat in between your legs, tucking the tail comfortably around him.

6. With the left hand stroke your cat's head, face, and mouth, explaining again what you're going to do as you do it. Then, with palm down, grasp your cat's face from above, the heel of your hand resting right between the ears, the thumb and middle fingers hooked under each cheekbone.

7. Pressing down a little on the heel of your hand and gently pulling up on the cheekbones, angle your cat's nose upward but not all the way. If you stretch the throat out too much, he won't be able to swallow.

8. Insert the dropper (or syringe) into the corner of the mouth for about one inch, back between the teeth and the cheek, pointing straight back toward the jaw hinge.

9. Using three to six successive gentle squirts (not all at once and not suddenly) empty the liquid into the cheek pouch and give ample time between each squirt for the liquid to dribble slowly back and down toward the throat. When you see the kitty swallow, you can give another small squirt. You and your cat may decide that it's best to let go completely and remove the dropper from the cat's mouth in between each squirt. That's fine. Remember, "slow makes neat." *Caution:* Never squirt liquid down the center of an animal's throat; this could cause him to choke.

10. Use the pieces of paper towel the minute any liquid soils the fur anywhere. Your cat will appreciate a fastidious attitude. When you finish, it is considerate to wipe again with a clean, warm, damp sponge.

11. Carry your friend back to his perch.

12. Pet and praise as he returns his face, ruff, and paws to his own high standards of cleanliness.

Taking the Temperature

Taking the cat's temperature is a useful skill to have. If you can do it smoothly, you'll be able to give your veterinarian valuable information by phone. Since a cat's temperature will often fluctuate, getting higher when she is excited or stressed by riding in her carrier or being examined at the vet's, a temperature taken at home will always be more accurate as long as it is taken correctly.

Here is one of those times when your practice of stroking all over your cat's body is going to pay off. Remember how she arches her back and lifts up her tail whenever you stroke strongly down her back from neck to tail. Try giving a few extra scratches at the end of the stroke right before the tail. She'll keep her tail up longer, and you can lean over and reexamine the anal area and locate the opening where you will be inserting the thermometer.

Now is a good time to do your therapeutic communication (page 204) with your cat, explaining in detail all the steps in the procedure below, asking her cooperation and telling her why getting an accurate temperature will be helpful to the two of you and to the veterinarian. Now you're ready to begin.

Here's what you'll need:

- Thermometer—use a rectal or baby thermometer or one of the new digital thermometers. *Never use an oral thermometer on an animal.*
- Petroleum jelly

Read though the entire procedure before you begin.

It would be nice to have someone else to talk to your cat, encourage her to stand fairly still, and do the back stroking for you, but it's not really necessary. Taking the temperature is done almost exactly the same way you would slide in an enema bottle applicator (see "Giving Enemas," steps 7 through 11, on page 231).

Here are the steps:

1. Begin, as usual, with therapeutic communication (page 204) and read all the steps below to your cat.

2. Shake the thermometer down—holding the end opposite to the silver tip. For safety, stand on a thick carpet if that's possible and shake the mercury down to the tip. The temperature should read below 95.

3. Liberally coat the thermometer with petroleum jelly from the silver ball at the tip to about one-third of the way up.

4. Have the patient standing sideways to you.

5. Stroke down the neck, continuing down the back and giving a few scratches on the lower back right before the tail. Your cat will probably react by pressing his lower back upward and raising the tail.

6. Continue the stroking and at the same time position the thermometer tip about three-quarters of an inch away from the anal opening. Tell your cat everything you're doing as you do it.

7. Continue stroking and angle the thermometer so it points *slightly* upward. Insert the tip plus about one-third of the thermometer into the anal opening, continuing to angle it slightly upward toward the middle back. If you encounter a block with only the tip inside the anus, take the thermometer out and try again in two or three hours. You don't have to succeed the first time. This is one of those techniques like wrapping the cat for medication that is best learned slowly, one step at a time, until you and your feline friend perfect the trick together.

8. After inserting the thermometer partway, just encourage your cat to stand fairly still and face the same way so you can hold the thermometer in. Don't press; just maintain the position loosely. After she readjusts her position and stands quietly again, you may be able to gently and steadily push the thermometer in a bit more, still angling upward, until about three-quarters of the thermometer has been inserted.

9. Keep hold of the thermometer end and wait at least one

full minute; two is even better. Continue stroking her neck and head and telling her how clever she is and how proud you are of her.

10. Slide the thermometer out slowly and steadily. Thank your cat for all her help. Wipe off the thermometer with a tissue or cotton that's been saturated in alcohol. Read the temperature and *write it down with the date and time* to be communicated later to the veterinarian.

Giving Enemas

People seem so awestruck and impressed by the thought that I would give a cat an enema. Actually it's no big deal. As with any procedure, proper preparation is half the job done. If a cat is badly constipated, there is certainly no safer or gentler way to alleviate the problem than giving an enema. Since dehydration frequently accompanies constipation, especially in older cats, the enema has the bonus effect of allowing the body to absorb needed fluids via the intestinal walls.

So, if your cat is constipated and if you and your vet do not want to use the old tube of habit-forming mineral oil preparations or other laxatives, perhaps you will decide to try the gentle enema.

Here's what you'll need:

- Fleet enema bottle for a baby is just about the right size for an average cat. Be sure to *throw away the Fleet enema fluid inside*. It isn't suitable for a cat and can cause kidney damage and death.
- Liquid acidophilus (from the dairy section of the health-food store)
- Liquid chlorophyll
- Distilled or spring water
- Petroleum jelly
- A medium-size bowl
- Towel

Read through the entire procedure before you begin.

1. Play with the enema bottle and get used to it. Hold it on its side as you would when giving an enema, and see how to keep the air bubble in back of the water so you don't squirt air into the cat's rectum (harmless but also totally ineffective). Practice rolling the bottle up like a toothpaste tube as the water goes out. Notice how you have to take the cap off when you're finished to allow air in so the bottle will return to its original shape. Get familiar with your equipment.

2. Into a warm mug or small glass measure one-eighth cup liquid acidophilus, one-eighth cup liquid chlorophyll, and one-half cup distilled or spring water. This makes what I call a "chlorodophilus solution."

3. Stand the container with the chlorodophilus in a bowl of hot water until it reaches "warm bath" temperature (warmer than a baby bath).

4. Transfer the warm chlorodophilus into the empty Fleet enema bottle and stand this in the same bowl of hot water. You may need to refresh the hot water in the bowl if it has cooled.

5. Prepare your cat by doing therapeutic communication with him: (a) assure him you understand how he's feeling (describe his condition in sympathetic terms); (b) describe how you want him to feel; tell him how easily the old stool will slip out, how comfortable his tummy will feel, and that he can take a lovely nap afterward; (c) describe and explain in detail and with love how you are doing to accomplish this—read steps 6 through 13 in the procedure to him and explain each step carefully. Remember, this not only reassures the patient but also greatly improves your technique.

6. Bring the cat, the chlorodophilus, and the bowl of hot water into the bathroom, the kitchen, or a small and pleasant confined space where you can close the door, and, as you proceed, communicate each step again.

7. Coat the tip and sides of the enema bottle applicator with petroleum jelly. Tell your cat why.

8. Place the cat on his side, or, if you have an assistant to stroke the cat and keep him still, you can leave the cat standing up. Obviously he cannot be seated.

9. Stroke strongly down the cat's back several times from the ears to the tail and give a few nice scratches just before the tail at

the base of the spine. This often makes him react by raising his tail and exposing the anal opening.

10. Continue to scratch the lower back and position the tip of the enema bottle applicator one-quarter inch from the anal opening, ready to go in. Angle the bottle as if you will be sliding the applicator in on a *slightly* upward path.

11. Continue scratching the lower back and firmly insert and slide in the enema nozzle. Now hold the bottle in place without starting to squeeze in any fluid while you give the cat a chance to readjust his posture if he wishes and settle down again. If you have an assistant, she should assure the cat he's doing beautifully and also direct his attention toward some pleasurable stroking in back of his ears and/or down the sides of the throat.

12. *Slowly*, taking a count of at least sixty to do so, begin to squeeze the plastic bottle, gradually emptying the chlorodophilus fluid into the cat's lower intestine. I always end up by rolling the bottle up like a toothpaste tube from the bottom toward the top.

13. *Slowly*, again, *slowly* slide the enema nozzle out. (Your assistant continues to stroke the cat's head.) Encourage the patient to remain where he is, retaining the fluid for sixty seconds or even three minutes. During this time he is free to change positions as much as he likes.

14. Place the patient near the litter box and wait for desired results.

After the first 13 steps have been completed, any one of the following may occur:

A. The cat will step into the litter box, give a hasty scratch or two, and pass a mixture of chlorodophilus, hard stool, and soft stool. If all of the above happens except that the stool part is hard only, be sure to continue using one-eighth teaspoon psyllium powder and three tablespoons extra water in the food twice a day as given in the section on constipation (page 293). A teaspoon of chlorodophilus mixture every day would also be wise.

B. The cat will walk away, lie down, clean his anal area, and nothing else will happen. No stool or liquid will appear. This usually means that the cat was dehydrated as well as constipated. All the liquid was needed by the system and is being absorbed. Fine. Let him absorb that good chlorodophilus fluid. Wait an hour or two and try again; or he may pass the stool later. In addition, remember that your cat was dehydrated and give him one or two servings of Chicken Super Soup (see page 244) between meals every day and also ask your veterinarian to take a blood test to check the kidney function, the pancreas, the intestine, or even the thyroid. Periodic subcutaneous hydration (see page 235) will ease the situation considerably even if kidney failure is not the problem.

C. When you insert the nozzle you may encounter a hard mass of stool. Don't force the nozzle. Even if you manage to slide by this hard mass and insert half of the nozzle, and begin squeezing the bottle, the liquid may go into the cat only an inch or so and then run out again onto the towel. (Don't worry, chlorodophilus washes out easily.) If this happens, call a veterinarian at once. The stool has probably become impacted. The doctor will want you to bring the cat in at once to be deobstipated—this means the stool is dug out while the cat is under anesthetic.

While the cat is under anesthetic, take advantage of the situation: Ask the veterinarian to scale the cat's teeth after he's done the deobstipation if the cat is still under anesthetic at that point. At the animal hospital that I use, the veterinarians will, at my request, have one of the interns clean the teeth at the same time that the vet does the deobstipation. If the two procedures are done simultaneously, no additional anesthetic need be given, a definite plus. The less time a cat spends under anesthetic, the safer he is.

In this case, after the cat returns home, continue the psyllium powder and water regimen plus one tablespoon chlorodophilus by mouth, follow the constipation diet, and watch the stool very carefully. If the cat goes more than two days without at least three inches of stool, give another enema before he becomes impacted again. (See also "Constipation," page 293, and "Irritable Bowel Syndrome," page 365.)

Hot Compresses

Hot compresses are used to raise the temperature in an area to kill germs, promote drainage, or relax muscles.

Here's how to administer a hot compress:

1. Use therapeutic communication (see page 204).
2. Place a nice soft towel on a place that is quiet, pleasant, and a convenient height for you to work—like a drainboard, counter, table, or a dresser top.
3. Put two washcloths into a large pan half full of hot water or a specific herbal solution.
4. Place the patient on the dry towel and, as you proceed, go through the communication again.
5. Wring out one of the washcloths. If it's not too hot for your hands, it's not too hot for your patient. Fold it in quarters and place it on the desired area.
6. When the washcloth cools, alternate it with the other one. Continue to explain how the nice warm cloth is helping his body feel better.
7. Dry the area; perhaps run a wide-toothed comb through the fur. Compliment and thank the patient and return him to a comfortable spot.

An herbal decoction or infusion (page 259) can be used to make an herbal hot compress. Simply heat the herbal decoction or infusion and follow the above instructions.

Cold Compresses

Prepare cold herbal compresses the same as hot compresses above, except wave the compress about in the air to cool it before applying.

Subcutaneous Hydration

This is a simple procedure that alleviates the dehydration that occurs in any disease, especially toward the end of a cat's life. Dehydration occurs most frequently in cats with kidney disease, but many other diseases such as irritable bowel syndrome, diabetes, and hyperthyroidism can also produce occasional dehydration, which can then be alleviated by the administration of subcutaneous fluids.

A subcutaneous fluids setup looks exactly like an intravenous (into the vein) setup, but the needle doesn't go into a vein; it's only slipped under a fold of skin (sub = under; cutaneous = skin). Any veterinarian can do this simple procedure in the office, and many owners have learned to do it at home, especially for kidney disease patients. A plain saline solution called Ringer's Lactate is dribbled underneath the skin by means of a small needle. The procedure takes about five minutes and is as easy as giving an insulin injection. A cat kidney patient will need from one hundred to two hundred milliliters of fluid from once a week to twice a day.

I have helped several vets here in New York teach hundreds of owners to do it themselves at home. There is nothing that will so dramatically improve the health, comfort, and well-being of a dehydrated cat as subcutaneous hydration. Knowing how simple it is, I always advise every owner whose cat had kidney disease to include it in their therapy program. The difference it makes is like night and day, and the joyful owner will see this improvement in fewer than twelve hours. Regular hydration and the appropriate diet add weeks, months, and often years to a cat's life. Indeed, the results must be seen to be believed.

One of my first experiences with subcutaneous fluids was with fifteen-year-old Suzi, a little red tabby shorthair. Her story is a good example of what to expect. Suzi had been the hostess with the mostest in her old home. Her owner was a highly emotional person who loved Suzi very much but could not deal with the extra care Suzi needed. She realized that Suzi's disease was terminal and wanted euthanasia to be carried out at the proper time in a proper way, but she knew she wouldn't have the emotional control to be there with Suzi when the time arrived. So, when Suzi entered the final stages of kidney failure, she was left with me for terminal nursing care.

She arrived dehydrated, anorexic, constipated, stiff in the joints, and so weak she couldn't always make it to the litter box. We put her on the kidney diet and began hydration with one hundred milliliters of Ringer's Lactate once a day. That was four years ago. Suzi is nineteen now. She's still a kidney patient and eating the special diet plus frequent treats of watermelon, cantaloupe, and Chinese broccoli. She still receives subcutaneous fluids (now only three times a week). But Suzi doesn't know she's sick. She feels just fine and has taken over as hostess at my place. When visitors arrive, they're greeted by fluffy, perky little red-haired Suzi standing tippy-toe on the antique highchair just inside my door, purring and arching her back to be petted and making everyone feel welcome and important.

Your veterinarian and/or his helper will show you how to set up and use the bottle of fluids, the tubing, and the needle. Arrange to have two or three "Sub Q" lessons, ideally with two or three different teachers (for example, the veterinarian, his technician, another owner). That way you can learn everybody's helpful hints. Here are mine:

Helpful Hints for Giving Subcutaneous Hydration

1. The fluid bottle can be suspended from a plain wire hanger, a drawer pull, a coat hook, or an "S" hook from the hardware store. Fluids should be three to four feet above the kitty.

2. Play with your equipment. Practice turning the flow valve on the tubing off and on and moving it this way and that along the tube so you can pinch out any crimp in the tube. Practice with an old number 18 or 20 needle on the leg of your slacks. Pull up the slacks away from your thigh and insert the needle into the "tent" you have formed (see step 6 below). Learn to push one-half of the needle into the "tent" very swiftly. Learn to slide the rest of it in and to hold fabric (hair) and needle in place with one hand while you play with the release valve or pet the patient with the other.

3. Heat the fluids to about 102 degrees (warm adult bath temperature; not baby bath). Most veterinarians don't have time to bother with this, but it makes the difference between a cat wiggling to get away from the cold feeling under his skin and a cat purring with contentment, lying on his fluffy towel while the comfortable warm liquid makes him feel better. I heat the fluids by placing the whole thing, tube and all, in the bathroom sink full of hot water until the fluids are warm enough. Test the heat by holding your hand against the container for about thirty seconds. It should feel pleasantly warm.

4. While the fluids are heating, do your therapeutic communication (page 204) with your feline friend, finishing up by reading

all of these steps aloud to her. Explain why as well as how each step will be done and ask her to help you out.

5. Veterinarians usually use a number 18 needle, which is large and lets the fluids run through freely. I prefer the number 20, which is thinner and works fine. If I want the fluids to run faster, I position the bottle higher above the level of the cat and let momentum and gravity do the rest.

6. The needle is inserted under the skin of the scruff or behind and to the side of the shoulder blades (never near the spine). Cat's skin is extremely loose and supple. There are a couple of different methods for picking up the cat's skin and inserting the needle. (Some owners find it helpful to think of pulling the skin over the needle rather than pushing the needle into the skin.) I like to lift the skin by taking hold of a small bunch of hair near the roots and pulling upward until I've lifted the skin into a "tent" about one and a half or two inches high. Practice this a few times. Pull straight up or a bit toward the tail (and you), not toward the patient's head. Explore how high a tent your particular cat's skin is going to make. Then, when you're actually giving the fluids, touch the tip of the needle to the side of the tent about halfway between the top and the patient's body. Point the needle toward the center space inside and halfway up the tent. Put your index finger halfway down the needle and *swiftly* push the front half of the needle in (up to your finger). (If you have an assistant, he should be scratching the patient's head and talking about mice and sparrows while the needle is being inserted.)

7. When the first half of the needle is in, release the fluid flow valve on the tubing; move it along the tube a bit, exposing the crimp it has made; and pinch out the crimp. Look inside the little bulb under the fluid bottle and see that the drops are flowing. Fast is okay as long as it's not an unbroken stream; you should see individual drops. Allow enough drops to flow to create a nice little pocket of fluid inside your tent of skin; then feed the rest of the needle into the bubble of fluid up to the hilt.

8. Allow the correct amount of fluid to transfer from the bottle down the tube through the needle and under the patient's skin. (Your vet will tell you how much fluid will benefit your friend.) Many owners like to go over the numbered lines on the bottle with a colored marking pen to be sure they can see them easily.

9. To end, turn off the flow valve on the tube; then find where the needle is going into the skin and pinch the surface of the skin firmly around the needle and draw the needle backward out of the skin. Keep holding the skin gently pinched closed for five or six seconds. Then pet and praise the kitty and carry her back to the perch where you got her.

10. Store the fluids out of the way. Loop the tubing over the hanger or hook and hang it in a closet or on the hook behind a door that isn't used.

Be patient with your cat. At first it's best to have a friend help you by stroking the patient's head and encouraging her to lie quietly. Cats catch on by about the third session that this new ritual is making them feel about three hundred percent better. They come to expect it and depend on it, and they become quite blasé about giving their quiet cooperation, even if, later on, you need to train a temporary replacement whom you and your cat will then have to encourage and reassure.

Be patient with yourself. Remember when you were first learning to give a pill or eye drops. Remember you didn't start out perfect; you made mistakes. Human beings make mistakes when they are learning something new. Don't be discouraged if you push the needle in one side and out the other so that the fluids go running down onto the counter. Just turn the fluid valve off, take the needle out, and try again. Everybody makes that mistake at least once. There are a whole bunch of other mistakes a person might make. Your veterinarian made them when he was learning; I made them when I was learning. It's no big deal. Just go back to your teacher, the veterinarian or his helper, and persevere. That's the kind of owner everyone admires; the one who won't give up but perseveres for the sake of the cat he or she loves. Owners like that always win in the end because love cannot be beaten.

Recipes, Formulas, and Extras for Home Nursing

The Snug Retreat

The snug retreat is great for cats who are elderly, stressed, ill, recuperating, thin, frightened, or lonely—or for any cat who loves warmth or privacy.

Create a "snug retreat" out of a cardboard carton (liquor cartons are sturdy) placed on its side. Put it in a quiet, secluded place near a radiator, and clip a reflector light (with a seventy-five-watt bulb) onto a pulled-out drawer or table leg and focus it into the box from only two feet away. Place a terrycloth towel or old wool sweater in the box for extra warmth and comfort. Launder the towel or clothing weekly or more often if needed.

Antistress Supplements

- *Vitamin E.* 100 units a day for two weeks; then 400 units once a week. Strengthens the heart, lowers the body's need for oxygen, helps prevent adrenal scarring during stress. Helps heal any damaged tissue and reduces scarring.
- *Vitamin C.* 250 units three to four (or more) times a day. Mix into each meal and into every snack one-sixteenth teaspoon ascorbic acid or sodium ascorbate powder or crystals. Cushions against all stresses. Vitamin C is used by the body in huge amounts during *any* stress situation. It's almost impossible to overdose vitamin C; it is lost in the urine.
- *B vitamins*—especially B-2, B-6 and pantothenic acid. Add to the food twice a day one-half of a crushed 10 mg level B-complex pill. Also, be sure to use the Vita-Mineral Mix (see page 55) as directed; it is a natural source of these same B vitamins. B vitamins, like C, are lost in the urine.
- *Calcium.* The bone meal used in the Vita-Mineral Mix (page 55) is usually a sufficient amount of calcium in the diet. Calcium calms nerves and raises the threshold for pain and stress. Your veterinarian may prescribe more calcium in

some cases. To absorb calcium the body needs vitamin D.

- *Vita Mineral-Mix (page 55)*. Be sure to include two to three teaspoons a day mixed into food.
- *Vitamins A and D*. Once a week give one capsule containing 10,000 units vitamin A and 400 units vitamin D.
- *Enzymes*. Make sure your cat will digest and use the good food and supplements you are giving him by adding one-fourth teaspoon feline digestive enzymes to each meal. (See Appendix, "Product Suppliers.")

Supplements for Infections and Wounds

The following supplements will help the body fight germs and viruses and promote healing of tissue that is damaged or scarred.

- *Vitamin C*. Give 250 units C in the form of one-sixteenth teaspoon sodium ascorbate powder or ascorbic acid crystals four times a day mixed in the meal or in a small snack. Vitamin C helps the body process out the invading bacteria and dead white cells.
- *Vitamins A and D*. Give one capsule containing 10,000 units vitamin A and 400 units vitamin D once a day for four to five days; then go back to giving it once a week as usual. Needed to help absorb calcium and helps the liver detoxify infection.
- *Vitamin E*. Give 400 units vitamin E twice a week for eight weeks; then go back to giving it once a week as usual—use alpha tocopherol *not* mixed tocopherols. Prevents scarring and helps body build healthy new tissue.
- *Vita-Mineral Mix (page 55)*. This basic to your cat's daily diet should be increased to three teaspoons a day during the crisis; then return to two teaspoons a day as usual. Provides calcium to build strong tissue, calm nerves, and help the body handle pain. Vita-Mineral Mix also provides water-soluble nutrients that are needed in larger quantities when the body is fighting infection and healing itself.
- *Snug Retreat (see page 240)*. Cushions cat from environmental stress and provides warmth to save the cat's energy and

calories. Mutes sounds and gives a feeling of protection and privacy.

Acid-Alkaline Swing

I have a little trick I use whenever I get a warning that my cat's body might be battling something. I reason that the invading organism has taken hold because the cat's body is either too alkaline (very rare) or too acid. So I proceed to swing the pendulum from acid to alkaline and back again, in an effort to disturb the attacking organism. I do this by feeding supplements that I know have an acid-producing effect for two days and other supplements that tend to alkalize on the next three days. I choose specific supplements that have lots of side effects—all of them beneficial.

On the acid days:
- Give 500 units of natural vitamin C twice a day. You can get it in the health-food store. Choose a tablet that is long and flattish, like a lozenge, for easy swallowing (see "Giving Pills," page 208), *or* use one-eighth teaspoon plain ascorbic acid crystals or sodium ascorbate powder added to the food. Besides acidifying the body, ascorbic acid acidifies the urine, getting rid of little bits of crystals and helping to destroy many germs that can breed in the bladder. It also helps build up the body's immune response and renders the system better able to deal with stress.
- Once a week on the acid day, squeeze onto the food the contents of a 400 unit vitamin E capsule and a 10,000-unit vitamin A and 400-unit vitamin D capsule.

On the alkaline days:
- Twice a day mix into food one-eighth teaspoon Delicious Garlic Condiment (page 256). This protects against parasitic invasion and actually contains a natural raw antibiotic.
- Give one-half teaspoon kombu broth (see page 256) mixed into each meal. Kombu is full of minerals and contains very little sodium, so it can be used even for heart patients.
- Give one extra teaspoon of alfalfa sprouts or one teaspoon

of finely grated raw zucchini or carrot on the alkaline days and none on the acid days.

Be conscious of how much time your cats spend in active play. It will help their circulation greatly if you can get them to join you in some high-energy sport at least once a day. If your cat is not the sporting type, you might try to get hold of a peacock feather. Florist's suppliers often have them. These feathers are so irresistible when waved or trailed in front of cats that cat show judges use them to elicit response from those blasé show types. The Cat Dancer toy is also a big winner. You can get it from your pet-food supplier or pet store.

High-Calcium Chicken Broth

Your own homemade chicken broth will be full of calcium and nutrients. Here's how to make it:

    2 to 3 lbs. chicken (I prefer thighs)
    1 lb. chicken necks and backs
    water to cover
    ¼ cup tomato juice (*not* V8 juice)

Put all chicken into a soup pot large enough so the chicken fills the pot only halfway. Cover with water until water is one to two inches above chicken. Cover the pot loosely (tip the lid). Bring to a low simmer. Simmer three to five hours, occasionally breaking up the chicken and adding more water if necessary. During the last hour remove the lid and let the water cook down until the chicken is barely covered. Broth is now deliciously strong. Pour off broth, cool to room temperature, and then store in refrigerator.

While the broth is cooling, pour enough cold water over the chicken left in the pot to cover. Then let it cool some more until it's cool enough for you to be able to touch. With your hands, knead, squeeze, and stir the chicken around in the water to get all the good out of the meat and into the water. The water will begin to look milky. Finally, take handfuls of chicken meat, wring out the liquid into the pot, and throw the meat away. (The hours of simmering have succeeded in transferring the usable nutrition from the meat into the broth. What little nutrition is left in the meat at this point would be largely indigestible.) *Leave the bones and the broth behind in the pot.*

Pour this broth off and store it with the first batch of broth. Transfer the bones into a smaller pot. Crack them up so they form a fairly compact mass in the bottom of the pan. Cover the bones with water and add the one-fourth cup tomato juice. Simmer one-half to one hour.

Pour off this broth, again combining it with the other broth. Throw the bones away. Store about two cups of the broth in a jar in the refrigerator; store the rest in the freezer in pint-size covered freezer containers to be thawed as needed. To thaw, stand the container in a bowl of hot water.

Chicken Super Soup

Here's how to make your homemade chicken broth even more nutritious.

Combine the following ingredients:

¼ cup High-Calcium Chicken Broth (see recipe above)
¹⁄₁₆ teaspoon ascorbic acid crystals (250 units of vitamin C)
½ teaspoon food yeast (flaked, brewer's, or tarula)
¹⁄₁₆ teaspoon feline digestive enzymes (see Appendix, "Product Suppliers")

Choosing Methods of Treatment

Homeopathy

Homeopathy is the medical science that cures by using the law of similars to stimulate the body's immune response. It was developed in Vienna during the late 1700s by Dr. Samuel Hahnemann. He found that giving the patient a substance that would produce the same symptoms as the disease he was suffering from would stimulate the patient's own immune system to fight the disease. Not only would the patient be cured, but he would also end up more resistant to the disease than he was before he got it.

If a patient has a cold with a runny nose and red irritated eyes, the homeopath might prescribe allium cepa, which is made from the juice of red onion. We all know how a red onion can make the nose run and the eyes feel irritated.

Dr. Hahnemann taught that symptoms of illness are the body's normal, constructive response to an intolerable situation. Homeopathy supports and enhances that response. Giving a homeopathic remedy is like sending a message loud and clear to the body's immune system saying, "Here's what's wrong; now wake up and *do* something!" More than 1,500 remedies exist.

Dr. Hahnemann made another major discovery: the principle of the minimum dose. He diluted his remedies by 1 part to 1,000; 1 part to 1 million, 1 part to 1 billion, and even more, and then shook them vigorously hundreds or thousands of times. His research revealed that the more a substance was diluted and shaken, the more potent it became. Diluting and shaking release and enhance the intrinsic curative energy in the basic molecules of the substance. It can even be diluted so far that no actual molecules remain and only the energy is present. The more dilute it becomes, the stronger it will be.

Homeopathic remedies often cause a slight increase of symptoms at first. Then the immune system kicks in and overcomes the disease. If drugs have been used in the past, the homeopath may first have to prescribe a remedy to undo their adverse effects and help the body expel the residue before he can begin to treat the disease.

One of my veterinarians, Dr. Richard Pitcairn, is a homeopath. He lives far away, so my local veterinarian and I consult him by phone. I have never found any disease or behavior problem that did not respond favorably to homeopathy. Tumors, skin rashes, wetting outside the box, attacking people, diabetes, kidney disease, or leukemia—I've seen them all turn into a dim unpleasant memory after a competent homeopathic veterinarian was consulted as part of a comprehensive program of natural treatment.

Because these remedies work on the level of energies rather than actual substances, they must be handled in a manner that is very different from the usual pills and liquids. If not handled correctly, they can easily be accidentally deactivated and neutralized.

Cautions for handling homeopathic remedies:

1. *Do not touch a remedy with your fingers or any part of your body.* The first time a remedy touches a body should be when it goes into the patient's mouth.

2. Remedies can be deactivated by odors. Do not store your remedies near peppermint, menthol, or coffee.

3. Keep remedies away from heat, electrical equipment, hi-fi speakers, and magnets. Don't store near radiators or stoves; do not administer with a hot spoon.

4. Never mix remedies with any food except a little milk.

5. Once the remedy is taken, it can be antidoted by extreme stress, or if the patient is treated with acupuncture, or if the patient takes a corticosteroid, peppermint, or catnip.

Administering Homeopathic Remedies—Pills
METHOD I
Before beginning, read all directions through once. Then read again, explaining each step to your cat.

1. Tip the correct number of pills from the bottle into the lid.
2. Take the pill-giving position (see "Giving Pills," page 208).
3. Do therapeutic communication (see page 204).
4. Reaching down from above, grasp the cat's head as for giving a pill.
5. Tilt head back so that the pill will naturally fall onto the back of tongue at the center line.
6. Holding your hand palm up, hold the lid of the bottle with the pill in it between your thumb and index finger, insert the tip of your middle finger or nail between the cat's front teeth, and, using the back of your finger or nail, press the lower jaw down to open the mouth.
7. Double-check the tilt of the head—see step 5 again.
8. Lightly toss the pill from the lid onto the back of the tongue near the center line of the tongue.
9. Let the cat's head and mouth go free. Press down on the top of the back of the neck just below the skull so the head stretches forward and down. Then stroke the throat.
10. Give loving praise and thanks to the patient.

METHOD II
(Spoon Method A)
Before beginning, read all directions through once. Then read again, explaining each step to your cat.

1. Prepare a tablespoon and a teaspoon by standing them in a mug of very hot water for about three minutes.
2. Rinse the spoons in cool tap water and dry on clean paper towels. Don't touch either spoon where it's going to be touching the pill.
3. Measure the pills into the lid of the bottle.
4. Pour the pills onto the tablespoon and crush them to powder with the back of the teaspoon. It is easier if you have the spoon handles sticking out in opposite directions.
5. With the tip of the teaspoon, scrape the powdered pill toward the tip of the tablespoon, and then dump the powder onto the front part of the teaspoon.
6. Take the pill-giving position (see "Giving Pills," page 208).
7. Position the cat's head as in steps 4 and 5 of Method I above.
8. Holding the spoon so the middle finger is free, pry the jaw down as in step 6 of Method I.
9. Toss the powdered pill across the cat's tongue.
10. Let the cat's head go free; stroke the head and throat.
11. Give loving praise and thanks.

METHOD III
(Spoon Method B)
Before beginning, read all directions through once. Then read again, explaining each step to your cat.

Follow Steps 1 through 5 of Method II above.
7. Add ½ teaspoon of room-temperature milk or cream to powdered pill in the tablespoon and stir carefully with teaspoon tip until nearly dissolved.
8. Offer the mixture on the tablespoon to your cat as a treat or an appetizer before a meal.

Note: Milk or spring or distilled water are the *only* substances with which you may mix a homeopathic remedy. Do not use soup or any food, not even butter.

METHOD IV

Before beginning, read all directions through once. Then read again, explaining each step to your cat.

1. Measure the dosage into the lid of the bottle.
2. Tip the pills onto a piece of clean white writing paper.
3. Roll the paper into a cone.
4. Take the pill-giving position (see "Giving Pills," page 208).
5. Grasp the head as in step 4 of Method I above.
6. Hold the paper cone so your middle finger can pry the cat's lower jaw down.
7. Tip the pills onto the back of the cat's tongue.
8. Release the head and stroke the cat.
9. Give praise and thanks.

METHOD V

Before beginning, read all directions through once. Then read again, explaining each step to your cat.

1. Follow steps 1 through 3 of Method II above.

   or

   Place pills between two sheets of clean white writing paper and crush by pressing down with the back of a spoon.
2. Then dump powdered pills onto another piece of clean white writing paper, roll into a funnel, and proceed as in Method IV, steps 4 through 9.

Administering Homeopathic Remedies—Drops

Drops should be given according to directions from your homeopathic doctor. Some are given straight from the bottle and can be administered as in giving liquid medication by dropper (see page 210). However, you must not touch the dropper from the source bottle to the patient's mouth. Instead use a second, independent dropper or syringe that you prepare as follows:

1. Fill a clean, well-rinsed mug half full of very hot tap water.
2. Fill the syringe or dropper with the hot water, and let it stand

in the hot water three minutes. 3. Flush with cool water. Now the syringe is ready for use. Don't touch the tip with your fingers. Use the syringe as in giving liquid medications, page 210. After using, stand syringe in hot water again; then dry and wrap in clean paper towel and it's ready for future use.

Bach Flower Remedies

Dr. Edward Bach lived in England between 1886 and 1936. In his practice of homeopathic medicine, he observed that his patients' physical ills were always preceded by mood changes. He reasoned that these emotional changes were a part of the disease and that a good doctor would be aided in his diagnosis by recognizing the moods and attitudes that usually accompany each malady. He believed that treating the emotional problem was a necessary part of treating the disease and, further, that treating the emotional problem before the physical symptoms began to appear could actually prevent the disease from ever developing further.

Dr. Bach developed thirty-eight remedies to treat emotions, moods, and mental tendencies. They are all made from flowers; they are dilute, natural, gentle, and perfectly harmless. If you use the wrong remedy, the worst that will happen is nothing—zero results.

When working with an animal, you can mentally put yourself in his place and try to recognize what emotions are prompting his attitude or actions. Because cats as a species are emotionally closer to the primitive, wild state than other domestic animals, their survival mechanism is more active. Nearly all negative emotions—anger, jealousy, hatred, and so forth—are based on some type of fear.

For example, if you are introducing a new cat into a household where the old cat is very attached to his owners and possessive of his territory, you would look up fear and possessiveness in the Bach flower book. You might settle on mimulus (fear of losing home and protection; fear of future) and holly (jealousy, suspicion, envy). You might give the newcomer rock rose if she is terrified; or star of Bethlehem if she has just been separated from her mother; gorse if she seems uncertain and hopeless; or vervain if she is overenthusiastic.

The most well-known and commonly used Bach flower remedy is a mixture of impatiens, star of Bethlehem, cherry plum, rock rose, and clematis; it is called Rescue Remedy. Most health-food stores carry it already mixed. It is used for all forms of shock, both physical and emotional. It can be given every five minutes in severe cases.

Most health-food stores carry the remedies and a book telling how to use them. I would suggest that you buy the book first; then buy the specific Bach flower remedies as you need them. It's best to use only two or three at a time. You'll gradually build up a nice little collection.

Bach flower remedies are prepared homeopathically. When working with them, it is best to treat them as you would any homeopathic remedy (see "Homeopathy," page 244).

How to prepare Bach flower remedies:

- Choose the Bach flower remedy or remedies you require. (Look in Chapter 10 under the appropriate health problem.)
- Into a one-ounce dropper bottle put two drops of each. Fill the bottle to three-quarters full with distilled or spring water. Shake vigorously 108 times. Keeps up to two weeks in the refrigerator.

Here are a couple of Bach remedy formulas that I use most often:

Bach Flower Remedy Formula II

For inflammation, pain, toxicity, restlessness; helpful for hemorrhoids, feline urinary syndrome, and abscesses.

- Buy these Bach remedies:
  water violet, crabapple, agrimony, olive, star of Bethlehem
- To prepare, follow directions above. Give two to three drops four times a day.

250

Bach Flower Remedy Formula IV

For weakness, exhaustion, long-term illness, or if patient is failing.

- Buy these Bach remedies:
  water violet, sweet chestnut, olive, clematis, gorse, wild
  rose
- To prepare, follow directions above. Give two to three
  drops every two hours.

Herbs

Herbs are one of the oldest sources of healing in the world. Thousands of years ago when history was first recorded, herbs were already in use, established, and respected. How long they were in use before that, no one can be sure. In 300 B.C. herbal medicine was taught and practiced in the famous medical school in the cultural center of Alexandria. In A.D. 77 Pliny the Elder completed his *Historia Naturalis* of over one thousand herbs. During the Dark Ages monks and herb women carried on the practice. During the Renaissance herbal medicine was refined and expanded; however, this knowledge was jealously guarded. Women and nonprofessional healers were forbidden to study and practice, and many were pronounced heretics and burned at the stake. Because of this, even today some people equate herbalism with superstition and quackery.

Today the knowledge is preserved; the art and practice of herbalism persists. The herbs are there for us to use, growing in the woods and along the highways and pushing up through cracks in the pavement. It seems that Mother Nature is determined that we shall never be without her help and comfort.

In the mid-twentieth century herbalism reached an all-time low, but as this century draws to a close people are concerned about the side effects of drugs and want to take greater responsibility for their own health care. Herbal medicine is experiencing a remarkable revival.

Like any tool that has strength and power, herbs must be carefully used. Some herbs are harmless and some can damage the system if used carelessly. The Chinese divide herbs into three categories:

1. *Poison herbs*. Very strong. Having very specific benefits. Only for short-term use and allowing no margin for error. (Examples: wormwood, hemlock, and rue)
2. *Medicinal herbs*. Strong. Having short-term specific benefits with wider margin for error but cause reversals if used too long or too much. (Examples: golden seal and catnip)
3. *Food herbs*. Give broader general benefits and can be used copiously and forever with no fear of negative effects and no reversals. (Examples: parsley, slippery elm, garlic)

Keep in mind that some herbs work differently on cats than they do on humans. Catnip, for example, is a stimulant and aphrodisiac for a cat, while we humans take the tea as a sedative. *Marijuana, cocoa, and marigold are all poisonous to cats.* So, before trying a new herb on your own, consult a veterinary herbalist to be sure the effect it has on your cat's system will be the one you want. I am not an herbalist, so I limit myself to a few tried-and-true remedies used and approved by veterinarians.

The cat's senses of taste, smell, and feeling are much more sensitive than ours. A sharp flavor, such as garlic, can feel like a burn on the delicate tissue inside the cat's mouth and throat. A syrup such as slippery elm, if made too thick, could awaken fears of choking. So first I like to "feel" each remedy on my own tongue or eye or whatever in case I need to alter it a bit.

If a drop on the tongue tastes too sharp or strong, you can dilute with a little water or chicken broth and add a drop of tamari soy sauce if necessary, or mix it into a flavorful pâté and finger feed it. Use your ingenuity and the refined good taste possessed by all cat lovers.

If an herb is being taken for its concentrated nutrients (such as horsetail tea for silica) or its aromatic oils (such as garlic for flea-repelling properties) or its antimicrobial properties (such as golden seal painted on ringworm), then the actual herbal preparation should be used. However, if the same herb is to be taken for its effect on a condition (golden seal for bladder infection or liver inflammation), then an elixir can be used. This is made in the manner of a homeopathic preparation (see ''Elixir,'' page 260). The healing properties of the herb are enhanced and strengthened while the taste is diluted almost to the level of water.

Herbs must be fresh or they lose their strength. Tightly covered, in a cool, dry, dark place, dried green herbs last six to seven months. Roots, seeds, and bark last two to three years. The very highest medicinal value will be received from fresh-picked herbs growing wild where nature has decreed. The more recently picked, the stronger they will be. However, herb identification is a specialized study. Dried herbs from a store that guarantees freshness and stores properly will work just fine. Herbal extracts and tinctures are found in most health-food stores these days. They are simple to use and, properly stored, will last for years. Herbs are best stored in colored glass containers with screw tops in a cool, dry, dark place.

Here are the herbs I use most often and the indications for use:

- *Arrowroot.* A food herb. The root, ground into a white powder, can be used to thicken liquids. Like cornstarch and the oriental kuzu, it should first be softened in a little cold water before mixing with the hot liquid and stirring at a simmer for two or three minutes. About one teaspoon thickens one cup of liquid.
- *Burdock root.* A food herb. This root is used cooked like a carrot but is also available as an extract. It is high in organic iron and vitamin C; it is alkalizing and soothing to stomach and intestines. The tea and the cooked root are used as a blood purifier for skin and liver conditions and are often included in diets for cancer, hepatitis, and bowel diseases.
- *Calendula.* A food herb. Used as an external wash, the tea made from this herb promotes incredibly fast healing of cuts, abrasions, and burns. Used as an abscess irrigation, it will close the drainage hole in a matter of hours, so don't use it until the wound has finished draining.
- *Caraway.* A food herb. Caraway seed tea aids digestion and is used as a remedy for flatulence.
- *Carrot.* A food herb. Like burdock root, carrot is considered

good for the intestine. Raw grated carrot is sometimes used in the treatment of roundworm. Alkalizing and high in potassium, it is excellent for use in diets for arthritis, heart disease, and other low-salt diets. The seeds made into tea are diuretic and tend to eliminate flatulence.

• *Catnip*. A medicinal herb. The leaves, dried and crumbled, act upon cats as a stimulant and aphrodisiac. Cats will eat them, sniff the dust, or roll on them and lick them off their fur. The effect can be increased if the young plants are transplanted once and then, later, allowed to go almost but not quite too dry once or twice before harvest. The mature plants are uprooted and hung upside down to dry. The tops will be most potent. The effect on the cat wanes if used more than once a week.

• *Celery seed*. A food herb. The tea made from celery seed is used as a blood builder and tonic because of its rich mineral content. It is also alkalizing and slightly diuretic. It is soothing to the intestines, stimulates appetite, and prevents flatulence.

• *Comfrey*. A food herb. This herb contains allatoin, which promotes cell production. The tea can be taken internally or used as a wash to aid healing of wounds and broken bones. It is also used as an expectorant and removes mucus from the intestinal tract. It is high in calcium, potassium, phosphorous, and, alas, also in sodium. It is used to quell internal hemorrhaging of lungs, stomach, intestines, and bladder.

• *Dill seed*. A food herb. The tea made from dill seed prevents flatulence, is high in minerals and low in sodium, and stimulates milk flow in nursing mothers.

• *Echinacea*. A medicinal herb. An antiseptic antifungal herb, the extract or tincture can be painted on ringworm to dry it up. The tea, taken internally, reduces fever, purifies the blood, and is widely used in cases of boils, abscesses, and circulatory diseases.

• *Eyebright*. A medicinal herb. The tea is used as an eyewash to soothe red itching eyes.

• *Garlic*. A food herb. Called "Nature's antibiotic," garlic richly deserves a place in any book on natural health care. This humble and inexpensive herb has been used for centuries for everything from nursing a cold to repelling were-wolves. Modern laboratory testing reveals that it does indeed have antibacterial, antiviral, antifungal, antiparasitic, and antithrombotic properties. It also tends to lower blood sugar, strengthen intestinal walls, alkalize the system, aid in the expulsion of intestinal parasites, and render the entire body unappetizing to fleas. I recommend it frequently throughout this book. But the question is always raised: how to give it. Cats' mouths are notoriously sensitive, and raw unadulterated garlic is so strong it can actually feel as if it is burning. Some holistic veterinarians and other natural practitioners have successfully used the mild "deodorized" version of garlic oil in capsules. They tell me these capsules will work for most things. However, purist that I am, I persist in using raw crushed, whole garlic. I want the patient to get all of the elements nature intended him to ingest along with the oil of the garlic. Science is continually discovering new elements that are indispensible to body function, and those of us who have been eating the *whole* grain, the *whole* fruit, and so on have been gratified to learn that we have been better off all along than those people who were eating only parts of the grain or only the juice of the fruit. And so, when a remedy calls for garlic, I feel more comfortable using a measured portion of fresh crushed raw garlic. Here are my methods for making it delicious when mixed into the food or making it tasteless when given as a pill:

Garlic Given as a Pill

1. Obtain a package of empty gelatin capsules from the health-food store. Separate the two halves of the capsule.
2. Carve two or three little pieces off a clove of garlic and insert them into one-half of the capsule.
3. Put the capsule halves back together and give it immediately as a pill (see "Giving Pills," page 208). Don't let it sit around or the capsule will get squishy.

Delicious Garlic Condiment
(If you're going to take garlic, you might as well enjoy it!) Into a teacup or a custard cup measure:
     ⅛ teaspoon distilled or spring water
     ⅛ teaspoon tamari soy sauce
     ¼ teaspoon raw garlic crushed in a garlic
        press.
Mix ingredients together and let stand two to five
minutes. Mix ⅛ teaspoon (or more) into cat's
dinner.

- *Ginseng.* A medicinal herb. An appetite stimulant, the tea made from ginseng is pleasantly sweet and very alkalizing.
- *Golden seal root.* A medicinal herb. The tea of golden seal provides a general tonic for all mucus membranes. It is a natural antibiotic, antiseptic, and fungicide. It soothes in-flammation and kills germs, viruses, and fungus in eyes, nose, throat, ears, or any mucous membrane and is used to treat yeast infection. The elixir made from golden seal is used by holistic veterinarians to treat kidney problems. It is also used as an alternative to corticosteroids. The extract or tincture can be painted on ringworm to dry it up. It is ex-tremely alkalizing, has a very bitter taste, and does stain fur. It is a golden color.
- *Horsetail.* A food herb. Taken internally, this tea acts as a tonic because of its high vitamin and mineral content. It is especially high in silica, and therefore it is used to strengthen hair and nails. Slightly diuretic, it is sometimes used for heart and lung problems.
- *Kombu.* A food herb. This seaweed is made into a broth and used in soups. Rich in minerals but low in sodium and very alkalizing, it is excellent in diets for diabetes, arthritis, and kidney disease. Buy dried kombu in the health food store. Break off a square inch and cut, break, or crumble it into tiny pieces. Put in a small pan and soak it in a cup of water for a half-hour. Then cover the pot and simmer it for another half-hour. Be careful that it doesn't boil dry. Let it cool; refrigerate. Add the kombu and the broth to the cat's

food. Don't try to keep it for more than two days. It is extremely perishable; make it up as you need it.

- *Myrrh*. A medicinal herb. Valued for its soothing and healing properties. The following formula will soothe and reduce swelling and redness of gums.

Healthy Mouth Formula
Mix together: ¼ cup spring or distilled water, ⅛ teaspoon salt, 3 drops tincture of myrrh. Apply liberally once a day to gums with cotton swab.

- *Nettle*. A food herb. This tea is slightly diuretic, good for digestion, and rich in minerals.
- *Parsley*. A food herb. Used externally the leaves make an antiseptic poultice, the root decoction a soothing eyewash. Internally, the plant and the tea are high in minerals, vitamins A, B, and C, and beta carotene. The extremely high potassium content makes the tea a strong diuretic.
- *Pennyroyal*. A medicinal herb. The oil of pennyroyal is used in many herbal flea collars, coat sprays, and flea shampoos. It has insect-repellant properties. Cats are not fond of the smell, so I don't suggest it.
- *Plantain*. A medicinal herb. A poultice of the fresh leaves can be used to cover, protect, disinfect, and speed healing of wounds. The tea is used to promote healing after internal injury or surgery.
- *Psyllium seeds*. A food herb. Psyllium seed is used as a stool conditioner. It is a mucoid; that is, it makes the stool slippery so it slides out easily. The husk of the psyllium gives the best result, with finely ground psyllium husks being the most effective. Psyllium husks are mild enough for infants and kittens, but they must be taken with large amounts of water (one-eighth teaspoon psyllium husks with two tablespoons water) or they can clog up the intestine.
- *Rosemary*. A food herb. A poultice of leaves or a hot compress of the tea draws blood to the area. It is used for arthritic joints. The tea taken internally is used to aid fat digestion. The tea also makes a nice rinse after shampooing; it leaves the hair shiny and free of soap residue.

- *Rue.* A poison herb. Rue is used in herbal worming treatments but always in combination with other ingredients, carefully measured, and for a carefully prescribed period of time. *Consult a holistic veterinarian.*
- *Slippery Elm.* A food herb. The powdered bark made into a syrup is very soothing for any inflammation or irritation in the digestive tract. For centuries it has been widely used for diarrhea, ulcers, and vomiting. It contains minerals and vitamins and has a pleasant mild taste well accepted by cats. Even sprinkling the powder into food will soothe the stomach and intestines.

Slippery Elm Syrup

Into a small saucepan place ½ cup *cold* water and 1 teaspoon powdered slippery elm. Whip with a fork. Bring to simmer over low flame, stirring constantly. Simmer 1 or 2 minutes or until slightly thickened. Cool and refrigerate. Keeps 7 or 8 days.

- *Stevia.* A food herb. The leaves or extract can be made into a tea that is extremely sweet-tasting. This can be mixed into food to tempt a cat who is habituated to a commercial food with a high sugar content. Despite its sweet taste, stevia is alkalizing, destroys yeast and fungus, and tends to lower the blood sugar. It is widely used in Europe and the Orient as a natural low calorie sweetener and as part of the diet for diabetes.
- *Valerian.* A medicinal herb. Valerian is called "Nature's tranquilizer." A cold decoction of the powdered root or even the smell of the powder calms the central nervous system. It is used as an antispasmotic and mild tranquilizer. Many cats enjoy the smell.
- *Wormwood.* A poison herb. Used under *veterinary supervision* in herbal worming preparations. Like rue, it is always carefully measured and used for a very limited time and in combination with other herbs.

258

Using herbs

1 teaspoon dried herb = 3 teaspoons fresh herb
1 teaspoon dried herb = 5 drops extract or tincture

Herbal remedies are usually taken three to four times a day; one to two teaspoons of tea for a cat or one-half teaspoon for a kitten. Continue three to four days for minor problems or for several weeks for chronic conditions such as arthritis or diarrhea. If, after long-term treatment, the condition improves, try reducing the dosage gradually.

Herbal preparations

Note: Do not use aluminum, copper, or "no-stick" pans or containers. Do not reuse a container for a different herb unless you wash it, sterilize it, and let it stand open for two weeks. Even then, if you still smell the first herb, you have to wash it all over again until there is no odor left. Also, take care not to mix up the lids. Label lids as well as the herb jars. Colored glass containers with nicely fitting lids are best.

INFUSION OR TEA
(for leaves and small stems)
- Into a heatproof container put 1 teaspoon dried or 3 teaspoons fresh herb.
- Add 1 cup boiling water (spring or distilled).
- Let stand, covered, 10 to 30 minutes.
- Strain, refrigerate in covered glass container.
- Keeps 3 days.

COLD INFUSION
- Soak 6 teaspoons bruised fresh herb or 2 teaspoons dried herb in 1 cup cold water for 8 to 12 hours.
- Strain and store as above.

DECOCTION
(for roots, bark, stems, or seeds)
- Put 1 ounce bruised or crushed herb into small saucepan with 1 pint distilled or spring water.

- Slowly bring to boil; simmer gently 30 minutes. (By this time water should be reduced to one-half or one-fourth. Add more water if it gets lower than this.)
- Turn off heat and let steep, covered, until cool.
- Strain and store as with infusion.
- Lasts 3 days.

PULVERIZING OR POWDERING
(for use in capsules or to sprinkle on food)
- Grind, bruise, or mash fibers or seeds in blender, mortar and pestle, or clean coffee grinder.

TINCTURE
(can often be bought already made)
- Put 4 ounces dried or 8 ounces fresh chopped herb into glass jar with tight cover.
- Add 1 pint brandy or vodka that is more than 60 proof. (Do not use ethyl alcohol, rubbing alcohol, or surgical spirits.)
- Stand jar in a warm dark place and shake twice daily for 2 weeks.
- Strain through double muslin, squeezing herb at the finish.
- Store in covered, dark-colored glass jar. Keeps for years.
- Dosage for cats is 1 to 2 drops. Because of strong taste, always dilute with broth or water or use as an elixir.

ELIXIR
(a homeopathic preparation to increase therapeutic effects while decreasing flavor)
- Into a new one-ounce glass dropper bottle put ⅔ bottle full of distilled or spring water and 3 drops of herbal tincture.
- Cover and shake vigorously 108 times, hitting bottle against a thick rug or padded arm of a chair each time.
- Shake 12 times before each use.
- Dosage is ¼ dropperful 20 minutes before meals.
- Keeps in refrigerator 7 days.

POULTICE
(Works like a compress [page 234], but stronger. Actual plant parts are used instead of liquid on a cloth.)
- Mash fresh plant parts, mix with small amount of boiling water, and apply to affected area as hot as can be tolerated.
- Hold in place with gauze.

POULTICE USING DRIED HERB
- Grind dried herb to powder and mix with a few drops boiling water to make paste.
- Follow poultice instructions above.

Traditional Remedies

In addition to homeopathy, Bach flower remedies, and herbs, I often recommend the following remedies:

- *Acidophilus.* This is the friendly bacteria always found in a healthy intestine. If it is killed by ingestion of antibiotics or by some infections, it can be replaced by eating yogurt or taking an acidophilus supplement in liquid or pill form. Acidophilus manufactures somes vitamins inside the intestine, prevents gas, foul odor, and diarrhea. The companies Plus Products, Ad-Vita, and Continental all market an unflavored acidophilus culture suspended in water, not milk (be sure to get the unflavored kind). Also, there are now available some acidophilus capsules made without lactose (that part of the milk that can cause a problem). These products are usually found in the refrigerator at your health-food store and should be stored there at home. Milk and milk products such as yogurt do not mix well with some antibiotics. Also, some adult cats can't digest milk, even when they're healthy. Because bottled acidophilus won't keep more than two weeks, even in the refrigerator,

I like to mix one teaspoonful of it into all of the cat's dinners when I have it in the house.

- *Chlorophyll.* Liquid chlorophyll inhibits bacterial growth, neutralizes foul odor in all parts of the body, and prevents putrefaction in the intestine.
- *Charcoal.* Absorbs poisons, sometimes used as an antidote. Absorbs putrefaction in intestines, prevents flatulence. Will turn the stool black. Charcoal also absorbs digestive enzymes so it should not be used for more than two or three days. It is usually given in pill form.
- *Lemon rinse.* A multi-purpose rinse:

   1 lemon, thinly sliced, including skin
   1 pint boiling water

   Put sliced lemon in a heat-proof glass jar. Pour boiling water over it. Cover tightly and let stand at room temperature for twenty-four hours.
- *White vinegar solution:* Used on healthy ears to discourage yeast infections and after other ear treatments to maintain an acid environment in the ear canal.

   Combine in a one-ounce dropper bottle:

   3 drops white vinegar
   Distilled or spring water to fill bottle

   Warm to 101 degrees before using by standing bottle in a bowl of hot water. Administer six drops in each ear twice a day. This should feel good. If ear is red or irritated, dilute by half before using. If your cat objects, it probably means the ear tissue is irritated. Until the ear is normal, use a saline wash with calendula (page 219) instead of the white vinegar solution.
- *Soaked Oat Bran.* Put one-quarter cup oat bran in jar; add one cup spring or distilled water. Cover loosely and soak at room temperature for twenty-four hours. Store covered container in refrigerator.

Affirmation and Visualization

> *Primum est, non nocere:* Above all, do no harm.
> —Hippocrates

* * *

This quotation from Hippocrates, the father of holistic medicine, is my first and guiding rule whenever I consider a therapy for a sick or troubled animal. *Affirmations* (repeating a positive statement) and *visualizations* (mentally seeing and experiencing a situation or thing) are so simple to do that there is virtually no chance of doing any harm with them. In addition, they are free and they require no extra time. You can design them while you're driving, riding on a bus, eating, or anytime at all.

They work on the philosophic principal that everything that happens must first be conceived of in the mind. Edgar Cayce, the great psychic, said, "Mind is the builder." So we go to our mind, our own thoughts, and make conscious decisions about what it is we really want to conceive of and have happen. We do this by making up a sentence describing what we want and/or constructing a picture or scene. We've heard for many years now about "the power of positive thinking." Affirmations are positive thoughts that we've chosen very consciously; visualizations are an extension of positive thinking and involve consciously *visualizing* in our mind's eye the positive outcome we want.

Because animals pick up our attitudes, emotions, and thoughts, it is fairly easy to see the effects of this on cat behavior. In addition, scientific experiments have been carried out to show that the effects do go farther to influence speed of healing and recovery.

When I first began to practice affirmations and visualizations, my attitude was "It doesn't sound logical to me, but wiser heads than mine have said it works so, since it won't do any harm and it won't cost anything, I might as well give it a try."

What fun I have had! It's like suddenly having a magic wand. I did make some mistakes at first; you can make mistakes. For example:

1. If you want something to happen now, think and speak in the present tense, not the future tense: "The skin is healing beautifully" *not* "The skin will heal."

2. You must be able to believe what you are saying and visualizing. Repeating the affirmation "The cut is healed; the skin is perfect" while you're looking at a newly sutured incision will definitely not work as well as the more realistic affirmation "Muffy has

marvelous recuperative powers; her skin heals fast." That's what I mean when I speak of designing your affirmation. Your sentence must say exactly what you want in a believable way.

3. When designing your affirmations don't concern yourself with *how* a thing will be accomplished: "because we found the right remedy" or "now that he's home with us." Why and how are not important. Focus only on the bottom line: what it is you want.

4. Negatives *do not work*. They only call to mind what you *don't* want and therefore strengthen the possibility of the *wrong* thing happening. For example: "The wound will not become infected." Forget the possibility of infection; forget what you don't want. Concentrate on what you do want: "The wound is healing beautifully."

5. Both affirmations and visualizations work best when you include a strong emotional feeling. This is easiest done by prefacing your statement with a positive phrase such as "I'm so glad that . . . ," "We're so relieved because . . . ," or "We're delighted because . . . ," and really feel it.

Affirmations can be used alone but work even better when combined with visualizations. The rules for both are the same, but when designing a visualization you involve as many senses as possible.

If I want an incision to be healed, in my mind I

- *See*   Myself stroking my index finger over the healed scar
- *Feel*   The soft new tissue and silky baby hair under my finger
- *Hear*   Muffy purr with comfort and satisfaction as I stroke her there
- *Taste* (Would not apply here but could be included if I were doing an affirmation about Muffy enjoying her new diet)
- *Smell* (Same as taste)

The more I practice affirmations and visualizations the more I enjoy them and the more clearly I realize what a powerful tool they are. Before long I found the rules had become automatic and I could design them on the spot as I needed them. Now, whenever I work with a cat, I think and speak in affirmations and visualizations.

When people ask me such questions as "How in the world do you get him to sit there so calmly while you . . ." or "However did you manage to (a) get his temperature down, (b) get his blood count up, or (c) stop the diarrhea," the answer is always the same: In holistic therapy we attack any problem in many ways at the same time, but one of the ways I always include is affirmation and visualization.

Vaccinations and Other Immunizations

A vaccination is made from a live virus or germ that has been weakened or killed. It is injected into the patient purposely to give him that disease but in such a mild form that the body should easily overcome it and build an immunity to that particular virus or germ. Vaccinations are never given if a cat is already sick or if he has only recently recovered from an illness.

The cat's body has not evolved to handle viruses and germs that are injected under the skin and go directly into the bloodstream. Microorganisms usually enter through the mouth, nose, or intestines. Nevertheless, vaccinations can work. However, a problem is created when more than one serum is given at the same time. This is the case with the three-in-one shot for cats, which is used all over the country. Most allopathic veterinarians will very conscientiously advise you to have your cat vaccinated for anywhere from three to seven or eight diseases in one day. Dr. Pitcairn, who has a specialty in immunology, warns that this is not practical.

The immune system works like a type of memory. Each disease has a different set of symptoms. Each vaccine "clues in" the immune system in advance to a particular set of symptoms so that if that set shows up in the body, the immune system will then remember what it did last time and automatically do it again so the disease will be defeated.

Multiple vaccinations given close together (within a few weeks) confuse the immune system's memory and disrupt the immune response at the same time that they are activating it. This frequently results in the immune system's becoming confused and turning against its own body, producing autoimmune diseases such as asthma, arthritis, allergic dermatitis, warts, tumors, gum disease, and irritable bowel syndrome.

Holistic veterinarians caution that a killed virus is safer than a weakened virus and that serums are best used singly, at least six weeks apart.

An alternative to vaccinations are *nosodes*. These are homeopathic preparations that contain only the energy of the virus or germ but not the microbe itself. They are taken as a series of drops by mouth at prescribed intervals over several weeks or months and serve to bolster gradually the body's immune response to that particular disease. Giving the nosode takes a little more time than a simple injection, but avoids the drawbacks and dangers of allopathic vaccines.

Antibiotics

Antibiotics are used to kill germs and sometimes viruses. If an antibiotic is taken orally in pill or liquid form, it will kill all the germs in the entire alimentary canal, from the mouth right on down to the anus, before it even begins to work on the germs it was sent after in the nose or the kidney or wherever the disease happens to be. Diarrhea is one way that the body reacts to the absence of all microorganisms in the intestinal tract. Not all bacteria are bad— a healthy body has lots of friendly bacteria in the intestines. They manufacture some of the B vitamins, help with the absorption of nutrients, and help regulate the acid-alkaline balance in the intestine. When the antibiotic comes through the alimentary canal, these good bacteria bite the dust with all the rest. The absence of the good bacteria disrupts the acid-alkaline balance, and this causes diarrhea. You can replace the friendly bacteria that were destroyed by feeding one teaspoon of liquid acidophilus or chlorodophilus (page 232) one hour after each dose of the antibiotic (see page 261).

Continue mixing the acidophilus culture into the food for two weeks after the course of the antibiotic is finished. It's very good for the insides of the intestines. Some antibiotics, such as Keflex, are so harsh and strong that the poor little pussycat will still get diarrhea even though he's getting the acidophilus chaser an hour after each medication. Keep it up anyway; he'd be a lot worse off without it. It will help him bounce back faster once the nasty medicine is finished.

To calm a troubled intestine and minimize the diarrhea, I always give a teaspoon of slippery elm syrup (page 258) five minutes before each meal.

Also, remember that diarrhea uses up a lot of fluids and washes many of the water-soluble nutrients out of the cat's body. I add one-sixteenth teaspoon of Adolf's salt substitute to supply extra potassium. Also add one-sixteenth teaspoon ascorbic acid crystals to supply 250 units vitamin C, a piece of a crushed B vitamins complex pill (about 5 mg worth), and one-quarter of a crushed mixed trace mineral tablet to each meal. Nature's Recipe has powdered trace minerals with digestive enzymes that I find more convenient. I like it so much I use it every day in the Vita-Mineral Mix. If your health-food store doesn't carry it, check the Appendix for product suppliers you can order it from.

Remember that if you and the veterinarian decide to use antibiotics you must be sure to follow the directions very carefully. Unlike diuretics and cortisone, antibiotics are not given for the shortest time possible. Once you start, you must give the full course of antibiotics that the doctor prescribes, finishing all the pills. If you're careless and stop too soon, a stray germ or two might survive, slightly injured, to breed an altogether new strain of germ, which is then immune to that particular antibiotic and a brand-new menace to all the pussycats of the world. (See also "Diarrhea," page 305.)

Diuretics

Diuretics are given to prevent water retention. They help the body drain off the liquid by promoting copious urination. If there is fluid present—in the lungs, abdomen, or around the heart—an herbal or chemical diuretic may be prescribed. Lasix is one type of chemical diuretic. Usually the cat will begin to drink copiously and urinate copiously. And, one hopes, the bad fluid will be drawn to the kidneys and bladder and make its exit with the good fluid. However, with all this washing of fluids through the body, many water-soluble nutrients, vitamins, and minerals will be washed out along with everything else. The biggest loss is potassium. If a cat is given a diuretic get some Adolf's salt substitute (potassium chloride) and sprinkle $\frac{1}{16}$ teaspoon onto the cat's food at each meal. Double the amount of Vita-Mineral Mix (page 55) with each meal and also add $\frac{1}{16}$ teaspoon ascorbic acid crystals (or 250 units vitamin C), a B complex vitamin (5 mg level), and $\frac{1}{16}$ teaspoon mixed trace mineral powder (or $\frac{1}{4}$ of a trace mineral tablet) as in the section on antibiotics above. Chemical diuretics are almost never given over long periods of time. The lower the sodium (salt) intake, the lower the amount of diuretics that will be needed. Parsley tea is a natural diuretic used by many modern veterinarians. It is so high in mineral and vitamin content that it replaces some of the nutrients washed out by the diuretic action.

Cortisone and Other Steroids

Steroids are sometimes used to reduce inflammation and swelling. They work by suppressing the body's immune system. (Inflammation and swelling are a normal part of the body's immune response.) Steroids do not cure anything; they only suppress the symptoms and drive them deeper within the system. They do nothing to address the cause of those systems. For these reasons most veterinarians dislike using steroids and will do so only in life-threatening situations, such as when a swelling is blocking an air passage; or at the very end of a terminal illness, such as cancer or kidney disease, hoping to buy a little time.

However, my own vet has pointed out to me and I have observed for myself that death, when it comes for an animal on steroids, is much harder. I counsel the owners of cats who have been treated with steroids to be aware of this and carefully plan in advance to have a veterinarian available twenty-four hours a day for a quiet euthanasia in case their pet takes a bad turn at any time of the day or night.

Since steroids suppress the immune response, great care must be taken to avoid all stress and not to expose the patient to any sort of germs, viruses or parasites. Any source of infection is potentially lethal to an animal on cortisone or any other steroid, whether natural or artificial. Now is definitely not the time to change his environment in any way. No trips and no new additions to the household should be contemplated at this time. Any visitors who have animals of their own should wash their hands well before touching the patient.

Steroids raise the body's need for vitamins A and C. Add 1/16 teaspoon ascorbic acid crystals or sodium ascorbate powder (250 units vitamin C) to each meal, and, for vitamin A, give a dropperful of cod liver oil every day *or* give a capsule containing 25,000 units vitamin A once a week. Because steroids are usually given to reduce swelling, you probably are already giving your cat extra vitamin C and cod liver oil to alleviate the condition.

One caution about steroids: Never stop them abruptly. Steroids, like diuretics, are always given for as short a time as possible, but, unlike diuretics, the dose is always tapered down at the end. Steroids can make cats feel depressed. Coming off the steroids too abruptly depresses them even more. I prefer not to use steroids at all. Modern veterinarians have found a homeopathic preparation of the golden seal elixir can sometimes be used in many cases to replace part or all of the corticosteroid.

Anesthetics, Tranquilizers, and X Rays

Vitamin C is manufactured by cats in their intestines. This takes care of the normal requirements. However, "normal" means hunting twice a day, eating raw food, and lounging in the sun—healthy, happy cats. It has been found that any stress can cause vitamin C to be totally depleted—extreme cold, extreme heat, fear, anger, after X rays, during any illness, after anesthetic, or when chemical preservatives such as ethoxyquin, nitrates, nitrites, and sodium benzoate are ingested. Even a disruption in the owner's life can be stressful to the sensitive cat. The vitamin C requirement during such situations soars. It is practically impossible to get an overdose of vitamin C, because it cannot be stored. Excess vitamin C is excreted in the urine. This is why it is sometimes used as a way to acidify the urine in cases of feline urologic syndrome. I give one-sixteenth teaspoon of ascorbic acid crystals or sodium ascorbate powder (250 units vitamin C) in the food twice a day for six days before a cat is to be either x-rayed or anesthetized. I give it three times a day for three days afterward and then I go back to twice a day for two weeks or longer if the cat is still in the hospital or on any sort of medication. I do this in hopes of keeping the cat's resistance to disease higher. Anesthetization is such a drain on the cat's body that all too often the cat picks up some unrelated infection that becomes evident a couple of days after he returns home. Adding 1/16 teaspoon Delicious Garlic Condiment (page 256) to the food once a day for three days before and one week after will offer some protection against invading germs and viruses. (See Chapter 8, "Seeking Professional Help.")

I think of vitamin C as a little additional cushion to help the beleaguered body cope with any serious stress. At the risk of belaboring a point, let me say again that the entire nutritional program must be of extra high quality during stress. Anesthetic is one of the worst stresses. Vitamin C is a big help, but vitamin C can't do it alone. You need the vitamin B family and vitamin E to complete the antistress group. (See "Antistress Supplements," page 240.)

Mineral Oil

Mineral oil washes the oil-soluble vitamins A, D, and E out of the system. Fur ball medications and laxatives in a tube contain mineral oils. If the doctor advises their use, choose a brand that does not contain the preservative benzoate of soda (sodium benzoate) or use a plain petroleum jelly and follow with a seven-day regimen of replacing those fat-soluble vitamins.

I give 400 units vitamin E (alpha tocopherol) and a low potency vitamin A and D pill (10,000 units of vitamin A and 400 units of vitamin D) every week, as a matter of course. If a product containing mineral oil must be given for some reason, I follow the veterinarian's directions precisely so I won't have to do it more than once, and I double the above amounts of vitamins A, D, and E for the next two weeks.

If a cat becomes constipated, I seldom use mineral oil. Instead, 1/8 teaspoon of ground psyllium husks from the health-food store plus two tablespoons water mixed into each meal for a few days usually does the trick. Psyllium is harmless enough to be used on human infants and can be kept up indefinitely as needed. It's great for older cats who tend to produce a dry stool, but be sure to mix extra water in the food: two tablespoons to every 1/8 teaspoon of psyllium husks (see "Constipation," page 293).

Surgery and Catheterization

I'll add a word here about nutritional support before and after surgery and catheterization. These procedures present the body with three problems: stress, danger of infection, and scarring. This means that nutrition should emphasize the antistress supplements. Give the antistress supplements found on page 240 for two weeks before and two weeks after surgery; however, *double* the amount of vitamin C. To speed healing of the incision, spray it twice a day with a saline solution with calendula (page 219). Also, to prevent the healing scar from itching, you can rub vitamin E directly on the scar once the scab is gone. Use a vitamin E capsule punctured with a needle. The vitamin E oil in a bottle goes rancid too quickly.

Shopping List of Home-Nursing Items

Here is a list of most of the items you will need for home nursing and health. To help in finding these items, I've noted those that can commonly be found in the health-food store (HS) and those that can be found in a pharmacy (P).

- Baby food lamb, vegetables and lamb, and creamed corn
- Bach Flower Rescue Remedy (HS)
- Bathroom and kitchen supplies:
    jars to store food, etc., with screw tops in half-pint and one-pint sizes
    measuring spoons (⅛, ¼, ½ and 1 teaspoon and 1 tablespoon sizes)
    paper towels
    mug (for foot and cuticle soaks)
    shampoo bottle, empty plastic bottle—to use as a squirt bottle or to fill as a hot water bottle with an old wool sock to use as a cover
    terrycloth towels—never use fabric softener
- Betadyne surgical scrub and Betadyne (P)
- Boric acid powder (P)
- Charcoal tablets or capsules (HS or P)
- Cardboard box (for snug retreat, see page 240)

- Carry case (see page 20 for the type to buy)
- Chicken broth in freezer (at least one pint of homemade High-Calcium Chicken Broth, see page 243)
- Cotton swabs (P)
- Droppers:
  - bottle, clean, 1-ounce size (P)
  - teaspoon-size dropper found in baby supplies (P)
- Enema bottle: infant Fleet brand, emptied and cleaned (P)
- Hair dryer, hand-held
- Heating pad (P)
- Herbs—the basic herbs that you'll be glad you have on hand at all times are:
  - garlic
  - psyllium husks in powder form (HS)
  - slippery elm powder (HS)
  - *See also* list of herbs on page 253
- Herbal extracts (tinctures):
  - calendula (HS)
  - echinacea (HS)
  - eyebright (HS)
  - golden seal (HS)
- Kaopectate—unflavored (P)
- Light—clip-on light for snug retreat (see page 240)
- Petroleum jelly (P)
- Salt—buy sea salt (HS)
- Syringes: ear syringe (P)
  - 3 cc hypodermic syringe (no needle) (P)
  - or large baby dropper (holds 1 teaspoon) (P)
- Thermometer, rectal type for infants or the new digital type is easy to use (P)
- Vinegar, white
- Vitamins (HS):
  - vitamins A and D—buy capsules containing 10,000 units vitamin A and 400 units vitamin D
  - vitamin C—ascorbic acid crystals or sodium ascorbate powder
  - vitamin E—buy 400-unit alpha tocopherol
- Water—distilled, filtered, or spring water
- Wheat germ oil in capsules (HS)

10

A Guide to Common
Feline Health Problems

Abscesses and Puncture Wounds
(see "Injuries")

Acne
(see "Feline Acne"; see "Skin Problems")

Allergies

An allergic reaction is not a disease in itself; it is a symptom indicating that a weakened or damaged immune system is reacting inappropriately to some harmless substance or to the body itself as in the autoimmune diseases (for example, arthritis, irritable bowel syndrome, allergic dermatitis, asthma).

The immune system is supposed to protect the body by causing vomiting or diarrhea if something irritating or damaging is swallowed. If the immune response is confused and causes vomiting every time something harmless such as wheat or turkey is eaten, that is an allergy.

Holistic veterinarians who have specialized in immunology point out that these problems are caused by a combination of factors:

1. Inbreeding. Dr. Alfred Plechner, in his book *Pet Allergies: Remedies for an Epidemic*, states: "The recent history of cosmetic breeding practices among cat and dog breeders is replete with bad news—animals with gross deformities, lost instincts, altered and bizarre behavior and specific health problems."[1]

2. Use of pet foods containing moldy and rancid meat and grain.

3. Use of foods containing preservatives and colorings.

4. Feeding a diet of all cooked foods. Dr. Richard Pitcairn warns that the immune system will be progressively weakened unless at least 50 percent of the diet consists of raw food. Between 1932 and 1942, Dr. Francis M. Pottenger headed a research project that showed that the progeny of cats fed only cooked food would be born with immune deficiencies and that within three generations, if little or no raw food was fed, the immune system deteriorated to virtual uselessness. Many of the kittens were diagnosed with various immune disturbance diseases.

5. The use of multiple vaccines. Dr. Pitcairn, who has a speciality in immunology, explains that the use of multiple vaccines, or the giving of frequent or repeated vaccines, can confuse the immune response to a point where it cannot distinguish between harmful and benign substances. Germs and viruses may be allowed to enter the body and thrive while the immune system begins to attack and destroy its own body tissue, as in irritable bowel syndrome.

Allopathic veterinarians will frequently treat allergies as isolated problems, separate from the rest of the cat's system. They attempt to "isolate the offending substance." The problem with this approach is twofold. First, it is often well nigh impossible to pinpoint which substance or substances are triggering the response. Because a cat is sneezing and has watery eyes does not necessarily mean that "the offending substance" is in the air or entering through the nose. Because a cat has allergic diarrhea does not necessarily mean he is reacting to something in the food. He could be reacting with diarrhea to an inhalant or he could be reacting to his own intestine. Second, even if the allergy-producing culprit is

[1] Plechner and Zucker, p. 7.

found and eliminated, the cat will most likely develop a reaction to several other things unless the basic problem of a weak immune system is corrected. By all means, eliminate "the offending substance" if you can, but, more important, strengthen the cat's adrenals, pancreas, and liver; turn him into a healthy animal with a normal immune response (see "The Immune System," page 195).

Symptoms

- Presence of any autoimmune disease: arthritis, asthma, irritable bowel syndrome, allergic dermatitis, feline leukemia, feline AIDS, feline infectious peritonitis. Cats with any of these diseases will be more allergy-prone.
- Any symptom that persists or is repeated without the usual accompanying symptoms such as runny eyes and nose, with no fever, no depression, no appetite loss.
- Many skin rashes are allergic responses to an insect, a fungus, or some food.

Recommendations

- See your homeopathic veterinarian for diagnosis. Allergies indicate that the underlying cause is deep-seated. This is precisely where homeopathy will have the greatest effect (see "Homeopathy," page 244).
- Avoid use of any corticosteroid drugs, which will further damage the immune system (see Cortisone and Other Steroids," page 268).
- Eliminate from the environment all possible causes of allergy such as insecticides, flea preparations, room deodorizers, strong chemical cleaners, fabric softeners, tobacco smoke, plants.
- Fasting is an important part of allergy treatment. Make a broth by simmering lamb or mutton bones or make High-Calcium Chicken Broth (page 243) but only with organic chicken. (See "Fasting," page 225.) Fast for two consecutive days per week, feeding three or four times a day ¼ cup of broth mixed with ⅛ teaspoon ascorbic acid crystals or so-

dium ascorbate powder (500 units vitamin C). Vitamin C in high doses has an antihistamine effect.

- Use only spring, filtered, or distilled water for drinking and in preparing broth.
- Feed ¼ to ½ cup of the following allergy diet two or three times a day:

> ¾ cup cooked lamb, mutton, or organic chicken;
>
> ¼ cup cooked organic millet, amaranth, teff, quinoa, buckwheat, barley or brown rice *or* organic oat flakes or oat bran that has been soaked forty-eight hours;
>
> 3 tablespoons organic raw finely grated zucchini or carrot.

Into each meal add:

> ½ low potency B complex tablet that is not made with yeast;
>
> ¼ teaspoon feline enzymes or ½ digestive enzyme pill (crushed);
>
> ⅛ teaspoon ascorbic acid crystals or sodium ascorbate powder (500 mg vitamin C).

- Hormones, antibiotics, fungicides, and pesticides that have been sprayed on, injected into, and eaten by food animals may cause allergic reaction when any part of that food animal is eaten by your pet. Until his system is strengthened, try to use only organic foods.
- After one or two months on the above allergy diet, add the following supplements one at a time, trying each one for two weeks to be sure it doesn't cause an allergic response before adding another supplement to the diet. Continue adding an additional supplement to the diet every two weeks until you have included all the listed supplements. *If a supplement causes an allergic reaction, stop its use, move it to the end of the list, and wait two weeks before trying another new supplement.*

> ⅛ teaspoon calcium gluconate powder twice a day;
>
> ¼ teaspoon lecithin twice a day;
>
> 1/16 teaspoon ground psyllium husks twice a day;
>
> 1/16 teaspoon mixed trace mineral powder or ground kelp twice a day;

a capsule containing 10,000 units vitamin A and 400 units vitamin D, given once a week. Try this for four weeks before adding next supplement to the diet;

¼ teaspoon fine wheat bran twice a day. When you add wheat bran, stop giving the psyllium husks. If the stool seems hard or dry continue the psyllium as well as the wheat bran;

• After two weeks, if there is still no adverse reaction, you may combine the following:

Mix together:

> 1 cup lecithin granules
> 1 cup wheat bran
> ¼ cup mixed trace minerals or ground kelp
> 1 cup calcium gluconate powder

Mix 1 teaspoon of this combination with food morning and evening.

• Try giving once a week one capsule of 400 units vitamin E (alpha tocopherol). Do this for four weeks and continue if there is no adverse reaction.

• Add ⅛ teaspoon brewer's yeast to each meal. If, after two weeks, there is no adverse reaction, you may add it to the lecithin, bran, trace mineral, and calcium mixture. Add one cup of brewer's yeast to the above recipe.

• Herbal remedy: For a stuffy nose, give three drops in each nostril of warm saline nose drops. If you add two drops of golden seal extract to ¼ cup of the solution it will kill germs and viruses and shrink swollen tissue. For red itchy eyes you can use the same solution for eye drops. (See "Giving Eye Drops" and "Giving Nose Drops," pages 212–16.)

• For itchy skin massage in Lemon Rinse (page 262) or spray the area and massage in Spritz (see Appendix, "Product Suppliers").

• For diarrhea and/or vomiting give one teaspoon slippery elm syrup before each meal. Slippery elm is very soothing.

• For asthma put three drops oil of eucalyptus in a cup of boiling water and let the patient breathe the fumes.

• Bach flower remedy: Give Rescue Remedy prepared as given on page 249 to soothe, calm, and cheer. Put three drops in each meal and six drops in water dish.

Arthritis

Arthritis, like asthma, is one of the autoimmune diseases. Usually it builds up for years before it becomes obvious. There are two types of arthritis. *Rheumatoid arthritis* is an inflammation of the membrane that surrounds the ends of the bones at the joints. *Osteoarthritis* causes deposits of calcium to build up within the joints. Bones become very brittle and sometimes wear away at the ends. Modern veterinarians who are holistically oriented now believe that arthritis is caused by a combination of things. As it is an autoimmune disease, we know that it cannot occur unless the immune system has been damaged to the point where the immune response begins attacking the body it is supposed to protect. This confusion can result from corticosteroid therapy or from giving repeated vaccinations or many different vaccines at the same time or very close together (see "Vaccinations," page 265). The question is: why does the immune system attack itself in a way that produces arthritis as opposed to asthma or one of the many skin diseases. A partial answer would be that the genes of this particular animal predisposed him with a weakness in that direction. If the animal's body also contains many toxic substances ingested as preservatives and colorings in commercial food and if there is also a big backlog of wastes in general due to a slow metabolism caused by the owner's leaving food down for the animal to smell all day long, it's a pretty sure bet that the poisons are going to back up and settle in the joints. Arthritis is the result.

Arthritis is a subtle disease. At first, the little stiffness that creeps into the hips or lower back may not be recognized for what it is. "Well, he's not a kitten anymore" or "We can't expect her to jump up and catch the pipe cleaner the way she did when we first got her" may be all that is said to remark the subtle beginning of a downward spiral in the health of a beloved pet.

The disease is augmented by stress and adrenal exhaustion. Cats living under stress, such as those that are declawed or those forced to live with incompatible humans or animals, or those who are frequently caged, are more prone to the disease. Treatment with cortisone, ACTH, or other drugs can give temporary relief, but larger and larger doses are usually required and, as stated above, the use of corticosteroids further damages the immune system and you soon find out you're caught in a snowball—rolling down hill.

The holistic approach to relief from arthritis uses exercise, diet, gentle fasting, supplements, herbs, and homeopathy to reduce stress, strengthen the adrenal glands and immune system, and stimulate the organs of elimination to detoxify the body. Improvement usually progresses at a moderate but steady pace and is permanent as long as bad habits are not resumed. Also, with the natural, holistic approach, the side effects are all beneficial.

Herbal remedies have proven very helpful to the arthritis patient. When giving herbal remedies, be alert to the flavors you are asking him to accept into his mouth and throat. You don't want to shock or stress the patient. Taste a drop yourself if it seems too strong a flavor, too alkaline or too acid, dilute it with water or chicken soup and slowly give however many dropperfuls you need to, depending on how much you have diluted the herbal remedy. Some herbs, such as celery seed tea, may be accepted mixed in the food. Others will have to be given as liquid medication. The action of herbs is slow and gentle. Since arthritis is a disease of long standing, don't expect to see sudden changes. Continue the herbal remedy for three to four weeks before judging its effect.

Arthritis is a painful disease so speed of improvement is important to the concerned owner. Homeopathic treatment will provide the therapeutic support that will enable the nutrition and other natural therapies to work more quickly. When dealing with arthritis, I always urge the owner to consult an experienced homeopathic veterinarian.

When a cat's activity is curtailed by arthritis, he may experience depression, especially if he has enjoyed entertaining the family with acrobatic feats in the past. The Bach flower remedies given below are both simple and effective.

Symptoms

- Stiffness of movement
- Seeking out warmth or, with some cats, seeking out cool spots

- Pain during movement of certain joints, when cat is held in certain positions, or when certain areas are touched.
- Objects to being picked up and/or held
- Loss of appetite
- Fatigue; much sleep required
- Swelling
- Constipation
- Skin rashes
- Fever

Recommendations

- Consult veterinarian for diagnosis.
- Check environment for stresses such as loud radios, careless children and pollutants (see "Stress," page 197).
- Provide a snug retreat (see page 240).
- Provide frequent reassurance and love.
- Encourage short gentle play periods chasing a sash or ball two or three times a day.
- Feed three small meals a day; remove all food between meals.
- Fast on High-Calcium Chicken Broth one day a week (see page 243). Under a veterinarian's supervision a longer fast might be used to start the program off.
- Feed the arthritis diet and supplements given below.
- Folk remedy: have cat wear a copper band collar. Use one that is narrow and has a break or open space (should not be a closed circle).
- Give one teaspoon of herbal remedies chosen from those below three times a day. Can be given as liquid medication (see page 210) or mixed in food.
  To alkalize the system:
    Kombu broth (page 256)—use up to ¼ cup per meal;
    Celery seed infusion—use 1 teaspoon per meal;
    Dandelion root decoction—use ¼ teaspoon per meal (strong flavor).
  Against pain:
    Chickweed infusion;
    Valerian infusion or capsule;

> Feverfew—chop one fresh leaf and mix into each meal for pain and swelling.
- Bach flower remedies: Give three drops four times a day of the following mixture prepared as given on page 249
    Crabapple—to promote detoxification;
    Hornbeam—to bolster confidence;
    Larch—to increase the sense of self worth.

Arthritis Diet

Prepare the I'll-Do-Anything-for-My-Cat Diet on page 57, choosing from the following for the listed choices:

- *Two parts protein:*
    Raw ground beef or organic chicken;
    Chicken or liver, lightly cooked;
    Tofu may be added—up to 20 percent of protein portion.
- *One part vegetable:*
    Raw is best—grated raw carrot or zucchini;
    Lightly steamed—string beans, carrot, zucchini, or celery,
- *One part carbohydrate:*
    Raw soaked oat bran (see page 262);
    Cooked millet, quinoa, amaranth, teff, buckwheat, barley, or brown rice.
- *Liquid:*
    Use High-Calcium Chicken Broth (page 243) mixed with one or more of the herbal remedies (such as kombu broth) listed above. Choose from the herbal remedies depending on (a) what the patient most needs and (b) what flavors the patient will tolerate. In general the measurements should be about one teaspoon of herbal remedy per meal.
- *Into each meal add:*
    ¼ teaspoon feline digestive enzymes;
    Vita-Mineral Mix—increase to 1¼ teaspoons (When you prepare mix, add an extra ½ cup of fine bran and an extra ½ cup lecithin);

$\frac{1}{16}$ teaspoon ascorbic acid crystals (250 units vitamin C);

$\frac{1}{8}$ teaspoon Delicious Garlic Condiment (see page 256);

One teaspoonful finely grated carrot or zucchini (if you're not already using raw food recipe).

- *Add to food once a day:*

  $\frac{1}{2}$ crushed alfalfa tablet or $\frac{1}{16}$ teaspoon Green Magma;

  2 mg zinc tablet (crushed into food);

  100 units vitamin E (alpha tocopherol) oil from a punctured capsule—after one month give 400 units once a week as usual;

  $\frac{1}{8}$ teaspoon psyllium husks (ground) and two extra tablespoons water;

  5,000 units vitamin A (the type that is marked fish liver oil). Give this only for the first month, then give 10,000 units vitamin A and 400 units vitamin D once a week as usual.

- *Add to food once a week:*

  After a month, instead of 5,000 units vitamin A, give vitamin A and D capsule (10,000 units vitamin A and 400 units vitamin D).

Bad Breath
(see "Teeth and Gums")

Bald Patches
(see "Skin Problems")

Blindness

Blindness can be caused by an injury to the eyes or brain by extensive cataracts, by long-standing infection, by kidney malfunction, or by a dietary deficiency of the amino acid taurine as in a vegetarian diet. Cats' dietary requirements are different from humans. Nature designed them to be predators. Without an adequate supply of good quality meat or poultry in the diet, they gradually go blind and then die. There is a new natural pet food company that has a vegetarian formula, supplying the amino acid that cats require and taurine, from sea vegetables. The idea sounds promising, but I have had no firsthand experience with this formula to date.

The cat's senses of hearing and smell are much more acute than ours, so he will be better able to compensate for a loss of sight than we are. Remember that the cat does not know that blindness is not normal; as far as he knows, a loss of sight is simply something to be accepted like a change in the weather. This allows the owner to eliminate most potential stresses without the cat ever suspecting that it's being done for him. The blind cat can live quite happily if given the additional protection and consideration he requires.

Furniture should always be kept in the same place; care should be taken never to leave packages, toys, or other obstacles lying about. New games can be invented—instead of "catch the mouse," you can play "find the source of the sound." In this game, you make an intriguing sound such as tapping on a lamp base, crinkling paper, or scratching the post. You make the sound every five seconds or so, never moving, until the cat "finds you." You then reward him with lavish praise and petting. Climbing rather than running should be encouraged as an exercise since a running cat might bump into something. Of course, a blind cat must be kept indoors or within a screened enclosure.

To prevent blindness have the cat's vision checked as part of the yearly exam, especially if he is being treated for diabetes. Have eye injuries examined by a veterinarian and treated promptly. And be sure the cat has sufficient taurine from the meat and poultry in his diet.

Symptoms

- Bumping into objects left about
- Falling off the edge of things
- Milky cloud over eye surface

Recommendations

- Keep all furniture in the same place.
- Don't leave boxes or children's toys on the floor.

- Give frequent demonstrations of love.
- Make yourself always audible by doing lots of humming or chatting so the cat will know you're around and can enjoy your presence even though he can't see you.
- Always make noise before touching the cat to announce your presence and your intention. (No surprises, please!)
- Invent new sound, touch, and smell games. Be sure the cat "wins" at least two out of three times.
- Install a good quality floor to ceiling climbing post or a ramp for climbing exercise.
- Give Bach flower remedies. If blindness comes on suddenly, there may be fear and/or confusion. Give three drops every two to four hours at first; then gradually reduce the frequency to two to three times a day, and continue until the cat has adjusted to the new lifestyle. Give the following mixture, prepared as given on page 249:
  Mimulus—for fear of darkness, of injury, of being alone;
  Hornbeam—to build confidence in physical ability.

Body Odors

A body odor indicates that there is putrefaction and germs present. There are several possible causes. Dirty teeth mean dirty saliva; a cat who needs his teeth cleaned will spread germs and odor everywhere he licks. Another cause of odor can be germs breeding on a dirty skin. If food is left available at all times, the metabolism slows down every time a hint of food odor reaches the cat's brain through the nose. Slow metabolism causes wastes to back up; the body handles the problem by shoving the excess wastes out through the pores as oil and dandruff. This looks and smells terrible. If pores become clogged and/or infected, the smell will be even worse. A low-quality or poorly balanced diet will compound the problem. Soiling is another common cause of body odor. Diarrhea can soil the bloomers on the back legs; long hair can be dirtied by dragging in a badly kept litter box. A discharge from overfull anal glands or infected ears or ear mites will also soil the hair and produce a bad smell. Since a smelly cat is always an unhappy cat and inevitably becomes a lonely cat, stress-triggered diseases often follow.

Symptoms

- Bad smell anywhere on body
- Skin irritations
- Oiliness, itching, dandruff
- "Scooting" rear along floor
- Discharge from ears or anal area
- Urine or stool soiling the bloomers
- Shaking head
- Dirty cuticles

Recommendations

- Have veterinarian diagnose and treat the underlying cause—clean teeth and check for pathological conditions (kidneys, liver, hyperthyroid, respiratory, intestine, ear infection or mites, anal glands, or intestinal virus). Also check on other cats in the household for dirty teeth.
- Fast on High-Calcium Chicken Broth (see page 243) one day a week.
- Feed high-quality diet; raw food is best (see Chapter 2, "Diet"). Be sure to include Vita-Mineral Mix and other listed supplements to diet.
- Feed twice a day; be sure to remove all food between meals, leaving only water available.
- Add to each meal ¹⁄₁₆ teaspoon ascorbic acid crystals or sodium ascorbate powder (250 units vitamin C)—to help body to process out the backup of waste materials;
- Extra ½ teaspoon lecithin once a day (in addition to lecithin already in Vita-Mineral Mix)—to emulsify fatty wastes and help eliminate dandruff.
- Reevaluate litter-box setup (see pages 79).
- Call groomer to remove mats, or, if cat is to be anesthetized for dentistry or other reasons, have mats and soiling removed at that time.
- For longhaired cats, trim hair around the anus to ¼ inch

length and trim a free-fall area under the anus by trimming down the bloomers directly below the anus and between the back legs.

- Reevaluate grooming methods on outer thighs, inner thighs, and bloomers (see pages 138 to 141).
- Institute regular exercise period each day to speed up metabolism and help anal glands to function normally.
- Bathe cat after underlying cause of odor is diagnosed and successfully treated (see "The Bath," page 157).
- Herbal: A final rinse of one part lemon juice to eight parts water helps eliminate dandruff, discourages mites, soothes itchiness, and ensures complete rinse-off of any soap residue, or use Spritz coat enhancer after the bath.

Broken Bones
(see "Injuries")

Burns
(see "Injuries")

Cancer
(See also "Feline Leukemia")

Modern research has shown that toxic chemicals in the cat's food and environment are a major factor in producing cancer. However, it is also true that the animal whose health is below par, or the animal living under frequent stress, or the animal whose immune system is not functioning at top efficiency is the most susceptible (see "The Immune System," page 195). Prevention is far easier than curing the disease, but if the disease has not progressed too far, many cats experience remission. Tumors shrink and symptoms disappear when the highest quality diet (see pages 53) is adhered to, supplements are added to build the immune system and detoxify the body of stored pollutants and wastes, and the counsel of an experienced homeopath or other holistically oriented veterinarian is sought.

However, if remission does not occur, care should be taken

that the animal does not suffer. Arrangements should be made with your veterinarian well in advance for painlessly putting your pet to sleep if you and the veterinarian and your cat decide that the time has come (see "Euthanasia," page 192).

Symptoms

- Symptoms for all types of cancer are very general. (See symptoms given under "Feline Leukemia," page 326.)

Recommendations

- Cats diagnosed with any type of cancer can benefit from the diet and treatment given under "Feline Leukemia," page 326.
- Folk remedy—if cortisone is being prescribed: As cortisone works only for a limited time, golden seal elixir (see page 260) can sometimes be substituted for all or part of the cortisone dose. Check with a holistic veterinarian.
- Provide a snug retreat (see page 240) because cancer patients usually need an outside source of warmth.
- If the patient becomes dehydrated, request that your veterinarian administer subcutaneous fluids (Ringer's Lactate) to raise the level of comfort and to permit the body to continue to function. Or you and the vet might decide that you should give subcutaneous fluids at home at regular intervals just as you would for a kidney patient or any cat who is having a problem with dehydration. See page 235 for directions.

Cardiomyopathy

Cardiomyopathy is an enlarging and weakening of the heart muscle and is the most frequent cause of heart failure in cats. Cardiomyopathy appears either as a thickening and stiffening of the heart wall or as a thinning and ballooning out of the heart wall. In either case, the result is the same: low blood pressure. Blood is not being pumped as quickly or as forcefully as before. Therefore, an insufficient supply of blood reaches the organs. As cardiomyopathy progresses, one or more of the other major organs usually begin to break down. Blood clots frequently occur, causing strokes and thrombosis.

Many cats with cardiomyopathy live long and happy lives if diagnosis is reasonably early, diet is tailored to the patient's special needs, and an experienced homeopathic or holistically oriented veterinarian is consulted. Unfortunately, early symptoms are so unspectacular and general (laziness, easy tiring, difficulty breathing, fast and weak pulse) that most cardiomyopathy cases are not discovered until they are well advanced. Even a veterinarian could overlook a fast pulse, thinking it's the result of nervousness over coming to his office. Cardiomyopathy is the leading cause of sudden death in cats.

If cardiomyopathy is suspected, the veterinarian can employ electrocardiogram and/or X rays, to get a clearer picture of the condition of the cat's heart. To treat the condition all of the usual nutrients must be supplied in extra large amounts. This is especially necessary to combat the side effects if old fashioned allopathic medications are used to control the condition. In any case, enormous amounts of minerals and B vitamins will be washed out of the cat's system by the copious urination that often occurs or is induced by diuretics. A low-sodium diet helps to correct this condition so that fewer diuretics need to be used.

Symptoms

- Easily tired, pants easily, sleeps more
- Bluish tongue and gums after exercise
- Fast, weak pulse
- Copious drinking and urination (see also "Kidney Disease," page 372, and "Diabetes," page 30)
- Poor appetite
- Prostration or sudden collapse
- If left side of heart is affected: dry cough, difficulty breathing, wheezing, and worsening symptoms during exercise or activity
- If right side of heart is affected: fluid retention in legs and/or abdomen (pot belly)

- Hind legs cold, bluish, and then paralyzed. *This is an emergency situation.* Cat can be saved by a veterinarian only if treated immediately—in less than one day.

Recommendations

- At first, if the disease is not too far advanced, frequent short, gentle activity periods. Walking or strolling—not running.
- Administer oxygen if tongue becomes blue.
- Eliminate all toxins and pollutants from environment, especially cigarette smoke, which immediately aggravates symptoms.
- Use spring water—no chlorine or fluoride in water, no softened water (softened water has a high sodium content).
- If cat is heavy, reduce weight (see "Obesity," page 387).
- Provide a snug retreat (see page 240), both to reduce stress and as a source of warmth.
- Feed three or four smaller meals a day so heart is not taxed by large meals.
- Feed kidney disease diet on page 374. Diet should be low sodium, low meat, high vitamin and mineral content.
- Add kombu broth (page 256) as liquid portion of food recipe. This provides minerals and alkalizes the system.
- Alter Vita-Mineral Mix recipe by substituting mixed trace minerals for the kelp.
- Give 1/16 teaspoon ascorbic acid crystals or calcium ascorbate mixed in each meal (250 units vitamin C)—do not use sodium ascorbate.
- Increase vitamin E (alpha tocopherol) to 100 units a day for one month to strengthen heart muscle and minimize body's need for oxygen. After one month, decrease to 400 units once a week.
- In each meal give:
    Vitamin B complex pill (crushed)—choose a low-potency-pill; strongest values should be 10 mg;
    ½ of a multimineral pill (crushed)—should be low potency and must include selenium and chromium (no sodium);

Give 2 to 3 mg zinc each day if not included in above multi-mineral pill.
- Herbal remedies:
    Parsley Tea—if veterinarian prescribes a diuretic (such as Lasix), the parsley tea will promote copious urination. Add it as part of the liquid portion of the food. Perhaps the vet will be able to lower the dosage of the diuretic or even eliminate it as a low sodium-diet is now being given;
    Dill seed tea or horsetail tea is rich in minerals. A teaspoon can be added to meals if your cat enjoys the flavor.
- Bach flower remedies: Give three drops four times a day of the following mixture prepared as given on page 249:
    Oak—to encourage patience with self when the patient is too tired to keep up with what he used to do;
    Hornbeam—to build self confidence.

Cataracts
(see "Eye Problems")

Claw and Cuticle Problems

There are three types of claw and cuticle problems:

1. *Nail loss* either from declawing or through an accident affects the cat physically by weakening the corresponding leg and shoulder muscles. Scratching serves to tone those muscles, and cats who cannot scratch have poor balance. Loss of claws affects the cat psychologically as well because the claws (not the teeth) are the cat's first line of defense. Cats without claws are more tense, careful, and suspicious, as a person would be if he had no fingers.

2. *Nail abnormality* can be either breaking, chipping, or overgrowth of claws or crooked regrowth of claws on a declawed cat. Nails break and chip because of a dietary lack of calcium, silica, or other minerals, vitamins C and D, protein or oils, or because the cat is not assimilating these nutrients even though they are present. This is a common problem in older cats. Nail overgrowth means the nails are too long. As they grow around and under in a curve,

they can grow up into the cat's paw pad, imbedding themselves deeper and deeper if they are not clipped. Old, sick, or injured cats who cannot wear the claws down with use or by scratching the post sometimes end up with ingrown nails.

The growth of deformed nails on declawed cats occurs because declawing is a delicate and difficult operation and is frequently done poorly. Instead of cutting the claw out of the joint and severing the tendons with a scalpel, an instrument resembling a miniature guillotine is frequently used and the toe joints are simply lopped off. Under these circumstances it is not unusual for one or more of the claws to grow back; however they never grow in a normal way. Usually the claw grows backward or sideward and into the paw. Often the cat does not limp but simply lives with the pain of having a claw through her foot, accepting the situation as normal because she has known no other life. Such cats are usually defensive about being picked up because they know it always hurts to land on their paws when you put them down again. The only hope they have that the condition will be discovered is if one of the deformed claws finally becomes infected and a second veterinarian is consulted.

If you should adopt a cat who has been declawed, be sure to have your veterinarian carefully examine the cat's toes to be sure the amputations were done carefully.

3. *Cuticle infection* occurs when dirt gets caught between claw and cuticle and neither the cat nor the owner cleans it out. A poorly kept litter box can cause such a problem either because it is dirty or because a spray or powder containing irritating chemicals was used (see page 79). But more often dirt under the cuticle is the result of a cat using the back claws to dig at waxy ears. Ear wax is too thick for the cat to lick off his claws thoroughly, so it builds up under the cuticle and causes swelling and redness. Ringworm often develops as well. If left untreated, infection can spread to the toe and foot.

Symptoms

- Limping or refusing to walk
- Not wanting to be picked up, not wanting to jump down from high places

- Frequent biting or licking at nails
- Pieces of thread or fabric caught on claw, claws catching on clothing and rugs
- Claws clicking on hard floors
- Claw tip imbedded in pad
- Redness, swelling of cuticle or pad
- Discharge (wetness) around cuticle or pad

Recommendations

- Have veterinarian examine toes for abnormalities.
- Gently remove any wax or dirt with a fingernail and clean cat's claws with almond oil or olive oil.
- Feed a high-quality diet with as much raw food as possible (page 53). Be sure to include Vita-Mineral Mix and other listed supplements to diet.
- Add to each meal:
  - ¼ teaspoon feline enzymes to insure assimilation of all nutrients;
  - 1/16 teaspoon ascorbic acid crystals or sodium ascorbate powder (250 units vitamin C) if there is an infection present.
- Provide suitable scratching post, such as the Felix Katnip Tree (page 89), or cover any other scratching post with carpet backside out; be sure scratching post is stable.
- Practice greeting ritual to reinforce use of scratching post (see page 93).
- Fondle feet and claws and examine them every day (see page 143).
- Clip tips of claws every two to three weeks (see page 144).
- Reevaluate litter-box setup to check for sanitation (see page 79).
- Do not use cleaning compounds such as Lysol, kitty box deodorant sprays, and/or baking soda. They can irritate cat's feet.
- For in-grown claws, seek help of veterinarian or groomer at once.
- Have veterinarian check for fungus or parasites in ears or on body.

- If dirt around cuticles has built up from scratching ringworm or ear mites, follow directions for cleaning cuticles
  (see page 221), and then soak feet in golden seal or echni-
  cacea infusion as part of the general treatment (see page
  222).
- If there is a wound and healing is desired, soak foot in calendula infusion. See "Soaking Feet and Cleaning Cuticles,"
  page 221.
- If, instead of a clean wound, infection is present or if an
  ingrown claw has been extracted, draw out the poison with
  a foot soak of one cup warm water with two teaspoons epsom salts twice a day until infection has drained. Always
  follow the epsom salt with a rinse of clear water. The cat
  should not lick the epsom salt solution. (See also "Abscesses," page 354.)
- Add to each meal one teaspoon horsetail tea (page 259)
  or kombu broth (page 256) for extra silica and other
  minerals.

Coccidia
(see "Parasites")

Colitis
(see "Irritable Bowel Syndrome")

Concussion
(see "Injuries")

Constipation
(See also "Irritable Bowel Syndrome")

Constipation, straining at stool or passing hard dry stools, has
become so prevalent among domestic cats as to be virtually universal. Commercial foods, all-meat diets, and fish are all low in
bulk (fiber) and result in a hard stool that passes slowly and with

difficulty through the intestine. Constipation can also be a symptom of hair impaction or of some disease that causes dehydration such as kidney disease, diabetes, pancreatitis, hyperthyroidism, cardiomyopathy, or irritable bowel syndrome.

Frequently when cats are sick, owners call to ask me what to do about the additional problems of constipation. Because a sick cat often stops eating, the desperate owner tries to get the cat to eat by offering baby food meat. This usually gets the cat to eat all right, but baby food meat is incomplete nutrition and such a low-bulk food that it forms into hard little balls inside the cat's intestine and causes constipation because there is no roughage whatsoever for the intestine to "grab onto."

If constipation is not treated, the intestinal walls will stretch and pockets will form as in diverticulosis. This will cause the cat to strain even more. In extreme cases the cat will be forced to take an unusual posture to pass stools, sometimes even standing with a paw up on the side of the litter box. Because a hard stool is held inside the body longer, some of the wastes will be reabsorbed and a coating of old stool will build up on the intestinal walls.

Both constipation and diarrhea are symptoms; they are not diseases in themselves but a sign that something else could be very wrong deeper in the body. If the intestinal tract is very badly obstructed, chances are that even the vet's laxative won't help. So don't wait more than three days, and make sure the vet knows it has already been three days since the cat passed a stool. The vet will have to wait an additional day after administering a laxative to see if it works before deciding whether to do an X ray, give an enema, or even resort to surgery. If the cat's diet is high quality and rich in fiber and the cat is groomed every day, such a situation almost never arises.

A healthy cat passes a stool once or twice a day. The stool color can range from medium to dark brown, and it should be in long pieces and soft enough to be easily flattened when pressed. It is natural for the stool to have an odor.

Good health can best be maintained and recovery from any disease can be speeded up to a great extent if attention is given to strengthening the intestine, balancing the friendly bacteria, and conditioning the texture of the stool.

Symptoms

- Hard stool, often black in color
- Stool formed of several small hard pieces or even balls
- Straining at stool
- Remaining in squatting position for a long time before and/or after stool is passed
- Blood in stool
- Crying out while passing stool
- Failure to pass stool daily

Prevention:

- Groom cat at least thirty seconds a day to prevent hair impaction.
- Reevaluate grooming tool (see Chapter 7, "Grooming").
- Feed a high-quality diet with as much raw food as possible (see page 53), being sure to include Vita-Mineral Mix, which contains bran to condition the stool.
- Three times a week add an additional one teaspoon grated carrot per meal to help clean intestinal walls.

Recommendations

After one day of not passing a stool

- Follow suggestions above.
- Prepare the following Stool Softener Treat and serve once or twice a day, sprinkled with brewer's or nutritional or flaked yeast if your cat is a yeast lover:

Stool Softener Treat
1 tablespoon baby food vegetables and meat mixture
½ teaspoon melted butter
⅛ teaspoon *ground* psyllium husks
⅛ teaspoon powdered or fine bran
2 tablespoons water (or more—use your judgment)

- Mix ½ teaspoon powdered bran with ½ teaspoon butter and serve as a treat.
- Add to food three times a week: ⅛ teaspoon Delicious Garlic Condiment (page 256). It will strengthen intestinal muscles.
- Add to one meal a day ⅛ teaspoon Yerba Prima ground psyllium husks and 2 tablespoons water (first choice) *or* plain, unflavored Siblin or Metamucil and 2 tablespoons water.

For serious constipation (no stool for two to three days)

- Follow suggestions above.
- Ask veterinarian to check for hair balls or disease.
- If laxative gel in a tube is prescribed, be sure to give the medication at least two hours before or after meals, never mixing with food. Try to find a brand that is not preserved with sodium benzoate or benzoate of soda. You can also use plain petroleum jelly. (See "Giving Paste or Gel Medications," page 210.)
- If the veterinarian suggests it, give an enema (see page 231).
- Ask your vet if your cat seems dehydrated. If he says yes and if your cat has no heart problems, request that he hydrate the cat with 100 ml or so of subcutaneous fluid (called Ringer's Lactate). This therapy is simple and very valuable and always serves to give the patient's body a wonderful head start toward perfect health. (See "Subcutaneous Hydration," page 235.)
- Herbal remedies: I do not use laxatives, herbal or otherwise. However, psyllium husks, especially when finely ground, are an efficient stool conditioner and mucoid. They help the stool to slip out easily and are not habit-forming. Be sure to add plenty of extra water when you use them.
- Bach flower remedies: Constipated cats tend to hold tension in their bodies and secret worries in their minds. Give three drops four times a day of the following mixture prepared as given on page 249:
    Crabapple—to help expel toxins;

Vine—to help relax;
Aspen—to dispel vague fears.

Corneal Ulcer
(see "Eye Problems")

Cuts
(see "Injuries")

Cystitis
(See "Feline Urologic Syndrome")

Dandruff

Dandruff is a waste product. As Chapter 2 discusses, when the smell of food triggers the brain to prepare the body for digestion, waste disposal is slowed down tremendously, along with the rest of the metabolism. So, if the owner leaves food available between meals, the cat constantly smells food and the metabolism is constantly slow. The result is that wastes build up and back up. Disposing of wastes and toxins is just as important as taking in food. When the primary avenues of excretion—the kidneys and the intestines—are not able to handle these large amounts of wastes, they get rerouted through the secondary organs of excretion: the lungs, as carbon dioxide, and the pores of the skin, as grease and dandruff. Germs then build up on the dirty skin surface, which becomes a home for funguses, parasites, and infections. In addition, the coat mats easily because it is oily and dirty.

Dandruff can also be caused by any of several deficiencies, disorders, or imbalances. Its appearance signals that one or more of the other organs of excretion or detoxification has become too weak to do its own job. Also, the cat might be ingesting a large amount of toxins (as found in semimoist food) or an excess of proteins (as in an all-meat diet). Dandruff or oiliness is also one of the first signs that the body's metabolism has become too slow. Ninety percent of all cats with dandruff have owners who allow their cats to smell food all day long by leaving some sort of food or a dirty food bowl on the floor between meals and/or by giving frequent snacks or treats. Dry food is the usual culprit here. Dandruff almost always disappears when owners begin removing all food between meals. The lecithin granules contained in the Vita-Mineral Mix help emulsify the fatty wastes so the blood and urine can carry them away and send them out through the urine and stool.

Cats with dandruff are not inviting to snuggle and pet. The rejection that results leads to depression—which is a stress. This lowers the cat's resistance and makes him more vulnerable to disease and parasites—a classic snowball situation. Matted hair prevents the cat's tongue from reaching his dirty skin to clean it, and, in areas where he can lick and clean himself, he will only be recycling his own wastes—a "can't win" situation.

Symptoms

- White or brown dandruff flakes on cat's coat, on floors, furniture, and your clothing
- Oily fur, tendency to mat
- Frequent throwing up of hair balls
- Excess shedding of hair
- Tendency to pick up fleas, mange mites, or ringworm
- Constant licking and/or scratching
- Body odor

Recommendations

- Have veterinarian check for illness—especially in kidneys, intestines, liver, and thyroid.
- Increase metabolic efficiency by feeding only twice a day and removing food between meals, leaving water always available (see page 44).
- Eliminate impurities in the diet by avoiding commercial cat foods that contain chemicals and by-products; feed a high-

quality diet with as much raw food as possible (see "Diet," page 53). Be sure to include Vita-Mineral Mix and other listed supplements in diet.

- Add to each meal:

  > Extra ¼ teaspoon lecithin (in addition to lecithin in Vita-Mineral Mix) to help body dispose of fatty wastes;
  >
  > Extra ¼ teaspoon bran (in addition to bran in Vita-Mineral Mix) to aid the intestines

- Use finely grated carrot or zucchini as the fresh vegetable in the meal at least once a day.
- Encourage energetic play before meals once or twice a day to help speed metabolism and facilitate normal waste disposal.
- Bathe every two or four weeks until condition is corrected to prevent recycling of wastes (see "The Bath" page 157). Finish the bath with an acid rinse: one part lemon juice to eight parts water *or* one part cider vinegar to eight parts water.
- Bach flower remedies: give three drops of crabapple prepared as given in page 249 four times a day to encourage cleansing.

Deafness
(See also "Ear Problems")

Deafness can be caused by wax impacted against the ear drum; an infection causing swelling around the ear drum; wax or swelling and/or injury due to ear mites; rupture of the ear drum due to infection or injury; or congential deafness as found in some but not all blue-eyed white cats and odd-eyed white cats. Deaf cats should never be allowed to wander free. They are missing a major sense, the one that gives them early warning of danger. Deaf cats are vulnerable to attack by dogs, wandering toms, coyotes, mountain lions, and other predators, and they are incapable of detecting an oncoming motor vehicle until it is too late.

Symptoms

- Cat does not react when others are responding to a sound stimulus
- Cat does not react to another cat's communication by sound, such as a hiss or warning growl
- Cat is easily startled by touch unless he has seen you coming or felt your vibration on the floor

Recommendations

- Ask veterinarian to determine cause.
- Treat any infection.
- Check for dirty teeth, which can cause infection.
- Use veterinary wax-dissolving oil followed by an ear flush (see page 219).
- If veterinarian is anesthetizing cat for another procedure, such as teeth cleaning, ask him to do an ear flush as well.
- Feed a high-quality diet with as much raw food as possible, including Vita-Mineral Mix and other supplements to the diet (see page 53).

If deafness is incurable

- Be sure *always* to signal before you touch the cat either by sight or by tapping on the floor or on the surface where the cat is sitting.
- Continue to talk to cat when you hold him or whenever you have his attention. He can still pick up on your mental attitudes and pictures. You convey these best when you verbalize them.
- Be alert to help the deaf cat avoid impending social difficulties that may arise with other cats because of his inability to hear a warning or challenge.
- Protect the deaf cat by confining indoors or to a screened-in area. Never allow cat to roam or be in the yard unsupervised.
- Devise vibration and sight signals to communicate. Here are a few examples:

1. To say "come," flick the lights off and on or stomp a particular number of times in a particular clear pattern;
2. To indicate "May I pick you up?" extend your hands palms up.

Diabetes

Diabetes is a disease of the pancreas, whose job it is to produce insulin. Insulin combines with the tissue cells making it possible for (a) sugar to enter the cells to be used, or (b) sugar to be changed into fat or starch for storage, or (c) stored fat to be burned up and used for energy. If the pancreas is not manufacturing sufficient insulin, the sugar remains in the blood until, with the help of copious drinking, it is passed off in the urine. Sugar in the urine is a sign of diabetes. Without sufficient insulin little fat is available for storage, and stored fat cannot be converted to energy. Because of copious drinking and frequent urination, most of the water soluble vitamins and minerals will be washed out of the system. Every time the insulin level falls, a stress situation results and *all* the antistress nutrients (vitamins E, C, B complex, and potassium) are rapidly depleted. Both extreme stress and cortisone therapy have been known to produce a diabetic like reaction.

The typical diabetes-related diseases and complications, such as fatty liver, clogged arteries, gangrene, obesity, retinitis, and cataracts, have all been prevented when the high nutritional needs are met. When a nutritional program is instituted that supplies all the nutrients the cat's body needs to build up the pancreas, heal pancreatic scarring, replace water soluble nutrients and those nutrients used up by stress, stimulate insulin production by the pancreas, and, at the same time, lower the body's need for insulin, then the dose of insulin the animal needs to take is always dramatically lowered. Often, the dosage can be completely discontinued except if a stress situation again occurs. It is essential to work closely with the veterinarian while you are building up your cat's health and his ability to produce his own insulin again. You are walking a very fine line between insulin shock and diabetic coma.

Insulin shock means that too much insulin has been given to

the cat. Insulin will always need to be reduced if the diet is improved and stress reduced, so again, be sure to work closely with your veterinarian. If you are also using an experienced homeopath, success will come more quickly, so be vigilant. Diabetic coma means that the body still needs more insulin therapy; perhaps a reduction can be made later if the pancreas can be built up more or stress further reduced. I repeat: I have always worked very closely with the veterinarian, who constantly adjusts the insulin level as the cat improves. It does take time and attention for a while, but you usually end up with a cat who is healthier than he ever was before the trouble began, because all sorts of small problems will automatically be corrected along with the diabetes.

Diabetes often produces copious urination as the body tries to wash the excess sugar out of the system. Copious urination is a sign that more insulin may be needed. If the patient becomes dehydrated, ask the veterinarian to hydrate your cat with Ringer's Lactate solution given subcutaneously. Because I have the Ringer's Lactate at home to hydrate the kidney patients, my own vet has agreed that I can give Daisy, my diabetes patient, a little fluid once a week by hydrating her with 100 ml of solution. If there is any extra sugar in the blood, this will help her body to wash it out; if not, she'll simply pass the fluids out with the urine. We first made sure Daisy's heart was strong and her blood pressure normal so we knew there was no danger of a build-up of fluids anywhere in the body. (See "Subcutaneous Hydration," page 235.)

Diabetes patients crave warmth, so it is wise to provide an outside source of heat such as a snug retreat, which also serves to cushion stress.

Symptoms

- Copious drinking and copious urination (*note:* this can also signal kidney disease, see page 372)
- Good appetite but loss of weight
- Repeated infections: feline urologic syndrome, respiratory problems, cysts, feline acne, and so on
- Wounds not healing
- Tendency to cataracts
- Urine tests high in sugar

- Urine tests high in xanthic acid (shows vitamin B-6 deficiency, which causes damage to pancreas)

Recommendations

- Consult veterinarian for a firm diagnosis and to set beginning insulin level.
- Feed diabetes diet given below.
- Groom and eliminate mats, fleas, ringworm, and the like to reduce stress.
- Be sure teeth are clean and anal glands normal.
- Provide a snug retreat (see page 240).
- Provide *regular* play and exercise—be sure it's regular or insulin needs will fluctuate.
- Give Bach flower remedy to reduce stress. (Stress raises the body's need for insulin.) Give 3 drops twice a day of the following mixture prepared as given on page 249:
    Hornbeam—to bolster self confidence;
    Mimulus—to reduce fear.
- Herbal remedy—give a teaspoon to a tablespoon of herbal tea added to all food. Ask your cat which he prefers: dill tea (increases appetite and provides minerals) or horsetail (gives strength and provides minerals).

Diabetes Diet

Note: the goal of this diet is to strengthen the pancreas, reduce scarring, reduce insulin needs, stimulate insulin production, replace nutrients lost in urine or because of stress, and prevent the main complications associated with diabetes.

FORMULA I

½ cup raw ground chuck or organic chicken (see precautions for freshness on page 58)

½ cup raw liver

½ cup cooked grain (brown rice, oatmeal, millet, cornmeal, or rye) *or* ½ cup raw oat bran that has been soaked in water for forty-eight hours

¼ cup finely grated raw zucchini or carrot *or* cooked green
beans, onion, winter squash, or peas
¼ teaspoon Delicious Garlic Condiment (see page 256)
Kombu broth (see page 256), vegetable broth, parsley tea, or
dill seed tea (see page 259) to moisten

FORMULA II

1 very soft cooked or poached egg (yolk runny, white cooked,
or raw yolk, white cooked)
½ cup grain (see Formula I)
¼ cup vegetable (see Formula I)
½ cup very rare chicken
Chicken broth or mixture of chicken broth and kombu broth
(see page 256) to moisten

- Combine ingredients in blender or food processor and
blend. Store frozen in one-meal portions in self-sealing
plastic bags. Thaw as needed by dropping bag into bowl of
hot water.
- Feed three to five small meals a day (¼ to ½ cup per
meal). Five is best, but stick to the same schedule every
day.

- *Add to each meal before serving:*
    1 teaspoon Vita-Mineral Mix (see page 55);
    1 teaspoon chopped alfalfa sprouts;
    ¹⁄₁₆ teaspoon ascorbic acid crystals or sodium ascorbate
    powder (250 units vitamin C);
    ¹⁄₁₆ teaspoon potassium chloride (salt substitute).
    1 drop stevia extract or 1 teaspoon stevia tea

- *Once a day (after breakfast) give:*
    100 units vitamin E (alpha tocopherol) capsule. After
    two weeks, reduce to 400 units once a week.

- *Once a week add to meal:*
    10,000 units vitamin A and 400 units vitamin D from
    an A and D capsule that you have punctured.

Note: If you must use canned food (a poor second choice), avoid fish and add the supplements and grated vegetables to each meal as with the homemade diet above.

Diarrhea
(See also "Irritable Bowel Syndrome")

Note: Diarrhea in kittens under three months old can be very serious. If a young kitten gets diarrhea, *do not wait* more than half a day; take him straight to a veterinarian. Dehydration from diarrhea can kill a tiny kitten in one day.

Diarrhea, the passing of frequent soft or watery stool, is usually a sign that the body is trying to rid itself of some unusually toxic waste material by passing it out through the intestine. This is as it should be, and if diarrhea in an adult cat does not continue for more than one or two days, it is not serious and often clears up naturally when the backlog of toxic wastes have all been excreted. If there are no other negative symptoms present, don't be too quick to run to the medicine chest and grab something that will stop it right away. Instead, help the body to handle the problems by smoothing the path and minimizing the discomfort and the negative side effects.

If soft or runny stool persists for more than two days, it may mean that the intestinal wall is irritated or that parasites are present. The veterinarian should be consulted because diarrhea can be a symptom of poisoning or of any number of diseases such as hepatitis, colitis, pancreatitis, or irritable bowel syndrome. Many adult cats cannot digest milk products and will get diarrhea if milk, cheese, or yogurt are included in the diet. The early stages of hair ball impaction can also produce diarrhea as can intestinal parasites. Oddly enough, extreme dehydration can also produce diarrhea, which clears up after the cat is hydrated (see "Subcutaneous Hydration," page 235).

Symptoms

> *Note:* If diarrhea is violent or accompanied by vomiting, withhold food and consult veterinarian at once. This is an emergency situation.
> - Passing stool frequently, three or more times a day
> - Passing of loose, unformed, soft or watery stool
> - Unusually foul odor to stool
> - Stool mixed with mucus
> - Straw-colored or yellow soft stool
> - Passing gas with stool
> - Lethargy or depression
> - Hiding
> - Refusal to eat or eating voraciously and not gaining weight
> - Soil on bloomers

Recommendations

Diarrhea for one day

> - At the first sign of diarrhea withhold all solid food and put the cat on a fast of High-Calcium Chicken Broth (see "Fasting," page 225, and broth recipe, page 243). The patient may have as much as he likes three to five times a day, but remove the leftovers between feedings as you would with any food.
> - Alkalize the system (diarrhea almost always indicates a hyperacid system). Add one tablespoon of kombu seaweed broth to the chicken broth each time you feed.
> - Soothe the intestine by giving one teaspoon slippery elm syrup before each meal (see page 258). Slippery elm is soothing, alkalizing, and full of minerals.
> - Restore the balance of friendly bacteria in the intestine by adding one teaspoon unflavored liquid acidophilus to chicken broth. (Ask your health-food store for vegetarian acidophilus that contains no milk or lactose.)
> - Alkalize and purify the entire intestinal tract by giving ⅛ teaspoon liquid chlorophyll or Green Magma three times a

day—either in the chicken broth or mixed with a teaspoon of the broth and given as a liquid medication.
- Herbal remedy: If there is irritation in the intestine, golden seal infusion will soothe and provide a tonic for the entire digestive tract. Put five drops golden seal extract into ½ cup water. Give one to two teaspoons twice a day between meals (at least two hours before or after food). Or give ¼ dropperful golden seal elixir twenty minutes before meals. Discontinue after five days. (See "Giving Liquid Medication," page 210, and "Herbs," page 251.)

Diarrhea for two days

- Follow suggestions above.
- Consult veterinarian by phone.
- Watch for any other symptoms.
- If stool has a strong smell or if there is flatulence, give a charcoal capsule or tablet after the slippery elm syrup (see above) twice a day.
- Continue to withhold solid food and fast on chicken broth.

Diarrhea persisting on third day

- Follow suggestions above; *and*
- *Consult veterinarian by phone or visit.*
- Continue chicken broth fast.
- Give 3 cc plain, unflavored Kaopectate three times a day using a dropper or syringe (see "Giving Liquid Medication," page 210).
- Be sure cat is drinking water or broth (at least 30 cc daily) to prevent dehydration.

Diarrhea continuing unabated on fourth day

- *Take cat to veterinarian for diagnosis.*
- Dehydration can sometimes cause diarrhea to persist. Ask veterinarian if your cat seems dehydrated. As long as your cat has no heart problems, you can request that he administer subcutaneous fluids (see page 235). This always gives the patient a nice head start toward recovery.

Dry Coat
(See also "Skin Problems")

An extremely dry coat is not as common as an oily coat. An oily coat that has collected large amounts of dust and dirt or one in which the oils have hardened and clogged the pores is often mistaken for dry coat. In true dry coat, the hair is almost always sparse, and the skin easily seen through the hair. The hair is characterized by a coarse feeling and will sometimes break off at varying lengths and is easily matted. The skin will be sensitive to grooming or touch because of damaged capillaries that are not adequately feeding the skin nerves and hair follicles. Poor circulation or a lack of vitamin A, vitamin C, bioflavinoids, minerals, or B vitamins can result in weak or damaged capillaries. Another possible cause of dry coat is a lack of usable fats in the diet, often the result of feeding too lean a diet, or the failure of the liver or gall bladder to process the fats present in the food. Malabsorption, anorexia, and dehydration can all produce the same effect (see "Weight Loss," page 420). Dry coat can also be a result of hyperthyroidism (see page 345).

Any skin or coat problem is a sign that the cat's system is not functioning properly. It is out of balance. Homeopathy as practiced by an experienced veterinarian is the fastest, most thorough way to balance the system and allow all of your other efforts to give maximum benefit (see "Homeopathy," page 244).

Symptoms

- Thin, sparse hair; skin easily seen through hair
- Dry skin easily sunburnt
- Sensitivity to grooming and to being touched
- Coarse hair, sometimes brittle and breaking
- Sensitivity to heat and cold
- Dandruff (sometimes)
- Ringworm or other fungus; mange mites or fleas (see "Ringworm," "Parasites," "Mange Mites," and "Fleas")

Recommendations

- Have veterinarian examine and run tests to diagnose for illness and/or parasites (intestinal or skin).
- Treat for any illness or deficiency diagnosed by vet.
- Feed a high-quality diet with as much raw food as possible (see page 53). Be sure to include Vita-Mineral Mix and other listed supplements to diet.
- Add to food twice a day:
    ¼ teaspoon feline enzymes to insure digestion of food and supplements;
    ¼ teaspoon skin and coat oil supplement from the pet section of your health-food store; *or* 10 minims wheat germ oil from a punctured capsule.
- Remove food between meals, leaving only water available.
- Groom lightly and frequently to stimulate skin capillaries. Use a soft brush at first until condition improves; then work up to wire slicker brush after cat is well. Use wide-toothed metal comb for longhaired cats. (See Chapter 7, "Grooming.")
- Be careful to protect cat from heat, cold, and sun.
- Have a regular daily play period to stimulate circulation.
- Give homeopathic treatments prescribed by homeopathic veterinarian.

Ear Mites
(see "Ear Problems")

Ear Problems
(See also "Deafness")

Just as a cat's sense of smell is so many times greater than ours, so are the ears much more sensitive. The sign of something wrong with the cat's ears is not always wax or discharge, although those are the most common. Any sort of irritation inside the ear canal, any kind of swelling down there, will cause an itch. The very first sign of trouble is a cat trying to relieve that unreachable itch by rapidly shaking his head or trying to dig into the ear with a hind claw. (Dirt build-up around the cuticles of the hind claws is frequently a sign of either ear problems or skin problems.) Sometimes sores on the forehead or around the ear are a sign not of trouble where the sores are but of the cat's desperate scratching in an attempt to reach a maddening itch deep inside the ear canal.

Wax in the ears—or any kind of discharge—can be caused by any one of a number of things. Ear mites produce a dry, dark brown wax; swelling and redness due to allergies or infection are often accompanied by a softer light brown or yellow wax. Untreated infections and wounds will produce puss and/or blood. *The only course is to take the cat to the veterinarian and let the veterinarian determine the cause.*

Ear problems are easier to treat if they are caught and diagnosed early—even before a discharge begins to form. Head shaking, head tilting, or digging with the back claw in and around the ear and above the eye are all signs of ear trouble. If left untreated, ear infection can spread to throat, eyes, gums, or even into the brain. Ear pain and itching are high-stress situations that weaken the body, rendering it easy prey to germs or viruses.

Ear Wax but No Mites

If your veterinarian determines that your cat's ear wax is not caused by mites, the other possibilities are germs, some sort of waste discharge or eruption inside the ear canal, an allergic reaction, or a yeast infection of already damaged tissue. First make sure that the problem is only in the outer ear canal and does not include the inner ear. If that is the case, my own veterinarian recommends a cleansing flush (see page 219) with Betadyne solution followed by the mild white vinegar solution (see page 262), which leaves the ear canal with a desirable acid balance. I have found that it takes about three weeks to completely clear up the problem.

I have found it important to clean the back claws and cuticles once a week. You can't look very far into the ear canal to see how well you're succeeding, but you will be able to monitor your progress by noting how much dirt has collected around the back cuticles.

By the third week there should be almost nothing for you to clean off. Cleaning the cuticles also prevents reinfection of the ear when the cat scratches with the dirty claws.

- Day 1—flush ears with Betadyne solution (page 219) followed by vinegar solution (page 262).
- Days 2 through 7—twice a day put ½ dropper of warm acid solution into each ear. If cat objects, dilute solution by half or a third for one week. Repeat for three rounds.

Ear Mites

Ear mites are nearly microscopic sluglike creatures. They burrow into the delicate tissue inside the ear canal and lay their eggs there under the skin. Ear mites cause wounds and scarring of the membrane. Therefore, when treating for mites, attention must be given to healing the tissue and treating and cat for stress (see "Antistress Supplements," page 240) as well as destroying the mites.

Dr. Pitcairn's herbal prescription for treatment addresses these problems very nicely. This is the method I employ to eliminate ear mites:

- Follow diet recommendations below.
- Flush ears and clean back cuticles as above for ear wax. Also use the Betadyne solution to shampoo around the ears, head, and the end of the tail, which rests near the ears when the cat sleeps. Mites and eggs are sometimes found there.

Dr. Pitcairn's Ear Mite Treatment

- Days 1, 2, and 3—heal the membrane inside the ear canal and smother some of the mites by using one dropperful of Dr. Pitcairn's healing ear oil (see below) in each ear once a day. Hold the ear flap closed over the oil and massage the oil around. Then let the cat go ahead and shake the excess oil out. Blot the fur dry with a paper towel. (See "Giving Ear Medication," page 217).

- Days 4, 5, and 6—rest. Do nothing.
- Days 7, 8, and 9—kill the mites. Put one dropperful of Dr. Pitcairn's Herbal Ear Mite Solution (see below) into each ear once a day the same as you did with the healing oil.
- Days 10 through 19—do nothing.
- Days 20 through 28—to catch any mites that have hatched since the first treatment, repeat the whole process, following directions for days 1 through 9 above.

Dr. Pitcairn's Healing Ear Oil

Into a one-ounce dropper bottle put:

¾ oz almond oil

¼ oz olive oil

400 units vitamin E oil (from punctured capsules), to preserve oil and heal tissue

Refrigerate. Warm before using by setting bottle in bowl of warm water.

Dr. Pitcairn's Herbal Ear Mite Solution

2 teaspoons ground dried rue

5 teaspoons witch hazel extract

1 cup boiling water

Steep rue in boiling water for fifteen minutes. Strain. Add witch hazel to liquid. Refrigerate. Warm before using by standing container in bowl of hot water.

If you decide to use a veterinary preparation for mites instead of the more gentle herbal method outlined above, here's a word of caution: when dealing with ear mites, be very sure to follow strictly the veterinarian's orders as to how often and how long to repeat the treatment. Mites are like fleas in that you can't kill the eggs. The veterinarian knows the life cycle of the organism and will gear the treatment so that you catch and kill the little horrors shortly after they hatch and before they can reproduce. When the prescribed time is over, before you heave a sigh of relief, a second test must be made by the veterinarian to see that all signs of the infestation are truly gone. It's a good idea to shampoo around the ears and tail tip as you would when doing the herbal treatment. Eggs clinging there could reinfest the ears. Many veterinary mite preparations contain steroids (see page 268), plus a very caustic chemical poison to kill the mites. If you decide to use one of these, *do not use a cotton swab to clean the ear first*. Rubbing against the very delicate ear membrane with the swab sensitizes the tissue. The mite medication may then feel like it's burning the inside of the ear.

However, beginning the treatment with a warm, gentle ear flush (see page 219) will give the patient relief and help the medicine to work faster (see "Giving Ear Medication," page 217). Here, too, it is wise to clean the cuticles as given above to prevent reinfestation.

Symptoms

- Ear exudation of hard brown wax, or flaky brown wax
- Head shaking after being touched anywhere near the ears
- Head tilt, stumbling and/or falling
- Digging into ear or over eye or on upper throat with back claws
- Wax under cuticle (which can cause toe infection)
- Bald patch or redness anywhere around ear or below ear on neck

Recommendations

- Determine the cause of the problem. Have veterinarian check for fleas; mites; bacterial, viral, or yeast infection; and so on. *Do not clean the ears before the examination.*
- Feed a high-quality diet (see Chapter 2, "Diet"). Be sure to include Vita-Mineral Mix and other listed additions to diet.
- Raise the cat's resistance by feeding as much raw food as possible (see page 58) and by removing all food between meals.
- Add an extra 1/16 teaspoon sodium ascorbate or ascorbic acid crystals (250 units vitamin C) to each meal to help the body process out the toxic ear mite medication.

- Add an extra ¼ teaspoon lecithin to each meal (in addition to lecithin in Vita-Mineral Mix).
- Add ⅛ teaspoon Delicious Garlic Condiment (page 256) to each meal food once a day.
- During any exudation, fast the cat for one day a week on High-Calcium Chicken Broth (see page 243; see "Fasting," page 225).
- Carefully follow veterinarian's directions for ear medication. This is especially important when treating mites. Do not clean ears with cotton swab before administering medication—you don't want to irritate the inner membrane (see "Giving Ear Medication," page 217). However, you may want to precede the treatment with a nice cleansing ear flush (see page 219).
- Clean wax off back claws and from under back cuticles with peroxide, almond oil, or sesame oil on cotton swabs, scrape with your own fingernail, or, better yet, soak the feet and clean the nails and cuticles (see page 221).
- Herbal remedy: after cleaning the claws thoroughly, if the cuticles are red, swollen or injured, add a final soak in warm calendula solution to soothe and heal. Mix two cups warm water, one teaspoon salt, and twenty drops calendula extract or tincture of calendula.
- Bach flower remedies: Give three drops four times a day of the following mixture prepared as given on page 249.
     Crabapple—to help expel impurities;
     Impatiens—to calm.

Emergencies
(see "Injuries")

Entropion
(see "Eye Problems")

Eye Problems
(See also "Blindness")

Eye discharge may appear temporarily if there is an eye wound or a foreign body is lodged there. The eye will then automatically secrete an unusually large amount of tears in an attempt to cleanse itself. However, if the discharge is constant, this indicates an abnormal condition. A back-up of wastes in the body may cause the eyes and/or ears to run as the system tries to rid itself of toxins through any door it can find. A diet high in chemicals (preservatives and other food additives) or a poorly balanced diet, such as an all-meat diet, can be the cause, as can leaving food available between meals, which slows the metabolism and causes wastes to back up. An infection in an eye can spread from dirty teeth or from upper respiratory problems. Conversely, infected tear ducts can spread infection into the mouth, nose, ears, or upper respiratory tract.

By far the most common cause of chronic eye discharge is blocked and/or malformed tear ducts. Persian cats especially are plagued with eye problems because of in-breeding to produce the congenital deformity of a very flat face (called the "peke-face"). The flat, straight nose of the very inbred Siamese can also produce the same problem because, as with the Persian's face, there is not enough room for normal tear ducts in the deformed skull structure. Many cats with eye problems come out of catteries where they are inbred to produce the specific facial structure that predisposes them to have this problem. This is done for profit because human beings have decided that a certain facial structure is more attractive. It is done without regard for the health or the comfort of the animal. To me, this indicates insensitivity on the part of the breeder.

A cat who has spent time under the care of an insensitive human may have had several uncomfortable or frightening experiences in life to deal with before coming to you, an owner who loves him and cares more for his comfort, health, and happiness than for the shape of his nose. The Bach flower remedies given below will help the cat put such negative emotional memories behind him.

(See below for specific eye problems: cataracts, corneal ulcer, and entropion.)

Symptoms

- Running eyes, red-rimmed eyes, squinting
- Brown-stained fur around eyes and nose
- White or yellow discharge from eyes
- Snuffling or sneezing, repeated respiratory infections
- Bad breath, red gums

Recommendations

- Have veterinarian check for infections, foreign objects, or wounds in eyes.
- Clip nails of all animals in the household to prevent accidental injury during play or scuffles.
- Give ½ teaspoon cod liver oil each day, or once a week give a capsule containing 10,000 units of vitamin A and 400 units of vitamin D (see "Giving Liquid Medication," page 210, or "Giving Pills," page 208).
- Remove all food between meals, leaving only water available.
- Feed a high-quality diet with as much raw food as possible (see page 58). Be sure to include Vita-Mineral Mix and other listed supplements to diet.
- Fast the cat on High-Calcium Chicken Broth (page 208) one day a week until discharge clears up (if you're not already doing a regular weekly fast) (see page 243).
- Add ¹⁄₁₆ teaspoon ascorbic acid crystals or sodium ascorbate powder to each meal to help the body rid itself of infection.
- Wash eyes with golden seal solution (see "Giving Eye Drops," page 212).
- Bach flower remedies: give three to four drops four times a day of the following mixture prepared as given on page 249:

    Willow—for overcoming past misfortune;
    Crabapple—for cleansing;
    Walnut—to break away from old patterns, memories, and ties.

- Herbal remedy: add five drops of herbal tincture or extract to ½ cup of normal saline eye wash (see page 260). Choose from those herbs below according to what you and your veterinarian decide and what makes your cat feel good.

     Calendula—to speed healing of wounds in or around eye; also soothes soreness and inflammation;

     Chamomile—to reduce inflammation and soothe;

     Golden seal—to reduce inflammation and swelling; also antiseptic and antifungal;

     Eyebright—to reduce inflammation;

     Echinacea—to reduce inflammation; also antifungal.

Cataracts

A cataract is a white cloudiness occurring in the clear lens of the eye where light and images are transmitted and focused. Cataract is most frequently found in old or diabetic animals, but it is sometimes seen in younger cats as well. It is often difficult to trace the cause, but any one of several dietary deficiencies have produced cataracts in laboratory animals. A vitamin B-2 deficiency can produce oily skin and lashes as well as cataracts. A cholesterol problem will clog all of the blood vessels, including the small capillaries feeding the eye, and cataracts can result. A diet lacking the amino acids histidine, phenylalanine, or any one of several others has produced cataracts. A cat forced to survive on a vegetarian diet will always go blind from lack of taurine, an amino acid found only in animal flesh; cats cannot manufacture their own taurine as humans can. Certain types of cataracts have been produced when vitamin C was lacking; the problem then improved when vitamin C was supplied.

Symptoms

- Cloudiness inside the eye behind the pupil
- Chewing and licking nonfood items such as glue, wires, plastic, bricks, belts, cat litter

Recommendations

- See veterinarian for diagnosis.
- Feed a high-quality diet (see page 53). Be sure to include Vita-Mineral Mix and other listed supplements to diet.
- Give ¹⁄₁₆ teaspoon ascorbic acid crystals or sodium ascorbate powder in each meal (250 units vitamin C).
- Increase vitamin E to 100 units a day for two weeks; then return to a maintenance dose of 400 units once a week.
- Wash eyes three or four times a day with an herbal eye wash solution (see "Giving Eye Drops," page 212).

Corneal Ulcer
(scratch on the eye)

A corneal ulcer is a minor or deep wound on the surface of the eye itself. The scratch is usually difficult to see, but it causes a runny eye for a day or two, then heals over if the animal is in a state of normal health. *If there is any blood in the eye discharge—any at all—the cat should be rushed to the veterinarian for treatment.* Blood in an eye wound is always serious and indicates that the very delicate inner eye has been injured and that the wound is very deep.

Symptoms

- Watery eye or eye discharge of yellow or brown
- Closing eye or squinting
- Bloody discharge—*see veterinarian at once*

Recommendations

- See veterinarian if blood is present or if symptoms do not disappear after three or four days.
- Give a capsule that contains 10,000 units vitamin A and 400 units vitamin D twice a week until healed; then reduce dosage to once a week. Puncture capsule and empty contents into food, or see "Giving Pills," page 208.

- Increase vitamin E to 100 units a day until healed.
- Place one drop cod liver oil into eye or inside lower lid four times a day.
- Wash eyes three or four times a day with an herbal eye wash solution (see "Giving Eye Drops," page 212).

Entropion
(lower eyelid turned inward)

When a cat's lower eyelid rolls permanently inward—*entropion*—the lower lashes will rub against the cornea and produce an ulcer that is sometimes visible as a white line from healed "old" ulcers or a crater in the cornea. In some cats, entropion is a congenital deformity. In others, it can develop slowly because of repeated inflammation or swelling caused by infections or injuries, washing while teeth are dirty, germ growth in blocked tear ducts, or infections spreading from the nose. When the lower lid swells and shrinks again and again, the tissues become abnormal in shape and can shrivel inward, producing entropion. This condition is easily corrected by surgery but will recur if the underlying cause is not cleared up.

Symptoms

- Constant tearing and eye discharge of colorless, brown, or white material
- Frequent blinking
- Sometimes a white line visible just under lower lid
- Lower lashes touching eye

Recommendations

- Ask veterinarian to diagnose, then perhaps correct the condition with surgery.
- Eliminate cause by treating any infections, cleaning teeth, and so on.
- Give 100 units per day vitamin E for two weeks; then re-

turn to maintenance dose of 400 units once a week to help normalize lower lid tissue.
- Wash eyes three or four times a day with an herbal eye wash solution (see "Giving Eye Drops," page 212).

Feline Acne
See also "Skin Problems")

Feline acne appears under the chin as a small lump or black debris or pimples. I have noticed during the shedding seasons in spring and autumn that there always seems to be an increase of feline acne cases. During the sheds the body processes shift into a sort of "clean-out" gear. Besides getting rid of the old hair, old body wastes are excreted through the pores. When the sebaceous glands under the chin oversecrete, filling the pores with sebaceous fluid, the pores can become clogged and feline acne results.

It is not a serious problem, it is simply a little warning signal to alert you that (a) there are too many wastes building up in your pet's body, and (b) the organs of excretion are not functioning at top efficiency and are not handling the wastes as they should. The problem always improves when you upgrade the diet, remove all food between meals, nurture all of the organs of excretion, and keep the area of eruption clean.

If the acne persists, let your veterinarian examine the area just to be sure it really is acne. If he confirms that it is indeed acne, persevere with the treatments below, especially the weekly fasting day and the improved diet. The added vitamins A and D will help the liver detoxify the old wastes; the vitamin C will help the lymph ducts carry off the old wastes; zinc and vitamin E will strengthen the skin and aid in its repair. As a general rule I always like to help the body get rid of wastes during the spring and autumn sheds by fasting the cats on broth one day a week. My chicken broth is very strong and delicious so the cats think of the fast day as a treat day.

My own vets caution against the use of antibiotics or other drug therapy for feline acne. I heartily agree. Homeopathic treatment administered by an experienced homeopathic vet has been very effective in speeding a complete cure.

Symptoms

- Small lump or black debris or pimples under the chin

Recommendations

- Upgrade the diet by eliminating all poisons, chemicals, and meat by-products from the diet by double-checking ingredients listed on the food you feed your cat. Do not feed any by-products (found even in some so-called "health-food" and veterinary brands of food), preservatives, colorings, or sugar (see page 47). Include Vita-Mineral Mix and other listed supplements.
- Help the body build resistance to disease by feeding as much raw food as possible (see page 58). Reread the section "Changing Over to the New Diet," page 68.
- Add the following supplements:
    ⅟₁₆ teaspoon ascorbic acid crystals (250 units vitamin C) to each meal;

    10,000 units vitamin A and 400 units vitamin D once a week;

    5 mg zinc to each meal;

    400 units vitamin E from a punctured capsule once a week.
- Follow the feeding rules on page 44, by feeding only twice a day, removing all leftovers after one-half hour and leaving only water available between meals.
- Fast the cat one day a week on High-Calcium Chicken Broth (see page 243) and see "Fasting," page 225.
- Add to each meal (in addition to the usual supplements):
    ¼ teaspoon bran (in addition to bran in Vita-Mineral Mix);

    1 teaspoon finely grated carrot or zucchini;

    ½ raw organic egg yolk (or 1 yolk per can of food)—to support the kidneys by keeping the urine acid to prevent the growth of germs.
- If the stool is quite smelly or if the cat has gas, give one charcoal capsule before breakfast.
- If the stool seems dry or hard or if it comes out in more

than two pieces, add $\frac{1}{16}$ teaspoon psyllium husks and 2 ta-blespoons water to each meal.

- If any antibiotics have been given in the last year, add 1 teaspoon liquid acidophilus to each meal.
- Keep the area of infection clean. Follow these steps:
    1. Clean away any old dried exudation by first using a hot compress (see page 234), then gently scraping away loose debris with your fingernail.
    2. Wash the area with a solution of $\frac{1}{2}$ cup warm water and $\frac{1}{2}$ teaspoon Betadyne scrub. Rinse *thoroughly*.
    3. Apply peroxide with a cotton ball (it will foam on contact).
    4. Rinse thoroughly.
    5. Apply White Vinegar Solution (see page 262) gener-ously with cotton ball. Repeat twice a day, except skip step 2 after first application.
- Herbal remedy: a poultice of mashed dandelion or water-cress leaves is cleansing and purifying.
- Bach flower remedy: Prepare as given on page 249 and give three drops four times a day of crabapple to assist the cleansing process.

Feline Infectious Peritonitis (FIP)

Feline Infectious Peritonitis, or FIP, is an immunological disease. The FIP virus itself is very fragile and cannot survive long outside of the warm moist body fluids. It can be destroyed in the environ-ment with a simple solution of one part chlorine bleach to thirty-two parts water. And yet FIP is considered a deadly disease, nearly always fatal once symptoms develop.

The reason is that the virus all alone does not produce the symptoms. The virus enters the body via intimate contact: washing, playing, biting, or being sprayed with infected mucus when a sick cat sneezes. The well cat's immune system then sends antibodies to combine with the invading viruses and destroy them. This is the normal immune system response, and this is what has always worked in the past. Unfortunately, this time the invader is an FIP virus. Instead of the antibodies combining with it and destroying it, the viruses and the antibodies bind together to form a whole new entity: a virus-antibody complex. These immune complexes, as they are called, attach to the walls of small veins, damaging the walls so that fluid leaks out into the body cavities.

Any veterinarian will tell you that FIP is difficult to diagnose. That is because the early symptoms, lethargy and a mild upper respiratory infection, look like the early symptoms of about twenty other diseases and are often so mild they are overlooked. The later symptoms, which can appear anywhere from weeks to years later, vary according to where in the victim's body the virus-antibody complex has taken hold. If the virus has settled in one of the abdominal organs, fluids will leak out and fill the abdomen. You will have a very skinny cat with a big belly. If the virus is in the pleural cavity around the lungs, there will be fluid in the chest cavity producing breathing difficulties. This is called the "wet" form of FIP. There is a dry form where fluid does not leak. Some veterinarians say the dry form is more common than the wet form; others say the reverse is true. The dry form is even harder to diagnose than the wet form, since there is no telltale excess fluid present. Symptoms will show up according to which organ has been attacked. If the liver is affected, you may see jaundice with personality changes; if the kidneys are being damaged, copious drinking and urination. FIP in the brain would produce seizures or paralysis. In the ear it would produce a head tilt and staggering. I have a theory that many cats have died of undiagnosed FIP, especially the dry form. They were probably treated for secondary diseases produced when the virus attacked one organ or another.

Any diagnosis is like putting together the pieces of a jigsaw puzzle. In FIP one important clue is a persistent high temperature. FIP is found mostly in cats under two or over thirteen and in cats who already have an immune system disease, such as feline leukemia, asthma, or arthritis. My own theory here is that the first autoimmune disease was a signal that the immune system was weak and needed serious attention. If poor diet continued or, worse yet, if the primary disease was treated with steroids or other strong drugs, this would weaken the immune system further so that a more serious illness could take hold. Cats under two have usually undergone a series of vaccinations, sometimes being vaccinated for three, four, or even seven diseases in the same week. The more modern and holistic veterinarians have warned us that this weakens and *confuses* the immune response. I put this information together with what we know about FIP and I became even more determined to immunize my own cats with homeopathic nosodes (see page 266) rather than with the shots dispensed by the standard allopathic veterinarian.

The blood test for FIP is not conclusive. FIP is one of several corona viruses. A positive result only means that the cat has one of the many corona viruses; the test is not specific. As for what to do if a cat of yours is diagnosed with this supposedly fatal disease, my advice is to pull out all the stops. I've done it; I've fought and lost, but I've also fought and won! But never alone. Every successful treatment of FIP (or feline leukemia) with which I've been involved has always been treated by what I call the winning team: the captain is my homeopathic holistic veterinarian, Dr. Pitcairn (who lives far away); we consult by phone daily if necessary. Supporting him is my local veterinarian doing the hands-on examinations, running the tests, and dispensing whatever he and Dr. Pitcairn together decide is right. Then there's me, coordinating the efforts, designing the diet, and making sure the owner understands what to do and how to do it and, most importantly, why. The owner is the key member of the team. It takes time and effort, patience and lots of determination, courage and, most of all, love.

Remember when you start out that your chances of achieving a cure are fifty-fifty or less. The bottom line is that you want to keep your furry friend as comfortable as possible for as long as possible. I like to help the owners turn this into a win-win situation. We work very hard and if our efforts help to achieve a cure, fine— we've won. On the other hand, if it becomes apparent that the patient's body is no longer able to sustain life without great discomfort, the owner and the rest of the team may decide that euthanasia (page 192) is the kindest and the most unselfish choice. As this means that you are still controlling the situation and you are still achieving your desire to prevent suffering, I call this another "win." You choose to prolong life; you refuse to prolong death. May the great Cat Spirit be with you.

Symptoms

- Begins with minor upper respiratory infection; then weeks or years later, it shows up disguised as some other disease, depending upon where in the cat's body the virus has settled
- High fever that persists despite all efforts to lower it
- Presence of another immune system disease: feline leukemia, cancer, arthritis, allergies, dermatitis, granular skin growths, severe gum disease, or asthma
- Presence of fluid in abdomen, distended abdomen
- Presence of fluid in chest, breathing difficulties

Recommendations

- Consult veterinarian for diagnosis.
- Consult homeopathic veterinarian for diagnosis and treatment (see "Homeopathy," page 244).
- If FIP is producing symptoms of another disease, read the appropriate section for help in alleviating those symptoms.
- If diuretic is prescribed (Lasix), read "Diuretics," page 267.
- Keep the patient warm; provide a snug retreat (page 240).
- If patient is eating, use all or as much raw food as possible in diet. Purée everything to aid digestion. Feed four to six small meals a day.
- Feed the I'll-Do-Anything-for-My-Cat Diet. For the vegetable portion, use finely puréed raw carrot or zucchini; for the grain portion use cooked amaranth, quinoa, millet, or buckwheat *or* raw soaked oat bran (see page 262).
- Add to each meal:
  ¼ teaspoon feline digestive enzymes;
  ¹⁄₁₆ teaspoon ascorbic acid crystals (250 units vitamin C)—do not use sodium ascorbate;
  ⅛ teaspoon liquid chlorophyll;
  ¼ teaspoon liquid acidophilus;
  ⅛ teaspoon Delicious Garlic Condiment (see page 256).
  10 mg CoEnzyme Q10
- If force feeding is necessary, see page 225.

- If only liquids are tolerated or if the patient refuses any of the above supplements, make Chicken Super Soup (page 244), using only spring or filtered water. Mix the above supplements into ⅛ cup of the soup and give by dropperful every two to four hours (see "Force-Feeding Liquids," page 225).
- Provide spring or filtered water to drink, and remove all chemicals from food and environment, including fabric softener on towels, room deodorizer, and so on.
- Keep stress low. Before giving any remedy or preparation, read the appropriate section in this book. Always explain to your cat everything you're going to do before you do it.
- Bach flower remedies: Give three drops four times a day of the following mixture prepared as given on page 249:
  Mimulus—to quell fears concerning bodily functions;
  Olive—to bolster energy;
  Gorse—to banish despair.

Feline Leukemia

Feline leukemia virus depresses the cat's immune system, causing lymphosarcoma and/or leukemia. Lymphosarcoma is a cancer of the cells found in the lymph nodes and tissue, thymus gland, or blood and bone marrow. Other internal organs can also be affected, but this is less frequent. Leukemia affects blood cells and is often associated with anemia.

There are several blood tests for feline leukemia virus. *This is not a test for cancer*. It simply tells whether or not the cat is *carrying* the virus. The results can be inconclusive, and no test is infallible. A positive result does not mean the cat has cancer; it means that the cat is carrying the virus that can sometimes cause cancer and that he or she can shed that virus in the urine and saliva and this may infect other cats. A carrier should be kept separate from other cats, especially the old, the very young, or the sick.

When a positive cat—one carrying the virus—comes into contact with a negative cat—one not carrying the virus—the negative, but exposed cat may:

- not become affected in any way;
- become infected (positive), develop immunity, and revert again to being negative;
- become positive, but not become ill and remain positive—thus becoming a new carrier of the virus;
- become positive and develop lymphosarcoma, leukemia, or other cancer; *or*
- become positive and be ill from the virus infection, much like flu; and then recover and remain positive or become negative.

A positive cat who has not developed cancer can be tested again in three months. If he has been treated by an experienced veterinary homeopath and put on a high-quality diet designed to build general health and strengthen the immune system, chances are good that he will have reverted to negative.

A negative blood test result means that the cat is not carrying the virus in his blood at that particular time. Yet it does not mean that he is immune. Furthermore, if the cat is in the very early stages of infection, presence of the virus may not show up on the test. A second test taken three to six months later that still shows negative results would be more conclusive. Other types of cancer may be present, but will not show up on the test.

The virus is not transferable to humans and is very perishable. It cannot live more than a few hours outside the cat and then only in a warm, moist environment. It is easily destroyed with chlorine bleach in water (use eight parts water to one part bleach). However, if a cat has died of feline leukemia-related cancer, veterinarians recommend waiting thirty days before getting another cat to be certain all the virus is gone from the environment.

The most recent cancer research has amassed a wealth of evidence linking a large percentage of all forms of feline leukemia to environmental pollution. Many chemicals in the air, water, and food; garden and household cleaners; and insecticides are carcinogens. Chemicals used directly on the cat, such as flea sprays and collars, can be even stronger factors. Modern veterinary immunologists warn that giving repeated vaccinations or several vaccinations together can depress and confuse the immune response (see "Vaccinations and Other Immunizations," page 265) as can any sort of steroid, whether used in an eye salve or given systemically as a pill (see "Cortisone and Other Steroids," page 268). The presence of other disease, viruses, or stress increases susceptibility. All of the above weaken the immune system.

One of the latest theories to come out of cancer research is called the "surveillance theory." In an article for *Prevention* magazine, Dr. Richard Pitcairn explains: "Cancer cells may be arising all the time in the body, but normally they are killed off by certain white blood cells which have the function of recognizing these deviants." He suggests, "If the immune system is healthy and strong, then it will do its job of eliminating any mutant cancer cells that arise." As with any disease, prevention is easier than curing, but in either case, the recommendations of Dr. Pitcairn and other holistically oriented veterinarians are the same: assist the body to protect itself and heal itself by (1) strengthening the immune system and (2) eliminating anything that depresses the immune system such as stress, chemicals, food colors, preservatives, concentrated hormones (found in meat meal, dry food, meat by-products), cortisone and other steroids.

Leukemia patients may have to travel to the veterinarian more frequently than other cats, and they will probably pick up your emotional tones. You will likely be experiencing worry and concern. These stresses can be minimized and cushioned a bit. Focus your mind on the positive aspects of what is being done. For example: remember that the veterinarian will help your cat feel better. Also try to emphasize short-term pleasures, such as the warm snug retreat and delicious homemade food. Do not dwell on negative possibilities and fears of the future.

Symptoms

Note: Early symptoms are general and similar to a number of other, unrelated diseases.

- Weight loss
- Depression
- Repeated persistent infections
- Failure of wounds to heal
- Persistent anemia
- Tumors revealed by palpation or X ray
- Fluid accumulation in chest or abdomen

Recommendations

- Consult veterinarian for diagnosis.
- Isolate cat; provide separate litter box and water and food bowls.
- Maintain a relaxed, supportive attitude.
- Groom daily (see page 126).
- Many leukemia patients crave warmth; if your cat is one of these, provide a snug retreat (see page 240).
- Protect the immune system by eliminating cortisone and all chemicals, which are found in commercial foods (especially dry and semimoist food); household cleaners; insecticides; air fresheners; fabric softeners; and cat litter treated with chemical deodorizers. Use only herbal flea products. (See Appendix, "Product Suppliers.")
- Feed diet of only 50 percent meat. Meat is at the top of the food chain and therefore has higher concentrations of DDT and other agricultural sprays (unless it is organic). If you can find organic meat or poultry, so much the better.
- Use only filtered or spring water.
- Feed a high-quality diet with as much raw food as possible to build the immune system (see Chapter 2, "Diet"). Use the following proportions and choices:
  1. *50 percent protein:*
     Raw hamburger or organic chicken or lightly cooked chicken, beef, lamb, turkey, or liver. Raw organic egg yolk and cooked egg white or tofu may be used as part but not all of the meat portion.
  2. *20 percent grain:*
     Oat bran soaked twenty-four hours in spring water or oat flakes soaked for forty-eight hours, or cooked farina, Wheatena, oatmeal, teff, amaranth, or quinoa.
  3. *30 percent vegetables:*
     Some can be cooked but raw is best. I use finely grated raw carrot or zucchini. The raw vegetables should be grated or puréed and added right before serving. If you use cooked vegetables, steamed carrot, celery, zucchini, and string beans are best, but

329

any other vegetable is permissible if your cat takes a fancy to it. Peas, broccoli, asparagus, mashed corn, squash, or raw finely chopped alfalfa sprouts or chives are all good.

- Add to each meal:

    1 teaspoon Vita-Mineral Mix (see page 55) for antistress factors and detoxification;

    1 tablet bioplasma, crushed into food;

    Contents of one capsule of liquid calcium or extra ¼ teaspoon bone meal;

    ¼ teaspoon feline enzymes to aid assimilation;

    10 mg CoEnzyme Q10

    ⅛ teaspoon olive oil to aid assimilation of vitamins A, D, and E;

    10,000 units vitamin A or ½ teaspoon cod liver oil (has been found to retard tumor growth in mice);

    2 to 3 mg zinc—to detoxify the body of heavy metals and helps body utilize vitamin A;

    1 teaspoon chopped alfalfa sprouts.

- Give a total of four doses of 250 units vitamin C each day (use 1/16 teaspoon ascorbic acid crystals or sodium ascorbate powder). Vitamin C is not stored in the body well so is most effective given in several doses throughout the day. Always mix vitamin C with a little High-Calcium Chicken Broth (page 243) or a teaspoon of a food the cat loves. Never give vitamin C without a little food.

- Once a week, with food or after meal, give 400 units vitamin E (alpha tocopherol) to help aid assimilation of vitamin A and protect body from the effects of some pollutants.

- Herbal remedies:

    1. Korean white ginseng increases resistance. When mixed half-and-half with caraway seeds in an infusion (tea), it tends to stimulate the appetite and provides extra minerals. Ginseng has a mild sweet taste. Try adding one teaspoon of this infusion to each meal.

    2. Give one drop golden seal elixir daily (see page 260). Discontinue if symptoms worsen (poor appetite, and the like); then resume dosage when cat's condi-

tion is stabilized. This is a powerful alkalizing agent and has been found to shrink swellings.

- Bach flower remedies:
  1. Give three or four drops Rescue Remedy (prepared as given on page 249) two hours before going to the vet and every two hours after that until you return home.
  2. On normal days (with no break in the routine such as trips to the vet) give three drops four times a day of the following mixture prepared as given on page 249:

     Mimulus—for fear of illness and of being alone;
     Aspen—for fear of the unknown;
     Crabapple—for cleansing;
     Hornbeam—for strength.

Feline Urologic Syndrome (FUS)
(See also "Kidney and Bladder Stones")

There are many misconceptions about feline urologic syndrome (FUS), sometimes referred to as cystitis. In FUS, crystals that irritate the bladder and urethra are formed in the urine. These crystals are sometimes called sand or gravel. They are made mostly of magnesium and phosphorus that have been ingested in the diet as ash. Dry food and fish are high ash foods that should be avoided. Other factors that can contribute to FUS include an alkaline urine. The cat's urine should be acidic; the crystals will dissolve in an acid urine. However, when owners leave food available all day long the mere *smell* of the food causes the body chemistry to turn the urine alkaline. Another cause of alkaline urine is a lack of digestible high-quality protein in the diet. Methionine, an amino acid found in protein, acidifies the urine. However, when protein is overcooked, overprocessed, or of poor quality, the cat cannot digest or assimilate it, so what methionine there is never gets into the cat's system but is passed off as a waste product.

The irritation from the crystals in the bladder and urethra causes redness, swelling, itching, and burning, and, finally, bleeding. It is first uncomfortable and then painful. In the beginning, the itching and burning make the cat think he needs to urinate all the time. He will run to the litter box three or four times in ten minutes and then squat and perhaps strain. He may pass up to a tablespoonful of urine, or only enough to moisten three pieces of litter—or there may be no urine at all. Often the urine is bloody. FUS is easiest to treat and cure if it is caught early. So if your cat runs to the litter box two or three times in one hour, take the cat to the veterinarian that very day—as always, better safe than sorry. At this early stage of the disease, when the veterinarian examines the cat, he will find that the bladder is small and hard because the urethra is not yet swollen shut and the cat is successfully voiding every drop of moisture as soon as it enters the bladder. If the disease is left untreated, the urethra will swell shut, and the veterinarian will discover a distended, full bladder.

There is a popular misconception that FUS is only a disease of male cats. This is not true. I've known of many female cats who have suffered from FUS. And I've met many people who know that dry food in the diet can bring on an attack of FUS and who still feed dry food to their female cat. They think that because she is a female she is therefore immune.

If your cat should begin the frequent litter-box syndrome (more than two or three times a day), be it male or female, move fast and get the cat to the veterinarian. FUS can end in a horrible death, and it happens all too frequently because it is such a quiet disease. There is no vomiting, no fits, no foaming at the mouth until the very end. There can be blood in the urine, but this is usually not noticed in the litter box. Usually that pitiful running back and forth to the litter box is the only apparent symptom. If you suspect blood in the urine, lay a white paper towel over the litter so any blood will show up clearly.

Sometimes the cat starts random wetting during the early stages of FUS. Several times owners have called to ask me what to do because their cat has suddenly begun wetting all over the house. They usually tell me that, in their opinion, their cat is trying to punish them for being away from home an unusual amount of time or for changing the brand of food or because they had a baby. I always advise them to have their veterinarian check for FUS. Then I explain that there is a fine distinction here. Cats do *not* use urination to express anger or dismay. Wetting outside the box is probably more distressing to the cat than it is to you. Here's what really happens: A stress situation results from your being away, or having the baby, or whatever. The stress target area in this particular cat is the urinary tract. The irritation and itching in the urethra force the cat to squat and urinate wherever he happens to be. The stress situation triggered it, but your cat certainly didn't plan it. Random wetting is so against the cat's nature that I always insist that there is some cause that has nothing to do with the cat's making a conscious statement. The ancient prohibition against drawing predators to the area because of the urine smell is far too strong. (See Chapter 3, "The Litter Box.")

There are two other reasons why the cat may wet outside the box. If the urethra has begun to swell closed, the cat may have to strain to pass urine. While straining he may straighten his hind legs, lifting the genital area up while he is still wetting, and spray the wall or floor outside the box. Finally, if the cat experiences discomfort, itching, burning, and so on of the genital area while urinating in the box, he may, in his little cat mind, decide to try to find a "safer" place, that is, a place that will not cause his genitals to itch or burn. He doesn't know why he's itching and burning; he just knows that it happens every time he goes into that litter box so he goes looking for a safer place.

As a precaution and, more important, as a convenience to your pussycat during a dreadful and painful disease, put at least one litter box in each and every room that your pet frequents. Your cat will bless you for it. I like to give a choice of one or two boxes lined with folded newspaper just as a precaution.

Another consideration with this disease is warmth. I always provide a snug retreat with a hot water bottle in it for an FUS cat (see page 240).

If this disease is left untreated and blockage occurs, the bladder swells with urine. The cat will crouch again and again in the litter box, straining to empty the badly swollen bladder, unable to pass one single drop of urine through the urethra, which is now swollen shut. If you call the veterinarian at this stage, he will undoubtedly tell you to drop everything and come *now*. My own veterinarian will come charging over to the clinic even in the middle of the night. The cat must be catheterized at once. The backup of poisons caused by the retention of the urine can kill the cat in a matter of hours.

Catheterization is painful and must be done under anesthetic, which is not only dangerous but also a drain on the cat's system. Catheterization poses a danger of bladder infection. It is a potential side effect, and veterinarians know they have to watch for it.

Because FUS is affected by emotions, hospital visits by the owner are of paramount importance. And once the cat is treated, the bladder emptied, antibiotics administered, and the disease controlled, the diet must be improved and the emotional environment altered to prevent a repeat performance. Repeated attacks can be a sign of bladder stones.

If the diet is not improved, or if the cat remains distressed, insecure, or unhappy and attacks recur, there comes a time when further catheterization is no longer possible. Too much scarring has occurred already. At this point, many cats are euthanized (put to sleep) rather than left to suffer while the poisons build up and permeate their entire body, bringing a horribly slow and painful death. The alternative at this stage is an operation called a *urethrostomy*, which some vets perform and some vets do not. It is major surgery and involves removing the urethra and widening the opening from the bladder. I have known several cats who had this surgery and did very well afterward. Of course, all of them were maintained on a very high-quality diet and were given a lot of conscious physical affection.

Symptoms

- Wetting outside the litter box or urinating all over the house
- Wetting on the wall or floor around the litter box
- Frequent trips to litter box, passing a small amount of urine, or none at all
- Blood in urine
- Crying out in litter box
- Licking the genital area
- Seeking warmth
- Loss of appetite
- Depression

Recommendations

- Give three drops of Bach Flower Rescue Remedy (prepared as given on page 249) every four hours for three days, then twice a day until disease is controlled.
- Contact your veterinarian at once and describe the symptoms. He will help you decide whether or not your cat needs to come in for treatment.
- If your cat goes to the litter box more than twice in one hour and passes no urine, *do not wait; rush to the veterinarian.*
- At first sign of urinary problem, withhold *all* solid food and administer 500 units of vitamin C or ⅛ teaspoon ascorbic acid crystals mixed with 1 teaspoon chicken broth. Also give 100 units vitamin E.

During attack and convalescence (in addition to veterinarian's treatment):

1. Fast on High-Calcium Chicken Broth (see page 243) three or four times a day for two days and give ¹⁄₁₆ teaspoon ascorbic acid crystals (250 units vitamin C) mixed each time into the broth (see "Fasting," page 225).
2. If antibiotic is a part of treatment, add ½ teaspoon liquid acidophilus suspended in water (from health-food store) to food and continue for two weeks after attack. Treat for temporary diarrhea by adding ¼ teaspoon powdered apple pectin to food until stools return to normal. Also give 1 teaspoon slippery elm syrup before each meal. (See "Antibiotics," page 266, and "Diarrhea," page 305.)
3. Eliminate all stress in cat's environment (see "Stress," page 197).
4. Provide a snug retreat (see page 240).
5. Keep a quiet, cheerful attitude when you're around the cat.
6. Feed a high-quality diet including as much raw food as possible (see Chapter 2, "Diet"). Be sure to include Vita-Mineral Mix (without the yeast) and

other listed supplements. From listed choices use carrots, green beans, or zucchini as vegetable; use High-Calcium Chicken Broth (see page 243) as liquid; choose chicken for the meat portion.

7. Eliminate yeast from Vita-Mineral Mix (see page 55). Instead, give ½ of a low potency (about 10 mg) vitamin B complex pill twice a day.

8. Eliminate all organ meats (liver, kidney, and the like) from the diet.

9. Add to diet:
   1 raw organic egg yolk each day;
   100 units vitamin E (alpha tocopherol)
       each day for a month; then give 400 units
       a week;
   ¼ teaspoon cod liver oil to each meal *or* a capsule
       containing 10,000 units vitamin A and 400
       units vitamin D once a week.

After attack:

1. Be sure never again to feed dry food or fish.
2. Organ meats may be used occasionally again a month after the attack is over.
3. Go back to regular Vita-Mineral Mix formula a month after the attack is over.
4. To keep urine acid and resistance high, feed only two meals a day and be sure to clean away dirty dish and all crumbs after a half hour. Continue adding to diet:
   1 organic egg yolk three times a week;
   Contents of a 400-unit vitamin E (alpha tocopherol) capsule once a week;
   ¼ teaspoon cod liver oil once a day or contents of a capsule containing 10,000 units vitamin A and 400 units vitamin D once a week;
   ¹⁄₁₆ teaspoon ascorbic acid crystals (250 units vitamin C) to each meal.
5. Continue to keep litter box very clean.

Fleas
(See also "Skin Problems" and "Parasites")

One scratch doth not a flea problem make. Many skin problems can cause itching. If you suspect fleas, groom your cat, save the hair in a pile, then spread it out and hold it up to the light. If you see debris—little black dots as if someone had sprinkled pepper on the hairs—this may be flea excrement. To be certain it's not just a bit of dust from the bottom of the closet or a little dirt from the potted palm where your cat occasionally lounges, you'd better do:

> *The White Towel Flea Test*
> Lay two white paper towels on the kitchen counter, one on top of the other. Moisten with water. Take a bunch of your cat's hair that has some debris mixed in and spread it out on the wet towels. Fold the towels over the hair, press them flat, and wait one or two minutes. Unfold the towels; if the black specks look like they're bleeding rust, your furry friend has fleas. The rust is your cat's blood, digested by the fleas and then excreted as those black specks.

Unless the infestation is very bad, you probably will not see fleas themselves as only 10 percent of the total flea population is on the cat at any one time. Ninety percent remain hidden in the environment, mostly where the cat sleeps, as eggs, larvae, and adults. Those few that are on the cat like to stay close to the skin. Under the chin and at the base of the tail are two favorite places.

Since fleas, like all parasites, are known to prefer sick, old, and weak animals, the presence of fleas is a sign that your cat's health is below par. A cat who is not in the best of health or one whose metabolism is slow because the owner forgets to remove food between meals will usually have oily, dandruffy skin. The fleas will love it, especially if there are a few convenient mats in the fur to hide under.

Fleas jump onto your pet because they need a drink of blood before they can lay their eggs. They lay the eggs on the cat and many eggs fall off into cracks in the floor and the spaces under and around large appliances and furniture. The places under or near where your cat usually rests will have the largest number of developing fleas. In one to five days the eggs hatch into larvae, tiny white worms with large toothy mouths. They feed on the debris existing in these dark crevices: dandruff, dust, mold, hair, and flea excrement (which is mostly your cat's digested blood). They will gobble up practically anything short of the missing pens and small coins that are also found there. The babies remain in the larval stage from ten to two hundred days depending upon the conditions. Then they spin a cocoon around themselves and in another ten to two hundred days they emerge as full-grown fleas ready to hop on your pet, chomp into his skin, drink the blood, and start the cycle all over again.

Using sprays, dips, powders, and collars may kill the fleas present on the animal, but they won't in any way inconvenience that large segment of the flea population lounging about, hatching, eating, and maturing in the environment. Furthermore, the commercial preparations contain chemicals that are debilitating and harmful to the cat and the humans he lives with. Labels warn owners not to breathe the fumes, not to allow the product to remain long on our hands, or to get it anywhere near our eyes or mouth. In the next sentence, they tell us to "soak the animal's coat thoroughly" and to leave the flea preparation on our beloved pet for an indefinite period of time! Many commercial flea collars use various forms of military nerve gas. Organophosphates are nerve paralyzers. Carbomates can cause vomiting, convulsions, and respiratory arrest.

Laboratory experiments assure us that use of these chemicals even in tiny amounts increases the chances of the animal developing cancer, allergies, nerve damage, reproductive problems, and breathing difficulties. Subjecting the cat's body to these toxic chemicals will even further damage the animal's state of health, weakening him and making him an even more attractive breeding ground for fleas. Thus, more of these toxic treatments will then be required and at more and more frequent intervals, causing the cat's health to deteriorate at an ever increasing speed and his immune system to become weaker and weaker. He will finally be laid low, not by the fleas themselves but by the treatments or by some "unrelated" disease that his damaged immune system hasn't the strength to fight. An unhealthy cat will always attract more fleas. Here we have a classic snowball situation. It's rather like trying to rid your kitchen of flies by shooting them off the wall with a bazooka. You'll certainly kill the flies, but the holes left behind will only let in more flies. The best you can say for the method is that soon you'll have no kitchen to worry about.

Happily for all of us, cats and owners alike, during the last few years several highly effective natural products have appeared on the market, and new methods of attack have been developed. Some of the products, like Spritz (now marketed as Natural Animal Coat Enhancer), are actually beneficial to the cat; others, such as the pyrethrin-based room foggers and carpet sprays, can be relatively harmless but only if used carefully, since most of these pyrethrins are synthetic and more toxic than natural pyrethrins. All have been thoroughly and repeatedly tested by me and all work as well as—if not better than—the poisonous chemical products.

To ensure your success in evicting all fleas from both pet and premises, you must follow three ground rules:

1. Cover all the bases. Leave no weak link in the chain. No one product or method will work well if used alone. Attack the fleas on the cat, in the house, and in the yard, and follow the suggestions given under each of these categories.

2. Thoroughness is very important. Do each step of your program as if it is the one and only method at your disposal. Vacuum as if you had no carpet spray; then spray the carpet as if you had no vacuum. Flea comb the cat's coat as if you cannot bathe; then bathe as if you had no flea comb.

3. Make the cat's body an unappetizing morsel for a flea by improving your pet's health and including in the diet those supplements having flea-repelling properties (see below).

Symptoms

- Scratching and biting, especially under chin, behind ears, and at the base of the spine
- Pulling out hair
- Shedding and bald spots, sometimes scabs

- Presence of small black dots, like black pepper, in hair
- Presence of fleas

Recommendations

Note: It is imperative that you incorporate treatments from each of the categories below to assure success in getting rid of fleas.

Diet

This is a must. Without this, nothing else will do much good.

- Raise the cat's resistance to parasites by feeding a raw-food diet (page 58), alternately with a high-quality diet (page 53). Remove all food after a half-hour and leave *only* water available between meals.
- Make your cat an unappetizing morsel for a flea. From three weeks before flea season until after the first hard freeze (or all year round in warm climates), include the following supplements in the food:
    1. Once a day add ⅛ teaspoon of Delicious Garlic Condiment (page 256)
    2. Into ten teaspoons brewer's yeast crush and add 10 mg thiamine (a B vitamin). Give ½ teaspoon of this yeast mixture twice a day in the food. This yeast mixture can be used as the yeast portion of the Vita-Mineral Mix (page 55) during flea season. Or crush the thiamine into PetGuard's yeast and garlic powder. PetGuard also has yeast and garlic wafers that make a great snack or treat and help the body to resist fleas (see Appendix, "Product Suppliers").
    3. If you plan to use a room fogger or carpet spray (listed below), add 1/16 teaspoon ascorbic acid crystals or sodium ascorbate powder (250 units vitamin C) to each meal.

Grooming and Bathing

- Remove mats and loose hair and stimulate circulation to the skin by daily grooming and massage.
- Buy a flea comb at a pet store or by mail (see Appendix, "Product Suppliers"). It is only about an inch-and-a-half long and has fine teeth that are very close together. Comb out fleas and debris with the flea comb, giving special attention to the top of the head, chin and neck, lower spine and skirts near the thigh. (See Chapter 7, "Grooming.") Submerge all hair and fleas in a bowl of hot water with a couple of drops of dish detergent to keep the fleas from crawling out.
- Kill all fleas remaining on the cat by spraying the coat with Natural Animal Spritz coat enhancer. Wait ten minutes before bathing.
- Bathe (see page 157) with Lightning Shampoo or Safers Insecticidal shampoo for cats or other flea shampoo for cats from the health-food store or from product suppliers listed in the Appendix. Shampoo twice. Leave second soaping on the coat for five to ten minutes before rinsing thoroughly.
- If cat's skin is damaged by flea bites or if he has scratched himself red and raw, Spritz will soothe the skin. If you can't get Spritz, use Lemon Rinse (page 262) after the bath to soothe and heal skin and repel fleas. *Or* add citronella or eucalyptus to the final rinse to scent the fur. These herbs are flea repellants.
- When cat is thoroughly dry, prevent further infestation by doing one or all of the following:
    1. Spray coat with Spritz three times a week during flea season;
    2. Use an herbal flea collar (see Appendix, "Product Suppliers"), or use citronella, or eucalyptus to scent a cloth flea collar.
    3. If you can't get Spritz:
        A. use the Lemon Rinse (page 262); *or*
        B. dust the coat with a yeast and garlic powder from the health-food store; *or*
        C. dust the coat with an herbal flea powder; *or*

D. dust the coat with a combination of diatomaceous earth and one of the other products.

On the Premises

Note: An ounce of prevention—if your cats have been outside or
boarding in your absence at a place where you suspect they may
have picked up fleas, confine the cats to a bathroom or the kitchen
(or any room without a rug) until you determine conclusively that
they have not brought back any unwelcome guests in their furs.
Then, if you, or the groomer, or the vet do find fleas, you won't
have to treat your whole house for larvae and eggs, only the one
room where the cats have been.

- *Treat every room where the cats have been for eggs, larvae and
  adult fleas.*
- Vacuum both carpets and floors thoroughly. Use the vacuum nozzle to clean every crack and crevice because eggs
  and larvae will be found there. Throw the vacuum cleaner
  bag away (out of the house) after each vacuuming *or* suck
  some flea-killing powder into the vacuum bag *or* burn the
  bag.
- Suffocate developing larvae and eggs by waxing the floors.
- Cut the protective shell of fleas and larvae so they dehy-
  drate and die by: (a) sprinkling diatomaceous earth in all
  cracks and/or (b) sprinkling the carpet liberally with salt.
  Leave overnight and vacuum up the next day. Choose a
  dry day to do this.
- Kill the fleas, larvae, and eggs by:
    1. Steam-cleaning carpet or steam-ironing carpet, so-
       fas, and so on;
    2. Putting pillows, pet bedding, comforters, and the
       like in clothes dryer on hot temperature for fifteen
       to twenty minutes;
    3. Laying old terry cloth towels on all the cat's perches
       and sleeping places to catch the larvae and eggs
       that drop off the cat. Wash all the towels once a
       week and dry on *hot* cycle.

- Kill fleas by spraying floors, furniture, and bedding with a 5 percent solution of Safers Insecticidal Soap. Do this every five days.

Several flea products use pyrethrins (made from crysanthemum) as the active ingredient. Products that contain synthetic pyrethrins or pyrethrins modified to be more toxic are acceptable but less safe than the natural pyrethrins. Some also use methoprene, a growth inhibitor, which keeps larvae from maturing. They live and die in their dark crevices and never develop to biting age. Both are relatively safe if used as directed. To make doubly sure of safety, I suggest that all people, animals, birds, fish, and plants vacate the premises for more than the length of time recommended on the can. My own vet suggests twelve hours. In addition, you and your cat should take extra vitamin C for two to three weeks after spraying—250 units twice a day will aid the body in processing out any residues. The products I use are:

1. Vet Chem Premis Spray;
2. Vet Chem Siphotrol Plus and Zodiac IGR Plus room foggers—both use pyrethrins and methoprene and have a ten-week extended-kill period;
3. Zodiac 120-Day Carpet Spray.

Fractures
(see "Injuries")

Gums
(see "Teeth and Gums")

Hair Balls

It is natural for cats to vomit up hair balls from time to time because they groom themselves with the tongue and swallow the hair. Some hair will be passed out with the stool if shedding is not too copious and the diet is adequate, with enough fiber, fats, and oils. However, during the shedding seasons when a cat swallows a lot of hair, he should from time to time vomit up a hair ball that looks like a small wet sausage. If he cannot vomit it successfully, the body will try to pass it out through the intestines. If intestinal action is weak because of poor nutrition or frequent snacking and smelling of food, the hair ball may stop somewhere along the way and form an impaction like a cork. The body may first pass a very runny diarrhea around the impaction; then complete constipation will set in. The cat will become lethargic and refuse food. Wastes will build up and, finally, serious infection will overcome the entire system.

Symptoms

Note: Vomiting hair balls is not a symptom; it is normal if it happens less than twice a week and only during the spring and autumn shedding seasons.

- Vomiting foam, vomiting many hair balls—more than one or two a week
- Diarrhea or constipation
- Bad breath
- Excess shedding (other than in spring and autumn)
- Unsuccessful vomiting attempts
- Lethargy, loss of appetite

Recommendations

Stage 1: To help cat successfully vomit hair balls

- Groom more often—once or twice a day (see page 126).
- Reevaluate grooming tool (see page 129).
- Feed a high-quality diet (see page 53). Be sure to include Vita-Mineral Mix and other listed supplements.
- Remove all food between meals; leave only water available.
- Include ⅛ teaspoon Delicious Garlic Condiment (see page 256) in food three times a week to strengthen intestinal muscles.

Stage 2: If cat is vomiting unsuccessfully and diarrhea and/or constipation are present

- Follow Stage 1 treatments above.
- Ask veterinarian if you should give cat an oral hair-ball lubricant. This is always given two to three hours before food. If it comes in a tube, administer approximately three inches. Choose a product that does not contain benzoate of soda *or* use plain petroleum jelly and give about ½ teaspoon.

Stage 3: If the cat has had no stool for three days, has no appetite, and is lethargic

- Don't wait—take the cat to the veterinarian immediately for treatment (enema or surgery may be required).
- After the veterinarian's treatment, when the cat comes home, give one charcoal capsule (wet on the tip) one time to absorb any putrefaction left behind. (See "Giving Pills," page 208.)
- For two weeks add to food ½ teaspoon liquid acidophilus suspended in water (not in lactose).
- Continue to groom thirty seconds every day all year.
- Follow all Stage 1 treatments above.

Hookworm
(see "Parasites")

Hyperthyroidism

Hyperthyroidism is a disease of middle-aged to older cats. "Hyper" means high or over. In hyperthyroidism the thyroid is overproducing the hormones thyroxin and/or, less commonly, tri-iodothyronine. Thyroxin regulates the speed at which all body functions proceed (the metabolism or metabolic rate). If there is too much thyroxin, the metabolism speeds up: the heart races, blood pressure and temperature go up, digestion speeds up, and cells die and are replaced more quickly.

Because many of the symptoms—skinniness, oily coat, copious drinking and urination—can be signs of other diseases (kidney disease and diabetes), the veterinarian will want to do complete blood tests that will reflect liver function and kidney and pancreatic function as well as the extra test, called a T3 and T4 test, for the thyroid. Frequently the doctor will be able to feel the enlargement of the thyroid in the throat, but more evidence than this is needed to make a firm diagnosis.

As with most physical problems, the cause is attributable to a combination of things. If there is insufficient iodine in the diet, the thyroid may become enlarged and overactive to compensate for the deficiency. Since vitamin E is needed before the body can absorb iodine, a vitamin E deficiency can sometimes provoke the same response. If there is not enough iodine in the food, the thyroid will absorb any radioactive iodine that is present in the environment and this will do further damage. Liver damage can also produce symptoms of hyperthyroidism because the liver supplies an enzyme that deactivates excess thyroxin. If that liver enzyme is absent or underproduced, too much thyroxin will remain in the blood.

The practices of in-breeding and of feeding a diet of heat-processed food that also contains chemicals and diseased tissue will weaken any animal as well as its progeny. If there is a predisposition to thyroid problems in the genes, which is then exaggerated by in-breeding, a low-quality diet added to this will be enough to do in the thyroid by middle years.

There are four orthodox treatments for hyperthyroidism:

1. *Surgery*. All or part of the thyroid gland is removed and the cat is maintained for the remainder of his life on thyroid hormones given orally. I have seen cats survive for years after thyroid surgery but only when the basic diet has been totally changed to the highest quality, mostly raw-food diet, with all supplements present. Also, the patient must be carefully monitored by the veterinarian to be certain the thyroxin level is properly balanced with the cat's ever-changing chemistry and metabolism.

2. *Thyroid-inhibiting drugs*. Drugs such as Tapazol (methmazole) inhibit the synthesis of hormones by the thyroid gland. They work

only while the drug is being taken. There are possible side effects: anorexia, vomiting and lethargy, rashes and facial swelling. If a drug must be used lest the excess thyroxin cause a heart attack or other life-threatening situation, every effort should be made to permanently correct the condition through homeopathy and nutrition in hopes of diminishing and then stopping the drug. Cats on thyroid medication should be monitored at least every six months; every three months is better.

3. *Iodine and propranalol.* This treatment, which decreases the heart rate and output, is seldom used because cats must be constantly monitored.

4. *Radioactive iodine therapy.* This treatment is seldom used because the cat must be quarantined for days or weeks after the treatment, and the radioactive urine and stool must be disposed of according to government regulations.

My preference, whenever possible, is a regimen of diet, herbs, and homeopathy, guided by a homeopathic veterinarian.

Hyperthyroid cats will have super-high nutritional requirements because the racing metabolism causes the body to use up nutrients very quickly. They often have oily coats because they tend to dispose of wastes through the pores and to produce excess oil. Also, the increased drinking and urination common to hyperthyroid cats washes the water-soluble nutrients out of the body. Besides supplying nutrients in large amounts, food should be easily digestible and extra digestive enzymes should be included to ensure that all the nutrients in the food will be assimilated, not just swallowed and passed swiftly through the digestive system and out the other end.

Symptoms

- Dull coat, sometimes very dry, sometimes very oily
- Skinniness despite large appetite
- Copious drinking and urination (as in diabetes or kidney disease)
- Slightly high temperature, seeks cool places
- Nervous energy, hyperactivity
- Hypersensitivity to sounds, movement, touch

- Hiding out of the way
- Fast pulse, high blood pressure
- Vomiting
- Diarrhea or an excessively large amount of stool
- Muscle weakness
- Veterinarian can sometimes feel enlarged gland in the throat

Recommendations

- Consult a homeopathic veterinarian for diagnosis and treatment.
- Feed a high-quality diet with as much raw food as possible (see page 55). Be sure to include Vita-Mineral Mix and all other listed supplements to diet.
- Add to each meal:
    ¼ teaspoon feline enzymes or ½ digestive enzyme pill;
    ⅛ teaspoon ascorbic acid crystals or sodium ascorbate powder (500 units vitamin C);
    ⅛ teaspoon granular kelp (in addition to kelp in Vita-Mineral Mix and in addition to your veterinarian's iodine pill);
    ½ of a vitamin B complex tablet, crushed (10 mg or lower).
- Once a day give:
    100 units vitamin E (alpha tocopherol) for four weeks; then reduce dose to 400 units once a week;
    10,000 units vitamin A in fish liver oil. Once a week substitute a capsule containing 10,000 units vitamin A and 400 units vitamin D. After one month, reduce dose to capsule containing 10,000 units vitamin A and 400 units vitamin D once a week.
- Herbal remedies: because minerals are being used up and lost in the urine, a teaspoonful of any of the following added to meals will be helpful:
    Kombu broth (page 256);
    Horsetail grass infusion (page 259);
    If diarrhea is a problem, give one teaspoon slippery elm syrup five minutes before each meal.

- Bach flower remedies: hyperthyroid cats are "hyper" every-thing—oversensitive, overactive, overhungry. They need to be calmed and protected. Give three drops three times a day of the following mixture prepared as given on page 249:

> Mimulus—to calm fear of noise, lights, motion, and the like;
>
> Impatiens—to sooth anxiety.

Hypoglycemia

Hypoglycemia used to be practically nonexistent in cats. Today, however, almost every product in the grocery store pet section contains some form of sugar: corn sweeteners, corn syrup, fructose, sucrose, and barley malt syrup are all high in sugars. The semimoist foods and semimoist treats are usually the worst.

Hypoglycemia (low blood sugar) can be caused by a malfunction of the pancreas or the liver. One of the jobs of the pancreas is to produce insulin, which neutralizes excess sugar in the blood. If large amounts of sugar or carbohydrates are eaten frequently (as in a diet of semimoist food), the pancreas is overstimulated. It becomes trigger-happy, as it were, and begins producing too much insulin—neutralizing all of the sugar instead of just the excess—and hypoglycemia results. Low blood sugar produces a big appetite so the cat reacts by overeating. This overstimulates the insulin trigger again, and the pancreas overproduces again, and a vicious circle results.

Another cause of hypoglycemia is liver damage. One of the liver's duties is to produce an enzyme that deactivates excess insulin. If the liver is damaged and does not produce the enzyme, excess insulin remains active to neutralize too much sugar and store it as fat instead of burning it for energy. Here again hypoglycemia will result. Hypoglycemia is a warning that diabetes is on the way.

Fortunately, hypoglycemia is simple to treat by natural methods once it is diagnosed. Frequent small high-protein meals that are easily digested and nicely balanced, along with the elimination of sugar of any kind from the diet, will begin to put things right. Progress will continue as long as the new regimen is maintained.

If the condition has progressed so far that water retention has become a problem, parsley tea used in the food will act as a gentle diuretic. If obesity has developed, do not attempt to fast the cat or put him on a reducing diet. The weight will melt away gradually as one of the many beneficial side effects of your furry friend's improved lifestyle.

Symptoms

- Depression, anxiety, or irritability
- Obesity with voracious appetite
- Laziness
- Leg cramps
- Arthritis
- Vertigo, dizziness, stumbling
- Trembling
- Indigestion
- Asthma
- Blood test may show low liver values and/or high pancreas

Recommendations

- Consult veterinarian for diagnosis. Have blood tested for sugar level, liver function, and pancreatic function.
- Feed *four* small high-quality meals each day.
- Eliminate all sugars from the diet—*no semimoist food or treats. Read labels.* Feed a high-quality diet. If you use canned cat foods, choose only those that are natural and contain no by-products, sugars, or chemical additives (see chapter 2, "Diet"). Better yet, feed a homemade food (the I'll-Do-Anything-for-My-Cat Diet) for a few months.
- Be sure to include Vita-Mineral Mix and other supplements to diet (see page 55).
- Add to each meal:
    - $\frac{1}{16}$ teaspoon ascorbic acid crystals or sodium ascorbate powder (250 units vitamin C);
    - $\frac{1}{4}$ teaspoon feline digestive enzymes—to ensure normal digestion and assimilation;

A few grains of salt substitute (for a week or two)—to replace potassium lost in urine.

- *Regular* exercise periods each day.
- Have another blood test done in three to six months.
- Consult an experienced homeopathic veterinarian (see "Homeopathy," page 244) to ensure speedy results.
- Herbal remedies:
    1. Parsley tea can be mixed in food if water retention or obesity is a problem. Use about 1 teaspoon per meal.
    2. Use 1 drop stevia extract or 1 teaspoon stevia infusion added to the food to help stabilize blood sugar and give a sweeter taste to food.
- Bach flower remedies: hypoglycemic cats will feel tired and lack energy. They will experience periods of depression, especially while the excess ounces are melting away and the old toxins stored in the fat are being processed out by their system. The following is a good general formula of Bach flower remedies for a hypoglycemic cat. Give three drops four times a day of the following mixture prepared as given on page 249:
    Crabapple—for those who need to lose weight;
    Larch—for those who expect failure and do not try;
    Clematis—for those who tend toward drowsiness and dreaming;
    Hornbeam—for those who need to be strengthened and encouraged.
- *Two months after symptoms disappear:*
    1. Cut number of meals down to three each day; then a week later, to two meals a day;
    2. Maintain high-quality diet with no sugar.

Hypothyroidism

"Hypo" means "under," as in hypodermic—under the skin. The thyroid gland produces the hormone thyroxin, which regulates metabolism—the speed at which all the other glands and all the body processes function. Hypothyroidism means that the thyroid gland is

351

not producing enough thyroxin so the metabolism is slow. This is the opposite of *hyper*thyroidism. The cause is usually a lack of iodine in the diet or an inability to assimilate the iodine that is present, because of a lack of vitamins E, C, B-6, or choline. The presence of radiation from color television, microwave ovens, nearby atomic energy plants, and so on will increase your cat's need for iodine.

Symptoms

- Fatigue, lethargy
- Cold ears, paws; seeking a warm place
- Slow pulse, low blood pressure
- Gains weight easily even though appetite is normal or poor
- High cholesterol level
- Chipping claws
- Oily coat

Recommendations

- Have your veterinarian make a firm diagnosis. A blood test will show hypothyroidism.
- Feed a high-quality diet with as much raw food as possible (see Chapter 2, "Diet"). Be sure to include Vita-Mineral Mix and other listed supplements.
- Remove all food between meals to help speed up metabolism.
- Have a short play period twice a day. Use your ingenuity to tempt your friend into activity. Try a peacock feather or a Cat Dancer toy.
- Add to each meal:
    ½ teaspoon lecithin (in addition to lecithin in Vita-Mineral Mix) to help rid the body of cholesterol build-up;
    $\frac{1}{16}$ teaspoon ascorbic acid crystals or sodium ascorbate powder (250 units vitamin C);
    ¼ teaspoon feline digestive enzymes—to ensure proper digestion and assimilation of nutrients.
- Three times a week add to food a raw organic egg yolk (as

a source of choline)—to help body assimilate iodine efficiently.

- Once a week give 400 units vitamin E (alpha tocopherol) from a punctured capsule.
- Provide a snug retreat (page 240). Hypothyroid cats will feel cold even on a warm day.
- Herbal remedies:
    1. Kombu seaweed (page 256) is an excellent source of iodine and other minerals. Give 1 teaspoon to ¼ cup mixed into meals, depending on how well your cat likes the taste.
    2. Horsetail tea—give one teaspoon three times a day mixed into food or mixed half-and-half with High-Calcium Chicken Broth (page 243) and given as liquid medication (page 210). Horsetail is high in trace minerals and tends to be strengthening.
- Bach flower remedies: hypothyroid cats will lack energy and enthusiasm. They will seek out the warm spots and sleep most of the time. Also, since the metabolism is slow, there is bound to be some backlog of wastes. Give three drops three times a day of the following mixture prepared as given on page 249:
    Wild rose—for those without enthusiasm;
    Crabapple—for cleansing.

Injuries
(including Abscesses and Puncture Wounds, Cuts, Burns, Concussions, and Fractures)

In any emergency situation your aim will be to get the patient to the veterinarian as fast as you can, keeping him as comfortable, calm, clean, dry, warm, and still as possible while you do so. There is no question of opting for home care; *a veterinarian must be consulted.* You must be able to act quickly and put aside your own feelings. Now is not the time to give in to your emotions; you can do that after your cat is safely in the hands of the veterinarian. Here are the steps to handling an emergency:

1. Reassure your pet that you understand that he is frightened and in pain. Tell him that you are going to help him feel better.
2. Call the veterinarian or ask someone else to call for you to warn the veterinarian that you are on your way with an emergency situation.
3. Ask for the assistance of others in obtaining any necessary items such as the carry case, towels, and so on.
4. Give your cat three drops of Bach Flower Rescue Remedy, prepared as explained on page 249 and take three drops yourself. Repeat every thirty minutes.
5. See appropriate heading below for the type of emergency— "Abscesses and Puncture Wounds," "Cuts," "Burns," "Concussions," and "Fractures."

Abscesses and Puncture Wounds

The most common sort of wound in cats is a puncture wound, because both the teeth and claws of other animals produce the typical puncture shape: a deep wound with a very small opening. Most punctures don't bleed much, and without that mildly antiseptic wash of the saline blood, puncture wounds become infected unless the cat is very healthy with a good strong immune response. If the cat is only moderately healthy, he will still be protected against serious harm because the body will form an abscess around the infection to seal it off.

My first experience with an abscess was atop the head of a sweet little blue cream shorthair named Tammy. Tammy had spent fifteen contented years quietly caring for an elderly invalid lady. I inherited Tammy when the lady passed away. During her introduction into my household of seven cats, someone (I'm naming no names) gave Tammy a ritual bop on the head. It was just a mitten-bop with sheathed claws; nevertheless one claw, sharper and longer than the others, pierced Tammy's scalp. An infection began and Tammy had a lump the size of a marble on the top of her head the next morning. Tammy's immune system was swinging into action; the body's defenses were being mobilized; an abscess was forming to protect Tammy's system from the spread of that infection. Millions of white cells were being carried to the area by the blood to battle the invading microbes and kill them. The dead white cells and germs formed the white pus that the abscess contained in a sort of flexible bubble. The longer the battle raged, the more cells and microbes would die and the bigger the abscess would become. By afternoon the lump on Tammy's head was the size of a ping pong ball. It looked grotesque. Tammy's temperature was 102—another good sign. The immune system was making the body uncomfortably warm for the invading microbes.

I called my veterinarian, Dr. Pitcairn, who prescribed two homeopathic remedies. He also told me to raise the temperature in the abscess area further by applying hot compresses four times a day (see "Hot Compresses," page 234). Tammy was a model of quiet cooperation; the compresses felt good.

When the body is fighting any infection, it is always helpful to put the patient on a light healing fast of chicken broth with supplements added. I also offered Tammy a snug retreat (see page 240) where she spent most of her time for the next three weeks.

There are three ways that an abscess can be resolved:
1. If the abscess is not very large the body can absorb the pocket of pus and carry the poisons away in the blood and send them out in the stool and/or urine.
2. The abscess can burst, discharging the pus, and then heal as any wound would. Often the patient will encourage this by frequent licking. When the abscess is ready to burst, it begins to itch; thus nature encourages the animal to lick. If this happens to your pet and he swallows a bit of the fluid, don't worry; the germs will take a direct route to the stool and urine and be disposed of there. Just keep giving the supplements for infections and wounds (see page 241).
3. If the abscess is very large, if you want to ensure that it will drain neatly, or if the abscess has burst but then closes up and again fills with pus, you can have your veterinarian shave the whole area, lance the abscess, and tie in a drain to keep the abscess from closing up before the pus is all gone. To do this the cat may have to be lightly anesthetized (as for teeth cleaning). The vet will make two clean incisions, one on each side of the abscess. A small rubber

tube is then looped in one side and out the other and fastened together on the outside. This holds the incision open so the abscess can continue to drain and be irrigated easily.

In Tammy's case the abscess was resolved on the fourth day in spectacular fashion. As we were finishing our morning compress ritual, Tammy's abscess suddenly started to itch. She reacted by giving her head a good shake, and with that the abscess burst and a stream of bloody pus shot straight across the room and hit the wall on the other side. Tammy just sat there, calmly waiting for me to finish doing whatever it was I wanted to do to her today. The pressure was relieved and the itch was gone.

After I cleaned the smelly mess off Tammy's neck, off the wall, and off my sleeve, I called Dr. Pitcairn to report the latest development. He gave me the formulas for abscess irrigation (see "Irrigating Ears or Abscesses," page 219), and I immediately began squirting formula number I into the newly opened abscess hole, filling up the pocket and then gently pressing to empty it out. By evening, when I went to repeat the treatment, the hole was healed closed. "Good," I thought. But Tammy's body was not finished dealing with the invading germs. She was older, had just come out of a stressful situation, and had never had the advantage of a high-quality diet. Her immune response was working slowly. The abscess filled up again. I know now that I could have just waited for it to burst again but after seeing all that nasty pus come out I couldn't stand the thought of leaving all that filth on Tammy's head. I was impatient; I did not let nature take its course. Instead, I again called my local veterinarian and got an appointment to bring Tammy over. The veterinarian shaved the area and put in a nice drain, as described above. He didn't even have to anesthetize her because the skin flap where he needed to make the incision was dead tissue that had no feeling. Now I could syringe out the abscess pocket twice a day without fear of it healing closed prematurely.

There is a marvelous hypodermic syringe that has a tapered curved plastic tip instead of a needle. It is perfect for abscess irrigation. Twice a day I would fill it with Irrigation Formula I (see page 219), insert the tip into one of the vet's incision holes, and inject the solution gently into the abscess cavity (see "Irrigating Ears or Abscesses," page 219). I would then carefully press the abscess flat, expelling the solution and any pus from the abscess pocket.

Tammy always knew that whatever I did would be completely comfortable. I always kept paper towels handy to sop up any dead white cells that had been washed out onto her fur by the irrigation solution. Then I'd dry her with a nice absorbent towel (paper towels work best).

We want the abscess to heal from the inside out, so it is important to keep the abscess pocket open and draining until no more pus is being formed inside. Leave the drain in place until the irrigation fluid comes out of the pocket clear or with only a little blood mixed in. You are then ready to switch to Irrigation Formula II (see page 219) with the added calendula. Calendula causes raw tissue to knit together and heal very fast. If you use Formula II with calendula too soon, the incisions will close up before the infection is gone inside and you'll end up with another abscess on your hands and have to start all over again.

After the abscess pocket is clean, irrigate with Formula II twice a day for two days. On the third day irrigate in the morning and then remove the drain. In the evening irrigate again only if you can easily insert the tip of the syringe into one of the openings. If the openings are healed shut, leave it alone and continue the supplements and remedies listed below. Here is a wonderful opportunity to do visualization (see page 262) and watch it come true as the body sloughs the old dead skin and manufactures perfect new skin with lovely silky hair growing out of it. Miracles do happen every single day.

Symptoms

- A deep wound with a very small opening.
- Balloon-like swelling around the wound which is filled with pus.

Recommendations

- Inform your holistic veterinarian of the situation and discuss what you are doing about it.
- Irrigate the abscess as described in paragraphs above.

- Give homeopathic remedies as follows:
  1. Silica 6X—give one tablet every four hours for two days; *then*
  2. Sulfur 6X—give one tablet every four hours for three more days.
  3. Be sure to read the section on "Homeopathy," page 244, especially on how to administer homeopathic remedies.
- Apply hot compresses (see page 234) four times a day.
- Instead of regular meals:
  1. For two days fast the cat on High-Calcium Chicken Broth (see page 243). Give three to six meals of ¼ to ½ cup a day, adding three drops of Pet Tinic to provide B vitamins and minerals *and* ¹⁄₁₆ teaspoon ascorbic acid crystals or sodium ascorbate powder to provide 250 units of vitamin C, which will help the body process out the toxins.
  2. *Then* gradually introduce a high-quality diet with as much raw food as possible (see page 53), adding to each meal the supplements for infections and wounds (see page 241).
- Provide a snug retreat (see page 240).
- Herbal remedies:
  1. Add five drops of golden seal to ½ cup of the first irrigation formula—it has antiseptic properties.
  2. Add five drops of calendula to the final irrigation formula to promote quick healing and closing of ruptured tissue.
- Give Bach Flower Remedy Formula II, prepared as explained on page 249. In Tammy's case I also added two drops of Bach Flower Walnut to help her break the old ties to her former home.

Cuts

A deep cut bleeding profusely can be frightening to the owner. But remember, blood is a cleansing and healing substance. It is better if a wound bleeds a little. When the skin is broken by a wound, the body reacts at once, sending blood to wash the area and carry healing antibodies to the site. After the first shock (and by the next day), the tiny cells of the skin begin to contract, pulling the wound as much toward a closed position as possible. White cells in the blood fight invading germs, lymph carries away dead germs and white cells, and the skin begins manufacturing a quick protective covering—a scab. Scar tissue, if needed, will be forming slowly inside the tissue. To aid and support this process we need to:

1. Stop any copious bleeding by applying direct pressure on the wound with a clean cloth folded into a square. If quick action is needed and you don't have a piece of cloth available, a piece of cloth can be torn from an article of your clothing or you can even use your fingers to apply pressure to the cut. If the wound is on a foot or lower leg and direct pressure is not working, make a tourniquet by looping a twisted dishtowel around the leg above the wound and twisting the ends together in a wringing motion until the towel is tight. This should slow the bleeding but not stop it completely. Loosen the towel or cloth every ten or fifteen minutes for five or ten seconds and then tighten it again. After a half-hour or so try using direct pressure again as it is safer.

2. Call the veterinarian (or ask someone else to call) to tell him that you are coming in immediately with an emergency.

3. If for some reason you must wait to see the veterinarian, carefully clip away any hair that is getting into the wound. Hair carries germs that will contaminate the wound. Then cleanse away any debris, dirt, and germs by squirting saline solution (page 213) or hydrogen peroxide onto the wound using an ear syringe, an empty clean shampoo bottle, or a hypodermic syringe without the needle. The solution should be body temperature. *Do not* use any solution containing alcohol or soap. If the wound is old, clots may have formed. Unless you see pus and obvious infection, don't disturb the clots to clean the wound because you might start major bleeding. Just get the cat to the veterinarian quickly.

The veterinarian may shave the area clean and then use either butterfly adhesive clamps or sutures (stitches). Sutures require that the cat be anesthetized. He will try to avoid bandaging the cut because it's best to let the air circulate around the wound. A clean dry wound heals fastest.

Do not put any oil, salve, or ointments on an open wound or scab. They collect debris and germs.

Recommendations

- To keep the wound clean and promote healing, wash twice a day with normal saline solution (see page 213), warmed to body temperature, squirted on with a syringe. You can add the following herbs to the solution:
    1. If there is pus (indicating infection) add five drops golden seal extract to each ¼ cup saline solution.
    2. To promote quick healing of a clean wound add five drops calendula extract to each ¼ cup saline solution. Keep the leftover solution in the refrigerator and, before use, reheat to body temperature by standing the container in a bowl of hot water.
- Once the scab falls off and the scar is formed, you can rub in a drop of vitamin E oil (from a vitamin E capsule that you've punctured) once a day for a week to encourage normal tissue growth.
- Add to your usual high-quality diet (page 53) 400 units vitamin E (alpha tocopherol) twice a week for one month; then reduce to once a week as usual.

    Minerals aid healing, especially silica. Add 1 teaspoon horsetail grass tea (page 259) to each meal.

    Vitamin C helps fight infection and garlic is a natural antibiotic. Once a day add ⅛ teaspoon Delicious Garlic Condiment (page 256) and ⅛ teaspoon ascorbic acid crystals or sodium ascorbate powder (500 units vitamin C) to food.

Burns

Burns are usually caused by a cat walking on a hot surface, by a hot fluid being spilled on the cat, by the cat biting an electric cord, or by his ingesting a caustic chemical. Burns cause extreme pain;

the patient should be treated for shock as well as for the wound. The burn area should be kept clean and moist while the cat is rushed to the veterinarian. Try not to touch the burn—it is too painful. If the burn covers more than an inch or two, dehydration may occur and the veterinarian may want to give the patient subcutaneous fluids (page 235) for a day or two.

Because burns cover a wider expanse than a cut or puncture, the skin cells will not be able to close the wound by contracting. Burns take a long time to heal and must be kept scrupulously clean while they do so. Your veterinarian will undoubtedly clip or shave the hair away all around the burn site.

Recommendations

- Call the veterinarian (or ask someone else to call) as soon as possible and let him know you're on your way with an emergency.
- Give three drops Bach Flower Rescue Remedy (prepared as given on page 249) every thirty minutes. Take it yourself as well.
- Assure your cat that you know he is in pain and that you are going to help him feel better.
- Using a rubber ear syringe or a clean squirt bottle, wash the burn area with either:
    ½ cup saline solution (page 213) and five drops urtica urens tincture; *or*
    ½ cup saline solution (page 213) and ten drops Bach Flower Rescue Remedy.
- *Do not use salves or ointments on burns.* Keep the wound moist while traveling to the veterinarian by squirting a little solution on the wound every three to five minutes. Be sure the patient is lying on several layers of towel. Don't touch the wound. The veterinarian will probably give a tranquilizer before he attempts to clean it.
- If the skin over the burn becomes hard and stiff, this means that the skin has died. It is best to leave it in place to serve as a natural protective bandage. You should irrigate all around the edges at least twice a day with one of the following solutions:

361

1. If pus or infection is present, use ½ cup saline solution (page 213) with five drops golden seal extract or tincture;
2. If no pus is present and any discharge looks clean, use ½ cup saline solution (page 213) with five drops calendula extract or tincture.

- Add to the food once a day for three weeks:

    An extra ⅛ teaspoon bone meal, calcium lactate, or calcium glutonate (in addition to that in Vita-Mineral Mix);

    10,000 units vitamin A (except once a week give a capsule containing 10,000 units vitamin A and 400 units vitamin D instead);

    100 units vitamin E.

- After three weeks, reduce above supplements to the following, given once a week:

    400 units vitamin E;

    10,000 units vitamin A and 400 units vitamin D.

- Feed a high-quality diet with as much raw food as possible (see page 53). Be sure to include Vita-Mineral Mix and other listed supplements to diet.

Concussion

A sudden, violent bump on any part of the head can cause a concussion. The most common cause is the "high rise" syndrome—falling from a window or balcony. Being hit by a car or something heavy falling on the cat are other possible causes of a concussion. If the blow injures an area of the brain causing swelling, then brain function will be partially impaired. It is to be hoped that the effects will be temporary. With rest, quiet, and gentle nursing, the swelling will subside and the whole episode can be relegated to the category of unpleasant memory. Homeopathy can do a lot to speed recovery.

A veterinarian should always be consulted as quickly as possible whenever any of the symptoms below appear, since they can also indicate other very serious conditions, feline infectious peritonitis and rabies among them.

Prevention

- Screen all windows.
- Never allow cat to sit out on balcony or window sill.
- Provide protected, screened run for outdoor exercise.

Symptoms

- Dizziness; falling to the side, circling or staggering
- Tipping head to one side
- Uneven size of pupils
- Vomiting
- Inability to lap food

Recommendations

- Confine cat to carry case and take straight to veterinarian.
- Give Bach Flower Rescue Remedy—three drops in mouth every thirty minutes until there is some improvement; then give three drops three times a day.
- After returning home confine to large cage or small room with dim light and quiet.
- Play soft classical music.
- Eliminate possibility of climbing until dizziness passes and balance returns.
- Finger-feed if necessary until balance returns (see page 225).
- Provide snug retreat (page 240).
- Herbal remedy: If there are tremors or spasms or restlessness give a teaspoon of valerian root decoction (page 259) or ½ valerian capsule every three hours.
- For one day (or longer if veterinarian advises) fast on High-Calcium Chicken Broth given three to four times a day (page 243). To each ¼-cup serving of broth add the following:
    - $\frac{1}{16}$ teaspoon ascorbic acid crystals or sodium ascorbate powder (250 units vitamin C);
    - $\frac{1}{16}$ teaspoon Pet Tinic from the veterinarian or pet supply company or one-fourth of a low-potency B vitamin pill (10 mg level);

$\frac{1}{16}$ teaspoon mixed trace mineral powder or $\frac{1}{4}$ mixed mineral pill.
- Once a day give 100 units vitamin E (alpha tocopherol); after one week reduce to 400 units once a week as usual.

Fractures

A fracture (a break in the bone) can be caused by the cat falling, by something falling on him, being struck by a car, or by the cat being crushed or caught in a slamming door. An actual break is less likely to occur when bones are kept strong by regular exercise and a high-quality diet rich in calcium, vitamin D, and trace minerals. The types of fractures are (a) hairline—the bone is cracked; (b) simple fracture—the bone is broken; or (c) compound fracture—the bone is broken and part of the bone is protruding out through the skin.

Broken bones are extremely painful. The injury can be made worse merely by allowing the cat to move about. If not tended by a veterinarian, infection can set in and the animal can be permanently crippled, lose the limb, or die from the infection.

Prevention

- Screen all windows. Do not allow a cat to sit on a balcony or unscreened windowsill.
- Look before you slam any door behind you.
- Provide a screened, protected run for outdoor exercise.

Recommendations

- Tell the cat you understand he hurts and that you are going to help him feel better.
- Give Bach Flower Rescue Remedy (prepared as given on page 249)—three drops into the mouth every thirty minutes.
- Confine the cat to the bathroom while you call the veterinarian and tell him you're coming with an emergency.
- If the cat cannot walk or if you are doubtful about the extent of his injuries, keep him lying in whatever position you found him and slide him onto a tray or board *covered*

by a towel. (A serving tray or the drip tray from under the broiler in the oven may be the right size.)

- If front leg is broken, very gently and carefully slide the inside roll from a toilet paper or paper towel roll over the leg to protect it. Do this only if the cat does not object.
- Keep the cat warm—cover with a towel or blanket.
- Add to food during recuperation:
     an extra ⅛ teaspoon bone meal, calcium lactate, or calcium glutomate (in addition to that in Vita-Mineral Mix);
     antistress supplements (page 240);
     1 teaspoon comfrey tea.
- Give one capsule containing 10,000 units vitamin A and 400 units vitamin D twice a week for three weeks; then reduce to once a week.
- While healing is taking place, devise ways of exercising that do not include the injured part. Use your ingenuity.

Irritable Bowel Syndrome (IBS)

Irritable Bowel Syndrome (IBS) is an auto-immune disease. The body's immune system has become overactive and is attacking the body itself—in this case, the inner walls of the intestine. Because the membranes lining the intestine are raw and sensitive, the body tries to rid itself of anything in the intestine as quickly as possible by increasing the force and frequency of peristaltic action and secreting copious amounts of mucus into the intestine. This results in frequent runny and/or gaseous stools. Sometimes the body will try to correct the situation by stopping peristalsis, causing the stool to remain in the intestine, dry out, and become hard—and then constipation will alternate with diarrhea. This always happens if the veterinarian resorts to an antispasmotic drug. Dr. Pitcairn, my own vet, counsels against the use of antispasmotic drugs for IBS. Because of the irritation and scarring, the intestinal walls become thickened. Nutrients cannot pass from the intestine into the bloodstream, and malabsorption results. IBS was once thought to be incurable, but it is now known that IBS "responds beautifully to a high-fibre diet" (*British Lancet*, April 25, 1987).

Any auto-immune disease is a signal that the immune system is weak and confused. Therefore, we must nurture and strengthen the failing immune system as well as the inflamed, swollen, and ulcerated intestinal walls. Modern veterinarians point out that auto-immune diseases appear most frequently in cats who have been treated at some time in their lives with corticosteroids or in cats who have been vaccinated frequently with vaccines combining several viruses (see "Vaccinations and Other Immunizations," page 265). Cortisone, Prednizone and other corticosteroids suppress the body's immune response (see "Steroids," page 268). Negative side effects of steroids sometimes show up many months or even years after treatment has been stopped.

IBS is *not* always incurable. I've seen it disappear time after time (but only when the owner insisted that *no* drugs be used). Some veterinarians try steroids or an antibiotic preparation called tylan that was developed for pigs. These drugs often suppress the symptoms for a little while, but then they always return, worse than ever. It's harder to effect a permanent and true cure after the animal's system has been drugged. Homeopathic treatment, guided by a good homeopathic vet, always enhances any other natural treatment and speeds the recovery. If drugs have been used in the past, homeopathy is indispensable (see "Homeopathy," page 244).

During IBS the body sometimes becomes dehydrated to a greater or lesser degree, especially if there has been much diarrhea and even vomiting. Hydration with Ringer's Lactate given subcutaneously will give the patient immediate relief and ensure that the body takes a giant step forward toward healing itself. I personally have never seen it fail in this. You can have the vet or his assistant do this procedure, or, like many of my clients, you can learn to give subcutaneous fluids yourself at home. All it takes is a desire to do it and patience with yourself while you learn (see "Subcutaneous Hydration," page 235).

Symptoms

- Constipation or diarrhea or both alternating
- Diarrhea consisting of thin, liquid, offensive stools that "sputter" when passed

- Much mucus with stool; sometimes blood in stool
- Constantly demanding food
- Voracious appetite
- Steady weight loss despite large appetite
- Vet will feel thickening of intestinal wall and lack of flexibility

Recommendations

- Nurture and strengthen the immune system:
  1. Change as quickly as possible to an all raw-food diet (see page 58). The immune system gradually fails without the enzymes that are present only in raw foods.
  2. Add ¼ teaspoon to ½ teaspoon powdered feline enzymes to all meals.
  3. Be sure to give Vita-Mineral Mix (page 55) and all additional supplements recommended in Chapter 2, "Diet"—especially vitamins A, C, D, and E.
  4. Encourage a rapid and efficient metabolism by removing *all* food between meals. Leaving snacks lying around will *not* help the cat gain weight—just the opposite. It's helpful to feed three or even four meals a day, but don't leave food around for more than one-half hour.
- Have vet or his assistant give subcutaneous fluids one, two, or more times a week, *or* ask him to teach you how to do it yourself at home (see page 235).
- Give 1 teaspoon slippery elm syrup (see page 258) five to ten minutes before each meal to soothe and calm the intestinal walls (see "Giving Liquid Medication," page 210).
- Give one charcoal tablet morning and evening for two or three days to eliminate flatulence and/or foul smell (stool will look black) (see "Giving Pills," page 208).
- To minimize putrefaction and encourage friendly bacteria in the intestine, add to each meal:
  - ⅟₁₆ teaspoon liquid chlorophyll or Green Magma; *and*
  - ⅛ teaspoon liquid acidophilus (or any acidophilus culture that is not suspended in milk or lactose);

or try mixing the chlorophyll and acidophilus with 1 or
2 teaspoons High-Calcium Chicken Broth (see page
243) and give as a liquid medication. Stool will look
quite dark.

- Bach flower remedies: cats with IBS tend to be rather
nervous and fearful. They are easily upset by other
animals or by people. Give three drops three or four
times a day of the following mixture prepared as given on
page 249:

    Gentran—to give courage;

    Aspen—to dispel undefined fears;

    Mimulus—to quiet fear of bodily discomfort.

- *If constipation is a problem:*
    1. Do all of the above.
    2. Add ⅛ teaspoon ground psyllium husks and 2 ta-
blespoons water to food twice a day until stool remains normal. It's okay to continue indefinitely.
Psyllium is just a ground-up seed and quite
harmless.
    3. Add an extra ⅛ teaspoon fine wheat bran to each
meal.
    4. See also "Constipation."
- *If diarrhea is a problem:*
    1. Whenever diarrhea appears, immediately stop feed-
ing solid foods.
        A. Give the patient all of the High-Calcium Chicken
Broth (see page 243) he wants three to four
times a day;
        B. Give one charcoal tablet twice a day for two to
three days (see "Giving Pills," page 208).
    2. Then gradually go back to solid food and:
        A. Do all of the above (except the steps under con-
stipation), especially chlorophyll and acidophilus mixture;
        B. Add to food once a day ⅛ teaspoon Delicious
Garlic Condiment (see page 256);
        C. Add to food twice a day ⅛ teaspoon powdered
apple pectin.
    3. See also "Diarrhea."

Kidney and Bladder Stones
(See also "Feline Urologic Syndrome")

Stones and gravel are really crystals that form in the kidneys and, more often, in the bladder. The razor-sharp edges slice and tear at the bladder or kidney walls, providing an ideal breeding ground for germs. If tiny pieces of the stones break off and pass out through the urethra, the scraping and tearing continue all the way, causing great pain and blood in the urine. Scarring of the urethra walls usually results, thickening the walls and narrowing the passage, making it even more difficult to pass the rest of the crystals. If a crystal blocks the urethra, or if the urethra swells shut, no urine or blood can get through. Then the wastes back up and a serious toxic condition quickly builds in the body. Repeated bouts of FUS (feline urologic syndrome), with its accompanying swelling and infection in the urethra, recurring despite all dietary and veterinary treatment, can sometimes be explained by the presence of bladder stones and gravel. (See "Feline Urologic Syndrome.")

One reason for the formation of these mineral crystals is the presence of large amounts of insoluble mineral salts in the diet, such as those found in tuna and other fish. Stones and gravel can also be caused by an alkaline condition in the urine. The smell of food triggers metabolic changes that produce an alkaline urine, so if you're not already doing so, feed only twice a day and remove all food, including the dirty food plate, after a half hour. An acid urine will dissolve mineral crystals and pass them out of the body as liquid waste. Urine also becomes alkaline if there is a dietary lack of vitamins A, B-6, or C, or if the diet does not contain enough of the protein methionine, or if the protein in the diet, no matter how copious, cannot be assimilated efficiently by the cat's system. The meat by-products and meat meal found in most commercial foods are so highly processed that it is questionable how much of the protein actually finds its way into the cat's system.

A nutritional imbalance producing stones can also result from stress as in cases of immobilization due to a cast or confinement in a cage, since stress uses up nutrients very quickly. Stones and gravel create a condition where pain is great, stress levels are high, and toxicity leading to death can build up quickly. If you see blood in the cat's urine, don't wait; get the cat to the veterinarian at once. A homeopathic veterinarian may be able to treat your cat successfully with homeopathy and diet (see "Homeopathy," page 244). However, if large stones are present that do not respond to treatment and your vet counsels that surgery is unavoidable, discuss the pros and cons of consulting a surgical specialist experienced in this particular operation. It is a bit tricky since the bladder is cut open and it must be sewn together again so that it will hold liquid. I've known many cats who have had bladder-stone surgery, and all have done fine afterward. You can ease the stress and help with a rapid recovery using diet, supplements, homeopathy, and the Bach flower remedies. (See "Surgery and Catheterization," page 271.)

Symptoms

- Crying out while at the litter box
- Repeated bouts of FUS or other urinary infection despite care and medication
- Blood in urine

Recommendations

- Ask veterinarian to test for stones (urine test, X rays, and blood test).
- Acidify the urine by giving veterinarian's medication, removing *all* food between meals, and carefully balancing the high-quality proteins in the diet. Methionine, the acidifying protein, is plentiful in egg yolk. Give ½ organic raw yolk in each meal.
- Stress level is very high because of pain—give extra demonstrations of love and provide a snug retreat (page 240).
- Eliminate all dry and semimoist food, tuna and other fish from diet.
- Feed a high-quality diet with as much raw food as possible

(see Chapter 2, "Diet"). Be sure to include Vita-Mineral Mix and other listed supplements to diet. Use liver as well as chicken for meat portion; half potato and half soaked oat flakes or brown rice for grain portion; half carrots and half peas for the vegetable portion. *Note: If FUS is present, along with the stones and gravel, your vet may want to eliminate liver and other organ meats and also the yeast from the Vita-Mineral Mix recipe until the crisis is past.* If so, you can supply the B complex vitamins by giving a pill from the health-food store. Buy a low potency B complex pill at about the 10 mg level, or divide a higher potency pill into smaller pieces. Do not use dolomite in the Vita-Mineral Mix; use bone meal, calcium lactate, or calcium glutonate.

- Add to each meal:
    ¼ teaspoon feline enzyme powder to ensure assimilation of all food;
    ¼ teaspoon bone meal, calcium lactate, or calcium glutonate (in addition to that in Vita-Mineral Mix);
    ⅛ teaspoon ascorbic acid crystals (500 units vitamin C) to help acidify urine and fight infection;
    Increase Vita-Mineral Mix to 1¼ teaspoons per meal.
- Once a day add to food ⅛ teaspoon Delicious Garlic Condiment (see page 256) to guard against the complication of infection.
- Once a week add to food:
    Contents of a 400-unit vitamin E capsule to help heal scarring;
    Contents of a capsule containing 10,000 units vitamin A and 400 units vitamin D to help assimilate the calcium.
- Bach flower remedies: bladder stone cats are frightened cats. They don't know why they're having this terrible pain or when it may strike again. They feel confused, helpless, and afraid. Stress level is very high; depression and loss of will to live are a constant threat.
    1. Give three drops Rescue Remedy (prepared as given on page 249) every two to four hours until the stones are gone.
    2. After stones are gone give three drops four times a

371

day of the following mixture prepared as given on page 249:

> Star of Bethlehem—for comfort after shock;
> Hornbeam—for courage and strength, *or*
> Gorse—to banish hopelessness;
> Mimulus—to dispel old fears.
> Walnut—to cut emotional ties to past experiences.

Kidney Disease

The kidney's job is to filter poisons and wastes out of the blood and send them to the bladder to be excreted in the urine. The kidneys of a cat filter hundreds of pints of blood every day. These hard-working organs will keep on functioning happily right into extreme old age if the diet is adequate and balanced and if no unusual stress is put on them by chemicals entering the body. Kidneys can be worn out early by processing excess amino acids from poor-quality protein such as is contained in most commercial cat foods or from eating too much protein as in an all-meat diet. The kidneys must also detoxify foreign chemicals such as preservatives and colorings in food, substances such as cigarette smoke, and some anesthetics. Chemicals such as phenol, which is contained in certain bathroom cleansers and deodorizers such as Lysol and PineSol, can damage the kidneys beyond repair. All the cat has to do is to walk on a surface where there is a residue after one of these products has been used and then lick his paws.

Kidney damage can take the form of fatty kidneys, scarred kidneys, or dead tissue. Symptoms of kidney failure include frequent, copious drinking and urination; pale, watery urine; periods of lethargy; and weight loss despite a good appetite. Often dandruff is also present. If the kidneys are failing, make their job as easy as possible by feeding less protein and by making sure that the protein you do feed is the highest quality, easily digested, and that the amino acids that make up the protein are as perfectly balanced as possible. Because leftover protein is converted to starch, you can aid the kidneys by adding more starch to the diet and using only enough protein to fill the actual daily requirements.

When treating a cat with failing kidneys, it is important to work closely with a veterinarian, preferably an experienced homeopath, who will guide you as to the amount of protein, salt, and fluid to include in the diet. Modern veterinarians have replaced the no-protein diet of the past with one in which a minimum of perfectly balanced protein is allowed. It has been found that a complete lack of protein in the diet will cause the body to rob protein from its own tissues. In cases where diuretics are indicated, some veterinarians are now using vitamins C and E and parsley tea to stimulate urine flow naturally. In cases where copious drinking and urination are occurring, all the water-soluble minerals, B vitamins, and vitamin C are rapidly lost with the urine so they should be replenished at least twice a day in the food. It is best to use only spring water or distilled water and to eliminate all chemicals from the cat's food and environment.

When kidney disease becomes advanced, the patient begins to urinate a great deal more than he can possibly replace by drinking. Dehydration results. The cat's face gets a pinched look; the coat seems rough and sheds easily. He dwindles to nothing, and, toward the end, even drinking stops. Often the cat suffers from diarrhea and/or constipation. Dehydration makes a cat feel nauseated and miserable; he aches all over.

Fortunately, cats experiencing advanced kidney disease can be spared all of the above if regular subcutaneous hydration is administered (see page 235).

Symptoms

- Frequent, copious drinking and urination (see also "Cardiomyopathy," "Diabetes," and "Hyperthyroidism")
- Colorless, watery urine
- Lethargy, depression
- Skinniness
- Greasy fur, dandruff
- Body odor
- Edema (water retention in tissues)
- Gouty condition
- Seeking out warmth
- Blood in urine

- Dehydration
- Hiding, turning face to the wall, sitting with head over water dish

Recommendations

- Have veterinarian do tests to determine type of kidney problem.
- Bathe cat once a week in plain castile shampoo from health-food store to wash off dandruff so cat does not lick it off and recycle his own wastes.
- Provide warmth and a snug retreat (see page 240).
- Provide plenty of fresh spring water or distilled water.
- Alkalize system by giving one or two drops of golden seal elixir before bed (see page 260).
- Feed diet high in carbohydrates with proteins carefully balanced, and eliminate all chemicals. See following recipes.
- Encourage exercise so breathing will deepen and the lungs will rid the body of more carbon dioxide and other wastes in the exhalations.

Diet for the Cat with Kidney Problems

Spring or distilled water

4 parts carbohydrate: Puréed barley flakes and/or baby food creamed corn

2 parts protein: Lightly broiled chicken or beef *or* raw organic egg yolk and cooked white (used with meat, not alone)—you can also use baby food chicken.

1 part vegetables: Chopped or finely grated raw vegetable or vegetable juice—carrots, zucchini, and alfalfa sprouts are best

2 tablespoons Vita-Mineral Mix

2 teaspoons soft butter

- Blend above ingredients together and store in glass jar.
- Because nutrients are washed out quickly in the copious urine, it is good to feed kidney patients three to four times a day.

Supplements:

• Each day mix the following into *each* meal or administer by dropper *after* the meal:

⅛ teaspoon mixed mineral powder;

1/16 teaspoon ascorbic acid crystals or sodium ascorbate powder (250 units vitamin C);

⅛ teaspoon Pet Tinic (a B vitamin and iron tonic available from the veterinarian) *or* ½ of a low-potency B complex capsule (10 mg level);

¼ teaspoon or ½ tablet mixed digestive enzymes.

• Once a week give:

400 units of vitamin E (alpha tocopherol);

A capsule containing 10,000 units vitamin A and 400 units vitamin D.

• Herbal remedies:

1. To add minerals to the diet moisten the food with 1 or 2 teaspoons of one of the following:
Kombu broth (page 256) or horsetail grass infusion (page 259).

2. If edema (water retention) is present give 1 teaspoon strong parsley tea four times a day before meals (this can also be made into an elixir [see page 260]).

• Bach flower remedies: kidney patients feel cold and shivery and weak. Give three drops three times a day of the following mixture prepared as given on page 249:

Hornbeam—to strengthen;

Aspen—to banish vague fears;

Crabapple—to encourage expulsion of poisons from the body.

Liver Disease and Liver Damage

The liver has many jobs. It detoxifies poisons in the system, such as drugs and chemicals; it detoxifies excess hormones, such as insulin and the male-female hormones; and it produces bile to digest fats, store them, and convert them to starch. Liver breakdown can be caused by a diet deficient in choline or magnesium.

It can also occur when the amount of outside poisons entering the body—such as antibiotics; toxic chemicals in household cleaners, food preservatives and colors; insecticides; or moth-ball fumes— becomes too great for the liver to handle, and too many liver cells are destroyed too quickly. Inflamed swollen liver (hepatitis) or fatty or scarred liver (cirrhosis) then occurs. When liver cells die, the liver swells and becomes inflamed and sore. In this stage the condition is called hepatitis. When liver tissue is replaced by scar tissue that cannot do the liver's work of detoxifying, further damage occurs more easily and then more scarring. This snowball effect is called cirrhosis. A lack of bile in the system causes digestion to break down, resulting in malabsorption of fats. Tissues become waterlogged and/or hypoglycemia develops because of the inability of the liver to deactivate excess insulin. An imbalance of the male or female hormones can also occur, resulting in bad temper or fearfulness.

The liver has a miraculous ability to regenerate itself if given adequate nutritional support and help from a homeopathic veterinarian (see "Homeopathy," page 244). But liver disease is seldom diagnosed early because the symptoms are so general that they could be confused with any number of other difficulties from hair balls to urinary disease.

Symptoms

- Lethargy or aggression
- Weight loss
- Random wetting or spraying, milky urine, diarrhea, light-colored (fatty) stool
- Digestive upsets, vomiting foam or yellow liquid, distended abdomen
- Yellow eye whites (often does not occur until late in the disease)
- Recurrent allergic reactions
- Tendency to pick up fleas and ringworm

Recommendations

- Ask veterinarian to do a blood test that includes a specific liver enzyme evaluation (e.g., SGPT).
- Seek the help of a holistic veterinarian experienced in homeopathy and nutrition.
- Follow veterinarian's treatment carefully.
- Together with veterinarian, try to determine the cause of liver trouble by examining:
  dietary deficiencies;
  presence of toxic substances in environment such as household cleaners; basin, tub, and tile cleaners; room deodorizers; litter deodorizers; moth-ball fumes; paint fumes; and
  chemical preservatives and colors in food such as BHA, BHT, propylgallate, nitrates, nitrites, sodium benzoate, and so on.
- Provide a snug retreat (see page 240) to eliminate stress.
- Feed a high-quality diet with as much raw food as possible. (See Chapter 2, "Diet.")
- Feed three or four small meals a day.
- Alter Vita-Mineral Mix recipe (page 55) as follows:
  1½ cups yeast;
  2 cups lecithin;
  1½ cups bran;
  ½ cup kelp or mixed trace mineral powder;
  2 cups bone meal, calcium lactate, or calcium glutonate.
- Add to each meal:
  1 teaspoon of special Vita-Mineral Mix recipe above;
  ¼ teaspoon cod liver oil;
  1/16 teaspoon ascorbic acid crystals or sodium ascorbate powder (250 units vitamin C);
  ¼ tablet digestive enzymes (crushed) or ¼ teaspoon feline digestive enzyme powder;
  ½ tablet low-potency B complex (below 10 mg level);
  ¼ teaspoon liquid acidophilus (not suspended in lactose).

- Add to food three times a week:
    200 units vitamin E (alpha tocopherol);
    1 soft cooked organic egg;
    10,000 units vitamin A—*for three weeks only*—then
        switch to a capsule containing 10,000 units vitamin A
        and 400 units vitamin D *once a week*.
- Herbal remedy: mix ¼ to 1 teaspoon rosemary tea into
  food to aid digestion.
- Bach flower remedies: liver patients feel tired and despon-
  dent, and all are subject to extremes of emotion, and some
  experience mood swings. Give them quiet cheerfulness and
  frequent gentle affection. Don't let their extreme or inap-
  propriate mood influence yours. You must be the Rock of
  Gibraltar providing the emotional stability they desperately
  need. Four times a day give three drops of the following
  mixture prepared as given on page 249:
    Crabapple—to help the cleansing process;
    Hornbeam—to give strength and courage;
    plus one of the following:
    Impatiens—for those who are easily angered
        (touchy) or seem to go looking for an argument;
    Aspen—for those who are fearful, seemingly without
        good reason;
    Scleranthus—for those who seem to have mood
        swings.

Mange Mites
(For ear mites, see "Ear Problems")

Mange is a skin condition caused by one of two types of mites:
sarcoptic mites, which burrow under the skin; or demodectic mites,
which live on the hair follicles. *Sarcoptic* mites cause terrible itching
and can be transferred to humans who have low resistance. Some
owners, including me, are sensitive to mites. If you discover you
have itchy red bumps like mosquito bites in straight lines but widely
spaced in places against which your cat has been resting, such as
the inner arm or side of the body, then you know your cat has
mites. Besides treating the cat you will want to treat yourself and

stop the itching. First of all, don't panic. Remember that cat and dog mites cannot reproduce on a human, so, unless you have the human variety, or unless you reinfest yourself from your pet or someone else's or from a piece of clothing where the mites have been lying dormant and waiting for you, the mites will gradually die out and the bites will disappear. Personally that's not fast enough for me. I've tried many different preparations and techniques, and I've found that the quickest, easiest, and safest way to get rid of a mite bite on humans and stop the itching at once is to brush the bite hard with a dry natural bristle bath brush. This works even after you've had the bites for a day or two, but you'll have to do it every few hours. If you do it when you first feel the bite, even before much of a bump has formed, you probably won't have any more trouble with it. If you finish up the brushing by stroking strongly in one direction: toward the body (or if the bites are on the body, toward the intestines), you will help the lymph ducts carry away the toxic itchy residues left by the little critters.

Mites proliferate on cats who are very old and/or sick. If I'm doing nursing care for such a cat, I protect myself by wearing a closely woven heavy blouse or smock. Mites will seek heat, so if they can't perceive your body heat, they'll stay on the cat. If it's too hot for a smock I put some citronella oil or Spritz coat enhancer on my arms.

My veterinarian showed me a young kitten infested with mange mites. The bizarre feature of this particular case was that the kitten was perfectly comfortable and maintained a normal coat of hair through it all. The infestation was discovered only because the owner was going through a positive agony of itching. The owner's dermatologist uncovered the cause and suggested that the cat be treated as the source of the problem. Any veterinarian I've ever talked to seems to agree that skin problems are by far the hardest to diagnose.

Demodectic mites are mites that live in the hair follicles. Symptoms appear as a bald patch above the eyes, around the ears, or on the chin, and therefore they are sometimes called head mites. They are usually transferred from one animal to another, or they can be carried by an unsuspecting human.

Mange is supposed to be very rare in cats, but, being a groomer, I have seen it with increasing frequency in the last few years. Holistically oriented veterinarians have found that mange mites take hold on animals with weak immune systems. As the liver is a key organ in the immune system, any cats with liver disease are prime targets for mange mites, as are any cats who are ill, on medication, or genetically weak because of in-breeding. If mange is diagnosed, the orthodox treatment has always been to apply a highly poisonous liquid to the skin. The solution is so toxic that only a part of the animal can be treated at one time. The liquid is specifically designed to be absorbed through the skin, killing the mites on the way. Unfortunately, being highly toxic, it also destroys many liver cells, doing further damage to the immune system. This is why cats once infested with mange seem to get it again and again.

Because mange is difficult to diagnose and as it is believed to be practically nonexistent in cats, it is often mistaken for some other condition or simply called an "allergy." Cortisone is frequently used to "stop the itching, at least" (see "Cortisone and Other Steroids," page 268). This is simply treating a symptom and not getting rid of the mites. The itching will return the minute the cortisone treatment is stopped. Also, it is well known that cortisone depresses the immune system even worse than the mange medicine. Once cortisone has been used, recovery from mites becomes very difficult. Since mange, like any parasite, is a sign that health is poor and resistance is low, a more effective solution is to build general health, with special attention to the liver to ensure strong resistence levels, and to treat the mites topically with natural preparations. Homeopathy can be invaluable in building up the immune system again (see "Homeopathy," page 244).

Symptoms

- Hairless patches around eyes, ears, or chin
- Hairless patches in long narrow lines on body
- Itching and scratching
- Pinhead-size scabs on neck, chest, or back, enlarging to large open sore after much scratching
- Red itching welts appearing in straight lines on owner's inner arm or body

Recomendations

- Consult veterinarian for a definite diagnosis of the condition. Mites are extremely hard to diagnose, even with a scraping examined under the microscope.
- Fast two to three days on High-Calcium Chicken Broth (see page 243 and see "Fasting," page 225).
- Feed diet and supplements given in section on "Liver Disease and Liver Damage," page 375, except include 10,000 units a day of vitamin A (for three weeks), which tends to inhibit the spread of mange.
- Feed twice a day and remove all food between meals, leaving only water available.
- Add to food once a day:
    5 mg zinc;
    ¼ to ½ teaspoon Delicious Garlic Condiment (page 256).
- Eliminate all dairy products from diet.
- Eliminate fatty treats such as butter.
- Bathe cat in natural flea shampoo daily (see Appendix, "Product Suppliers").
- After shampoo, sponge on Lemon Rinse (see page 262) or spray with Spritz.
- Herbal remedy: make Lemon Rinse with herb tea as the liquid instead of water. Use golden seal, plantain, or lavender—all tend to kill mites. Massage it into the skin once a day.
- Bach flower remedies: itchy mites make a cat feel out of sorts. If it goes on very long, they become nervous and depressed. Four times a day give three drops of the following mixture prepared as given on page 249:
    Crabapple—to aid in cleansing;
    Aspen—for those who are nervous;
    Gorse—to banish hopelessness.

Matting Fur

Matting occurs when the body sheds hair, but the hair is not groomed out—by either the cat or the owner. The loose hair will eventually build up into first soft and then hard mats. Matting is more common in longhaired cats because the cat's tongue cannot reach all the way down to the roots of the hair. Only a wide-toothed metal comb can groom a longhaired cat thoroughly. During spring and autumn, when heavy shedding occurs, any cat can mat, especially if a poor-quality diet has produced a poor-quality coat; or if frequent snacking has produced an oily coat; or if any spray, powder, or "cream rinse" has coated the hair follicles, making them sticky. Also, fleas encourage matting by leaving eggs and debris on the skin and coat. Finally, mats can form around dirt, debris, or soiling on the fur.

Soft mats are often not noticed by the owner. A comb with teeth too close together will simply skip through the top half-inch of the hair and not reveal the trouble building up at the roots. If the partially matted coat is then bathed or treated with a flea preparation, the soft mats immediately become hard mats. Never bathe, spray, or powder a matted cat; instead comb thoroughly and remove the mats first. Hard mats can inhibit free movement of limbs and are favorite places for fleas and ringworm. No air can reach the skin under the mat, and the cat cannot wash himself there, so he always suffers from itching, irritation, redness, and dandruff in those areas. Mats are unsanitary, uncomfortable, and a constant source of stress.

Symptoms

- Lumps near skin in the armpit or on the chest, inner thighs, outer thighs, lower back, around the ears and neck, or around and under the anus
- Scratching with hind foot
- Pulling on hair with teeth
- Bald spots where cat has torn the mat out
- Impaired motion at joints, inability to jump or land properly
- Unpleasant odor
- Demoralization and depression

Prevention

- Feed a high-quality diet with as much raw food as possible (see Chapter 2, "Diet"). Be sure to include Vita-Mineral Mix and other listed supplements to diet.
- Remove food between meals, leaving only water available.
- Use proper grooming tool and methods (see Chapter 7, "Grooming").
- Establish a regular grooming schedule:
    For longhaired cats: at least sixty seconds a day;
    For shorthaired cats: at least thirty seconds three times a week.
- Keep hair clean.

Recommendations

- To remove mats, see page 145.
- After the mats are removed, begin prevention program as outlined above and have veterinarian check for cause of any diarrhea. Treat for fleas, parasites, or fungus, if necessary.
- Herbal remedy: to keep hair from matting again after a shampoo and make it easier to comb out, rinse with one cup of a decoction (see page 259) made with either burdock root, comfrey, stinging nettle, *or* sage tea. Make the tea doubly strong. Also, add one teaspoon horsetail infusion to all meals to provide extra minerals used by the body to build healthy hair.
- Bach flower remedies: because mats made it uncomfortable to be picked up, a matted cat will be feeling a little lonely and his self-esteem will be low. Start before the grooming and continue for two weeks after he is clean and silky again by giving three drops four times a day of the following mixture prepared as given on page 249:
    Walnut—to forget old thought patterns and troubles;
    Crabapple—for those whose diet was only recently upgraded, those who had food left available between meals, or those with dandruff.

Mites
(see "Mange Mites")

Mites, Ear
Ear (see "Ear Problems")

Nervousness, Hiding, and Ill Temper

Nervousness, hiding, and ill temper are all warning signals that the cat is either afraid or ill or both. Nervousness is nearly always caused by a combination of things: environmental stress, a congenital predisposition, chemicals in the diet or environment, and/or a physical disease. The most ubiquitous cause of feline tension and nervousness (sometimes referred to as hypersensitivity to stimulae) is the presence of chemicals in literally *all* of the cat foods on the supermarket shelves—and even in those sold by most veterinarians. These preservatives, colorings, and flavor enhancers actually abrade the cat's nerve endings. When you change over to one of the pure foods that have no chemicals, you will always see a change for the better in your cat's temperament. There are no exceptions to this rule. Even cats who already seem perfectly fine and happy will become more mellow or jocular or playful. You should also eliminate the possibility of chemical residues such as air fresheners, moth-ball odors, and floor or bathroom cleansers containing phenol. Vaccinosis, caused by frequent and/or multiple vaccinations, is also a frequent cause of nervousness.

Causes of a nervous temperament nearly always include some discomfort, pain, or weakness. If a cat is not feeling up to par, he knows he cannot escape as easily if need should arise. What if someone picks him up carelessly or puts him down wrong and he is accidentally hurt? What if he is squeezed too hard or held in a position where breathing is difficult or his skeletal structure unsupported? All these circumstances take on greatly increased importance to a cat with an undiagnosed illness. Cardiac disease, lung disease, arthritis, and liver problems all require very special handling of the cat's body. A nervous cat, or one who "doesn't like to be picked up," should have a very thorough physical examination to determine whether or not disease is a part of the problem.

Now check out the following list of possible environmental causes, looking at them from the cat's point of view. Remember that a cat's acute hearing and sense of smell render him much more sensitive to noises and odors than you are, and yes, a cat can even be afraid of an odor. A noise level that is normal to you may be loud and startling to a cat; a noise that is loud and startling to you is probably downright painful to the cat's ears. The smell of a dirty litter box is a source of great tension to a cat. In the wild the smell of urine attracts predators, so over the millennia cats have developed an instinctive fear that makes them bury their wastes. This instinct continues to operate in the cat's subconscious even when he lives in a city apartment where, we would assume, there is a total absence of predators. The smell of a dirty litter box will still make him tense and afraid.

Also, remember that a cat is ten to fifteen times smaller than you. Imagine how you would feel if you were living with a family of elephants. Wouldn't you be afraid of their feet—especially if there were several elephants in the same room with you, or if they were moving about too quickly? What if there were young elephants who picked you up suddenly and put you down carelessly? Prolonged exposure to stresses like this will make any animal nervous and irritable, and finally weaken him to the point where he becomes an easy target for disease. Also, nervous animals are not a pleasure to handle, therefore the nervous cat usually lacks the physical affection he badly needs and so becomes even more withdrawn.

Symptoms

- Hiding, trembling
- Scratching and/or biting others with little or no provocation
- Defensive behavior, hissing
- Unwillingness to be held or touched in one or more places

Causes

- Dirty litter box
- Disease or pain
- Declawing (see page 94; see also "Claw and Cuticle Problems," page 290)
- Improper diet (see page 43)
- Possible liver damage, arthritis, or heart or lung problem
- Excess or prolonged stress (noisy household, unusual household activity, children, or adults who don't handle cat properly)
- Congenitally weak nerves and/or congenitally low intelligence due to careless breeding (in-breeding)
- Previous negative life experiences: early separation from mother, lack of human contact, careless or brutal handling
- Fear of other animals, members of household, objects such as vacuum cleaner, strangers, or anything else new and unknown
- Cat being deaf or blind without owner being aware
- Hypoglycemia (see page 349) or Hyperthyroidism (see page 345)

Recommendations

- Have veterinarian examine carefully for any painful or diseased conditions such as ingrown claw (especially on declawed cats), dirty teeth, swollen anal glands, and constipation, or have blood test to reveal any more serious disease.
- Homeopathy has the most immediate and powerful effects of any therapy used in cases of emotional problems.
- Eliminate all commercial pet food. *Read labels* even on food bought in health-food store or from veterinarian (see page 47).
- Feed a high-quality diet with as much raw food as possible (see Chapter 2, "Diet"). Be sure to include Vita-Mineral Mix and other listed supplements.
- Add antistress supplements (page 240) to diet.
- Reevaluate litter-box position and condition (see page 79).

386

- Reevaluate stress level in cat's environment (see page 197).
- Reevaluate items used to clean your home and eliminate any containing phenol.
- Begin practicing good cat etiquette: no surprises, ask cat permission to pick him up, give warnings, approach with hand below cat's nose level, control children, allow cat to sniff before you touch him, instruct all humans to speak softly and move slowly.
- Provide a snug retreat (see page 240).
- Try to structure as much sameness and repetition as possible into cat's life.
- Herbal remedy: use only as *part* of total program. Include all of the above suggestions as well. Give one teaspoon valerian tea for nine days only. Can be mixed half-and-half with High-Calcium Chicken Broth (see page 243) and given as liquid medication (see page 210) *or* can be mixed in food.
- Bach flower remedies: nervous cats, whether they attack or hide, will always benefit from a program of detoxification to expel irritants from the system. Give three drops four times a day of the following mixture prepared as given on page 249:
    Crabapple—to encourage detoxification;
    White Chestnut—to banish unfounded worries.
    Aspen—to cushion hypersensitivity;
    Mimulus—to quell fears.
- Also add any appropriate remedies listed under any disease that is diagnosed by your veterinarian.
- Also see "Dealing with Abused or Neglected Animals," page 17. For more detailed instructions on calming and re-patterning "attack cats" or scaredy-cats, see "Maizey's Story" in our book *It's a Cat's Life*.

Obesity

Obesity is another problem that can be caused by leaving food available between meals. If cats are on a low-quality diet, their bodies will be craving nutrients that are missing in the food. They will eat and eat in an attempt to get those nutrients. The low-quality diet has an overabundance of unbalanced cheaper proteins, which the body converts and stores as fat.

Cats may also become obese if their diet is too rich in fats, sugars, or salt. Almost all commercial cat foods contain large amounts of sugar or salt, or both, often hidden under such pseudonyms as sodium chloride (for salt) and sucrose, dextrose, corn sweetener, corn syrup, molasses, fructose, or malt syrup (for sugar). Also, the processed foods available in grocery stores are usually deficient in any number of trace elements that the cat requires and would normally ingest if he were hunting in the wild. Furthermore, the alarming percentages of chemical colorings, toxic preservatives, and high hormone by-products in these foods create an additional need for these missing nutrients because they are required by the body to help detoxify, process, and dispose of these chemical nonfood items. The cat tries to supply his body with those missing nutrients by eating more and more of the only food available, the poor diet. Thus, he gets enormous amounts of some elements, and almost none of the others, creating an ever greater imbalance.

Cats fed on all organ meat are usually not only fat but also greasy. It's such a sad thing to see an overweight cat. It is not only the drain on the cat's laboring heart that saddens one but also the fact that the cat can't play and therefore the circulation is slower. And what really tears at my heart is to see a cat so overweight that he cannot bend enough to wash and clean himself properly. The suppleness of the cat is as legendary as his cleanliness. It is criminal to allow the cat's body to get into a condition where he cannot reach his own anus to clean it. I cry inside every time the owner of an obese cat says to me, "Oh, well, she's been spayed, that's why" or "He's old and fat, there's nothing we can do." A cat that is properly cared for keeps a beautiful figure his whole life through. It's never too late to correct the problem. A finicky owner will jump at the chance the minute he or she finds out what to do.

I do not believe in crash diets. When confronted with an obese cat and contrite owners, I explain to the owners that changing to the recommended diet will automatically slim the cat down, albeit very slowly. This will happen because after a few days he won't *want* to eat as much; those missing nutrients he was reaching for will now be amply supplied. Also, the high-quality protein and fat in the new diet have a stick-to-the-ribs effect, which is another reason he will not feel hungry. Coming at the problem from another angle, the fact that you are removing food between meals means that the metabolism will speed up again. The cat will have more energy to play, exercise, and burn up calories.

Once they are aware of the dangers and discomfort that come with obesity most owners are eager to do little special things to speed up the weight loss and to make it easier on their cats.

I recommend feeding any one of the diets given in the diet chapter. Let me caution again: DO *NOT* try at first to reduce the quantity of food your cat eats. When the nutrients he needs are first made available to him, he may gobble them up and ask for more. It's okay to feed a third meal during the first two weeks on the new regimen. Just don't leave the food available for more than a half-hour at each mealtime. When your cat's body has had a chance to absorb all the nutrients it has been missing, he won't need to eat as much and will taper off of his own accord. In fact, at this stage some owners get worried and call me to complain that he's gone right off his feed. "How are his spirits?" I ask. "Is he using his litter box as usual?" If the answers are positive I tell the owners not to worry. He won't need to eat as much now that you're giving him food rich in high-quality nutrients. He's eating quality as opposed to quantity.

If your veterinarian has advised you to set about the weight loss program with all possible speed because of danger to the heart or pancreas, then *do it*.

I caution the owners to provide extra attention at this time, not only petting and cuddling but also frequent casual eye and voice contact. If, without realizing it, you have been teaching your cat that "food is love," you must now introduce him to some of the other delightful ways that love can be expressed. Attention is love, too, you know.

Often a lonely pussycat comes to his owner for attention, and, without thinking, the owner assumes that the cat is asking for food. If your cat is overweight, you may have trained him to do just that. So when he comes to you and cries, distract him with an alternate pleasure. Get out a brown paper bag and throw it on the floor—or roll a ping-pong ball. Or pick him up and hug him. Be sure, too, that you approach him with petting and praise at times when he's *not* expecting it. The more secure and relaxed he feels, the easier it will be to change the undesirable pattern of his eating habits.

As the weight goes down, everything else will improve. The eyes will be brighter, the fur silkier, the skin pink and clean. It's easier to pick up a lighter cat. When you do, and you snuggle your nose into the ruff, take a good sniff and enjoy the delicate aroma exuded by the furs of a healthy cat. Don't be surprised at the change in temperament. Your cat may well become more gregarious and alert, yet at the same time more mellow—relaxed but not lethargic.

Owners are always surprised when a correction in the diet produces an improvement in temperament. To me, it's only logical. A fat, uncomfortable cat who can't clean his own anus is bound to be nervous, grouchy, and lethargic. I frequently tell such owners that they're wasting their cat. They don't know what a beautiful animal they really have. It's not a matter of creating anything new. You're simply uncovering the reality that's already there.

Symptoms

- Looks overweight, thick waist, head and legs appear to be too small for the large body
- Inactivity
- Inability to bend enough to clean himself, causing dirty bloomers and unpleasant smell
- Anal gland impaction
- Dandruff and/or oiliness
- Bad disposition—due to discomfort and feelings of rejection
- Heart disease
- Digestive problems
- Constipation
- Overeating—the result of attempts to supply missing nutrients

Recommendations

- Have veterinarian check for illness.
- Feed a high-quality diet with as much raw food as possible

(see Chapter 2, "Diet," page 53). Be sure to include Vita-Mineral Mix and other listed supplements.

- Remove *all* food between meals; leave food out only one-half hour.
- Add to each meal:

　　1 extra teaspoon bran;

　　1 extra teaspoon finely grated carrots or zucchini;

　　2 tablespoons water;

　　$\frac{1}{16}$ teaspoon sodium ascorbate or ascorbic acid (250 units vitamin C).

The added carrot and zucchini are low-calorie ingredients that will expand the portion and fill up the tummy. They also give a beneficial side effect of conditioning the stool.

- Spread food on an extra large plate so it takes longer to eat. The increased area will make it seem like a bigger meal. Remember that the cat is a small animal so he needs only $\frac{1}{4}$ to $\frac{1}{2}$ cup of food, twice a day.
- Express your love with petting, hugging, play, and kisses, instead of snacks.
- Build a feeling of security by giving honest compliments while physical appearance improves (beautiful eyes and whiskers).
- Schedule regular play periods to make sure your cat is active each day, or, better yet, get an energetic kitten for your cat to romp with.
- *For kittens:* feed smaller meals more often so kitten's stomach is not stretched—six meals a day before three months; four meals a day before five months; three meals a day before seven months; two meals a day after seven months.

Oily Coat
(See also "Skin Problems")

Skin, functioning as an organ of excretion, normally discharges small amounts of oily wastes through the pores. Oily coat indicates that, for some reason, the skin is eliminating much larger amounts of oily wastes. Either the body is attempting to lubricate an irritation or infection on the skin, such as eczema, or the oil is being used to carry an overload of toxins out of the body. These toxins usually result from a backup of wastes due to failure of an organ, such as the kidney or liver; ingestion of an unusual amount of toxic wastes; a dietary imbalance; a lack of minerals or fatty acids; a diet that is too rich, such as an all-meat regimen; or a slowed metabolism caused by leaving food available between meals. The expelled grease coats the hair and clogs the pores. The oily hair collects dirt and germs like a dust mop; matting can occur. When the cat tries to clean himself, he recycles his own wastes. Resistance is lowered and disease can result.

Symptoms

- Dandruff, excess shedding
- Greasy fur, fur holding dust and dirt ("dust mop" effect)
- Mats in fur
- Frequent vomiting of hair balls
- Tendency to fleas and parasites
- Tendency to skin conditions such as hair loss, itching, redness, rashes, fleas, mange, and ringworm
- Constipation

Recommendations

- Have veterinarian check for problems in kidneys, lungs, intestines, liver, thyroid, and all major organs.
- Especially when diagnosis is vague or inconclusive, homeopathic treatment often succeeds where all else fails. Consult with a homeopathic veterinarian.
- Remove food between meals to aid in establishing normal metabolic tempo.
- Feed a high-quality diet with as much raw food as possible (see Chapter 2, "Diet"). Be sure to include Vita-Mineral Mix and other listed supplements.
- Add to each meal to help intestinal efficiency:
    ¼ teaspoon feline digestive enzymes to aid in assimilation of nutrients;
    Extra ½ teaspoon raw grated carrot;

Extra ½ teaspopn bran (in addition to bran in Vita-
Mineral Mix);

⅛ teaspoon liquid chlorophyll and ¼ teaspoon liquid
acidophilus (suspended in water, not lactose)—continue with these until bottles are finished; then stop.
The chlorophyll and acidophilus mixture can be
mixed with 1 tablespoon High-Calcium Chicken
Broth (page 243) and given as liquid medication
(page 210).

- Eliminate low-quality and highly chemical foods such as
dry food, semimoist food, fish, and other commercial cat
food.
- Increase exercise and schedule two regular play periods a
day.
- Add to food ¼ teaspoon Delicious Garlic Condiment (see
page 256) three times a week.
- Encourage circulation by grooming and massaging at least
thirty to sixty seconds a day.
- Always thoroughly groom out any mats or loose hair before bathing cat (see Chapter 7, "Grooming").
- If extreme oiliness or very thick waxy oil is present on tail,
lower back, or armpits, use a dry shampoo before bath
with corn starch or herbal combination given below.
- Bathe weekly to prevent recycling of wastes as cat washes
himself.
- If dandruff is present, rinse with a mixture of 2 cups water
and 2 teaspoons white vinegar or lemon juice, and massage into skin.
- Herbal remedies:
    1. Dry shampoo between baths or before a bath with a
       mixture of 4 tablespoons each of powdered orris
       root and powdered arrowroot. Leave on ten min-
       utes and then brush or comb out. (Cornstarch also
       works, but not quite as well.)
    2. Calm overactive sweat and oil glands and reduce ir-
       ritation with a rinse of calendula tea (see page 259).
    3. Horsetail infusion strengthens sparse, damaged
       hair. Give 1 teaspoon twice a day in food or as liq-
       uid medication (page 210).

4. Lemon Rinse (page 262) or lemon balm tea are mild disinfectants and fungicides. Use as a rinse after bathing.
- Bach flower remedies: cats with oily coats are usually nervous because of a backup of irritating toxins in the system. Give three drops four times a day of the following mixture prepared as given on page 249:

>   Crabapple—to aid in the expulsion of wastes from the system;
>
>   Larch—to encourage self-confidence.

Pancreatitis

The pancreas has two functions: to produce digestive enzymes, which are sent to the stomach through the pancreatic duct, and to produce insulin, which neutralizes excess sugar and makes it possible for the body to burn and use sugar, to change it into starch or fat, or to burn stored fat for use. Literally *pancreatitis* means inflammation of the pancreas; however, the term is also used to refer to a swollen, fatty, or scarred pancreas. Damage to the pancreas can occur in several ways. Long-term poor nutrition will cause the cat to overeat as he attempts to supply the missing nutrients. The consumption of excess fats, sugar, or carbohydrates will overwork the pancreas, and the pancreatic duct may become inflamed and swollen shut. The cat will continue to overeat even though no digestive juices are getting through to the stomach. As inflammation worsens, the pancreas cannot produce the digestive enzymes at all. Gas is then formed in the stomach, and fat is excreted in the stool. Hemorrhaging can occur in the pancreas, followed by scarring and calcification, impairing insulin production, and potentially causing diabetes. Cortisone, ACTH, or radiation therapy can damage the pancreas, as can a vitamin B-6 deficiency. Stress, which automatically leads to the release of large amounts of cortisone into the system, is also very hard on the pancreas. Finally, because digestion is poor in pancreatitis patients, the nutrients needed to rebuild the pancreas and reduce scarring are not assimilated from the food, and recovery is often pitifully slow.

Symptoms

- Food not digested; gas
- Fat, blood, or mucus in stool
- Constipation or diarrhea
- Depression or grouchiness
- Pain
- Poor appetite
- Poor coat quality
- Vomiting
- Weakness or coma
- Diabetes or hypoglycemia

Recommendations

- See veterinarian for diagnosis and treatment.
- Keep stomach's workload low by feeding four small meals a day.
- Feed Pancreatitis Diet given below (best choice) or feed a high-quality diet with as much raw food as possible (see Chapter 2, "Diet," page 53). Be sure to include Vita-Mineral Mix and other listed supplements.
- Double lecithin in Vita-Mineral Mix recipe to help with digestion of fats.
- Add to each meal:
    ¼ teaspoon feline digestive enzyme powder to aid in digestion;
    ¹⁄₁₆ teaspoon ascorbic acid crystals or sodium ascorbate powder (250 units vitamin C);
    ¼ crushed bioflavinoid pill;
    ¼ teaspoon Delicious Garlic Condiment (see page 256);
    1 drop stevia extract or 1 teaspoon stevia infusion (see page 259).
- Add to food twice a day ½ of a crushed vitamin B complex tablet—10 mg level.
- Keep fat intake low (that is, butter, oils, and the like).
- If necessary, reduce gas by giving:
    1 charcoal tablet, moistened at the tip, one hour before dinner (see "Giving Pills," page 208); continue for

three days. Charcoal turns the stool black but don't
worry;

½ teaspoon liquid acidophilus (suspended in water,
not lactose) *or* 1 teaspoon yogurt, if cat does not get
diarrhea from milk products.

- If diarrhea (page 305) or constipation (page 293) are present, follow suggestions given in those sections.
- Reduce scarring by giving contents of a punctured 100-unit
vitamin E (alpha tocopherol) capsule in food once a day for
two weeks; then reduce to 400 units a week.
- Exercise gently to stimulate metabolism and lower stress.
- Bach flower remedies: pancreatitis cats are sometimes out
of sorts because of discomfort. Give three drops four times
a day of the following mixture prepared as given on page
249:

Impatiens—for anxiety over illness and lack of
patience;

Mustard—for those who feel gloomy.

Pancreatitis Diet

Note: This diet is high in B vitamins, antistress vitamins, protein,
and calcium, and low in fat. It is easily digested.

3 cups High-Calcium Chicken Broth (page 243)
2 cups cooked grain: choose from amaranth, quinoa,
barley, or brown rice. (Do not use white rice.)
1 cup raw peas
1 tablespoon bone meal, calcium lactate, or calcium
glutonate
2 organic eggs, separated
1½ cups raw liver chunks
½ cup finely grated raw carrot or zucchini

Combine broth, cooked grain, peas, and egg whites in a
pan. Simmer for 3 minutes. Turn off heat and add liver
chunks. Cover and let cool. Add bone meal, raw egg yolks
and remaining raw vegetables. Blend in a blender or food
processor. Store one-cup portions (one day's supply) in re-
sealable plastic bags or plastic storage container in freezer.
Thaw, as needed, by dropping bag (or standing container)

in bowl of hot water. Serve ¼ cup servings 4 times a day. Add special supplements suggested above just before serving.

Parasites
(Roundworm, Hookworm, Tapeworm, and Coccidia)

The four most common intestinal parasites are roundworm, hookworm, tapeworm, and coccidia. It's sometimes hard to tell which kind of worms a cat has. You have to take the stool to the veterinarian and let him examine it under the microscope.

If worms are diagnosed, there are two ways that you can handle the problem. You can let the doctor give you the medication to administer, with specific instructions about fasting a number of hours beforehand and further instructions about what the first full meals should consist of. He may also prescribe a laxative. Alternately, under certain circumstances, the doctor may advise that the cat be hospitalized because worming medicine is caustic and toxic and the cat may vomit. The veterinarian may want to be sure that the medication stays in the cat to do the job. Do not buy any kind of worming preparations over the counter. Worming preparations are all poisons, and you must be very careful how you use them. *Worming should always be supervised by a veteriniarian.*

Here are specific details on these intestinal parasites.

Roundworm and Tapeworm

If the cat has roundworms or tapeworms, you have the choice of using the herbal worming procedure formulated by herbalist Juliette de Bairacli-Levy, which is given in *Dr. Pitcairn's Complete Guide to Natural Health for Dogs and Cats* (Rodale Press). I did this with my Big Purr, who had tapeworms. I had been horrified to see those awful wiggly, maggoty things in his stool. Gingerly I sliced off a chunk of stool, dropped it into a plastic bag, and, sealing it very tightly, dropped that into *another* bag and left it in the refrigerator until I was ready to leave. Purr seemed healthy as a horse, pert and chipper as ever, so I knew that this was not an emergency situation. I dropped off the stool sample at the veterinarian's, saying that I suspected it was tapeworm.

Tapeworms are carried by fleas, but Purr has no fleas; I asked the doctor where in the world Purr could have picked up tapeworms. He said that they could have been lying dormant in the intestine for years. As the standard worming medication is so toxic, my local veterinarian agreed that I should first try the natural herbal remedy along with the fasting and herbal laxatives that he recommends. He was enthusiastic and curious to see if the natural method would work, and both he and Dr. Pitcairn agreed that if it didn't work we could always give the standard chemical treatment afterward.

The herbal worming procedure took about a week (see "Treatments," below). The hard part was not so much stuffing powdered herbs and wet, gooey, crushed garlic into empty gelatin capsules or even tracking down a health food store that could supply such esoteric ingredients as wormwood and powdered rue (see Appendix, "Product Suppliers"). The hardest part was keeping myself from feeding Purr during the fast days as required. Purr was several ounces overweight, and I knew it. That fast did him a world of good, and he took it very well. But even though I knew that what I was doing was really great for him in every way, still I found it very, very hard not to feed him. It certainly made me understand the "food is love" syndrome that many owners fall victim to.

I waited a couple of weeks after it was over, examining Purr's stool every morning for signs of wiggly, maggoty things. When everything still remained normal-looking, I told my veterinarian that the herbal worming seemed to have worked. Like all holistic treatments, it benefited Purr's general health as well.

The herbal remedy is more trouble, but the big plus is that it is safe and the side effects are all beneficial. A fast of a couple of days renews the cat's youth. The backlog of wastes and toxins in the system is cleaned and flushed out. Purr was much more playful and jaunty after the experience. I would recommend the herbal worming to any owners who are able to give pills to their cat (see "Giving Pills," page 208). If we can avoid giving poisonous chemicals simply by spending some extra time, I feel that it is a very small price to pay and results in huge dividends in health for the cat.

Symptoms

- Weight gain or loss; loss of appetite or voracious appetite; a big, fat distended abdomen or a bony appearance
- Dull coat or hair loss
- Egg sacs in the stool or around the anus—about the size of a sesame seed or a grain of rice, they are white, and they sometimes move in a maggotlike fashion
- Dragging the anus along the carpet (this could also be a sign of impacted anal gland)
- Constant licking of anal area
- Vomiting—sometimes worms can be seen in the vomitus

Recommendations

- Have veterinarian check the cat and run tests on stool sample.
- Administer medication according to veterinarian's instructions *or* follow this breakdown of the herbal worming procedure:

Herbal Worming Procedure

What you need:

Rolled oats—soak 1 cup oats in water 24 hours; repeat every day

Herbal deworming capsules *or* make your own. Buy large gelatin capsules at your health-food store or a product supplier listed in the Appendix. Open the capsules and fill with:

    1 part raw crushed garlic
    1 part wormwood powder
    1 part rue powder

Capsules containing ¼ teaspoon senna and a pinch of ginger

Castor oil

Charcoal tablets

Deworming slurry. Into a small pan mix:
  1 cup raw milk or skim milk
  1 teaspoon slippery elm powder
  Bring to a simmer and stir until thickened.
  Add ¼ teaspoon honey and 3 tablespoons soaked
    oats.
Cool and refrigerate.

FISH AND OAT FOOD

½ cup soaked oats
2 tablespoons cod, haddock, or halibut simmered one
  minute in a small amount of water
1½ teaspoons Vita-Mineral Mix (see page 55)
Garlic, raw crushed—a piece the size of a pea

Here's the plan:

• Days 1, 2, and 3	Feed morning and evening meals of fish and oat food
• Day 4	Fast on water (see "Fasting," page 225)
	Before bed give 1 teaspoon castor oil (see "Giving Liquid Medication," page 210)
• Day 5	Fast on water
	Early evening—give 4 deworming capsules (see "Giving Pills," page 208)
	30 minutes later give 1 teaspoon castor oil
	45 minutes later give ½ cup deworming slurry
• Days 6, 7, and 8	Give 3 meals a day of deworming slurry
	In morning, 30 minutes before meal, give 2 deworming capsules
	Before bed give ¼ teaspoon senna with a pinch of ginger (in capsules)

- Days 9, 10, 11, and 12   Feed fish and oat food twice a day
- After 12th day   Feed normal high-quality diet. Be sure to include some raw food at each meal and ⅛ teaspoon Delicious Garlic Condiment (page 256) daily for 1 month, then 3 times a week

                           Give 1 charcoal tablet in the morning 3 times a week for 3 weeks

Hookworm

Hookworms are found mostly in hot humid areas of the country. They enter the cat through the mouth if he eats something that is contaminated with hookworm larvae such as prey or partially rotten meat. Kittens can become infected from the mother's milk. Larvae can also penetrate the skin, usually around the toes. They then migrate to the small intestine, where they chew into the intestinal wall and suck blood and tissue, leaving small ulcers that bleed and become infected. Large numbers of eggs are laid, most of which pass out in the feces.

Hookworms are a serious matter. They cause anemia, dehydration, and, finally, death. If your vet diagnoses hookworms in your cat, follow his directions to the letter and have your cat retested every three or four months now that you know you are living in a hookworm area. Be sure to keep his resistance high by feeding a high-quality diet.

Symptoms

- Weakness; listlessness
- Dehydration
- Weight loss, eating voraciously but not gaining weight
- Diarrhea or loose stool, dark red or black stool
- Rash between toes
- "Scooting" on floor

Prevention

- Feed as much raw food as possible in regular high-quality diet or, better still, feed the all-raw-food diet (see page 53).
- Add ⅛ teaspoon Delicious Garlic Condiment (page 256) to food every day.

Recommendations

- See veterinarian for a firm diagnosis and proper treatment.
- After treatment follow suggestions for prevention above.
- For a few weeks after treatment add to each meal:
  1/16 teaspoon ascorbic acid crystals (250 units vitamin C);
  1 teaspoon liquid acidophilus.

Coccidia

Coccidia are microscopic intestinal parasites. Consequently, they are the most difficult of the parasites to diagnose. Like all parasites they are a sign of a weak immune system. If you acquire a stray or a cat whom you know has been fed a poor-quality food and you see a bloated abdomen on a skinny cat—ask the vet to do a general physical exam and to include a fecal smear under the microscope for coccidia.

Follow the vet's directions to the letter. Recheck the cat a few weeks after the treatment to be certain no coccidia remain. Your vet will tell you when the best time would be for this follow-up exam.

Symptoms

- Voracious appetite but skinny cat
- Distended abdomen
- Persistent soft stools or diarrhea

Recommendations

- See the veterinarian for firm diagnosis and treatment.
- Follow additional treatment suggestions under "Hook-worm" above.

Respiratory Infections

Respiratory infections can range anywhere from a sniffle and a sneeze to bronchial congestion or the lungs filling up with fluid. Often the first symptom is the appearance of eye discharge or runny eyes. If the lungs are filling up with fluid, the cat cannot breathe, and you will need to have the veterinarian relieve this condition by tapping the lungs. A high temperature is a good sign that the immune system is responding as it should. Germs and viruses will not thrive if the body temperature is higher than normal.

Respiratory infections can be frightening because they do tend to spread to other cats in the household. As with all ailments, an ounce of prevention is worth a pound of cure. If any cat in the house exhibits respiratory symptoms, isolate the patient, keep him warm and snug, and then dose all of your cats with garlic and commence the acid-alkaline swing for six to eight days. Repeated respiratory infections indicate that the immune system is weak; germs and viruses are finding it easy to take hold and multiply. Like any other disease in the feline, the earlier you catch it, the easier it is to cure.

Symptoms

- Sniffle, sneeze, or cough
- Runny eyes
- Spraying runny mucus from nose
- Change in stool
- Elevated temperature
- Appetite loss
- Listlessness
- Rattling when breathing
- Coughing up phlegm
- Breathing with mouth open

Recommendations

- Have veterinarian make a diagnosis to make sure the problem really is an infection and not a tumor or asthma.
- For all cats in the household add ⅛ teaspoon Delicious Garlic Condiment (page 256) to all meals until infection is cleared up.
- For all cats in the household commence the acid-alkaline swing (see page 242) for six to eight days. Increase the vitamin C to 500 units per cat per meal on the acid days.
- If possible, isolate the patient.
- Provide a snug retreat (see page 240).
- Give eye and nose drops before each meal, using normal saline solution (see page 213). Because the tear ducts run from the inner corner of the eyes into the back of the throat, by giving eye drops you also treat the throat. Nose drops, if done well, treat the nose, the sinuses, and also the throat. Also, because some cats refuse to eat when they can't smell their food, giving nose drops before the meal can help the cat who has a stuffy nose smell his broth.
- For two to three days stop all solid food and put patient on High-Calcium Chicken Broth (page 243) three to four times a day. If the patient refuses the broth, let him fast for one day. Then on the second day you may flavor the chicken broth with a one-inch piece of sardine in tomato sauce so he can smell the broth even with his stuffy nose.
- Give ¹⁄₁₆ teaspoon ascorbic acid crystals mixed with chicken broth or 250 units vitamin C as a pill (see "Giving Pills," page 208) four to six times a day.
- Mix ⅛ teaspoon Delicious Garlic Condiment (page 256) with ½ teaspoon butter. Give morning and evening. Most cats lap it off your finger. If not, give it as a pâté (see "Force Feeding," page 225).
- Check the teeth. Tarter and filth in the mouth create an excellent breeding ground for germs that can spread disease to the nose and/or throat.
- If the infection persists for more than a week, or if it seems

to be spreading into the lungs, you should consult a homeopathic veterinarian if you have not already done so (see "Homeopathy," page 244), or you may need to resort to antibiotics (see "Antibiotics," page 266).

- Herbal Remedies:
    1. If the patient has a stuffy nose and a nasal discharge, golden seal will kill germs and help shrink tissues. Give three drops herbal nose drop solution containing golden seal in each nostril twice a day. See "Giving Eye Drops" and "Giving Nose Drops," pages 212–17, and follow directions for herbal solution with golden seal.
    2. If the veterinarian says the patient's throat is red and sore, add five drops chamomile extract or tincture instead of golden seal and give as both nose and eye drops (page 213) since the tear ducts run into the back of the throat.
    3. For bronchial congestion Dr. Pitcairn has recommended golden seal elixir (page 260) taken ¼ dropperful twice a day twenty minutes before meals. Also, the patient can inhale the vapors of eucalyptus oil in hot water.
- Bach flower remedies: cats with respiratory problems feel gloomy and tired and can become depressed. Give three drops four times a day of the following mixture prepared as given on page 249:

    Mustard—to dispel gloom;
    Crabapple—to help cleanse;
    Hornbeam—to strengthen.

Ringworm
(See also "Parasites")

Ringworm is not a worm; it is a fungus like athlete's foot. Once it infects an area it usually grows outward, spreading in a circle and then starting other new little circles. I have seen ringworm as a tiny little spot on a healthy cat's nose or as extensive areas of baldness all over the body of an old or sick cat. Ringworm patches may be hairless or the hair may break off to a stubble. The skin may become thickened and gray or pink to red in color and sometimes will be scabbed from scratching. It may itch but often it does not. Ringworm is mildly contagious and can spread to other animals or to humans whose resistance is low.

I always deal with any fungus or parasitic infestation in three ways: topically, with an application on the skin; systemically, by alkalizing the system and making sure the overall quality of health is improved; and environmentally, by using a safe fungicide.

Ringworm is around us all the time. You and I probably have ringworm spores on our skin right this moment. So why don't you and I have ringworm lesions? For the same reason that we don't have a virus cold even though we are frequently breathing viruses into our nose and lungs. We are healthy, our resistance is high, and our acid-alkaline balance is such that our bodies do not make a good home for viruses, germs, or parasitic infestations. If I see ringworm on a cat, my main concern is not the ringworm. Ringworm can be cured. My main concern is to discover what has caused the cat's immune system to become weak and to allow the fungus to take hold. Has the cat perhaps been eating foods with preservatives or a protein source where the amino acids are not properly balanced? Commercial semimoist and dry foods are good examples of that. Cats who eat commercial dry or semimoist food seem much more prone to pick up fungus and parasitic infestations. Or perhaps someone new was taking care of the cat, and food was left available between meals several days in a row. The resultant slowing of the metabolism could cause the pores to exude an unusual amount of wastes and so change the pH (acid-alkaline) balance of the skin. All of these things are easy to correct.

The other possibility is that the cat is under some sort of stress or the cat's system is currently fighting some other infection somewhere in the body. Perhaps the cat's system will win out in the end, but in the meantime the battle is depleting it and giving the ringworm a chance to take hold. The thing to do, along with your topical application at the site of the ringworm, is to mobilize and arm your cat's body with extra vitamins in addition to the super-high-quality diet. Now is the time for all those additional supplements you occasionally add to the food.

Fulvacin (gresiofulvin) is a drug in pill form that stops growth of ringworm fungus. It passes through the digestive system into the blood, and some of it is deposited in the keratin layer under the skin. From there it is incorporated into the hair follicle. Some of the Fulvacin will be excreted in the urine and some in the stool.

In very resistant cases some veterinarians will sometimes shave the cat, treat the ringworm topically, and then give the cat Fulvacin for several weeks. This always gets rid of the ringworm on the cat. However, the animal can be reinfected from spores in the environment after the Fulvacin is stopped. There is a long list of possible complications that can result from the use of Fulvacin: loss of protein through the kidneys, skin rashes and hives, diarrhea, lowered white cell count, lethargy, brain and nerve damage, mental confusion, vertigo, vomiting, or foaming at the mouth, or painful tongue. I have never used Fulvacin on a cat under my care.

Symptoms

- Bald patches spreading outward in a ring—usually starts on forehead and around ears and muzzle but can appear on toes or anywhere
- Skin is gray or red or scabbed
- Sometimes itching and scratching (but not usually)
- Usually (but not always) shows up fluorescent under veterinarian's ultraviolet light (but so do petroleum jelly and golden seal!)
- Always shows up purple after five days in veterinarian's test tube culture

Recommendations

- Fast one day a week on High-Calcium Chicken Broth (see page 243).
- Feed high-quality diet and as much raw food as possible (see Chapter 2, "Diet," page 53). Be sure to include Vita-Mineral Mix and other listed supplements. If preparing homemade diet, choose from the following for the vegetable portion to alkalize system: finely grated raw zucchini or carrots *or* steamed celery or green beans.

- Add ⅛ teaspoon Delicious Garlic Condiment to morning meal to help alkalize system (see page 256).
- Add to each meal:
    1 teaspoon chopped alfalfa sprouts;
    ½ teaspoon acidophilus culture in water *or* 1 teaspoon plain yogurt if cat tolerates dairy products well;
    Extra ¼ teaspoon yeast (in addition to yeast in Vita-Mineral Mix) or feed two or three yeast and garlic treats (see Appendix, "Product Suppliers").
- Once a day give 5 mg zinc (crush pill and divide into 5-mg portions and add to meal).
- Once a week give 400 units vitamin E capsule (alpha tocopherol) and a vitamin A and D capsule (10,000 units A and 400 units D).
- An all-raw-food diet is best of all (page 58), but at the minimum feed one tablespoon raw liver or raw organic egg yolk three or four times a week.
- Feed twice a day; remove all food between meals, leaving only water available.
- Bach flower remedies: cats who contract ringworm are often oversensitive, reticent types. This can manifest itself either as withdrawal to secluded nooks or as an overreadiness to strike out for very little apparent reason. Give three drops four times a day of the following mixture prepared as given on page 249:
    Crabapple—to help expel toxins;
    Mimulus—to allay fears;
    Aspen—for those who retreat and hide;
    Holly—for those who sometimes lash out.

Treating the Skin

- Clip hair away on and around affected areas.
- Bathe the cat (see page 157), soaping twice using Betadyne surgical scrub instead of shampoo. Allow the second soaping to remain on the cat for five to ten minutes before rinsing thoroughly. While you're waiting, thoroughly clean the claws and cuticles (see page 221). The ringworm spores will be concentrated in the dirt around the cuticles and can reinfect the cat whenever he scratches. You can finish with

a rinse of golden seal or echinacea foot-soaking solution for ringworm (page 222).

If ringworm patch is small (all patches together would be smaller than a fifty-cent piece in size), paint it (them) with iodine. Then, in three days begin painting area with golden seal or echinacea extract or tincture (see page 260). If ringworm is extensive *do not use iodine* because cats are very sensitive to too much iodine, so substitute the golden seal or echinacea extract or tincture for the first application as well.

- Bathe on and around affected areas four times a day with a cotton ball saturated with golden seal or echinacea elixir (see page 260) *or* six drops golden seal or echinacea extract in ¼ cup water.

Treating the Environment

- Chlorine bleach kills ringworm spores. Wash bedding (yours and the cat's) with 5 percent chlorine bleach solution. Dry bedding and pillows in the dryer on hot temperature.
- Wash windowsills and floors with 5 percent chlorine bleach solution.
- Continue adding chlorine bleach to all cleaning water for a few weeks *after* all signs of ringworm are gone from the cat.

Roundworm
(see "Parasites")

Skin Problems
(See also "Dandruff," "Feline Acne," "Fleas," "Mange Mites," "Parasites," "Ringworm")

Bald patches can be caused by any number of things. Sometimes a cat will try to scratch a mat out of his fur, pull too violently, and end up with a bald patch where some of the hair was torn away. This is not serious, and eventually it grows back in. However, most skin conditions, including some cases of bald patches, are symptoms of more serious underlying problems. Poor circulation to the skin due to a heart condition or clogged capillaries can cause thinning hair or bald patches. Many medications can also cause hair loss, especially on cats eating low-quality diets.

The term "skin allergy" has become a catch-all phrase used whenever the cause of a skin problem cannot be readily diagnosed. The cat is usually treated with one of many cortisone preparations that cause the symptoms to disappear immediately. This can be very satisfying to all concerned—the doctor, the cat, and the owner—until the medicine is used up and the same old problem comes back, worse than ever. It then becomes apparent that the cortisone has merely suppressed the symptoms. It has done nothing to cure the cause of the problem. The cause—and therefore the problem—is still there. Furthermore, this suppressing of the symptom tends to make the problem more and more difficult to treat and cure.

Cortisone, because of its side effects and temporary efficacy, has acquired a rather dubious reputation among more modern, health-oriented owners and veterinarians. Sometimes it will be called something else such as steroid, corticosteroid, anti-inflammatory, anti-itch, de-sensitizer, allergy shot, and the like. So always ask the veterinarian if the ointment, shot, or pill is a cortisone derivative (see "Cortisone and Other Steroids," page 268).

As the skin is the largest organ of excretion, the body will attempt to eliminate excess wastes or poisons out through the skin if there is too much for the kidneys, intestines, and so on to handle or if one of these other organs weakens or breaks down. For example, kidney-failure patients usually have terribly oily, dandruffy skin and coat. Alter the diet to "cushion" the kidneys, and the skin will improve. The skin will do its best to pass the poisons out of the body until the load becomes too much for the pores to handle and clogging occurs. Then dirty skin becomes inflamed and/or parasites and/or germs infest the buildup of oil and dirt lodged at the base of each hair and infection sets in. Nervousness, frustration, and loneliness are the leading causes of stress-triggered skin problems; so single cats and unneutered cats are more prone to problems in this area. Cats on poor diets will always have large amounts of wastes for the body to dispose of because of the nutritional imbalances. An all-meat diet is a good example: protein imbalance overwhelms the kidneys, while the absence of sufficient bulk and roughage clogs the intestines. The chemicals in commercial foods will overload the organs of excretion as well as the liver and, here again, the skin will bear the brunt. The use of aluminum utensils or fluoridated water can compound the problem. The sugar in semimoist foods promotes an acid system where funguses and parasites can thrive. The use of powders, compounds, sprays, ointments, creams, or rinses adds to the burden of wastes the overworked skin must try to slough off and the condition worsens.

But take heart—the skin renews itself rapidly. So once the quality of the diet is improved, toxins are eliminated, stress is reduced, and regular exercise is begun, you should see a definite improvement in just three to six weeks (unless cortisone treatment was used; in that case a change for the better will be more gradual).

Treatment by an experienced homeopathic veterinarian will always speed up the cat's healing. Homeopathy works very fast on skin problems (see "Homeopathy," page 244).

Symptoms

- Scratching or biting at the skin
- Bald patches
- Pus, scabs, or inflammation
- Excess ear or eye discharge
- Inflamed gums
- White or brown dandruff
- Oiliness
- Bad odor
- Redness, thickened skin, grayness
- Nervousness

Recommendations

- Have veterinarian check for parasites, fungus, or problems with liver, kidneys, intestines, glands, or other internal organs.

- Upgrade diet and begin internal cleansing to decrease wastes in system and take the burden of waste disposal off the skin:
  1. Fast on High-Calcium Chicken Broth (see page 243) for one to three days; then one day every week;
  2. Feed high-quality diet with as much raw food included as possible (see Chapter 2, "Diet," page 53). Be sure to include Vita-Mineral Mix and other listed supplements;
  3. Remove all food between meals, leaving only water always available;
  4. Add extra cup of bran to Vita-Mineral Mix recipe (see page 55) and increase amount of Vita-Mineral Mix in each meal to 1½ teaspoons;
  5. Add antistress supplements (see page 240) to diet;
  6. Add to each meal ¼ teaspoon skin and coat oil supplement for pets from the health food store (see "Product Suppliers" in Appendix).
  7. Eliminate all preservatives and other chemical additives and coloring from diet (check labels carefully— even on brands purchased from the health-food store or from the veterinarian);
  8. Never store food in can; lead sealers can "bleed" into food once can has been opened;
  9. Give 5 mg zinc once a day for two weeks; then decrease to 2 to 3 mg a day to strengthen skin and help body process out toxins.
- Feed fresh homemade food whenever possible. Use alkalizing vegetables such as garlic, kelp, kombu seaweed, carrots, celery, zucchini, and string beans.
- Neuter or spay, and eliminate other stresses in the environment.
- Bathe every one to four weeks—use only natural preparations on the skin.
- Stimulate the flow of blood in the small capillaries that feed the skin by grooming and massaging vigorously once a day (see Chapter 7, "Grooming").
- Encourage exercise. Have a play time once a day.

Skinniness
(see "Weight Loss")

Stud Tail

Stud tail is a disease of the sebaceous glands found along the top of the tail and up the base of the spine. It happens when these glands oversecrete sebaceous fluid and the pores become clogged. The excess fluid becomes hardened into a substance closely resembling half-dried ear wax. It is waxy rather than oily and usually dark brown or black.

Stud tail, as the name implies, is found on almost all unneutered males, but unfortunately it is not limited to them. I've seen it on neutered males and females, too, when food is left available between meals and the diet is not up to par. Neutering or spaying almost always clears up the condition provided the diet is adequate and food is removed between meals. A cat with stud tail will be supersensitive in that area. If left untreated, the pores and glands on the tail become inflamed, clogged, and infected. Pain and itching result, and the cat may bite the tail until it bleeds, so be extremely gentle. The fur over the area usually becomes matted and often falls out because hair roots lack nourishment.

I have noticed that every year at the cat show someone comes up with what he or she claims is a surefire cure for stud tail. These cures always involve spraying, powdering, or dipping the tail into something. The reason why there is always a new cure every year is that none of them work. Many breeders who show cats have their own private "secrets" that they hold to despite their inefficiency and the possible health hazards involved in implementing some of the more bizarre solutions. I have been made privy to such secrets as the use of dishwashing detergent, kerosene, and Windex. Forget it. Stud tail is a result of what is happening inside the cat's body because of a backup of wastes. It is caused by poor feeding and a slowdown of the metabolism combined with overactive sebaceous glands. You can't cure stud tail from the outside alone; you must also neuter the cat and improve the diet.

However, I too have a secret remedy, temporary though it may

413

be. This is the best method I have found to date and is to be used in the beginning while you are waiting to get an appointment to have the cat neutered and while the new, improved diet is slowly doing its work to permanently eradicate the condition. That hard, waxy grease cannot be washed off by any kind of detergent, soap, alcohol, or you-name-it. It's impossible. So don't wash it off. Instead, powder the area heavily with finely ground cornmeal and let it set for five minutes while it absorbs the greasy exudation. Then comb, shake, and jiggle the greasy cornmeal out. Do it again a few more times; you can use cornstarch for the last round for a more thorough cleaning. Then wash just the tail and lower back with Murphy's oil soap. Rinse and follow with a complete shampooing with a shampoo for oily hair from the health-food store. This cornmeal and cornstarch trick can also be used around the ears after an oily ear medication. Cornmeal and cornstarch are harmless—because they have no perfumes or conditioners. Here's another case where the cheapest and easiest also turns out to be the best.

Symptoms

- Copious oily or black waxy exudations from base to halfway down tail
- Discolored, oily, waxy tail hair that is prone to clumping and matting
- "Dust mop" effect—hair on tail attracts dirt and dust
- Skin on top of tail and on lower spine is red and very sensitive
- Sebaceous glands are inflamed and swollen
- Cat gnaws tail with teeth

Recommendations

Temporary

- Gently comb out loose hair and remove any mats.
- Powder liberally with fine cornmeal; wait five minutes; then comb out (as described above).
- Wash tail with Murphy's oil soap or dishwashing liquid.

- Shampoo three times with a castile shampoo for oily hair.
- Rinse with water and then with Lemon Rinse (see page 262).

Permanent

- Have cat neutered or spayed.
- Feed high-quality diet with as much raw food included as possible (see Chapter 2, "Diet"). Be sure to include Vita-Mineral Mix and other listed supplements.
- Add to each meal:

  ½ teaspoon lecithin (in addition to lecithin in Vita-Mineral Mix);

  ½ teaspoon cod liver oil *or* once a week give the contents of one capsule containing 10,000 units vitamin A and 400 units vitamin D.
- Fast on High-Calcium Chicken Broth (see page 243) one day a week until condition is completely normal.
- Increase exercise.
- Shampoo, and rinse with Lemon Rinse (as given in "Temporary" treatments above).
- Herbal remedies:

  1. Instead of cornstarch, you can powder the tail with a mixture of 4 tablespoons each orris root and arrowroot;

  2. Instead of using the Lemon Rinse after bathing, use a strong tea of witchhazel and burdock root *or* use calendula tea if there are sores and scabbing.
- Bach flower remedies: stud-tail cats are usually tense from not being neutered or from irritating chemicals in the diet. Give three drops four times a day of the following mixture prepared as given on page 249:

  Crabapple—to aid in cleansing the system;

  Impatiens—to calm anxiety;

  Walnut—to help change old thought patterns.

Tapeworm
(see "Parasites")

Teeth and Gums

Cats develop tartar on their teeth just as you and I do. And, like you and I, some produce more tartar than others, and some produce tartar that is soft and can be flicked off with a fingernail, while others, like my Priscilla, produce tartar that resembles granite. It amazes me how often I find tartar-covered teeth on the cats I groom. I always check the teeth and gums at the end of the grooming, especially on new clients. What really surprises me is when I find tartar coating the teeth of a cat who has just been to the veterinarian for a yearly exam. Either the veterinarian's examination leaves much to be desired, or, if he indeed saw the tartar and didn't suggest doing anything about it, that veterinarian's standards for feline oral health are a lot different from mine.

Tartar leads to inflamed, infected gums because it is full of germs. Germs make the mouth smell bad. (I've often seen my own veterinarian open a cat's mouth, put his nose up to it, and sniff.) Germs and infection in the mouth can lead to infection in the nose, throat, and upper respiratory tract, or, at the other end, in the anal glands—in fact anywhere the cat licks to wash himself.

When I see tartar on the teeth, I always try to scrape off a nice big piece with my thumbnail and show it to the owner. I then invite the owner to examine the cat's gum while I open the mouth and lift the lip. I point out the inflammation at the gum line, and I explain that this hurts. Mouth pain can make a cat nervous and irritable. Because eating hurts, this is a possible reason why a cat is off his food and getting thin. New clients often respond that they have been giving dry food every day, so they can't understand why the teeth are not in perfect condition. *Dry food does not clean the teeth*. It never has, and it never will. Even the dry-food companies have never claimed that dry food cleans the teeth. Cats fed an exclusive dry-food diet for years frequently have the worst tartar in the world. Dry food can exercise the teeth and jaw muscles, which is also important. But because commercial dry food has so many drawbacks—low protein quality and abundance of poisonous chemicals—it is much more rational to provide other substances for teeth and jaw exercise that have only beneficial side effects and no drawbacks. As discussed in Chapter 2, in the section "Acceptable

Crunchies" (page 65), I prefer such things as brewer's yeast tablets, raw or broiled chicken neck vertebrae, and the many wholesome treats packaged by reputable natural-pet-food companies.

Whether or not I am able to get some of the tartar off the cat's tooth with my thumbnail, I always recommend a visit to a veterinarian who will make a really thorough and complete examination. If the condition of the mouth was passed over, one wonders what else might have been passed over as insignificant. Several vets here in New York City will scale (clean) the teeth during the yearly office visit without using anesthetic. If a cavity is discovered or if the teeth have deteriorated to such a pass that an extraction is necessary, then the patient can be admitted to the hospital for dental cleaning and extraction under anesthetic. Follow the usual procedure for caring for the cat in the hospital and after arriving home (see Chapter 8 "Seeking Professional Help").

If I find that the red gums persist, as often happens with cats who have been for many months on a low-quality diet, I have good results using the acid-alkaline swing and the raw-food diet. The first time I tried this on a cat with inflamed gums, I figured it couldn't hurt, because all the side effects are beneficial anyway.

I have seen red and swollen gums respond immediately to treatment with cortisone (see "Cortisone and Other Steroids," page 268). However, the response lasts only as long as the cortisone is being taken. In other words, cortisone does not cure but only masks the symptoms. Cortisone, as everyone agrees, is death on the immune system. It's like killing a fly with a blow torch.

The persistent swollen gum problem is prevalent today. My own feeling had always been that this is simply a weakness a particular cat has that bubbles to the surface and explodes when the diet is overprocessed, low in quality, and laced with too many artificial colors, artificial flavors, artificial scents, and poisonous chemicals used as preservatives. However, Dr. Pitcairn, who has a specialty in immunology, has pointed out to me that although the diet is certainly extremely important, the real underlying cause is vaccinosis: a chronic disease state caused by repeated vaccinations. A combination of diet, homeopathy and topical therapy is the only way I know to gradually correct the problem.

Perfect health is a body's natural state. It is a rule of nature that the body will proceed toward perfect health when we eliminate all poisons and other destructive elements and give it all the support we can to build the perfect health that is its birthright.

Symptoms

- Inflamed, infected, swollen, and/or bleeding gums
- Bad breath
- Brown or yellow deposits of tartar on upper teeth, particularly on back teeth
- Bad smell on fur or on fur of cat friends
- Loss of appetite or weight loss
- Can lead to infection in the nose, throat, upper respiratory tract, or in the anal glands, or anywhere the cat licks to wash himself

Recommendations

- Visit vet to have teeth cleaned. Try to find a vet who has high standards and who will try to clean the teeth without anesthetic during the exam. If he then finds reason for use of anesthetic, give extra supplements (see "Anesthetics, Tranquilizers, and X rays," page 269).
- Add to each meal:
    1/16 teaspoon ascorbic acid crystals or sodium ascorbate (250 units vitamin C);
    1/4 teaspoon Delicious Garlic Condiment (see page 256).
- Put cat on acid-alkaline swing (see page 242) using kombu seaweed (page 256) on the alkaline days and twice as much vitamin C on the acid days.
- Inflamed gums are usually a sign of a weakened immune system. To help build up the immune system switch to a raw-food diet (see page 58).
- To prevent serious immune deficiency diseases, consult a homeopathic veterinarian (see "Homeopathy," page 244).
- There are some new tooth sprays and pastes now available from veterinarians. They are very new so I haven't yet finished testing and working with them. If you'd like to try them I suggest you read the sections on communication (page 204) and administering medications (page 202).

- Herbal remedies: to soothe and heal sore and bleeding gums, add ¼ teaspoon salt to ½ cup strong lukewarm calendula or plantain infusion (page 259) and pat on gums with a cotton ball *or* use Healthy Mouth Formula (page 257) to cleanse teeth and gums daily.

Urination, Random Wetting
(see "Feline Urologic Syndrome")

Vomiting

A cat's alimentary canal is relatively short, so vomiting is fairly common. If it does not frequently recur, it is usually not serious. Cats often vomit hair balls in spring and autumn when shedding is copious (see "Hair Balls," page 343). Eating food that is too hot or too cold or wolfing too much food at once can all cause vomiting. These things are very easy to check out and to correct.

Vomiting becomes serious if it is prolonged or repeated, because fluids and minerals are lost. The resulting dehydration can produce coma and death. Repeated vomiting is always a symptom of a serious problem within the body. Adverse drug reaction or poisoning by chemicals such as bathroom cleaners, sprays, or flea treatments will all provoke violent vomiting. Vomiting is often a symptom of disease or inflammation of certain organs, such as in hepatitis, gall bladder inflammation, and pancreatitis.

In the case of repeated or prolonged vomiting, telephone a veterinarian immediately. Before you call, make a list of pertinent facts to tell him: (1) any other symptoms, such as lethargy, diarrhea, constipation, or bad temper; (2) what the vomit consists of—food, white foam, hair balls; (3) if the vomiting was unsuccessful; and (4) when it occurred (before or after meal) and how often.

Symptoms

- Vomiting unsuccessfully (dry heaves)
- Vomiting of foam, food, mucus, or hair balls

Recommendations

- Check to be sure food is not too hot or too cold.
- Be sure food is not spoiled.
- Be sure cat isn't eating too fast—spread the food around on a large platter.
- Be sure cat did not swallow a foreign object or plant leaves.
- Withhold food for three hours and if no vomiting recurs, give ¼ cup clear broth (chicken or vegetable) with one teaspoon slippery elm syrup (see page 258). Continue to fast the cat on the chicken broth and slippery elm for one to two days; then gradually reintroduce regular food (see "Fasting," page 225).
- If vomiting recurs, call veterinarian and describe symptoms as suggested above.

Weight Loss

Weight loss, especially sudden weight loss, is always a sign that something is wrong. The wise owner will immediately begin to look for any other symptoms such as copious drinking, frequent urination, soft stool, restlessness, voracious appetite, lack of appetite, craving heat, seclusion, or any change of normal behavior. If one or more additional symptoms are present, make a note of them and call your vet for an appointment. If the cat who is displaying two or three of these symptoms is over ten years old, I always recommend asking for a complete blood test including thyroid values. Weight loss can be an early symptom of kidney disease, liver disease, hyperthyroidism, or irritable bowel syndrome. In all cases, diagnosis is made twice as easy with a blood test. If your cat is diagnosed as having any of the above diseases, look that disease up. There is much you can do to smooth the path toward recovery.

If skinniness is not a result of obvious starvation or of a large litter draining nutrients from the mother cat and if there is no tumor or other disease, then it is a symptom of *anorexia*—refusal to eat—or *malabsorption*—inability to utilize food even though large quantities are eaten.

Anorexia

Anorexia, or refusal to eat, can have a physical cause, such as bad teeth or gums, intestinal blockage by hair or tumor, or pain anywhere in the body (as in postoperative anorexia). Several antibiotics can cause anorexia.

If your feline friend seems fairly normal in all other ways, another possibility is that he may be suffering from what I refer to as the "finicky eater syndrome." Because the smell of food triggers the brain, if the cat is smelling food every time he passes the food dish or a vagrant breeze wafts the odor his way, sooner or later that trigger mechanism wears out and the cat begins to eat less. Ninety percent of all finicky eaters have owners who leave food available between meals or give frequent snacks. Often finicky eaters also have dandruff. Add to this a slowed metabolism, which results in inefficient digestion, and you have a skinny, undernourished cat surrounded by food. Because circulation and respiration also are slower, less blood and oxygen are reaching the organs. Less blood pumping through the organs means the cat will age earlier. A cat who smells food all day long cannot live as long as he could have if his owner cleared away all food between meals.

Anorexia can occur if a cat is unable to smell his food due to a stuffy nose (see "Respiratory Infections," page 403) or it can also result from a psychological shock, most often the loss of a playmate or beloved owner. The cat decides that life is finished and begins to move toward death.

Malabsorption

Malabsorption is the inability of the body to process and extract nutrients from food consumed, even though the diet may be of high quality and large amounts are eaten. Possible causes include a lack or imbalance of digestive enzymes or hydrochloric acid in the stomach due to disease or old age; overstuffing the stomach so digestion is inefficient; overactive peristaltic action, which passes food through the stomach and intestine too quickly, as in irritable bowel syndrome; coating and clogging of the intestinal walls resulting from lack of roughage in the diet; or a slowed metabolism caused by leaving food available all day long. Poor circulation due to heart disease can also cause malabsorption, as can the failure of a major digestive organ such as the pancreas or the liver. The cat's resistance to heat, cold, stress, and disease becomes dangerously low, and the undernourished system is easy prey to any disease, germ, or virus that happens along.

If a cat is not eating because he is suffering from a disease or recovering from illness (some antibiotics tend to suppress appetite), a very good way to tempt him is with Chicken Super Soup (see page 244). I used to bring this soup along with me when I was working night duty at Dr. Rowan's Cat Practice. Very often cats who could not be tempted even with baby food would break their fast for Chicken Super Soup. The liquid will help keep a sick cat from dehydrating. Also, it is high in protein, calcium, phosphorus, the B vitamins, and vitamin C.

When trying for weight gain in elderly cats or cats depleted from sickness, give three or four moderate-size meals a day. Don't feed large meals, because they are too hard to digest and assimilation will not proceed efficiently. Always leave at least four hours between meals for the same reasons.

A word about the finicky eater syndrome: if you acquire a cat who refuses your delicious high-quality food, you have probably inherited a finicky eater addicted to the taste of sugar and/or salt and/or the rotten taste of sterilized spoiled meat and/or MSG or any of the other items commonly found in supermarket cat food, which we do not use for obvious reasons. Do not despair; just be patient and read the section in Chapter 2, "Diet," on making the change to a new diet (page 68). Don't be afraid to add one or two of the bribe foods for a week or so.

No matter what the cause—or even if the cause is undiagnosed—a homeopathic veterinarian will be a great help in remedying the situation.

Symptoms

- Skinniness, boniness
- Nervousness, easy startling, trembling
- Copious drinking

- Refusing all food—even favorite treats—or eating only a lick or two
- Recurrent health problems (eye, ear, respiratory, and so on) or infections, such as ringworm
- Porous bones that break easily, hip dysplasia
- Lethargy, oversleeping, lack of stamina
- Seeking warmth and seclusion, easy chilling
- Excess shedding and/or dandruff
- Tooth and gum problems

Additional symptoms of anorexia

- Refusal to eat or only eating small amounts
- Urination and defecation slow almost to a stop

Additional symptoms of malabsorption

- Voracious appetite but skinny body
- Diarrhea or constipation

Recommendations

Note: Anorexia and malabsorption are always symptoms of a serious underlying problem. Consult a veterinarian to determine and correct underlying cause, such as tooth problems, pancreatitis, hairball impaction, and so on, otherwise any treatment will merely be a stopgap measure.

- Provide warmth and security so cat will burn up fewer calories (see "Snug Retreat," page 240).
- Feed high-quality diet with as much raw food as possible (see Chapter 2, "Diet"). Be sure to include Vita-Mineral Mix and other listed supplements.
- Never leave food available between meals.
- Give ¼ teaspoon feline enzymes or ½ digestive enzyme tablet (from health-food store) crushed into all meals or as a pill before the meal.
- Add antistress supplements to each meal (see page 240).
- Eliminate stress in cat's environment; provide calm reassurance and love (see "Stress," page 197).
- Massage the cat's body lightly all over, especially on the

sides of the spine, thighs, throat, and shoulders to stimulate blood flow and speed up metabolism.
- Invite cat to gentle play two or four times a day to speed metabolism. Before the meal is the best time for play.

Additional treatments for anorexia

- Give ginseng royal jelly mixture (found in health-food stores, some pharmacies, Chinese stores). Serve two to three drops twice a day (can be mixed into one teaspoon High-Calcium Chicken Broth (page 243) and given as liquid medication (page 210).
- Force-feed four to five times a day until appetite returns (see page 225).
- Feed ¼ cup or less at a time; *do not overfeed* (see "Force Feeding," page 225).
- Be sure cat gets plenty of liquid. Serve Chicken Super Soup (see page 244).
- Bach flower remedies: If anorexia occurs because of sadness due to the loss of a friend, give three drops three times a day of the following mixture prepared as given on page 249:
    Walnut—to help break old bonds and encourage a smooth transition;
    Sweet Chestnut—to banish anguish and despair.

Additional treatments for malabsorption

- Fast for one day on Chicken Super Soup (see page 244) to help cleanse the system.
- Add extra ¼ teaspoon bran (powdered or flaked) to all meals to help clean intestinal walls.
- Be sure there is some fat in the diet to slow emptying of stomach. Add ¼ teaspoon butter (not margarine) to food if in doubt.

Worms
(see "Ringworm"; see "Parasites")

Wounds
(see "Injuries")

Appendix

Product Suppliers

This list of suppliers is for the convenience of the reader. At the time of this writing, the companies listed supply one or more products that are acceptable within the guidelines of this book. This does not necessarily mean that the authors recommend *all* products made by or sold by these companies.

Product quality can change from year to year; companies can change management or policies or standards. We urge you to keep this in mind, to be continuously alert, and to *read labels* and product brochures carefully, even for products you have been using for a long time.

There may be other fine suppliers or new companies not listed here. Our not listing certain suppliers does not necessarily mean that we wouldn't recommend them if we knew about them.

Pet Foods, Supplements, and Pet Care Products

All the Best, 8074 Lake City Way, Seattle, WA 98115. Phone 800-962-8266. Distributor of natural pet foods, supplements, homeopathic remedies, and supplies.

Eco Safe Products, P.O. Box 1177, St. Augustine, FL 32085. Phone 800-274-7387. Manufacturer of Spritz (now marketed as Natural

Animal) Coat Enhancer, which kills fleas and acts as a repellent, and Natural Animal herbal products formulated for pets, including herbal flea collars.

Felix Company, 3623 Fremont Ave. N., Seattle, WA 98103. Phone 800-24-FELIX or 206-547-0042. Suppliers of the famous Felix Katnip Tree and Felix Fine Ground Catnip and other products.

HALO, Purely for Pets, 3438 East Lake Road, Suite 14, Palm Harbor, FL 34686. Phone 813-787-4256. Manufacturer of herbal pet care products. Ear Wash, flea dip, food supplements, etc. Mail order. Write for catalog. When ordering, mention *The New Natural Cat* for information on special offers.

Natural Life Pet Products, 12975 16th Avenue, North, Suite 100-B, Minneapolis, MN 55441. Phone 800-367-2391. Manufacturer of natural pet foods. Available in health-food stores, pet-supply stores, and veterinarians. Call for list of suppliers in your area.

Nature's Recipe, 341 Bonnie Circle, Corona, CA 91720. Phone 800-843-4008. Manufacturer of natural pet foods, including Optimum Feline brand for cats. Available in your health-food store or ask them to order for you.

Optimum Feline. Cat food manufactured by Nature's Recipe (see above).

PetGuard, Inc., P.O. Box 728, Orange Park, FL 32073. Phone 800-874-3221. (In Florida, call 904-264-8500.) Manufacturer of natural pet foods, supplements, herbal flea collars, shampoos, and so on. Also carries a flea comb and books we recommend. Available through health-food stores or call for free catalog.

Very Healthy Enterprises, P.O. Box 4728, Inglewood, CA 90309. Phone 213-672-3269. Manufacturers of feline enzymes and other supplements.

Westward's Herb Products Company, 12021 Ventura Place, P.O. Box 1032, Studio City, CA 91604. Phone 213-877-1050 or 213-761-1112. Suppliers of herbal products forumulated for pets.

Wow-Bow Distributors, 309 Burr Rd., Northport, NY 11731. Phone 516-254-6064. Distributor of Vita-Mineral Mix natural pet foods (Nature's Recipe Optimum Feline), Wow Meow Treats, and supplements. Also carries Spritz (now marketed as Natural Animal) Coat Enhancer, a flea comb, and books we recommend. Call for free catalog.

Wysong Medical Corporation, 1880 N. Eastman, Midland, MI 48640.

Phone 517-631-0009. Suppliers of natural pet foods and supplements.

Suppliers of Bach Flower Remedies

Ellon Bach USA, P.O. Box 320, Woodmere, NY 11598. Phone 800-433-7523. (In NY call 516-593-2206.)

Suppliers of Herbs

Indiana Botanical Gardens, Inc., P.O. Box 5, Hammond, IN 46325. Phone 219-947-4040. Write or call for free catalog.
Nature's Herb Company, 110 46th Street, Emeryville, CA 94608. Phone 415-601-0700. Call or write for free catalog.

Suppliers of Homeopathic Remedies

Dr. Goodpet Laboratories, P.O. Box 4489, Inglewood, CA 90309. Phone 800-222-9932 or 213-672-3269.
Homeopathic Education Services, 2124 Kittredge St., #11Q, Berkeley, CA 94704. Phone 415-653-9270.
Standard Homeopathic Company, P.O. Box 61067, Los Angeles, CA 90061. Phone 800-624-9659. (In CA call 800-992-9659.)

Recommended Books

Our books *The New Natural Cat* and *It's a Cat's Life*, as well as *Dr. Pitcairn's Complete Guide to Natural Health for Dogs and Cats*, can be purchased in most bookstores or by mail from the following companies (addresses and phone numbers given above): PetGuard and Wow Bow Distributors.

The book *Pet Allergies: Remedies for an Epidemic* can be ordered from the publisher, Very Healthy Enterprises, P.O. Box 4728, Inglewood, CA 90309. Phone 213-672-3269.

The following publications by Dr. Dean Black may be difficult to find in a bookstore. They can be purchased from the publisher,

Tapestry Press, P.O. Box 653, Springville, UT 84663. Phone 800-333-4290:

Health at the Crossroads: Exploring the Conflict Between Natural Healing and Conventional Medicine (book)

Regeneration: China's Ancient Gift to the Modern Quest for Health (booklet)

Healing Currents: Trends in the Art of Health (newsletter)

Holistic Veterinarians

American Holistic Veterinary Medical Association, 2214 Old Emmorton Rd., Bel Air, MD 21014. Phone 301-838-7778. Professional organization explores nontraditional techniques in veterinary medicine—including nutrition, homeopathy, and acupuncture. Publishes quarterly newsletter for members. Send self-addressed stamped envelope for list of holistic veterinarians in your area.

International Veterinary Acupuncture Society, c/o Meredith Snader, V.M.D., 2140 Conestoga Road, Chester Springs, PA 19425. Phone 215-827-7245. Educational membership organization; promotes research on and acceptance of acupuncture and its role in veterinary medicine. Brochure contains order form and prices for list of veterinary acupuncturists in the United States and other countries and other information.

National Center for Homeopathy, 1500 Massachusetts, Ave., N.W., Suite 42, Washington, DC 20005. Phone 202-223-6182. Nonprofit membership organization; makes referrals to directory of homeopathic practitioners (including veterinarians) and distributes list of homeopathic pharmacies.

Bibliography

Bach, Edward, M.D., and F. J. Wheeler, M.D. *Bach Flower Remedies*. New Canaan, CT: Keats Publishing, Inc., 1952, 1979.

Ballard, Juliet Brooke. *Treasures from Earth's Storehouse*. Virginia Beach, VA: A.R.E. Press, 1980.

Black, Dean, Ph.D. *Health at the Crossroads: Exploring the Conflict Between Natural Healing and Conventional Medicine*. Springville, Utah: Tapestry Press, 1988.

———. *Regeneration: China's Ancient Gift to the Modern Quest for Health*. Springville, UT: Tapestry Press, 1988.

Boone, J. Allen. *Kinship with All Life*. New York: Harper & Row, Publishers, 1954, 1976.

———. *The Language of Silence*. New York: Harper & Row, 1970.

Bragg, Paul C., N.D., Ph.D. and Patricia Bragg, Ph.D. *The Miracle of Fasting*. Santa Barbara, CA: Health Sciences, 1983.

Bremness, Lesley. *The Complete Book of Herbs: A Practical Guide to Growing and Using Herbs*. New York: Viking, 1988.

Davis, Adelle. *Let's Eat Right to Keep Fit*. New York: Harcourt Brace Jovanovich, 1970.

———. *Let's Get Well*. New York: Harcourt Brace Jovanovich, 1965.

deBairacli-Levy, Juliette. *The Complete Herbal Handbook for the Dog and Cat*. New York: Arco, 1986.

Frazier, Anitra, and Norma Eckroate. *It's a Cat's Life*. Rev. ed. New York: Berkeley Books, 1990.

Gallico, Paul. *The Abandoned*. New York: Knopf, 1950, 1987.

Gawain, Shakti. *Creative Visualization*. New York: Bantam, 1978, 1982.

Gray, Robert. *The Colon Health Handbook*. Oakland, CA: Rockridge Publishing Company, 1983.

Healing Currents Newsletter: Trends in the Art of Health. Tapestry Press, P.O. Box 653, Springville, UT 84663. (800) 333-4290 or (801) 489-3265.

Home Research Projects. Membership service of Association of Research and Enlightenment, P.O. Box 595, Virginia Beach, VA 23451.

Integral Yoga magazine. Satchidananda Ashram, Yogaville, Rt. 1, Box 172, Buckingham, VA 23921.

Lappé, Frances Moore. *Diet for a Small Planet*. New York: Ballantine, 1971, 1982.

Lazarus, Pat. *Keep Your Pet Healthy the Natural Way*. Indianapolis/New York: Bobbs-Merrill Company, 1983.

Lorenz, Konrad. *King Solomon's Ring*. New York: Crowell, 1952.

———. *On Aggression*. New York: Harcourt Brace Jovanovich, 1974.

Maltz, Maxwell. *Psycho-Cybernetics*. Englewood Cliffs, NJ: Prentice-Hall, 1960.

Milani, Myrna M., D.V.M. *The Body Language and Emotion of Cats*. New York: William Morrow, 1987.

Muramoto, Naboru. *Healing Ourselves*. St. Louis: Formur International, 1973.

Ohsawa, George. *Macrobiotics: An Invitation to Health and Happiness*. Ohsawa Foundation, 1434 Corson, Los Angeles, CA 1971.

Pitcairn, Richard H., D.V.M., and Susan Hubble Pitcairn. *Dr. Pitcairn's Complete Guide to Natural Health for Dogs and Cats*. Emmaus, PA: Rodale Press, 1982.

Plechner, Alfred J., D.V.M., and Martin Zucker. *Pet Allergies: Remedies for an Epidemic*. Very Healthy Enterprises, P.O. Box 4728, Inglewood, CA 90309, 1986.

Plummer, George Winslow. *Consciously Creating Circumstances*. Kingston, NY: Society of Rosicrucians, 1939.

Prevention Magazine. 33 East Minor St., Emmaus, PA 18049.

Bibliography

Sivananda, Swami Paramahansa. *Yoga, Health and Diet*. Rishikesh, India: Yoga-Vedanta, Forest Academy, 1958.

Venture Inward magazine. Association for Research and Enlightenment, P.O. Box 595, Virginia Beach, VA 23451.

Wilbourn, Carole C. *The Inner Cat*. Briarcliff Manor, NY: Stein and Day, 1978.

Index

433

Index